HANATSUMI NIKKI
Flowers of Italy

HANATSUMI NIKKI
Flowers of Italy

⌣ Masaharu Anesaki ⌣

Translated with an introduction and notes by
Susanna Fessler

KURODAHAN PRESS

ISBN 4-902075-27-X
ISBN 978-4-902075-27-4
NS-J0022-L20

KURODAHAN PRESS
KURODAHAN PRESS IS A DIVISION OF INTERCOM LTD.
#403 TENJIN 3-9-10, CHUO-KU, FUKUOKA 810-0001 JAPAN

CONTENTS

List of Illustrations

Acknowledgements

I FIRST came upon *Hanatsumi nikki* while I was researching Japanese overseas travelogues from the Meiji period. At the time, I knew next to nothing about Masaharu Anesaki and his world, but I knew, once I had read his travelogue, that I would need to revisit it in greater detail in the future. Clearly it had a richness and depth that spoke of intellectual society both in Japan and Western Europe at the turn of the century.

In the course of regular correspondence on other matters with Chris Ryal at Kurodahan Press I mentioned that I thought *Hanatsumi nikki* deserved to be translated, and was both pleased and surprised that Chris agreed. Although it has taken longer than either of us anticipated to bring this work to a broader, English-speaking audience, the fact that it has happened at all is largely due to Chris's enthusiasm, support, and excellent editing.

In addition to the staff of Kurodahan, there are several individuals I would like to thank for their help in getting the project off the ground and onto the bookshelf. Two of Anesaki's grandsons, Professor Masahira Anesaki and Professor Yukio Kachi, have provided immense support, both in the form of family memories and information, and also in introductions and assistance throughout the course of the project. It has been an honor to meet them (both virtually and in person) and have the opportunity to help their grandfather's work live on in the twenty-first century.

The Italian School of East Asian Studies (ISEAS) in Kyoto, headed by Professor Silvio Vita, provided a platform for the early dissemination of my work on Anesaki by inviting me to their 2007 conference "Itaria-kan no isseiki: tabi to chi to bi" イタリア観の一世紀・旅と知と美, where I delivered a brief paper on Anesaki's views of Italy. Professor Jun'ichi Isomae has also been very helpful in providing further resources on Anesaki's life and work. Mr. Hara Takahashi and Mr. Naofumi Annaka not only pointed us to the source of the Anesaki passport photo seen on the cover of the book, but also sent us a very good, clean copy of the image. I would also like to thank the Institute of Nichiren Buddhist Studies at Risshō University who gave us permission to use the image.

The bulk of this translation was done while I was living in Kyoto, teaching on the Associated Kyoto Program at Dōshisha University as a Visiting Foreign Faculty member in the spring of 2006. That was made possible in part by the Freeman Foundation's Undergraduate Initiative, which helped facilitate my leave that year from the State University of New York at Albany.

Of course, my colleagues, friends, and family, although too numerous to mention individually here, have been invaluable to me in their support. In particular, Anne Rose Kitagawa of the Harvard University Art Museums tolerated quite a number of art-related questions, and when she did not know the answer always managed to find someone who did. Professor Olimpia Pelosi at SUNY Albany very generously offered to help me with some of the more obscure Italian poems that Anesaki quotes in *Hanatsumi nikki*. Professor John Monfasani, also at SUNY, read an early draft of the manuscript and made many helpful comments.

This translation is dedicated to the memory of Anne Rose's father, Professor Joseph M. Kitagawa, who led the next generation of scholars in promoting the study of the religions of Japan.

Albany, New York
October 2008

Translator's Introduction

HANATSUMI NIKKI (A Journal of Gathering Flowers) is an early twentieth century travelogue of Italy. It is a memoir of viewing art in Florence, a visit to the rustic town of Assisi, and a pilgrimage to Rome. But it is not a romantic novel, or a coming-of-age story; rather, it is a tale of spiritual and artistic pursuit, one that tries to define and absorb the beauty found in religious art. One may ask what makes this work distinct from the many other European travelogues written at the time – works such as Henry James's *Italian Hours* – and the answer is that it was written by a Japanese, not a Westerner. Masaharu Anesaki 姉崎正治 (1873–1949), who published *Hanatsumi nikki* under his literary pen name Anesaki Chōfū 姉崎嘲風, was a scholar of religion. He was well known both in his native Japan and abroad, where he traveled and worked during his long, prolific career. *Hanatsumi nikki* represents but one of his many publications, most of which were scholarly books and articles on world religions. Anesaki is often credited with having educated the West about Buddhism through such works as *History of Japanese Religion* (1930), which was first written in 1907 for *Encyclopedia Americana* and then later presented through lectures at Harvard University in 1913–15.[1]

In the late fall of 1907, Anesaki left Japan to travel around the world as a Boursier of the Kahn Foundation, a philanthropic organization that funded scholars' overseas travel in the interest of promoting international understanding. Three months of his journey in the spring of 1908 were spent in Switzerland and Italy. He wrote at length about his experience, focusing on a few key subjects: St. Francis of Assisi (1182–1226), whom he admired, the painter Fra Angelico (1395–1455), whom he also admired, and their connection (as he saw it) to the Japanese Buddhist saint Hōnen 法然 (1133–1212). The text is lyrical yet dense with cultural and historical references, both Western and Japanese.

How should we read this work, a hundred years after its initial publication and in a world where the political and cultural borders have shifted significantly?

In the Western context, Anesaki was traveling in an Italy which had recently undergone unification under one monarch and which had reduced the Papal States to the territory of the Vatican. He was writing during a time in which governments (mostly Western) were making new, promising efforts toward a World Peace. European intellectuals were discovering the "Far East," and were beginning to understand some of its traditions, including Buddhism. Finally, Anesaki was part of a wave of travelers throughout Europe who took advantage of a robust travel industry, led by *Cook's* and *Baedeker's*. His impressions are well highlighted when compared to what other tourists saw and heard, and this is my reason for choosing *Baedeker's* travel guides from the same period as a main contrast object. Anesaki and *Baedeker's* foci are not always the same, and Anesaki's gaze reveals his true interest in traveling.

In the Japanese context, Anesaki was writing for an erudite audience of peers. Like many of his contemporaries in the Meiji period (1868–1912), he lived in a highly-educated if not rarefied world that blended Japanese and Western traditions in such a way as to be opaque to the modern reader. The original travelogue had no footnotes or citations of any kind, but that is not because the content is clear or self-explanatory. Rather, the text is peppered with references to historical events and figures. This translation attempts to fill in the rifts that time and cultural shifts have caused, but one still wonders how much Anesaki's audience really understood and/or appreciated his text. On the one hand, it is possible that the self-deprecating author's preface was sincere, and that Anesaki did not expect a large audience for his musings, which often read more like a personal journal than a formal travelogue. On the other hand, Anesaki regularly produced scholarly articles and books each year, and if indeed *Hanatsumi nikki* was meant as a *personal* work then it would be the exception to the rule. In the years surrounding his journey he published articles on many subjects that he also raises – at least in passing – in *Hanatsumi nikki*, such as an article published in June 1907 titled "Wagner's Roman Empire," [2] an article in September 1907 titled "Zola's *Paris* and Fogazzaro's *The Saint*," [3] an article in January 1909 titled "Social Change and the Problem of Faith," [4] and an article in July 1909 titled "Dante and *The Tale of the Heike*." [5] So it would seem that *Hanatsumi nikki* was a less formal presentation of Anesaki's scholarly thoughts as he traveled through the locales of ancient Western civilization. Whether the reader understood each and every reference was not the point: the references provided the textured canvas on which Anesaki could paint broad strokes of cultural criticism.

I have written elsewhere about how *Hanatsumi nikki* fits into the larger picture of modern travel writing by Japanese abroad [6] and so shall refrain from doing so here. Suffice it to say that this work incorporates a number of traditional forms (poetry, allusions, etc.) while maintaining its modern personality. To put the work in a clearer context, I provide here a brief introduction to Anesaki and his work.

BIOGRAPHY

Masaharu Anesaki[7] was born in Kyoto on July 25, 1873. He lost his father at age nine, which, as he notes in his autobiography, resounded with him when he realized that Hōnen lost his father too at the same age.[8] He attended a series of schools in the Kansai area during his childhood. He recalled studying the Chinese classics, and in his early teens he began to read philosophical works in their original English, by such authors as Hume, Spencer, and Mill.[9] He took a particular interest in Spencer's treatise "Education" (1861) and claimed to have memorized various passages from it. During this time, as he recounts bemusedly in his autobiography, he took an interest in studying electricity. He had heard that the writer Kōda Rohan 幸田露伴 (1867–1947) had also at one time taken an interest in telegraphy, and was inspired to do the same. He also became interested in a newly-published book by Miyake Yūjirō 三宅雄二郎 titled *A Drop of Philosophy* (*Tetsugaku Kenteki* 哲學涓滴). In order to pursue both his interest in electricity and philosophy, he had to order books from Tokyo on the subjects. He ordered two: one a book on the history of philosophy[10] by Albert Schwegler (1819–1857), and one a book on electricity. In the end, the Schwegler book arrived but the electricity book did not, and with this serendipitous event, his career course was determined.[11]

At the age of twenty he enrolled in the Philosophy Department of the Imperial University (what is today Tokyo University). One of his classmates was Takayama Chogyū 高山樗牛 (1871–1902), to whom *Hanatsumi nikki* is dedicated. Anesaki began publishing in 1895 at the age of twenty-two, when he produced no less than eight articles on religion and philosophy in such journals as *Taiyō* 太陽 and *Teikoku Bungaku* 帝國文学. His topics included the fate of the character Margaret in *Faust*, the character and conduct of Schopenhauer, and comparative research on spirituality. He continued publishing throughout his undergraduate career on similarly broad-ranging topics and graduated in July of 1896. He then entered graduate school to focus his research on the "Development of Religion." One must remember that "religion" (*shūkyō* 宗教 in Japanese) specifically referred to organized religion, and it was a relatively new concept, one that was introduced when the Western term "religion" was translated into Japanese.

Thus Anesaki was entering a new discipline, and would help that discipline progress not only in Japan but also overseas. Two years into his graduate studies he married Inoue Masu 井上マス, the niece of Inoue Tetsujirō 井上哲次郎 (1855–1944), an established philosopher at the Imperial University.

As a young scholar, Anesaki continued to publish on religious topics and became an assistant professor in the Faculty of Humanities of the Imperial University in 1900 at the age of twenty-seven. In May of the same year, he left for Europe, where he would stay until June 1903. During his time abroad, he studied and traveled in Ger-

many, Holland, England, Italy, and India, occasionally writing articles and participating in scholarly conferences. While he was gone, his good friend Takayama Chogyū passed away – an event that profoundly moved Anesaki. He helped compile Chogyū's works for publication, and he also wrote his own essays about Chogyū, including one published in *Taiyō* in March 1904 titled "Takayama Chogyū and Saint Nichiren 高山樗牛と日蓮上人." Anesaki credited Chogyū with single-handedly reviving Nichiren Buddhism in the year before he died, and with charismatically leading the youth of Japan toward a kind of spiritual renaissance. One of Chogyū's major essays compared Christ and Nichiren, "especially in respect to their dignified aloofness from earthly powers, in which Takayama saw the kernel of veritable spiritual leadership."[12]

From mid-1903 until 1907, Anesaki continued pursuing his scholarly career, eventually being promoted to professor of Humanities at Tokyo Imperial University. In September of 1907 he was one of the fortunate scholars chosen to receive funds from the Kahn Foundation. His journey took him from Japan to New York, Paris, Switzerland, Italy, Austria, Germany, and London, finally returning home in October of 1908. As on his previous journey, he participated in scholarly conferences and produced a number of publications while traveling. In the course of *Hanatsumi nikki* we see him having informal scholarly conversations, and he mentions writing some essays, although he certainly does not seem to be working hard on them every day. Rather, Anesaki took his trip (at least the portion in Italy) for the purposes of contemplating the past and integrating it in his current cultural milieu. Thus, *Hanatsumi nikki* is by no means a scholarly product, but it does show us the process whereby a Meiji period mind incorporated Western ideas and

traditions into a coherent whole with a Japanese base.

After his trip to Italy, Anesaki continued in the same vein for the rest of his life; that is, he spent considerable time abroad as a scholar, but maintained his academic base in Tokyo at the Imperial (Tokyo) University. He became one of the most well-known names in Religious Studies in Japan, and his work is still respected today. Later in his life he shifted his philosophical focus from Hōnen to Nichiren, then to Prince Shōtoku of the seventh century. The last two moves, often interpreted as acts of nationalism, seem to have doomed him to a sort of academic obscurity despite his

insight on Japanese cultural trends of his time and his intellectual integrity as a scholar. He maintained his overseas contacts even during the Sino-Japanese war of 1894–5, the Russo-Japanese war of 1904–5, the First World War (during which he taught at Harvard University) and the Second World War, the opening days of which saw him forcibly repatriated from England. He witnessed the end of the last war, maintaining his foreign friends all the while, and passed away in 1949, four years into the post-war era of modern Japan.

PHILOSOPHY

Reading Meiji period texts is a fascinating journey through a time of philosophical upheaval the likes of which I find difficult to imagine in the twenty-first century. Of course, in the late nineteenth and early twentieth centuries Japan was incorporating outside ideas at a rapid, even chaotic, pace, but in addition to that her own indigenous ideas were mutating at a similar speed. A study that did justice to it all would certainly be beyond the scope of this essay, but as a case study perhaps Anesaki's background and personal experience can show how one Meiji intellectual's ideas took shape.

Anesaki's first trip to Europe was a formative one: he went to Germany because it was seen in Japan as on the cultural forefront of the Western world. He had great hopes and expectations when he arrived, but these were quickly destroyed as Germany entered the frothy era of Wilhelm II, who identified the "Yellow Peril" as a major threat. In an open letter to Takayama Chogyū, published in the magazine *Taiyō* (which Chogyū edited), Anesaki railed against German culture. German culture *had* been great, but it was now the latter days. He writes:

> But there are few in Europe who possess an understanding of philosophy...
> In particular, the world of German thought in the late nineteenth century
> was akin to the declining *Man'yō* age [in Japan]. The brilliant French cul-
> ture of the eighteenth century had moved the German spirit, and the early
> nineteenth century was the classic age of philosophy and letters. But after
> the irresistible force of thought and literary production had overflowed into
> the spiritual world, now we find ourselves in the next age where there are no
> geniuses, where there are no great minds of production besides those who
> simply embellish and ornament what had come before. What is more, the
> unification of the country and its consequent prosperity are, contrarily, dis-
> tanced from the people's basic self-discipline, and we find ourselves in an age
> of increasing conceit and outward patriotism.[13]

Of course he took offense at the Yellow Peril concept, but in addition to that he was dismayed at the Kaiser's appropriation of religion for nationalist purpos-es. It is worth noting that Anesaki's keen ability to differentiate between differ-ent Christian camps – Protestant and Catholic – was unusual in his generation. For him, Christianity held much promise but had been wrongly interpreted by the Kaiser and the Lutherans in a parochial and xenophobic way. He continues:

> When I was in Japan, I had not studied things in depth and I thought that
> Christianity was the basis of civilization. The Roman Catholic Church had
> misinterpreted the Gospels and because it had held ecclesiastical authority
> in shackles, the Catholic countries had consequently forfeited their culture.
> But, having shed the restraints of the Church and revived Christian spiritual-
> ity, the Protestants had regained their true spiritual worth and thus, recently,
> civilization had flourished in England and Germany. It was because I was

thinking thusly that I came to Germany to encounter those products of civilization myself. When I saw how the new Christianity was spreading the Gospels I truly could not but be awestruck; it was truly the opposite of what I had expected: I saw that the new German Christians were promoting their civilization by being the bitter enemies of spiritual freedom, and by fighting spiritual independence.[14]

The experience in Germany left Anesaki bitter and any admiration he had for Germany and German culture had been disabused. That said, he still held hope that some philosophical bridge could be built between Japan and the West.

In the years between his stay in Germany and his trip in 1908 to Italy, Anesaki published largely on the subject of finding a reconciliation between Western traditions – chiefly Christianity – and Japanese traditions – chiefly Buddhism. In "How Christianity Appeals to a Japanese Buddhist" in *The Hibbert Journal* (which we have included here as an appendix), he argues that Christianity and Buddhism are compatible, that "The differences [between the two] are necessary consequences of the historical circumstances in which the two religions have grown up, and of the different demands of the peoples they were intended to lead; *but the religious foundation of both is the same*"[15] (emphasis mine). He continues that "we Buddhists are ready to accept Christianity; nay, more, our faith in Buddha is faith in Christ. *We see Christ because we see Buddha*."[16] He saw an affinity between Buddhism and Christianity, which were, in his opinion, natural results of religious evolution from Hinduism and Judaism. Perhaps more importantly, he implies that Buddhism and Christianity are qualitatively better than Hinduism and Judaism, which he describes as "[lacking] living moral truth"[17] in the sense that they have no human manifestation of the faith. In short, Anesaki was looking for a way to reconcile two major world traditions that would bring their faithful together instead of pushing them onto opposing sides in a religious argument. The conversations that he has in Italy mirror this desire, and he often reports that he is not alone in finding similarities between Buddhism and Christianity.

Politically, Anesaki was a product of his time. The major political movements against which he argued in *Hanatsumi Nikki* were Socialism, the Papacy and the Roman Catholic Church, and Capitalism. Of the three, he disliked Capitalism the most. To him, it contained no spirituality and thus was void of value. Those who constantly strove for financial security and wealth were misguided and spiritually impoverished, and he wanted nothing to do with them. Chief among the Capitalists in his mind were Americans. In Switzerland he writes, "There were many emigration offices. They all took care of the Italians from this area who wanted to emigrate to America. I wondered if there could be many people who were unhappy in this Italian and Swiss paradise and who wanted to go instead to live in the coal smoke of America solely to make money; what a tragedy it is" (see page 27). In his essays on the United States in *Teiunshū*, he echoes this sentiment and goes on to say that the United States was, in a sense, rushing into social folly. To be fair, one should note that these essays are about California, largely San Francisco, which was not a "typical" city in that it was only months into its recovery from the Great Earthquake of 1906. The bustle and reconstruction underway when Anesaki saw it would have been a surprising sight to any observer, not least of all a highly religious Japanese intellectual. In any event, Anesaki saw the United States as bereft of a deeper, longer tradition such as existed in Europe, and he closely associated the United States with Capitalism, which to him also represented a shallow approach to life. That his benefactor, Albert Kahn, was a financier and able to practice philanthropy thanks to Capitalism does not attract a mention.

Given his strong affinity toward compassion as expressed in Christianity and Pure Land Buddhism, one might expect Anesaki to embrace Socialism, but he does not. His feelings on the subject are not as strong as those on Capitalism, but he seems to mistrust the Socialists, perhaps because he sees them as enemies of the Roman Catholic Church. Moreover, in early twentieth century Italy, the Socialists were, at least in a very superficial way, associated with the Freemasons and Garibaldi, all of whom had had a hand in reducing the Papal States to the territory of the Vatican. Anesaki is not explicit about his feelings; rather, he makes occasional comments that show he disapproves of political philosophies of all kinds. This is most clear when he tours the Roman ruins, which appear to him as clear evidence that man's vanity cannot build permanence in an evanescent world. He writes,

Even though we know that there are undoubtedly palaces below us, now a stand of trees grows here and if one walks on it, it seems to be nothing more than a hill. When one begins to dig here, one finds that beneath the brick walls of the age of the Empire is the rubble from the age of the Republic, and beneath that is a layer from the old days of the monarchs which contains bits of building stones. This single wall speaks of all of Roman history, and shows the vicissitudes of over a thousand years.

And although this history fascinates him, he is not philosophically seduced by it. The only constant, in the end, is faith and religion. This is not to say that he was a Papist. He viewed the Papacy as corrupted by politics, and he was openly critical of Pius X for his distance from the common people. The rhetoric, established by Pope Pius IX, of the pontiff being a "Prisoner of the Vatican" in the face of Italian monarchial hostilities was so well established by 1908 that Anesaki writes of it as if it extended much further back than the mid-nineteenth century. As discussed below, dogma and formality in religion – qualities certainly possessed by the Roman Catholic Church – did not appeal to Anesaki, who was looking for the spirituality and faith in Italy, both in her religious history and in her art. Thus, the Catholic Church represented to Anesaki the shallow, political side of religion, one that had lost sight of the spiritual bond to the human soul.

It should be said that although Anesaki opposed much of organized religion, he could not quite bring himself to reject all authority, for that would bring a state of anarchy as was advocated by many of the popular fiction writers of the early twentieth century. He equated this anarchy with the Naturalism movement, which explains why, in *Hanatsumi Nikki*, he notes that Zola was sometimes wrong about his interpretations of the Church. In *History of Japanese Religion* he writes,

[A] feature distinguishing the last part of the first decade [of the twentieth century] was the rise of what was called naturalism. Though its expression was chiefly limited to the sphere of literature, it represented a strong stream of thought operating against the authorized teaching of ethics and religion. The artificial method of imposing official ethics upon the youth worked, as we have seen, to arouse a spirit of discontent and even revolt among the young people of independent spirit. The impatient among them demanded total emancipation on the contention that the genuine "natural" meaning of life could be realized only in a full play of the instinctive nature of emancipated individuals. Theorizing or arguing did not suit their temper; to expose life in its naked reality seemed to them the only method of arriving at a satisfactory solution of human problems, because all entanglements were understood to arise out of artificial means of control. By "naked reality" were meant the actualities of life stripped of all conventionalities, and the literature produced for this cause aimed at a relentless exposure of all compromise and hypocrisy. The literary movement was, in its negative aspect, a bitter protest against every kind of authority, and was on its positive side a declaration of emancipation of the individual. This movement of individualism and naturalism prepared a way for the rising of socialism as an idea...[18]

If Capitalism, Socialism, and the Papacy were bad, what, then, was good about Italy for Anesaki? What *was* his philosophy? At this stage in his life,[19] he was still focused on the Pure Land leader Hōnen (1133–1212), one of the first advocates of salvation for "sinful and depraved beings" through the compassion of Amida Buddha. This stood in contrast with, in Anesaki's words, "the 'Way for the Wise,' the wise who could go through severe training... [This] was the regular religion of Buddhism, hardly within the reach of the people of the latter days [of the Buddhist Law]."[20] One could turn to any number of Christian parallels, but Anesaki chooses the promise of salvation and compassion provided by St. Francis of Assisi to the common man. Thus, on the one hand sit elite forms of religion, limited by their demanding nature to the educated elite; on the other hand sit common forms of religion, available to a wide group regardless of their economic or educational background. One could certainly argue that Anesaki was mistaken in his interpretation of both Catholicism (at least the Papacy) and non-Pure Land forms of Buddhism, but this would not change our reading of *Hanatsumi nikki*. The salient point is that Anesaki was drawing a connection between Buddhism and Christianity in an effort to illustrate a universal characteristic found in both.

As mentioned earlier, Anesaki was not alone in finding this affinity between Buddhism and Christianity. In *History of Japanese Religion*, he writes that "young Buddhists [of the late nineteenth century] found that the Buddhist conception of the world as a perpetually flowing process and the continuity of Karma had anticipated the Darwinian theory of evolution; that the dialectical method of Buddhist philosophy in analyzing all conceptions and dispelling the idea of permanent entity was quite congenial to Spencerian agnosticism; that the Hegelian logic of reaching a higher synthesis over the concepts of being and non-being was exactly the kernel of the Tendai doctrine of the Middle Path."[21] In other words, it was possible to integrate many of the current, leading ideas of the West into Buddhist ideology without difficulty, aiding the assimilation of Western culture and ideas, and thus also aiding the amorphous but important goal of "modernization."

In sum, Anesaki felt that there was a unifying factor connecting all humanity: the need for spirituality. But political authority did not satisfy mankind's need for spiritual order; rather, such satisfaction could most readily be found *outside* the normal confines of organized religion. Moreover, the expression of faith that sat at the core of this expression was to be found in art, specifically pre-Renaissance art, as described below.

ART AND THE AUTHOR'S PURPOSE

As mentioned above, Anesaki received funding for his trip from Albert Kahn, the French financier and philanthropist. Little remains today of Kahn's legacy, but at the peak of his philanthropic activity (between 1910 and 1931) he contributed large sums to universities and scholarships for the purpose of improving international understanding. As vague as that dictate seems – and there was at least one scholarly reviewer who felt the money wasted[22] – there were many professors from the United States, France, Germany, Japan, and England who took advantage of Mr. Kahn's offer. Benefactors were given funds to be used for overseas travel "for the performance of high duties in the instruction and education of the youth of their country, and not as affording a mere vacation or pleasure trip."[23] In short, Anesaki's responsibility to the Kahn Foundation was to visit many countries, confer with scholars, learn about the West, and take that knowledge back to Japan to disseminate it to college students. He was not affiliated with any specific institution of higher learning in Europe and he did not attend classes or give regular lectures. He does not disclose how much money the Kahn Foundation gave him for this endeavor, but it was probably not much different from what Americans who traveled abroad on Kahn fellowships received in 1913: US$3,000, an amount which compares favorably to a senior academic's yearly wage in today's terms.

There was a certain amount of networking that helped Anesaki form his itinerary. Albert Kahn was friends with Charles Marie Georges Garnier, a scholar of English literature who lived in Paris. Anesaki became close friends with Garnier (Anesaki's collection of travel essays, *Teiunshū*, was dedicated to Garnier), whom he visited often in Paris on his trips to Europe. His itinerary in Italy has him visiting some scholars, such as Enrico Bignami and Paul Sabatier, and traveling on his own to famous locales, largely to contemplate history and see artwork, much like other travelers of the day. This does not, however, make Anesaki one of a crowd of common travel writers. He differs in one significant way: the European travelers of the time (if the popular travel guidebooks such as *Baedeker's* are any indication) focus more on the artwork and architecture of the locales than anything else. But the guidebooks describe the art as an art historian would, with names, dates, sponsors, and so on. Anesaki instead focuses on the religious air of the paintings – for him, "art is the universal language of the human heart, and through that channel the heart of religion may be communicated incomparably better than through that of dogmas or of reason."[24] His objective in viewing religious art was already set in his mind years earlier, when he wrote the following:

> we find painting, especially that of the Quattrocento, remarkable in its depth and vitality. In this respect, the works of the Quattrocentisti appeal to our inner heart incomparably more than the later European art, excellent though this be in execution. There is in them nothing comparable to the gracefulness of a Raphaelian Madonna, but these earlier artists knew how to paint the deep store of faith or emotion, to attract the beholders and to assimilate their hearts to the inner hearts of the figures depicted. One expects in vain to see the skilful shadings and colourings of modern French painters in Lippi or Bellini, but their naïve sincerity and sometimes childlike freshness are truly products of piety. I find no necessity of saying more on this subject to the English public, whose taste is now much influenced by Ruskin and who are true lovers of Italian art. What I wish to enforce is the wonderful similarity existing between the art of the Quattrocento and our old Buddhistic painting. My impressions when I first saw Angelico's Madonna in the National Gallery of London, and then in Florence, were simply the feelings I had when I looked at the old paintings of the Tak'ma school. Not only in intention and depth, but in treatment and colouring, they show a striking similarity. They depicted their piety in figures and colours, and have appealed to the heart of the same emotion. Their paintings were not for the sake of amusement or of dilettantism, but for worship. For them art was not a merry thing, but serious as life.[25]

And, when Anesaki went to Italy the second time he swore off viewing anything *but* the early fourteenth century art that he felt showed such a fervent faith. In this sense, his art-based journey differs significantly from his contemporaries' journeys. This view of painting was mirrored by his view of architecture:

> The most visible and tangible product in which a religion manifests its actual influence upon human mind and civilisation is art. The one thing

which strikes most the mind of an Asiatic in Europe is the grandeur of religious architecture. It has not the impressive but overwhelming grandeur of an Egyptian sepulcher, nor the gigantic but extravagant magnitude of a Mohammedan mosque, but grandeur in proportion, sublimity with harmony. The Gothic tower of a Strassburg or Rouen Cathedral, pointing imposingly to heaven, rising from among the roofs of human dwellings or along the undulating hillside, appeals to us as something grand and elevating. Standing among the pillars of a cloister like that of the Lateran, or sitting under the vault of a Cappella degli Spagnuoli, no one could restrain himself from uttering a prayer to Him, or singing in praise of Him, who has caused a pious architect to plan this or that impressive building in His service. God does not dwell in a temple built by human hands, but there is the Divine exhibited to us in these harmonious grandeurs or in these serene beauties. At the same time, while we are impressed and inspired by the sublimity and beauty of the Christian architecture, we cannot but admire the same power expressed before us in the graceful temple of Hōryūji or meditatively serene building of the Zen-Buddhism. I shall not enter into description of this Japanese Buddhist architecture, but the similar plan and idea, expressed, though on a smaller scale, in the Buddhist buildings, never fails to excite my wonder. Certainly there is a gap between the tastes of the West and the East, but it is not an insurmountable one, when we examine into the very root of religious faith which has produced such similar grandeur and harmony.[26]

This passage does much to illuminate Anesaki's gaze in Italy. Without it, his long descriptions of Angelico's paintings seem at times inarticulate or unfocused. With it, we understand the essence that he was trying to isolate and describe. His distaste for the synagogue of Rome and the over-sized proportions of the Vatican, which on the surface seems to be the product of petulant whim, is perfectly clear. And, as stated earlier, his constant focus on artistic expressions of faith and on faith itself are for him also political and philosophical statements.

It is also clear that Anesaki was influenced by the aesthetic currents of the day, to which Takayama Chogyū was a vocal contributor. At the forefront of aesthetics and artistic movements in the Meiji period were Ernest Fenollosa (1853–1908) and Okakura Kakuzō (1862–1913). They were influenced by the Arts and Crafts movement and the ideas of John Ruskin (1819–1900), one of the most notable art critics at that time. Ruskin was prolific and a polymath so it is difficult to quickly sum up his approach to art, but for Anesaki the salient point was that Ruskin celebrated art and architecture that was not beholden to long-standing traditional methodology but rather expressed the artist's inner spirit. Moreover, Ruskin was opposed to the type of architecture that resulted from the industrial revolution – those buildings that were oversized and thus oppressive to the individual soul. This could also well describe Anesaki's feelings about painting and architecture, such as St. Peter's of the Vatican. Ruskin's feelings about art extended to religion, and are echoed in Anesaki's criticisms of Germany in his letter to Takayama. Ruskin gives us this example:

Take a sentence, for example, from J.A. James's "Anxious Inquirer": "It is a great principle that *subjective religion, or in other words,* religion *in us,* is produced and sustained by fixing the mind on *objective religion, or* the facts and doctrines of the Word of God."

Cut entirely out the words I have put in italics, and the sentence has a meaning (though not by any means an important one). But by its verbosities it is extended into pure nonsense; for "facts" are neither "objective" nor "subjective" religion; they are not religion at all. The belief of them, attended with certain feelings, is religion; and it must always be religion "in us," for in whom else should it be? [27]

Thus, religion is not doctrine or the understanding of doctrine, but rather the belief and feelings attendant to it. The dichotomy of "subjective" and "objective" also appears in Anesaki's letter:

The philosophers of the world say that they are seeking objective truth; the pedagogues and logicians try to complete their theories based on a foundation of objectivity. Theory is precious and truth is important, but what is truth in the first place? How can one find objectivity, divorced from subjectivity? Individual spirituality is sincerely experienced, sincerely believed; how can there be objective truth outside of what one experiences? [28]

Thus for Anesaki both religion and art were expressions of an individual subjectivity, by which he meant an emotional response to the outside world.[29] This all connected to his motives on this journey: in addition to the obligation he had to the Kahn Foundation to further his knowledge of the West in order to disseminate it in a Japanese university, he also wanted to see and appreciate the deep spirituality of both Christianity and Buddhism as expressed in fourteenth century art, particularly that of Fra Angelico. He argues in his entry on May 22 that art is necessarily a product of religion, and that non-religious art is vacuous. He is not charmed by the realism and refinement of the Renaissance, preferring instead the expression of fervent faith he finds in Giotto and Fra Angelico.

WESTERN INFLUENCES

Anesaki was working with a wide spectrum of resources. We know that he read Sabatier's biography of St. Francis and used it as the primary source of information on Francis's life. He refers explicitly to works by Fogazzaro and Zola, and incorporates them indirectly in his work. For example, while touring the Vatican grounds he mentions that he comes across a "small version of the Grotto of Our Lady of Lourdes," and follows this comment with negatively critical comments on the Pope to the effect that he had ideas of grandeur but was really a small man – two apparently unrelated events. Similarly, Zola, in his novel *Rome,* depicts his protagonist coming across the same grotto and then commenting, "I was told of it, but I thought that the Holy Father was of loftier mind – free from all such base superstitions." In Rome, Anesaki laments the corruption of the Papacy: "The sun shone so strongly on the world, but the Pope was shut up in the Vatican on the hill, never setting foot outside of this little walled fortress. It really is incredible that he is heir to Christ, who walked across the hot fields of Judea to save mankind. That the Pope has come to strictly protect this walled city is the product of a very narrow world-view..." and in *Rome,* Zola writes, "Assuredly it was Rome, the soil of Rome, that soil where pride and domination sprouted like the herbage of the fields that had transformed the humble Christianity of primitive times, the religion of fraternity, justice, and hope into what it now was: victorious Catholicism, allied to the rich and powerful, a huge implement of government, prepared for the conquest of every nation."

Anesaki also shows evidence of Western influence in his artistic descriptions. His statement that "art is the universal language of the human heart, and through that channel the heart of religion may be communicated incomparably better than through that of dogmas or of reason" is markedly similar to Schopenhauerian and Ruskinian ideas on art and the artistic experience as substitutes for structured religious practice. It comes as no surprise that in the years immediately following the journey to Italy, Anesaki translated and published Schopenhauer's *Die Welt als Wille und Vorstellung* (*The World as Will and*

Representation). And in *Hanatsumi nikki*, he attempts to convey his personal religious revelations as brought about by Fra Angelico's art, not through textual and/or scholarly understanding of Franciscan doctrine.

Although Anesaki was certainly reading from a wide variety of sources, one of the central publications through which he made many academic acquaintances and whose themes appear in his works was the Italian philosophical journal *Cœnobium* (1906–1919). In its pages we find articles by Paul Sabatier and Alessandro Costa on Catholic reform, another by Costa on Schopenhauer's religion and philosophy, one by Guiseppe Rensi on Hegel – a veritable list of Anesaki's friends and acquaintances and their works. The focus of *Cœnobium* lay between the philosophical and the religious, with occasional political pieces; the same description could be applied to Anesaki's works. In any event, Anesaki's connection with *Cœnobium* (in which he too published) was central to his journey in Italy, where he visited the editor, Enrico Bignami. If we want a quick survey of the influential articles that Anesaki was reading while he wrote *Hanatsumi nikki*, we had best begin by reading the table of contents of *Cœnobium*.[30]

In the end it would be a fruitless endeavor to identify *all* the influences in this text – as it would be for almost any text of the Meiji period – so suffice it to say that Anesaki was well read on the current arguments and theories of his day, a time when modernization in its various forms was sweeping not only Japan but the entire globe. Earlier travelogues by Japanese who traveled to the West were often written with limited cultural knowledge, but Anesaki's observations are fully informed in both the Japanese and Western traditions.

LANGUAGE

Many of the Meiji period literary travelers were hampered by a language barrier, as indeed travelers from all countries to all countries often are. Anesaki, however, was a polyglot who took some joy in language. He mentions what languages are spoken in various conversations in *Hanatsumi nikki*, and occasionally offers a normative comment. Although it is difficult to assess his fluency today – essays can be edited, and sound recordings are rare – we can make some judgment based on his own evaluations and memories. He seemed most comfortable in English and German, but was also fluent in French. He knew a few words of Italian but often made errors in transliteration of it. His published recollections of language learning in school are inconsistent, but by the time he was a college student he seems to have mastered English to such an extent that he no longer required formal language classes in it. He mentions that he and his classmates all enjoyed studying German, but that their French class met too early in the day and so he did not attend. Latin did not enthrall him, but he was interested in how English had some of its roots in it. His first stint abroad, largely spent in Germany, clearly cemented the linguistic grounding he had received in the classroom in Japan. How his French improved to the level that he felt comfortable in conversations and in writing scholarly articles is not clear, but it seems to have done so.

What this all means for Anesaki the traveler is that his interpretations and impressions of the landscape, both figurative and literal, were colored more by English and German speaking fellow tourists and expatriates than by the locals. His meaningful conversations were almost exclusively conducted with these other "foreigners"; even those Italians with whom he spent time, such as Bignami, were the product of a cosmopolitan society that was in some ways distant from what one might consider "typical" Italians. Bignami and Anesaki communicated in French, not Italian. In this respect Anesaki was both like his European counterparts, who toured Italy with a focus on the history of civilizations past, not on the contemporary culture, and like his Japanese predecessors in the genre of travel literature, who traveled to view poetically famous locations (*utamakura*) and vicariously experience earlier poets' rapture, almost always to the exclusion of the local culture.

I should note that Anesaki was writing at a time of rapid linguistic change. The Japanese lexicon experienced a large influx of neologisms during the Meiji period thanks to the mass importation of Western concepts. Even so, Meiji writers (Anesaki included) often faced the need for a word that did not yet exist, or was not yet in wide usage, in Japanese. Particularly in the case of Christian terminology, Anesaki chooses a Buddhist term that is a close approximation of the Christian meaning when there is not a "proper" (i.e., widely recognized by the readership) term available. For example, when referring to churches he uses the Japanese term *tera* (寺), which today is usually translated as "temple." The term *kaidō* (会堂 "church building"), popularly used now, never appears. As the translator, I do not interpret this as an attempt on Anesaki's part to impose Buddhist ideas on Christian objects. Rather, I think he was simply creating the least awkward text possible given the linguistic limitations of the time. In this translation I have tried to use the most natural sounding English, not a literal translation. Moreover, if there is a specific Catholic term, I chose that over a descriptive term. Thus, *tera* is "church," (not "temple"), *yakusō* is "sacristan" (not "attending monk"), and *Seibo* is "the Virgin Mary" or "the Holy Virgin" (not "Holy Mother").

STYLE

Finally, a word on the style of this travelogue. Anesaki, following a long-held format in Japanese travel literature, creates diurnal entries in a personal journal. On some days there is a larger theme, such as the fall of the Roman Empire or the piety of St. Clare, but not to the exclusion of quotidian events. This diary form has its roots in tenth century Japanese literature, specifically the *Tosa Diary* by Ki no Tsurayuki. Over the centuries the diary/travelogue form has survived with a few modifications, and is largely accepted as a legitimate literary genre in its own right.

For the reader, the diary presents an intriguing if not vicarious view of another's experience. It is not without its idiosyncrasies, though, chief of which is an assumed knowledge on the part of the audience. We are expected to know *who* the author's friends are, *why* they are his friends, *how* they met him in the first place, and so on. We are expected to know what the author cares about, what his education consisted of, what his philosophical stance is, and what physical ailments he may have. In short, the writer is writing either *to himself* (as in a diary entry) or to a familiar friend (as in a letter), but in either case the amount of background information missing is daunting for uninitiated readers such as ourselves. It is a challenge for the author to simultaneously maintain the guise of a personal essay while providing just enough information so as not to alienate his larger audience. In all of *Hanatsumi nikki,* Anesaki breaks the guise but once when he says, "If I do not give the history here my reader will not understand" (see entry for April 25). In other passages he provides the history, but without explicit acknowledgement that he is doing so.

It is also worth noting, from a stylistic standpoint, that Anesaki includes both poetry and prose in this work. This, too, was the format used in *Tosa Diary* (indeed, *Tosa Diary* was really a vehicle for poetry, with prose added on, and not vice versa). Most of the poems are in traditional *waka* meter, and those that break from it do not follow what is known as "new poetic form" (*shintaishi*), which is comparable to free verse in English, but rather retain a syllable-based rhythmical form. Eventually Anesaki leaves poetry behind and writes exclusively in prose, but that is not to say that his diction becomes dry. Rather, it continues to be lyrical in its attempt to capture the sublimity of his surroundings and the profundity of the spirituality he finds.

The reaction to this work in the Japanese press was favorable, with one reviewer describing it as "melting nature and man together into a harmonious whole." [31] Another reviewer praised his prose as harmonizing the feeling of the landscape, making it easy for the reader to indulge in the author's wittiness and lightness. He concluded by saying that one could easily feel as if one had traveled to southern Europe simply by sitting down with the book. [32] In short, Anesaki's audience found this work accessible and intriguing.

This essay introduces the context in which Anesaki wrote *Hanatsumi nikki*, but it does not attempt to neatly package Anesaki's conclusions, if indeed he had them. That is for the individual reader to do, based on the text itself. One could argue that the work, not being an academic piece, contributes little to Anesaki's scholarly opus. But if we follow Anesaki's dictum that "art is the universal language of the human heart," then perhaps *Hanatsumi nikki* is closer to capturing the author's human heart than any of his other theses.

HANATSUMI NIKKI

FLOWERS OF ITALY
DIARIES OF A PILGRIMAGE [1]

I'll take home as a souvenir
This simple flower I plucked
Perhaps it will inspire a tale
Of the fields I passed

Tornasti, o Primavera,
E l'erbe verdi e i fiori
E i giovanili amori
Tornarono con te;
  E il mio felice stato,
Teco una volta nato,
  Col dolce tuo rinascere
  Tornò più dolce a me.
Sulla nativa spina
  Aspetta già la rosa
  Che l'alba rugiadosa
  Tempri il suo bel color.
  Son nati i bei giancinti,
Gli anemoni dipinti,
Le mammole, i ranuncoli
E ogn' altro amabil fior.

. . . .

  E in seminati solchi,
Speranza de' bifolchi,
Della messe giovine
Le foglie verdeggiar.

. . . .

Dei geli dell' inverno
  A compensarne il danno
Ringiovenisce l'anno,
  Torna ogni bel piacer;[2]

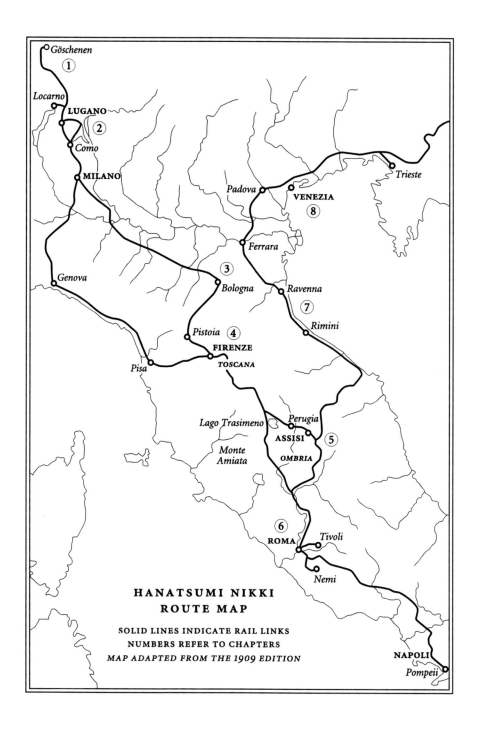

**HANATSUMI NIKKI
ROUTE MAP**

SOLID LINES INDICATE RAIL LINKS
NUMBERS REFER TO CHAPTERS
MAP ADAPTED FROM THE 1909 EDITION

Preface

EVERY YEAR on March 31 I think about the first time that I left this country for foreign shores.[3] Nine years ago on this day I bade goodbye to my friends in Yokohama, and that evening, as I gazed at the large island of Izu that seemed to be a shadow lying in the evening sky, and at the ocean's surface in the setting sun, I thought of my friend who had been enveloped in the sadness of parting. Three years later, when I returned home, he had already joined those who have left this world, his bones buried in the mountains on the opposite shore.[4] On this day of remembrance I have come here once again and arranged my diary of gathering flowers in Italy; I remember he told me, "Whatever else you do, come back with an interesting diary." This diary does not exactly meet his wish, but it is a record of what I saw and did each day on my journey, and is a memento of my sincere feelings of friendship toward him.

Here in Kiyomigata,[5] where I have come to edit the manuscript of my diary and remember my late friend, I realize that I must also give thanks to the man who made my journey last year possible, Mr. Albert Kahn. He donated funds to various universities for a world tour (*la bourse pour la tour autour du monde*), and his aim – of having scholars travel around the world – of making people study the condition of various peoples – was truly for the sake of world peace for mankind.[6] As each country's condition and situation becomes known through scholarly research, so too does empathy grow between the scholars of different countries, and in the end we can avoid calamities such as international misunderstandings and wars. I was able to go abroad again thanks to the endowment that was born of this logic, and here I will tell of both my studies of the religions and civilizations I observed, and also the kindness I received from the people I met. I would like to say that although the civilizations of East and West are different, the human emotions therein are the same. I also felt a duty to convey to my compatriots the things I learned about Western civilization and human emotion. With this intent, my diary and the other materials I collected on my journey over the past year came to be voluminous, but at this point, for the purposes of disseminating these publicly, I will begin by publishing one volume on my journey to Italy, that beautiful country in southern Europe. I have such warm memories of the flowers that I gathered in Italy and throughout Europe, and if my audience reads this "record of gathering flowers" and reaches the true conclusion that "There are no devils in this world,"[7] then I have stayed true to Mr. Kahn's intent, as well as shown my deep affection for my late friend. I would like, in due time, to present the results of the thoughts and observations I made outside the realm of this diary, both in Japan and in France.

> Tonight
> The wind is quiet
> The moon faint
>
> The faint moon at
> Kiyomigata
> The spring night's
>
> Dream tranquilly
> Sleeping
> Sea and mountains

In this realm, recollecting the flowers of Italy, I feel as if I were in a trance remembering a dream. Meeting the spring in another country made me recall my own country's landscape; returning to Japan and reading my diary of those times, I yearn for the flowering fields of southern Europe. Being able to taste these happy memories of deep affection and reminiscences in such a sad fashion is a gift for my late friend and mentor.

Kiyomigata
March 31, Meiji 42 (1909)

CHAPTER ONE

THE SNOWS OF GOTTHARD

TEUFELSBRÜCKE, ANDERMATT, SWITZERLAND

April 5 [1908]
Mountain Climbing in the Snow

THINKING THAT I wanted to see the spring moon on the shores of Lake Lugano,[1] I passed this evening surrounded by snow in the mountains of Göschenen.[2]

I had left Zürich at ten in the morning. It was cloudy again today but the mountains along Lake Zürich were visible, trailing above the water. I caught sight of the Enge home of Wagner,[3] which I had seen the previous day, as the train gradually ran along the foothills and up into the mountains. The lake vista was expansive. Houses with green glass windows lay between the fruit orchards and pastures of green grass. The lakeside at Zürich was truly a peaceful paradise. I passed through a tunnel to come out between two mountains, then passed through another tunnel and came out at Lake Zug. At this side of the lake was Mt. Rigi; its top was sheathed in clouds, and below the clouds the cliffs were layered in snow, making for a speckled effect of white snow on the rocky mountain. We arrived at Arth-Goldau on the lakeshore. Last year when I was on Rigi, the weather was fine, and I was able to see the peak to the right, Lake Zug at the foot of the mountain, and the sharp cliffs of Mt. Mythen to the left, away across another lake. But this time it was cloudy and I could only see the lonely surface of the two lakes. Turning toward the south we came to the shore of Vierwaldstatter. The waters of this lake are a deep blue that seems bottomless and fill the space between the carved mountains as if in eternal sleep. Looking at this lake reminds me of the play about Tell.[4] The free spirit of the strong and stouthearted people who live around this lake are the foundation of Switzerland's independence. To the south of the lake sits the village of Flüelen. I recalled vividly that six years ago I crossed this lake by boat and went by horse carriage from this village to Altdorf, said to be the village of Tell, where I spent the night. I could also see the Altdorf steeple which I had seen on the evening of All Souls' Day in November.[5]

The train ascended gradually through a mountain pass. On this plateau, the foliage was not withered from frost, but verdant instead; yellow dandelions and primroses bloomed riotously. The mountains on either side did not look like they were capped with lingering snow, but rather the falling snow seemed like clouds, and the snowflakes clung to all the trees of the copse.

> Blossoms of snow on the trees on the peak
> Golden primroses in the field
> The change from winter to spring
> Is confused in the clouds of the Swiss Alps [6]

As we continued along through the mountains, which were tall and distant on both sides, the layers of peaks hidden among the clouds occasionally poked through the mist. Waterfalls poured down the mountains from the midst of the clouds, like something falling from the heavens. Spring began to come from the blanket of snow deep in the mountains, and the snowmelt had begun.

> Spring has come
> The white Alpine snow
> Has begun to melt.
> Between the crags
> A white thread of a waterfall

Once I had ascended close to the clouds, I saw that what had seemed like clouds was actually entirely whirling snow. The world above 800 meters, outside the winding tunnel, was silvery on all sides. I could still see fallen snow and piles of ice here and there among the shadows of the cliffs where the "clouds" had cleared. When I looked up I saw that there were even more peaks layered above those that already seemed to be touching the sky.

> Looking up
> I saw peaks that
> Seemed to have fallen from the sky
> I could see amidst the clouds
> Above, more peaks

Above were white peaks of snow in the clouds; below were valleys of snow that had fallen in avalanches. Before we knew it the place we had just passed was below us and we arrived in the village of Göschenen, which sits at an altitude of 1,000 meters. Here we all entered a dining hall and had lunch. I had intended to go as far as Lugano today, but upon seeing the snow covered village and recalling my regret at not stopping here the previous year, I decided to stay here one night. After my meal I arranged for my luggage to be taken to the Göschenen Hotel. The previous year while waiting for my train I had dined at this establishment, and I had thought that only I would remember such a thing. But the hotel manager, a fat old man, came and said, "You were here once before!" I was surprised that he did remember, but then of course he would – it was a place where few Japanese came, so he remembered a Japanese who had come before, and to whom he had recommended mountain climbing. Although I had not done it before, this time when he asked if I would climb the mountain I said, "Of course. Bring me some climbing shoes!" I settled on a room and unpacked my bags. The bellboy who came to light a fire in the heater of my room had characteristically kind Swiss eyes (although they share the same language, the eyes of a Swiss are different from those of a German). Inside the room was the crackle of the burning fire; outside was the silence of the snow. After a while I could hear the sound of jingling sleigh bells – of the sort that are hung around a horse's neck. The sleigh was waiting for me when I went downstairs. I left the inn at three o'clock and ascended the mountain. After a bit the snow was very deep and the mountains on both sides soared high and steep. There were so many clouds that I could not see the summit, but the cliff sides appeared here and there through the clouds. More than simply mountains against the clear sky, they were mountains that were high, large, and steep. Some of the cliffs had been entirely worn away by the accumulation, leaving nothing but valleys of snow, but outcroppings survived the snow and stood out here and there. An ice pillar came down the cliff face like a saber blade.

> Rain and snow
> Enduring the millennia
> Are dangerous
> Hanging down from
> The soaring cliffs

As I ascended, the landscape became increasingly steep, and the snow very deep. The wind was at my back but still I pulled the collar of my overcoat closed against the cold snow storm. My driver was happy with a single shirt and no overcoat. When I asked him if he was not cold, he said that he had been born and bred in the snow and was not cold. When we came to a place along the summer mountain road where snow had fallen in an avalanche, our conversation turned to avalanches. The unflappable driver said that he himself had once survived being buried in an avalanche. He said, "Today is safe – we won't have an avalanche. Tomorrow, if it is bright and sunny, there will be many dangerous places." Directly above the road was a deep valley where two or three days earlier there had been an avalanche. The snow had fallen in a direct line from the mountainside into the valley; on the opposite side a similar avalanche had occurred, leaving the river in the valley buried from both sides. Only the road had been cleared of snow. My driver looked at the mountains beyond the valley and said, "Ten years or so ago I tended sheep every day in those mountains. I herded them from May to October. Each head brought three francs." He had lived his summers herding sheep from morning till night in the rocky mountains, and winters were spent in the snow. No doubt he had a good constitution. I thought to myself that the Swiss must come by their rich spirit of freedom naturally.

We came to Teufelsbrücke, which means "The Devil's Bridge." A stone bridge spanned the deep valley. The driver said legend had it that the devil had built this bridge. The people of Uri canton had tried to build a bridge across this valley, but to no avail. Then the devil came and told them that he could build the bridge if they paid him much gold. With a promise of gold the bridge was built but the gold was never paid. So the devil became angry and said that he would grab the first person who tried to cross the bridge and throw him into the river. A wise old man drove a sheep across the bridge. The devil grabbed the sheep and threw it in the river, leaving the old man to cross the bridge safely. It is said that from that time forward, all those who cross the bridge have done so in safety. After finishing his story, the driver added, "It is just a legend – not a bit of truth in it." I thought to myself that country folk are honest, if not amusing. On a boulder at the side of the bridge there is a drawing of a fire-breathing black devil. There is also a hole carved in that boulder where an image of San Antonio de Padua is placed for worship. When I looked from the bridge, I saw that above the river was a solid mass of rapids, but below I could see that the rapid currents ran beneath and through the covering snow. I passed two tunnels that had been dug to get around avalanches. At the bend there was a stronghold where it seemed that batteries had been built at the base of the mountain, and guards stood at the entrance in the snow. It was a scene out of Tang Dynasty frontier poetry.[7]

Past the front of the northern battery, there was a wide field that spread out between the mountains, and which, like Senjōgahara at Nikkō,[8] had at its base a lake in a gorge. The wide field was covered in a blanket of white snow. At the base of the mountains I could see a small group of houses and the tops of trees, poking out here and there from the snow. Mountains surrounded the field on all four sides. I could only see the foot of the mountains – the rest was obscured by the clouds. The driver said that the snow in these mountains was quite nice in good weather. Presently we arrived at the village. Once I saw how the houses were buried I understood the snow's depth. Nothing but the tip of the metal railing of the hotel, which was only open in the summer, showed through the snow. The army came to a barracks here in the summer, and its gun carriage sheds had snow up to their eaves. It was a Sunday, so in the village I found soldiers and young girls sliding along the snow on the long wooden shoes they call "skis." The village children had gathered on an elevation to throw snowballs. I headed to an inn called "Krona" and went in. Villagers and soldiers were gathered here. I had a cup of tea and sent postcards to everyone. I sent postcards that showed snow falling from the April sky.

I rested for about half an hour, then went out. The sky, which I had earlier thought had cleared a bit, was completely covered with snow clouds and a strong northern wind was bringing a snowfall. We turned into the blowing snow and headed north. I turned neither my face nor anything else. From time to time I looked through the fingers of my gloves, which I held up in front of my face, and on one of those occasions I saw two sleds in front of us. The one nearest ours had a Franciscan monk riding in it, and one was carrying the mail. The Franciscan monk wore a pointed hood – called a capuchin – over his head. Apart from that remarkable brown hood, everything in all directions was an entire world of snow. The horse kicked the snow powerfully down the slope as it moved along. The wind blew the snow from the side. On the winding road the wind was very strong on my hands and on the exposed rocks, and it blew about the snow that had accumulated on the ground. The feeling was exactly that of being enveloped in a snowstorm.

> Waves of snow,
> Kicking, crumbling,
> The sky above
> The sleigh's destination
> Enveloped in snow

We passed the fort and the tunnel in no time, went over the Devil's Bridge, and came to a bend in the road. The horse went too quickly down the slope, and the sleigh slid over on its side. Both driver and passenger rolled into the snow, leaving the horse to pull the empty sleigh forward. Because we fell into the soft snow, we had no injuries. The driver ran ahead to catch the horse while I picked up the cushions and chased after the sleigh, which was headed down the slope. When the driver cracked his whip in an effort to overtake the sleigh, the horse pulled with all its might. In the end, we did not slip and were able to catch up. Because we were considerably further down the mountain by this time the blowing snow lessened and the clouds seemed to lift a little. Soon I could see the Göschenen railroad and the village; it was past five o'clock when I returned to the inn. When I got down from the sleigh in front of the inn and looked at myself, I discovered that my overcoat, my moustache, and my eyebrows were covered with snowflakes, making me look like a polar bear. I brushed the flakes off and returned to my room to warm myself by the fire, feeling like I was coming back to life. The ascending trip up the road took an hour and a half but the return trip took only half an hour.

In the surrounding silence of the accumulated snow I could hear the sound of children's playful voices and the occasional bells of a passing sleigh, but I could not hear the sound of the nearby railroad. When I looked out my window I could see the blowing snow flitting about in the wind coming down off the mountain. Here I was viewing the snow while it was cherry-blossom viewing season in Japan.

> In the mountain wind blowing from the peak
> I watch the white snow falling
> I am lost in thoughts of my hometown
> Surely adrift in cherry blossoms[9]

Surrounded by snow I read the philosophy of Rosmini as the sun set.[10]

> A mountain village
> In the quietly
> Falling snow
> Not a bird chirps
> As the sun sets

I am writing this entry after dinner. The church bells ring from time to time, but all in the inn are fast asleep and the heavens are quiet. There is no sound, save the scratching of my pen and the voice of the devoted prayers I say within my own heart.

April 6th
Leaving the Shadow of the Mountain

I SLEPT in this morning, and when I got up and looked out the window I saw a snowy sky. Yesterday the snow fell heavily, but today it flew about quietly. I felt not the least bit cold even though I had opened the window to take a look outside. The serving boy came to stoke my fire after morning tea. I read Rosmini inside my warm room while outside it was snowing. Just before noon I went out for a little walk and found the slightly melted and muddy road covered with lines of snow; my feet made a heavy sound with each step. The wind that accompanied the quietly falling snow gently caressed my face and filled the air with a delightful kind of feeling, just like the sensation of being wrapped in silk wadding. I breathed in the air of heaven and earth with zest. I left the village and went gradually up into the mountains. Beneath my feet was only white snow that sparkled and was bright to my eyes. Looking up I saw snow clouds clinging to the mountains, and no matter where I turned all I could see through the clouds were rocks and copses covered in snow. Just ahead slopes came down from both sides, and I could just see a wooden cottage nestled in the snow. Once at the cottage I looked back and could see the village of Göschenen below. Ahead of me the mountains continued in the same fashion, and if the sky had been clear I would have been able to see the Damma glacier in the valley, but no matter how high I stood it was pointless today.

I covered my eyes from the snow and returned to the inn, occasionally picking up snow from the roadside and putting it in my mouth. The clock struck one. The sun had come out a bit and I wanted to stay here another day, but I regretted how few days I would have in Italy, so I boarded a train at two o'clock and headed south. I anticipated that, once I passed through the four-*ri* tunnel[11] the Italian sky would probably not be snowy: within a moment I would go from the depths of winter to meet spring.

CHAPTER TWO

SPRING ON THE LAKE

LOCARNO, MADONNA DEL SASSO, LOGGIA, TESSIN, SWITZERLAND

April 6
Southern Exposure Flowers; the Italian Sky

AFTER POSTING the morning's letters I left Göschenen at two o'clock and went through the four-*ri* tunnel. I thought that when I did so it would be spring-like on the other side, but there was still snow, and there was more falling. However, it was not as deep as it had been in Göschenen. The train went down through the mountains; here the mountains, unlike in the north, did not encroach upon but rather bordered a valley that was open on many sides. On each side of the valley, mountains jutted forth and the snow clouds seemed lost between the peaks in a spectacular manner. I wished that I could borrow Sesshū's brush.[1]

The train ran down along the mountain road through the valleys where I could see a few fruit blossoms. The sun began to peek through when we reached Faido at 700 meters. On the mountain that was our destination the sun shone on the white snow and the peaks reached the clouds; the snow-covered mountains soared to the blue skies. By and by we arrived in Italy.[2] Whenever the train stopped people were speaking Italian outside the cars. Even within the train cars the conductor would announce the stops or transfers first in Italian and then in German. I could see hermitages and churches up in the mountains – their roofs were tiled in slate. The sun's rays gradually became stronger. The snowy peaks were far away in the distance. By the time we reached Bellinzona it was clearly springtime, and the evening sun coming through the window even felt hot. The surrounding fields were all verdant, and the peach blossoms were in full bloom in the meadow. Peach blossoms directly at the foot of a snow-capped mountain!

> The flowing snowmelt from the peak
> Passes through the bosom of the earth
> On a peach tree growing in a sunny place
> Bloom light pink flowers

I gazed at the evening sun reflected on the lake by Locarno as the train began to ascend from Bellinzona to Lugano. All the mountains I had passed in the north had been tangled in clouds, below which were dark valleys. Here in an azure sky, crimson rays of sun struck red peach blossoms in green fields. It was an entirely different world. Yesterday I urged my horse on through the snow and had lived, until this morning, in a snowy world, passing exhilarating days; now in this spring landscape, looking back at the mountains from whence we came, I did not feel like entering them once again. The intrigue of the snow was in no way inferior to that of the spring sun, but after coming here I did not want to return to the mountains. The lofty mountains and snowstorms had made me strong and strengthened my resolve. But the spring sky was sweet and captured my heart. Like the gentleness of Christ and the strict faith of the Jewish prophet; like the devotion of Zoroaster and the quietude of the Buddha; like the majesty of Nichiren[3] and the gentleness of Hōnen;[4] in each case, the pairs seem to be incompatible, but the two sides instead complement each other. This thought struck me all the more today when I saw the change from snow to flowers.

We arrived in Lugano at five thirty. The lake is directly outside the station, the deep blue waters filling the space between me and the surrounding mountains. Around the lake shore red brick houses were clumped together here and there. I will stay at a certain inn today, but the view – despite it being on an elevation – is of nothing but the railroad, so tomorrow I think I will change accommodations.

I left the inn to call on Signor Bignami,[5] but I could not find his place despite searching all quarters. I asked two or three people on the street and after much struggle with incomprehensible Italian I found his house. The graying gentleman in his fifties came out and bade me welcome, saying that he had been waiting for me. His wife and children also came out to greet me. We spoke briefly, exchanged letters, and promised to meet again the next day. There was a letter from my home among those I received.

I returned to the inn and wrote letters in the sitting room. The sun set in the west, shining on the mountains surrounding the lake, dyeing them a dark red. To the north were what looked like storm clouds gathering above the tall, snowy peaks.

At dinner there was a performance of Italian music and songs. Among the many people in the dining hall were two ladies who were eating their meal with a nurse. Perhaps they were here because one of their husbands was ill. One of them shot me a frightening look, which at first I took for rudeness. But then, I thought perhaps her face had become stern naturally as a result of dealing with her husband's illness and I felt sorry for her.

I went out after dinner. The air was chilly, even though there was no breeze. The new moon was in the western sky and the stars were twinkling, as were lights from boats on the lake; only the mountains remained in dark shadow. I would sleep from this night forward on this quiet Italian lakeside.

April 7
A Distant Friend

I CHANGED inns today. The inn where I stayed last night was a German inn, and when I entered the dining hall the Germans all gawked at me and made me uncomfortable. The inn I came to today is full of English guests and run by Swiss so I am comfortable here.[6] The inn is on an elevation, and there is a garden in the front with a copse of trees and a lake, above which one can see the tall mountains of the lakeside. My room has a wide veranda, and when I go out on it the view of the copse and the lake make it feel like my own garden.

I was invited to Signor Bignami's house for lunch and enjoyed a pleasant meal with his family. In addition to Signora Bignami, there were three girls, the eldest about ten years old and a small son, plus the Signora's younger sister in the family. Lunch was an Italian rice dish. During lunch the children sat attentively when I spoke about Japan (the children can all understand French). The small boy said he was *contento* (happy) when I spoke to him in my limited Italian. Although our countries are far apart and our languages are different, we share the same human emotions, and I had the feeling that, through correspondence, we would nurture a feeling of exchange for many years. We had a candid conversation over our meal in which Signor Bignami told me, "Since I heard the news that you were coming I have been showing the children your photograph, and telling them that their uncle from Japan would come visit. We've been waiting every day, and I'm sure my friends will be coming to meet you, too." The next day was *uzuki yōka*,[7] so I invited them to my inn. But he said that there were others who wanted to meet me and who lived far away so Sunday would be better. So I postponed my invitation and decided to go for a walk.

After returning from Signor Bignami's house I went down the mountain in the rain at sunset to the town center where I looked out at the lakeside landscape. The clouds were tangled above the mountains and the lake waters were darkened by the gentle rainwater. I walked through the village under the roofs which formed a kind of corridor, and then returned to the inn.

April 8
Gathering Flowers on the Lake Shore

TODAY IS *uzuki yōka* – the birthday of the Buddha.[8] I rose to find the sun shining a bit and the birds singing. After breakfast I put a chair out on the veranda and perused a biography of St. Francis.[9] I left the inn after ten o'clock and walked along the road on the elevation looking at the lake, then I descended to the lake shore. Unlike the day before it was sunny, and many people were taking strolls along the lake. After walking all along the lake, I arrived at the church of Santa Maria degli Angioli. The exterior architecture is simple and inside there is very little decoration, save for a fresco depicting the death of Christ. The individual figures are good enough, but the piece as a whole is muddled.[10] There is also a painting of the Virgin Mary in a small grotto – the artist is Luini, the same artist who painted the wall painting.[11] I have a print of this painting hanging in my home. The colors of my print are a little too bright, but the original's colors are more subdued, as it is a fresco. In the painting the Virgin Mary lovingly caresses two innocent children (John the Baptist and Christ). As a post-Raphaelite work it has nothing to be ashamed of, and it clearly shows the Franciscan faith in an admirable way. It surely was not coincidence that I was admiring a painting of Christ and the Virgin Mary in a Franciscan church on the birthday of the Buddha.[12] I climbed the hill home once more, gathering flowers on the way back to my inn, where I had lunch.

I had an appointment with Signor Bignami in the afternoon, so I went to his house directly after finishing lunch. His children were waiting in the garden for me, and we went inside and spoke for a short while. His younger sister played "Elisabeth's Prayer" from *Tannhäuser*[13] on the piano and, after we had some coffee, I walked down the mountain with the Signor, Signora, and two of their daughters to board a steamship that went out onto the lake. We left the town of Lugano behind; up on the hill where the church of Castagnola is situated there was a sort of country cottage on the lakeside where many peach blossoms were in bloom. The view from the boat in the middle of the lake was of mountains on all four sides, the water opening wide toward the southwest. After about thirty minutes we got off the boat at the village of Oria.[14] This is Italy proper (Lugano is in Switzerland) so at the landing an Italian customs officer conducted an inspection. Immediately ashore was the country house of Fogazzaro.[15] The landscape and village here feature in his novels. The country house was small, but the walls were painted an Italian-style color and the cypress trees in the garden stood forlornly, reaching for the sky. The houses in this village are all built and layered tightly against the mountains, so the roads and spaces between houses are narrow, as is the space between walls. Beneath the houses are tunnel-like cobblestone ways; all in all they are curious streets. Nonetheless, the streets all have names, and the main street (the "Via Principale") is a slope about three or four *shaku* wide which winds between people's houses.[16] There is a church on an elevation above the lakeshore away from the village of Oria. There are various frescoes on the outside walls of the church, as is particular to Italy. From there we followed the bluff road along the cliff. There were various flowers blooming in the field on the bluff. The children, who had heard me talking about how this was *uzuki yōka* and thus Flower-Gathering Day,[17] picked these various flowers and gave them to me. There were violets, cherry blossoms, dandelions, and a kind of wild chrysanthemum. I thought I would dry them for the children as a memento of our outing this *uzuki yōka*. We came eventually to the lakeshore village of San Mammette, which looked like the painting I had seen of it. At the village entrance was a bridge across the Solda River that was like the sort of bridge one would see in a Chinese landscape painting. The view of the water of the Solda and the deep, craggy cliffs was just like a Sesshū ink painting, with its great boulders and roiling clouds.

The priest in Fogazzarro's novel spent his youth in the Solda valley. I stopped for tea in San Mammette and sent postcards to everybody. The people of the village looked exactly like they had stepped from a medieval painting; women in blue garments hugged children in red. The wooden shoes that the children wore were just like Japanese *geta*; there was practically nothing there from the contemporary world. The proprietor of the store where I bought my postcards was painting a painting. Villagers gathered around to watch him. There were various paintings hung outside the shop. The surrounding cypress trees, the stone walkways between the walls, the church dais and lake view from the tea shops' veranda – all composed a landscape out of a painting or poem. It occurred to me that the Nature and Human Life that painters and poets celebrated came from this landscape. The steamship arrived and we left Mammette for Lugano. I never tired of gazing at the villagers working in the mountains, the cypress groves, the red-walled lake villas, and the boulders in the Solda valley. On board I spoke with Signor Bignami about the Buddhist faith and Italian politics; presently the boat reached Lugano. His younger sister and other children came to greet us and we all together climbed the mountain back to his house. After parting from the Bignami's I met up with an Englishman who was staying at the same inn as I and we returned there together, gathering flowers along the way.

After dinner I conversed with the other Britons at the inn, and then I returned to my room to write this letter.[18] On this, the day of *uzuki yōka*, I went for a walk on the lake shore instead of having tea, I picked flowers, and I spent the day with an Italian family and their children. It was truly an enjoyable *uzuki yōka*.

April 9
On Lake Como

TODAY THE sun shone in the morning and the weather was very spring-like. I spent the morning on the veranda reading a book, and at ten o'clock I left the inn to go by boat out on the lake.[19] At first I followed the same route as I had yesterday. However, the villages layered among the cliffs, the red-walled villas that I could see among the cypresses on the lake shore, the red peach flowers and yellow dandelions, and the white snow in the deep valley recesses all had a new charm to them. The boat passed nearby villages and distant shores and arrived in Porlezza on the far eastern end of the lake. From there I took a train through a mountain pass, past a small lake and a peach orchard, to the shores of Lake Como to the east. I could see the whole lake as I descended from above it. The fleeting view comprised the snow covered peak of Monte Muggio soaring high on the opposite shore, the Bellagio peninsula jutting out into the lake, dividing the waters into two fingers, and on the right the Cima mountains. Next to the descending railroad were, of course, peach trees among cypress.[20] Soon the train came to the village of Menaggio on the lakeshore. I bought some postcards and wooden shoes of the type worn by the folk of these parts while I waited for the steamship. It was not a large purchase, but the shop girl gave me a camellia and thanked me for my patronage. There are many camellias in this area now, but originally they all came from Japan so the flowers here are all the grandchildren of Japanese camellias.[21] I put the camellia in a buttonhole and boarded a boat.[22]

The boat headed for Bellagio. The mountains around this lake are rather high and are all snow-capped, but they are not steep like the mountains around Lugano. The snow flows abundantly from the peaks down to the lake at their feet, where I could see lakeside villages of rows of white houses with red tile roofs. To the east was Monte Muggio, to the north the high peaks of the Alps; they created a pure white skyline gleaming in the sunlight of the azure sky. A gentle breeze blew from the south, raising waves on the lake surface. It was a tranquil, gentle scene.

The boat arrived in Bellagio. On shore there were tables lined up beneath the trees on the lakeshore where many tourists sat to read the newspaper or have after-dinner coffee. The village women who walked up and down the shore wore red kerchiefs on their heads and wooden shoes. The houses had white walls and green doors, all of which combined into a most interesting color combination. On top of the mountain behind the village I could see a famous villa situated among the cypress trees. I was told that from its prospect the view of the lake was the best to be had, but I did not have time to go ashore to see. After some village men loaded many olive branches used for Easter decorations on board, the boat headed for the opposite shore. The village on the opposite shore, Tremezzo, also had rows of inns and villas behind which were hills of olive orchards with various flowers, and above which were the Cima mountains. From Tremezzo the boat headed south. There was also a villa on Avedo promontory.[23] It is built on the shore in a Roman architectural style, with stone arched walls and statues along the stone railing of the observation platform. There were, of course, cypress trees in the garden, and one of them at the front of the grove jutted out in a lonely way over the tip of the promontory, its reflection showing on the water. If one were to stop one's boat in front of such a villa and play a flute on a moonlit night it would be exactly like a scene from a romance. On the Island of St. Giovanni, or in the village of Colonna, the scenery was also straight out of a painting or poem. As I lamented that these mountains obscured the view of the snowy mountains up to the north, an Englishman who had boarded the boat in Bellagio came up to me and asked, "Which is better – this or Mt. Fuji?" I replied, "Fuji is Fuji, the Alps are the Alps; they each have their own charms, so I never tire of looking upon them." We laughed and spoke further for a while. During our conversation the boat arrived at a village along an old wall built against a mountain cliff. The Englishman said, "This is the village of Nesso, which dates back to the days of the Roman Empire. Caesar came here once. We are staying in Bellagio and taking outings around the lake occasionally. Today we have come to see Nesso." With that he got off the boat with three colleagues. I waved my handkerchief to the four travelers who climbed the mountain road to the top of the cliff as the boat proceeded around the promontory to the south. The lake wound to the left and to the right. There were villas on each little promontory. The boat arrived in Como at about half past three, while I was napping in the cabin cooled by the breeze. I went ashore directly to see the *duomo* (in France a big church is called a *cathédrale*; in Italy it is called a *duomo*). It was an odd mixture of Gothic and Renaissance architecture, with a white marble façade and fine carvings on the columns of each corner. Inside it was entirely Renaissance – more than a church, it was like a palace, with tapestries hung between the pillars and paintings by Luini above the altars.[24] The feeling I had was entirely different from that of having entered the deep majesty of a Gothic church – instead I felt that I had entered into a gaudy and neatly organized space. The parishioners who come to this sort of palace do indeed worship. There were many confessants in the confessionals, both men and women. Voices of confessions were slightly audible in the shadows of the pillars and walls. It seemed fitting to hear these voices in the Gothic darkness surrounding the tall pillars. I left the church to take a look at the entry way and the carvings on the pillars. These too were in the style of Renaissance palatial decorations, but they also had a certain appeal to them. I had tea in the café in front of the church while I gazed at the church's façade. Rays of sunshine toward the west gleamed on the white marble and I was loath to leave the sparkling walls and pillars that soared toward the azure sky.

I walked through a narrow street. On either side, sandwiching the road, were houses in the old style with few windows and interior gardens full of statues, creating a veritable tunnel. After passing along this street I came to a path through trees among which were remnants of the old castle walls. There were many churches along the street. All of them were done in an old Romanesque style, except for the façades, which were done in a strange Baroque style. There were monasteries next to the churches and, passing along the opposite barracks, I went to the train stop on the bluff. Looking down from there upon the town I saw red tile roofs jumbled together, and from the center of them rose the majestic round steeple of the *duomo*; beyond the town the houses situated high up on top of the mountains gleamed in the sun. I was told that if I climbed these mountains I would be able to see the Alps to the north and the Lombardo plateau to the south, but I did not have time so I did not go.

The train left Como at five o'clock and soon arrived in Chiasso. This is on the Swiss and Italian border, so there is a customs inspection. I was told to leave the train and go through customs, but, I said, I have no luggage. Luggage or no, I was still told to go through customs. If such were the case then, I told the customs agent, inspect my camellia flower if you like, and I got off the train and went through customs. In the little time left before the train's departure I toured the town for a bit. There were many emigration offices. They all took care of the Italians from this area who wanted to emigrate to America. I wondered if there could be many people who were unhappy in this Italian and Swiss paradise and who wanted to go instead to live in the coal smoke of America solely to make money; what a tragedy it is.

The train headed north after leaving Chiasso and arrived on the shores of Lake Lugano. The evening sun shone on the snow-capped peak of Monte Generoso and I returned to Lugano under the cover of the darkness of sundown on the lake's surface.

After dinner I again gazed out at the darkening mountain landscape. The moon sent out bluish-white light across the wide sky. The driver of a horse cart passing in front of the inn tranquilly sang an Italian song.

I received a letter from Garnier. He wrote about the similarities between *uzuki yōka* and the Christian Easter, and also of the child Eveline.[25]

April 10
The Mountain View; Schools; Music; Family

TODAY IS clear again, with warm, spring-like temperatures. In the morning I rose and, after briefly soaking in the rays of spring sunshine on the veranda, I boarded a train at nine o'clock headed for the south end of town where a cogwheel train climbed Monte San Salvatore. The mountain is not very tall – just 600 meters above lake level – but because it has hills and fields on one side and the lake shore directly on the other side there was a good prospect all around as I ascended. I could see the range of the Alps to the northwest. At the summit I went out on a ledge to take a look. The boats passing by on the lake looked exactly like tree leaves on the water's surface and tall mountains were visible all around. To the east were the rocky mountains of Solda. Also visible were the snowy mountains above Lake Como where I went yesterday, and the mountains surrounding Lugano on all four sides. The Alps stretched from the north to the east; a line of snowy, rocky mountains that soared halfway up to the sky extended west from the highest of the peaks, the Jungfrau. Those snowy peaks faded off into the distant west, their tips floating in the azure sky, dissolving as if they were ice floes floating on water. I bathed in the warm sunlight and was caressed by the spring breeze; I forgot myself as I gazed enraptured, and I felt as if I myself would melt into the heavens. On the distant mountains, snow; in the nearby fields, flowers; on the lake, deep blue. And on the mountain that stands in the midst of this the villagers built a chapel to celebrate Christ and called this mountain Salvatore (Savior). In a sunny place by the chapel I picked a small flower as a memento and then went back to the foot of the mountain by the cog-wheel train, eating my lunch upon my return to the inn.

After lunch I went with Bignami to a girls' vocational school in the town. The principal was the wife of Rensi[26] (with whom I had become acquainted through the magazine[27]) and she showed us the school's facilities and classrooms. The two most popular occupations taught are carpentry and sewing, but the carpentry is not like the American style where the lines are taken from nature; rather, students are taught patterns and historical methods and they are made to create decorations and sculptures such have been made since the olden days. As they progress, they are allowed to make their own carpentry spontaneously. This is the Italian way. In America, which is a country with no history, students begin with spontaneous depiction, but in Italy, which is a country with history, of course there is a need to follow history. I sat in on the Italian class in the language classroom, and I read a section of the reader that had a travelogue of an Italian who went to Yokohama. Hearing about beautiful Japan, about the colors of the children's clothing and the patterns of the marketplaces, described in beautiful Italian in this distant foreign country made me feel like I was recalling a dream of something I had seen in the distant past. I also sat in on an English lesson and found fourteen or fifteen girls who had made great progress in no more than a year. I bade them a simple farewell in English and went to see other classrooms; then, I said good bye to the principal and left the school.

I had promised to go hear Frau Schablitz's daughter play piano at three-thirty. Mrs. Bignami, her sister and one of her children came and waited for me in front of the school, then we all went together to the Schablitz's house. Mrs. Schablitz is from northern Switzerland, a German speaking area, therefore we spoke in German. A music teacher also came, and the young lady played piano while the teacher played violin – they played many pieces by Tirindelli.[28] I found the works "Pierrot Triste" and "Mistica" most interesting of them all – the style of all Italian works is colorful. "Pierrot Triste" was melancholy, but there was a passion in the sadness and a certain tonality, as if it were celebrating the sadness and being driven mad by it. "Mistica," more than being deep, had a mysterious harmony; it had an Italian passion to it. The final piece she played for us was

Beethoven's "Moonlight Sonata," in which a deep sound resounded through the skies of colorless moonbeams. It had no color, no feeling, but it had an inner depth and thus a power. It was just a little musical performance, but I felt as if I had been shown the contrast between Italy and Germany. We talked about various things and by the time I left their house it was close to sundown, the evening sun dyeing the mountains red as always.

I was invited to dine that evening at the Bignami's house, with Mrs. Rensi also in attendance, and we had a feast of Italian *udon* and conversed throughout dinner on various subjects.[29] Mrs. Bignami thought that Zen meditation was interesting; Mrs. Rensi held the opposite view, saying that Zen meditation emptied one of desires and was a method of anesthetizing the self. At this, I said the following: "It is easy to make one's self clever, but it is difficult to pursue foolishness. People are especially prone to being taken in by their surroundings and are wont to show off more cleverness than they actually possess. Zen meditation is useful in that it helps right prejudices and helps one pursue foolishness." I proceeded to trot out numerous examples and our conversation flourished, but the children were getting sleepy and it was past ten o'clock, so we left off and Mr. Bignami and I took Mrs. Rensi to the foothills to see her on her way. The moon in the cloudless sky gave off a blue hue, casting a dark indigo all around. In that light the snow on the mountains seemed to be floating in the sky and the lake waters below the mountains were dark, as if slumbering. I looked up at the moonlight, and walked home remembering Beethoven's "Moonlight Sonata" that I had heard that afternoon.

As I wrote this letter in my inn, I could hear the sound of a flute coming from below. I went out on the veranda and looked at the moon, and the shadow of the snow in the mountains; then I went to bed.

April 11
Locarno; Madonna del Sasso; the Representative

I WOKE early and opened the window. The white light of the coming sun shone faintly above the shadow of the dark mountains. The birds were chirping, announcing the arrival of the spring morning. It was Regatta Day in Tokyo, and I wondered how it would turn out this year.[30] I finished breakfast after eight o'clock and as I gazed out at the lake I thought that just about that time on the Sumida River the results of the Faculty of Humanities' race were being decided.

Although it was thousands of miles away, I could see everyone waving their flags and shouting. I read about St. Francis on the veranda, soaking up the warm spring sun. At ten o'clock I left for Locarno by train. The Bignami children came out into their scenic garden and waved their handkerchiefs at the departing train. On the road to Biasca, from a prospect on the cliff, I saw a delightful view of the Ticino valley, the lake by Locarno, peach orchards at the foot of the mountains, and the morning shadows of springtime. From Biasca I passed by the Ticino river, past the broad fields to the west and along the Locarno lakeshore. On the right were mountain villages full of blooming flowers; on the left were snowy peaks beyond the lake waters. I arrived at Locarno at eleven thirty. From there, I directly ascended the mountain by cogwheel, past inns and villas with green gardens and through thick copses, higher and higher up the mountain. Ahead of us soared the church of Madonna del Sasso, and along the road that led to it were small chapels along the upward slope. We got out of the car beside the church and went to an inn that was built on top of the cliff where the church was located. From the veranda there I gazed out over the lake. The church juts out from the rocks, and the red tile roofs of the village are clearly visible against the blue lake waters. At that moment the noontime bells chimed. The sound of the bells reverberated off the lake and echoed throughout the mountains. When the last note had stopped, I felt as if my spirit had floated up into the vast sky along with the sound of the bells.

> The sound of the bells
> In the mountain church
> As the mist rises
> Crosses the waters
> They are silenced

After I had a leisurely lunch while gazing out at the lake, I went to Madonna del Sasso. The church is on a rocky outcropping and as I passed by it I also saw that the Franciscan monks' monasteries were similarly built on the rocks. Coming out of a monastery hallway that ran along a stone stairway, I came upon a small garden in front of the church. I saw that there were many frescoes painted on the two-story front wall. On the walls of this church, which is replete with pillars and arches, are red and yellow paintings, and these, contrasted with the blue sky, make the church really quite charming. Inside there is too much decoration. There are stars painted on the deep blue ceiling, and there are many paintings hung among the pillars and on the walls, showing the realization of desires. It is said that five hundred years ago the Virgin Mary appeared on this mountain and all convalescents were miraculously healed. Thus the church was built and in their faith the villagers in this area dress images of the Virgin Mary in brocade, put a crown on her, and prostrate themselves just as worshipers would do in Japan. They also place paintings of the Virgin Mary next to sickbeds. The women of the village pay visits to the church, and those of deep faith appear to supplicate. That aside, in the left grotto there is a painting by Ciseri.[31] It is a well-arranged and calm painting viewed from any angle.[32] I knew the painting from photographs, but standing in front of the real thing held a new kind of charm. Having only looked at photographs for many years, I stood as if in a dream in front of the painting and squinted my eyes, then gazed, then squinted my eyes again. My interest increased as I looked at each color, and the points of each figure. One thing in particular that I had not noticed before was that although in this painting Christ is dead, his face seems to be not dead but rather sleeping, and his body forms the core of the painting, with the other figures gathered around this core. I realized for the first time, standing in front of the actual painting, that there is a connection between all this and the size of the painting. I did not tire of looking at it, even though I did so for close to an hour, but I knew that I had to go. I left the church with the feeling that I was parting from an old friend.

There was a passageway along the side of the church above the rock. Looking through the pillars of that passageway I soaked up the sun and gazed at the scenery of the lake. Paintings are paintings; Nature is Nature; I never tire of gazing upon them both.

I went to the center of the old town to call on Signor Pioda, who was the representative of the region's prominent family.[33] In front of his house was an old monastery. Behind the monastery was the house, which had a thick garden with a commemorative stela. I knocked on the door and presented my calling card at the old house. I was shown to the second story reception room, which was decorated with old weapons and the like, giving it an old-fashioned feel. An old woman who introduced herself as the master's niece came into the reception room and told me that the master currently had guests, so would I please wait a little? She asked me about Japan. Presently Signor Pioda came down from the second floor.[34] He was diminutive and close to sixty years old. He said, "I have read your essays, and have been waiting for your arrival here. Let us go to my study and talk," and he went up to the second floor study. The passageway and staircase were like something from an ancient castle, and there were many books in the study; I saw upon closer inspection that there were some about Buddhism. This man was not a scholar, but he was fond of history and philosophy, particularly Buddhism, so he knew quite a bit about India and Japan. We spoke for over an hour and a half about the state of the Roman Church, Rosmini, contemporary Switzerland, etc., before I took my leave.

There was still an hour before the train left, so I went for a walk along the lakeshore path, rested in the shade of the willows that drooped over the water,[35] turned toward the mountains and went through the vineyards, then returned to the village and left Locarno at five thirty. A dark shadow rose on the peak to the west, and the setting sun pierced the clouds to cast a long ray upon the lake waters. I arrived back in Lugano after seven o'clock. Two of the Bignami children waved their handkerchiefs when they saw my train pass. When I got off the train I saw that Bignami himself and the two other children had come to meet me, and we returned together to his house.

We had Italian food again this evening, and I ate with the entire Bignami family. We spoke about my trip to Locarno and my conversation with Pioda, then one of the daughters played the piano. She played a Norman song about ancient Druids lining up before an altar on a moonlit night; it was remarkable, and it was a tune for which there was also a dance. Then she played a popular Sicilian tune, and, as it was past ten o'clock, I took my leave. When I left the house it was raining but the moonlight seeped through the clouds and the lake looked like it had died between the mountains, it was so dark and quiet.

There was nothing I could do about my yearning to know how the Boat Race had turned out today. Tomorrow I shall invite guests for the Birthday of the Buddha.

April 12
A Tea Party for the Buddha's Birthday

THE RAINY weather from the previous evening had not dissipated much, but in the morning I could see sunlight coming through the clouds. It being Sunday, the church bells rang across the lake and echoed across the mountains. I passed the morning writing letters and reading.

I lunched at the Bignami's and was joined by a man whose acquaintance I had also made through the magazine, a Mr. Finch, who had come from Milan.

Together we ate a goodly amount of the rice dish that was served. I wanted to have a picture of the Buddha for today's celebration of his birth, but I did not have one. Signora Bignami had suggested that I be accompanied on this day by their *bambino* (the youngest son) instead of a newborn Buddha, but he had been febrile since the night before and was resting. After the meal the *bambino* woke up and we all went to check on him. He was lying down in his bedroom and playing with a toy, and he smiled when he saw us all. He pointed at Finch and said, "Who is this?" and we said, "Your uncle from Milan." He pointed at me and said, "Who is this?" and we said, "He is 'Ane,'" which set him to thinking. "Sleep well," I said and waved to him as I went downstairs. I returned to the inn and began preparations for inviting people for the celebration of the Buddha's birth.

I rented a room and put flowers on the table, flowers on the wall, and because I did not have an image of the newborn Buddha, I put Hōgai's painting of Kannon in the center,[36] plus an image of Bonten[37] and Mujaku[38] on each side, with flowers all around.[39] With this, the room was ready. Next, I donned my Japanese attire and waited for my guests. Presently, Mrs. Schablitz and son, the entire Bignami family, Mr. Finch, and a British man named Scott who happened to be in Lugano, all arrived. We spoke about the Birthday of the Buddha, Japanese painting, etc. Today, because there was an Englishman who spoke Italian well, whenever my Italian failed me I could speak to him in English and have him translate. We drank tea, ate sweets, and spoke about various and sundry ideas; both they and I spent an enjoyable afternoon, everyone leaving for home before seven o'clock. I went out on to the veranda to send them all off, waved my handkerchief and repeated, "A rivederci."

Having come to Lugano, where there was to be built a Buddhist retreat suitable to house monks in pure robes,[40] I felt replete even though I had only invited a few intimate friends and put up flowers as decorations to celebrate the Birthday of the Buddha. My guests were also happy and they took the flowers home. I, too, felt somehow good, and spent this day in a state of happiness. My only regret was that the Rensis could not attend, and that another friend, a Roman Catholic priest who was a friend of Bignami's had a prior engagement and also could not come. But for those who did come there was a lively conversation in English, German, and Italian among the flowers; we thought not about the different religions or peoples there, but rather simply drank tea to celebrate the Buddha's birthday. I thought that it would probably be the highlight of this journey.

After dinner I went to call on an Englishman in my inn who had developed a fever the night before, and I took him a flower from the afternoon's gathering. The moon shone dimly through the clouds onto the lake and clouds tumbled over the mountains. The flowers on my desk were fragrant.

April 13
An Englishman's Family

IT WAS cloudy in the morning but the birds, as always, twittered from morning on, as if they were singing a song. In the morning I wrote letters and packed my bags; the cloudy weather produced rain intermittently and I spent half the day happily in my inn, without venturing outside.

In the afternoon I went to Bignami's house and read magazines and the like, then just past three o'clock I went with Signora Bignami to Mr. Scott's house. Scott lives in Castagnola, which is more than half a *ri* from Lugano, so we boarded a boat and went to that village, climbing up the mountain from the lakeside. On the mountainside, above a stone fence, there was a country house in the Swiss style. This was Scott's house. A young girl came out to greet us as we entered the garden, followed by Mrs. Scott and two boys, and we all went to the second floor. On the grounds there were cedars, of the kind that grow in the high Alps, and also hemp palms and loquats, in between which grew many varieties of roses. The view of the lake from the second story was even better, with the face of Monte San Salvatore straight ahead. To the south I could see a bridge over the lake in the distance, and to the left Monte Generoso; it was a landscape like an enlarged Ishiyama in Ōmi.[41] Mrs. Scott is Dutch, and she had Dutch paintings and Japanese lacquerware in her house. They lived a quiet life in the quiet mountains above the lake. We drank tea. We spoke Italian and English, as each pleased. I noted that the British, the Dutch, and the Japanese were the peoples of the world who liked tea, and Scott and I intently drank ours while Signora Bignami expressed surprise that we could drink such a strong libation. I spent a very enjoyable time at the house until sundown. The setting sun shone through the clouds on the mountains around the lake. The town of Lugano to the west appeared as a dark shadow, and to the east the mountains were dyed crimson. We said our farewells and returned by train to Lugano.

After reaching my inn I was halfway through dinner when a Swiss singer came and sang like a bird. It would not be long before I would not hear such Swiss songs any more. After dinner I conversed with an Englishman who had lived for fifteen years in India, then I went to call on the British man who had taken to his sick bed, and whose fever had returned. I consoled him, then returned to my room.

April 14
My Last Day

RAIN AGAIN today. I read about Saint Francis in the morning, then before lunch went for a walk in the village above the hills. I thought, as I rambled along, about how this would be my last view of Lugano.

I spent the afternoon writing a response to criticisms of Buddhism for publication in Bignami's magazine.[42] The local shepherds had been upset by recent rumors that there was a Buddhist group in Leipzig[43] and that a Buddhist retreat was to be built in Lugano,[44] so occasionally negative criticisms of Buddhism appeared in the local newspapers and magazines. Each and every one of them was lacking as an argument, but I thought it would be better to offer clarification than to dismiss them out of hand so I wrote this piece. Rensi had returned in the evening from Italy, so we were all invited to Bignami's house for dinner. We spoke about Japanese Buddhism during and after dinner. Rensi likes Indian philosophy more than Buddhism, and a long discourse ensued about the differences of morals between East and West. Mrs. Bignami and her daughters asked me to write something in Japanese, so I wrote a poem that Hōnen composed while in exile, "Here it is frightening – my dew-like existence has come to an end" and appended an explanation.[45] But those who meet must eventually part[46] and I had to part from the people who had shown me such kindness these many days, not sure when I would meet them again. I left the spring warmth and gentle rainy weather of Lugano, and continued on my journey. From here I would continue on to Florence, Assisi, and other locales I had dreamed of for years, but I would eventually leave them, too. It is often said that "Living life is like staying at a travelers' inn,"[47] and indeed life is like this journey of mine. Even on the road, even in foreign countries, human emotion and feelings are the same, and I have made friends. That evening everyone down to the last child gave me their best wishes. I reflected on how impermanent and beautiful life is.

As I headed back to my inn the sun broke through the clouds upon the deep lake that slept between the high mountains. I am sure anyone would be at peace in their soul among such nature. I wished that the critics of Buddhism with whom I had conversed that afternoon could leave their prejudice behind and admire the Buddha. I would head to Bologna the next day, then Florence the following day, and would pass Good Friday in the Church of the Cross. On Sunday I would go to Fiesole to pass the Easter Holiday where the artist Angelico saw God before his eyes.[48]

This would be my last evening on the shores of Lake Lugano, and I wondered when I would next come here. I expect that when I do come, I will be accompanied by a monk of Right Vision,[49] and we will be able to read the Pali sūtra along with the priests at the retreat.[50]

> *Odorosa foriera d'aprile,*
> *Dalla terra sei nata pur ora*
> *Come in petto di donna gentile*
> *Nasce il primo pensiero d'amor.*
> *Il tuo fior sulla zolla appassita*
> *È la speme che il mesto rincora,*
> *Il sorriso che manda la vita*
> *Al cessar d'un acuto dolor.*
> *Fra le nevi che l'aura discioglie*
> *Io ti colgo, o romita de' prati,*
> *Io delibo dall' intime foglie*
> *La tua molle fragranza vital.*
> *E mi duol che parola non sia*
> *Quest' arcano d'effluvii beati.*
> *Oh sonasse nell' anima mia*
> *Come nota di spirto vocal!*
> — Andrea Maffei[51]

~ CHAPTER THREE ~

BOLOGNA: CITY OF ARCADES

PIAZZA OF THE CATHEDRAL, MILAN, ITALY

April 15
From Milan to Bologna

Today I left Lugano for good. The Bignami family saw me off as far as the station. I had stayed a mere nine days, but I had spent them in a comfortable home, and I felt as if I were leaving my own family.

I looked down on Lugano and the lake from the train. I could see the Scott house on the lakeshore. The inn and Bignami's house were behind me. The train went through a tunnel and when it emerged on the other side I had a different prospect of the lake, in which I could see the Valsoda peaks amidst the clouds, just like a *sumie* painting. Soon the view was entirely obscured by the mountains. I passed flowers at the foot of Generoso, and then countryside villages, and arrived at the border town of Chiasso before ten o'clock. The Italian customs inspection this time took over an hour, and was really quite absurd. While the inspection took place, I read St. Francis's biography and thought to myself that it would not do for me to be so short tempered, for St. Francis did not become angry even though he was repeatedly put upon by others.

The train left Chiasso after eleven o'clock and soon passed by Lake Como. I gazed at the lake and the villas on the shore; it seemed like a painting to me. We passed through a long tunnel and came out onto the Lombardo Plain. Dark clouds gathered here and there overhead, and there were occasional squalls. The grasses on the plain were green as far as the eye could see, and there were many new plants budding in the copses. The rains watered them, and the sun, seeping through the clouds, shone down upon them. I felt that summer was near.

We arrived in Milan at one-thirty. I had been there once before but there were still many things that I wanted to see. Moreover, Mr. Finch had invited me to come. But I wanted to get to Florence by Easter so I did not stop over in Milan but rather spent the two hours I had there touring the cathedral before the train departed at three-thirty. I went by streetcar into the city center. The squalls had lifted and the sun shone brightly, the trees in the park were beautiful, and there were many people out and about in the city. I passed through a neighborhood I recognized, and soon I could see the cathedral dome and turrets. The streetcar went past it and I got off in front of the church. The main hall, which is entirely white marble, gleamed in the sun. Statues of the saints were lined up on top of the turrets, all standing straight toward the sky. The pillars, the walls, the windows, and the entrance were all decorated with statues of one kind or another. All these decorations were gathered into a triangular center, and from its center rose a grand turret that soared to the heavens, and behind it soared a diadem tower. It is truly a work of architectural perfection. The carving in the entrance and the bronze figures by the door (that show the lives of the Virgin Mary and Christ), none of which I remembered from before, are very splendid carvings all. They do not have, however, the grand, dense, Gothic style of France or Germany; rather they are simply impressive, beautiful, and neat – there is something missing. If it were in the northern Gothic style, instead of the turrets piercing the sky as far as the eye can see, the fundamental spire would have a human figure on it that would look like a child climbing a tree. I felt that even this impressive, perfect piece of architecture had not taken on the true Gothic spirit.[1]

Inside the cathedral there were many worshipers because it was before a holiday. Those many parishioners looked small under the high ceiling of the great hall. The pillars and ceiling of the main hall are also marble, and carved in the shape of flowers. There are paintings of beautifully colored glass[2] that are in no way inferior to those outside, but it is not a refined interior like that at Notre Dame in Paris because the windows are too big and the glass pictures appear jumbled together. Nonetheless, the decorations are neatly arranged and I think it good that these disparate decorations have been gathered under one roof.

I went outside and looked all around. The view of the side of the cathedral was the best, with the turrets all together and the tall dome especially complimentary. From the rear I could see nothing but windows. And the front, except for the unfortunate side view of the flat triangle, showed a building that was built from faith to praise God in the heavens.

I stopped for tea and to write postcards in front of the cathedral, then it was time to go so I took another streetcar back to the station. The train departed for the southeast at forty minutes past three o'clock. I traveled in a verdant world – the grass and trees in the fields were all a deep green. It began to rain again and the western sun poked through the clouds. The Po River bed cut through the landscape toward the south and we arrived in a place called Piancenza. From here toward the south I could see the Apennine mountain range extending into the distance. In front of me was yet another flat plain with a carpet of green grasses; there was some sort of short tree – what kind was it? – planted in straight rows and in between each tree were grape vines. Looking over those rows of trees into the distance I could see, here and there, reddish-brown country houses with green doors. There was also a splendid landlord's house that looked like a palace, before which was a grove with straight, even, long rows of trees. No matter where I went I saw the same landscape with the same plains. Those plains received both rain and sun; over there were dark clouds with rain beneath, over here the sun shone on the green grasses. Here too, I thought that summer was nigh. Parma, Modena, wherever I went I saw the same thing – countless old church steeples standing in the towns. From a distance it looked like meetings of steeples. I felt sad because we have no such view in Japan.

The mountains grew closer as we continued on our way southwest. The sun was setting and darkness fell; I could see the red walls of a castle-like church above the green trees on the hill to my right. The train arrived in Bologna at seven-thirty. I saw gas lights in the streets as I rode in the horse cart provided by my inn. Upon entering the city I saw the old city walls, the white marble towers, the stelae in the marketplace, and roads on both sides that were like corridors; it was like something out of a poem, or something that one only sees in histories. There were many people in the city's central marketplace, where blue electric lights were hung beneath the white canopies of shaved ice vendors. It was as if I had come to a city in the tropics.

After arriving at my inn and having dinner, I read the newspaper for a while then went out sightseeing in the city. I went to the marketplace where I had seen the ice vendors before. An old, castle-like building rose in the west, and to the east and north were houses with corridor-roadways running between them. Ahead of me was a large, dark church that touched the sky. Drawing closer I could see a statue in the entrance that had darkened with age over the centuries. Turning north from the church I saw, between old palaces, two towers that reached toward the sky. They were shaped like square pillars, and were hundreds of *shaku* tall; one slanted a little to the west, and the other slanted considerably to the southeast. If one stands between the two it seems like big poles have been thrust out of the earth at an angle through the power of something like a demon. The light of the full moon poked through the clouds, and the two towers stood grandly in the dim light of the sky. It was truly a strange sight.[3]

April 16
Churches; Mementos of an Old City

TODAY I felt all day as if I were living in a world four hundred years earlier. Bologna was at its peak in the late sixteenth century and was the site of Renaissance art's final finishing; to this day it retains that old flavor. Not only churches and halls but also houses and streets have a very old feel to them. I spent my day in this intriguing world.

There were many old-style pictures hung on the walls of the hotel, and among them was one by Raphael. The walls and flagstones were made using many kinds of marble, and the style of the houses was palatial. I went into the city and went to see the marketplace I had seen the night before. It was no different than what I had seen at night, [and indeed it turned out that] the old castle-like building was City Hall.[4] The surrounding houses all had deep eaves and the corridors (they are called "arcades") compose the passageways. The walls are all brown, and the window shutters green. The window curtains are not hung on the inside of the glass but rather on the outside, and they are all a dark brown color. In the streets there were women who wore cloths tied around their foreheads instead of wearing hats, and men who wore as overcoats towels that looked like a Buddhist priest's stole, both leisurely rambling along. Some of the women's kerchiefs are black with blue and red threads woven in; others are just brown. My field of vision was taken over by a dark world of brown and green, interspersed with the walls of old buildings. From the marketplace I went to the church I had seen the night before. It is called San Petronio,[5] and it is a half-finished, big church named after the patron saint of the city. The bottom part of the wide façade has columns made of black and white marble and between those columns are statues done in a Gothic style that had yet to mature. The top half of the façade as well as the side are simply brick, and on top of that are bricks jaggedly set such that marble could be attached to them later. However, this half-finished state[6] seems to add to the size of the building, and I felt like I was standing in front of a giant. Inside the decorations for tomorrow's celebration were in place. There were many worshipers, as well as tourists with tour books in hand puttering about. In the chapels to the left and right were many statues and pictures of the ages. When I went to the left to view these, a caretaker in a ceremonial hat opened the chapel door and provided the tourists with an explanation of the statue. I went in with them to take a look. That chapel was called Cappella Baciocchi, and contained the sarcophagus of some aristocrat. The marble carvings were recent, but they were really very good.[7] I then went to see a different chapel. Here was the oldest painting in the cathedral, dating back six hundred years. To the left was a painting of heaven and hell, and the saints in heaven all sat lined up at desks like students at school. Below was hell with various demons and sinners. There were covetous and starving demons, and misguided sinners. The large mouths of the demons, their hands like swords, the shape of the sinners' heads and feet, and the starving demons' distended stomachs were all very interesting.[8] As I looked, I noticed something new. The others all left the chapel, leaving behind me and another person who spoke Italian well. We stood and looked for a long time and when I engaged him in conversation I learned that he was from Vienna and that he was an historian. Having found an excellent person to guide me, I went to another chapel. I cannot write individually of all the things I saw: the cross of the old gate, the picture of the battle between life and death, all the various carvings on persons' sarcophagi, etc. The Viennese had learned from a teacher of art history with whom he had come, so he was quite knowledgeable and explained many things to me. He also listened to the caretakers' explanations, and conveyed them to me. I found, upon speaking with him, that he was on his way to Rome to research some ancient manuscripts, and that he was in Bologna to see a manuscript that had some relation to the house of the Duke of Bevilacqua.[9] He had an appointment to see the manuscript at one o'clock, so until then we walked about without interruption and he asked me also about Japan. He was an historian who spoke Italian well, and I could not have asked for more so I asked him to go with me and we headed for the church of San Francesco. This church too had an inelegant brick exterior.[10] Behind the building there is a strange thing like a roadside shrine held up by pillars. This is the grave of a professor of a local university, some scholar of law from long ago. In Bologna there are many graves like this. There are tens of pillars about two *ken*[11] high, on top of which is placed the coffin in a strange manner. Inside the church there was a service in progress, with flowers and lights on the altar. Fortunately, although the main altar was being restored and was surrounded by scaffolding, the caretaker opened it up and let us in. The altar had a giant marble relief carving, done by the Messegne brothers in the fourteenth century. It dwarfs the altarpiece of the cathedral in Milan and is a work done in the style of a large *byōbu* screen, a true embodiment of the early Renaissance. There were other things in the cathedral, but I looked at them hastily and headed off into the city to the east to stand beneath the slanting towers I had seen the night before. Dante, in Canto XXXI of his *Inferno*, compares the tower to a giant peering down from above his head; as I passed by

I felt as if two big ghosts were toppling over above my head.[12] I went further east to the church of San Giacomo Maggiore. In this city the streets on both sides are arcades, like the corridors of a palace, and the pillars have interesting sculptures at their tops. Old stones jut out of the walls here and there and as I walked through the arcades I wondered where the city would end. The exterior of San Giacomo is unremarkable, but at the base of the entrance pillars there are some interesting statues of lions. Inside the building there are recent paintings and the walls have been recently refinished. Behind the altar there is yet another grave of a law professor and the sarcophagus has a carving on its side of students wearing loose jurist's robes, all lined up to listen to a lecture. In an altar to the rear is a painting by Francesco of the Virgin Mary.[13] Francesco was a famous, passionate painter of the Renaissance, so his painting is full of spirit and he showed a lively skill. The mouths on his figures have a certain sobriety to them, and I was told that this is Francesco's special mark. It is a strange countenance to be sure, but there is a power in it. The woman caretaker rushed ahead and opened a door on the side of the building, then went out. We followed her through the courtyard and into a dark corridor which led to another church. Here there was no altar, but on both sides were walls with paintings. This was the oratory of Santa Cecilia, where there are many paintings by Francesco, Costa, and the like, all of which have been well preserved so that they are bright and pleasant to view.[14] In some paintings there are odd poses or irrational distribution of figures, but the colors harmonize, and beginning with St. Cecilia, the expression of faith on people's faces and the landscape give these paintings true merit and spirit. These are pre-Raphaelite masterpieces, full of faith, with advanced skill; they are flowers of Renaissance painting. Behind this church there is an old remnant of the city wall where, strangely, people sell firewood out of hovels.

The university is just beyond St. Cecilia's. The buildings are not only old, but the school itself, along with that of Paris, is one of the oldest universities in the world.[15] I went into the building but it was more like a palace than a university; it was especially quiet because school was in recess, and I felt like I had somehow returned to an ancient world.

From there I went in yet another different direction, but no matter which way I turned I ended up in a city of arcades. The streetcars traveling in the narrow spaces between these arcades truly did not match their surroundings. Winding around these arcades I ended up in front of the old palace court, to the side of which was the church of San Domenico. Here there was a small plaza with the usual reddish-brown square houses. Beside them were rows of green trees which made for an interesting contrast of color. There was a large statue of Galileo, and in front of both the church and the house there were typically towering grave markers. The statue of St. Dominic at the entrance was rather good, but otherwise the scene had nothing but artless tile roofs. The interior was the opposite [of the exterior] with gold decoration on white walls. Each of the little chapels had some painting or sculpture of good quality, but I did not look at each individually; rather, I looked at the most important of them: the chapel that held St. Dominic's sarcophagus. Everything was done in the overly ornate Renaissance style. The front of the sarcophagus was decorated with a white marble screen depicting the life of St. Dominic. Above that were statues of the saints and on both sides were angels holding candles, all of which indicated that it was done at the height of the Renaissance.[16] The altar at St. Francesco's was reserved, but this sight here was rather powerful.

At the front of this church was a small chapel and on its altar was a painting I liked very much by Filippo Lippi[17] of the Virgin Mary and four saints. In comparison to the works of Francesco, which had a lingering quality of the theater, Lippi's works were refined and showed a power and colorful skill that made them in no way inferior to Francesco's. People tend to praise only Raphael, but there were others who came before him, and when I think of the famous works that came before I realize that Renaissance art has great breadth. I left San Domenico and went to see the house of the Duke of Bevilacqua.[18] Here too, the exterior had minor relief carvings but the pillared arcades around the court and the verandas above, plus the scholar's stream in the center of the garden, were all superior Renaissance works. It was the sort of place that seemed eminently livable, one that would safely conceal the lifestyle of the medieval aristocracy. I had a lunch of rice and macaroni with the Viennese and after chatting a bit we agreed to meet again in Rome. I then returned to my inn.

Squalls came again in the afternoon. While I waited for the weather to clear I went to San Giovanni in Monte in the mountains. Although it is said to be in the mountains, it is really on a place that is just slightly elevated, and is surrounded by a wall that also encompasses a number of houses. I wanted to see the Madonna by Costa in this church, but it was too dark and I could not see it well. There was also a painting of St. Francis praying. As a painting it was unremarkable, but because it was an image of St. Francis I took a look at it in the gloom. I passed between the arcades of the houses and left the church. From there I walked along a dirty street and went out of the city through an old gate in the wall. I went along the hills to the south of the city and found red and yellow houses among the trees there. I rested in the rain in the park at the foot of the hill, then started my ascent. The forest became denser, and there were successive views as I climbed. At the top of the hill was an old church and from the top of a mound in the garden of a house that had been converted into a hospital I could see all around Bologna. From the slanted towers to the church steeples, to the red tiled and red walled houses, the entire city of Bologna came together. And before it stood the green grass fields, and the reddish brown houses among the vineyard trees, all of which composed a colorful palette. In the far distance I could see a small mountain. In the immediate sweep of my eye I saw only fields, but the composition of the colors and the shapes of the churches and red walls were most interesting. The mound on which I stood was above a steep cliff, and from there looking out toward the mountains in the west I could see the green new leaves of the horse chestnut interspersed with the dark color of the cypress. In front of the trees there were white flowers blooming along the road that meandered along through the mountains. On the one hand it was a very Italian scene; on the other, the flowered mountains were right out of a Shijō school painting.[19] I gazed here and there across this landscape for a long time, then I went down the hill. The road ran into a park where the meadow's new grasses and the cypress trees mixed together, and among the grasses marguerites and crocuses bloomed in profusion. Looking up the mountain at the church once I had descended, I could see the old, red-walled monastery nestled in the cypress above the stone walls covered with ivy. As something man-made, it added a charming element to nature; it also added a painterly quality to the Italian landscape.

I returned to the city center from the mountains by streetcar, and went to the cathedral.[20] The interior and exterior of this cathedral are not in a particular style; rather it is a kind of cosmopolitan architecture. The service for Maundy Thursday had finished; incense smoke wafted through the church and parishioners gathered in groups in the chapels. There were also people who had come to worship the relics that were in a pit below the altar. The gold colored altar and alcove shone in the candlelight and in front of them people kneeled in prayer in the darkness of the pit. This was a strange sight. From there I went through a small neighborhood to a park in the north. On my way were the palaces of the aristocracy and the hovels of the poor thrown together. The houses of the poor were two story wooden structures whose roof trusses jutted out into the street, just like in an old painting (such as in Lippi's *Peter's Distribution of Alms*).[21] In the park was an absurd *kyōgen*-like display,[22] in front of which stood a soldier in a black-feathered hat and a street urchin. All around the park were the usual brown-walled houses; the scene was like a painting. I looked to the northern plain from a high point in the park, then I returned to the city center and bought some postcards before returning to my inn.

I went to view the moon at the slanted towers once again after dinner, and after seeing their shapes like a ghosts in the moonlit shadows I returned home. From the afternoon on today the people began their holiday, so even though evening had fallen they were out on the streets, singing songs beneath open windows. The tunes were somehow like the songs of India. I shall sleep now. Tomorrow I will go to the city of flowers, Florence – the thought of that alone makes me happy.

April 17, Morning
The Cathedral and Picture Gallery

I SPENT the morning in Bologna. Of the frescoes in San Petronio,[23] I never tire of looking at the one of heaven and hell. In the small chapel to the side there is a sixteenth century[24] painting that is interesting, albeit clumsy. It is centered on a figure of Christ on the cross; the four points of the cross take the form of extended hands in red sleeves. The top hand grasps a key and points to the gates of heaven; the lower hand holds some sort of stick and raps on the door of hell; the left hand holds a sword and points it at the foreheads of the person below, who represents Judaism; the right hand holds a crown and is placing it on the head of a young girl, who represents the Roman Catholic Church. The Jew is riding a sheep whose body is weak and whose legs are broken; the Roman Catholic rides on a feathered lion. It is all very powerful. Whereas the Jew wears a kerchief on his head and has his eyes closed, the Roman Catholic has a happy countenance, holds out a basin in which she catches the blood from Christ's bosom, and in the middle of the blood in the basin is drawn a round, white piece of bread from the Last Supper. That the Roman Catholic faith emphasized the idea of blood in the sixteenth century is evident in this painting.[25] I left the church and went to the Picture Gallery[26] by streetcar through the typical streets lined by arcades. In the first room were works by Guido Reni.[27] When I saw his lesser pieces, such as the *Magdalena*, in Paris I thought that he was a master, but his larger pieces show only a struggle to compose colors and a total lack of spiritual power, making me feel like I was looking at an old fashioned theater poster from Japan.[28] The next room held more of the same.[29] The next room, or perhaps it was the one after that,[30] held Perugino's[31] *Coronation of the Virgin*[32] and Raphael's *St. Cecilia*[33] – these were the only works I looked at. Perugino's painting was in the same style as the painting I had seen earlier in Toulouse, and the human figures were praiseworthy. The expression on their calm faces and their collected countenances are typical of Perugino. Raphael's *St. Cecilia* depicted four saints surrounding St. Cecilia, who is the musical muse of the church.[34] She is a young woman standing barefoot and dressed in a pale yellow singlet. In her hands hangs an organ that she has just played and her face is turned upwards as she listens to the echo of her music resounding and echoing from the distant heavens. Her face has a divinity to it. Her resounding music transcending the blue sky is represented by a group of angels forming an ensemble (Raphael struggled with the [metaphysical] border between the sky and the heavens, and the crack he made in the azure sky was an unavoidable device [for depicting that], even for a master painter). In the middle of the saints gathered around Cecilia is the beautiful Magdalena on the right, dressed in pink robes. She cranes her neck, enraptured, to hear the same resounding music. On the left is St. Paul, a large (perhaps too large here), strong man with one hand on the hilt of a sword resting on the ground, and one hand propped below his chin, silently lost in thought about the music. I sat in admiration of Raphael's work for a long time. There were many other paintings, but Francesco's *Madonna* was most interesting. It was particularly so in comparison with the similar painting I had seen the day before in San Giacomo. It had almost the same qualities as Perugino's work. There were also works by Costa, and in a separate room a work in the style of Cimabue,[35] but I glanced at most and then returned to take one more look at St. Cecilia before leaving the hall.

On my way home I went to San Giacomo and compared the paintings by Francesco that I had just seen with the paintings in that church. I also went to see the paintings in San Cecilia that I had not seen enough of the day before. *The Marriage of Cecilia* (by Francesco) is good but Costa's painting of Cecilia giving alms was the best; it had a refined quality in its depiction of nobility giving alms to the poor. The landscapes I saw there were also rather good.

On my way back to the inn I went one more time past the slanting towers.

CHAPTER FOUR

THE HOME OF FLOWERS;
THE CAPITAL OF PAINTINGS

THE CATHEDRAL AND CAMPANILE, FLORENCE, ITALY

La Gloria di Colui che tutto move
  per l'universo penetra, e risplende
  in una parte più e meno altrove.
Nel Ciel che più della sua Luce prende
  fu'io; e vidi cose che ridire
  nè sa, nè può chi di lassù discende;
perchè appressando sè al suo Desire,
  nostro intelletto si profonda tanto,
  che retro la memoria non può ire.
                              – Dante, *Paradiso*[1]

DANTE SAW the figures of the saints in the light of heaven, then returned to the world to tell of that glory in his poetry. His sentiments in doing so were much like my feelings at making public my reminiscences of Florence. In his thirty-three cantos about Paradise, Dante rejoiced in the "glory of God in the heavens"; I have nothing but my own recollections of the "Home of Flowers, the Capital of Paintings, the Hometown of Poetic Saints" in my pitiful diary to console me.

April 17, Afternoon
Arrival in Florence; Church of the Cross

AH! TODAY I arrived once again in my long beloved Florence.
Bologna has its interesting places, but I had Florence ahead of me in my sights, so I finished my two days of sightseeing, feeling like a heavy burden had been lifted off my shoulders, and said my hasty goodbyes to board a train at one o'clock. I would always remember the churches of Bologna, especially San Petronio and the slanting towers, but as we entered the mountains and the city was obscured from view, the current of the wide Reno River gradually quickened [carrying me away]. Up in the hills, the bones of rocky cliffs instead of the flowering fields of the lowlands were strewn across the landscape; it was quite a mountainous view. The good weather of the morning was replaced by evening squalls. We passed a hot spring called Poletta which looked like Shūzenji,[2] and also went over the highest place on this railroad line (more than 600 meters in elevation), Pracchia, in the rain.[3] We went through countless tunnels, then turned southwest into a large valley which opened up before us, and through the rain, onto the Tuscan Plain. Coming down from the mountain we once again entered the world of flowers, and interspersed in those flowers were dark green olive trees and yellow dandelions among the cedars. Once we had descended from the mountain, directly in front of us was the town of Pistoja – a group of buildings in the middle of the plain – with its steeple prominently visible. When that steeple was directly above us the train turned toward the east and ran across the Tuscan plain. To the north was the Apennine mountain range with soaring snow-capped peaks in the middle. There were villages and grand villas on the plain where it met the foot of the mountains. I could see old city walls and towers here and there, olives groves, and cypress copses. The fields were not orderly like they were on the Lombardo plain, but rather there were groves and fields and villages scattered about, all of which was charming. The walls of many of the houses were a light brown rather than red. The charm of this area was the exact opposite of that in the northern mountains. As we went along I wondered if the seasons came earlier here, as there were many buds and flowers blooming. The young birch leaves were especially beautiful, and they reminded me of the

young zelkova trees on the Musashi plain. I wondered if the zelkova in my garden in Japan was budding like this now.

> The light green leaves
> of the birch tree
> in Tuscany
> I liken
> to the spring in Musashino

The villages, old castles, and steeples all grew closer as we ran through the
foothills. To the east of us I could see a snow-white peak. I was just thinking that
it must be Monte Prato above the Arno River when suddenly a large dome and
square tower came into view. This was the cathedral of Florence, and the bell
tower that Giotto built.[4] I felt that I had arrived in the city of flowers (*Firenze*
is the Italian for the Latin *Florentia*, which means city of flowers). Once again
the vision of Italy's old capital rose before my eyes – the city on the banks of the
Arno, which I had left reluctantly five and a half years earlier.

> For five years
> I saw it in a dream
> Thousands of miles away
> Now it is not a dream —
> The city of Fiora

> To move
> My hometown here
> To the city of flowers —
> Oh to say I was going!
> Oh to say I was returning!

> I return to
> The capital of painting
> In the spring, flowers blooming —
> And spend many days here
> A citizen of its world

The train arrived in the station. I had my bags carried to a horse cart that took me to the inn. The horse carts there had large umbrellas over them and the drivers napped underneath, none of which made one feel like it was the twentieth century. The horse cart passed by the Church of Santa Maria Novella, and I arrived at the same inn I had stayed in five years earlier. I got settled in my room and went out. With a sidelong glance at the majesty of the great monastery of the cathedral, built in black and white marble, I hurried to Santa Croce.

When I left France I had intended to spend the Easter holiday week in Assisi, the hometown of St. Francis. But many days were spent in transit and I fell behind schedule, so I decided to spend this Friday – Good Friday – in Santa Croce in Florence, a city with which St. Francis had a deep connection. I had cut short my sightseeing in Milan to hurry here, and I wanted to come to this church before seeing anything else. I saw the statue of Dante in front of the church, and the white marble façade done in an old style, but I had a certain burning desire and so I went into the church, without looking at Dante's grave, and went directly to the deepest recess, to the Cappella Bardi.

This chapel has a statue of St. Francis at the front, and on the side wall there is a depiction of Francis's life by Giotto.[5] The painting shows the saint on his deathbed and when I saw it, I thought, "I will spend the entire day here." I stood before the painting enraptured. I had photographs of this painting at home, and I had gazed long upon them. The scene and the figures were all well done, but they all gained a deeper significance when, in front of the painting, I could see the brushstrokes made more than six hundred years ago. The face of the saint, who had ceased to breathe and whose spirit was on its way to heaven, still looked half alive; he did not smile, but rather he looked very peaceful. His high cheekbones showed the remnants of a hard life; the line of his nose showed the revered spirit of the saint who had moved thousands of people; his eyes, which were closed but still overflowed with happiness, wore a look of self-renunciation and consecrated joy between God and Man. His closed lips still showed signs of his last drawn breath with which he had praised God, taught his disciples, and prayed to Christ. An older disciple standing next to Francis's pillow and looking skywards to see the spirit of the saint ascend to heaven showed that he was fully convinced of the saint's worthiness. Ah, this painting shows a yearning for this saint's virtues, and the mature power of a lifetime flowing from Giotto's brush. The day was close to its end and the inside of the church grew dim, but I could still see the image of the saint clearly. As I closed and opened my eyes, the figure of the saint on his deathbed moved with life.

Many tourists came to look as I stood before the painting. Some would merely take a step into the chapel and then leave as if there were nothing of importance there. Others would simply say that this was a painting by Giotto and with that leave. Some were led by guides who said that this was a bad painting because it had been restored, and with that they would withdraw. As I saw and heard these people, I pitied them, but I also became a little angry. My heart was stirred at the sight of the dying saint's figure. But, the more I thought about it, the irritation I felt at these sightseers prevented me from entering a state of spiritual concentration on St. Francis. That I could not calm down, and that I let others' business concern me, showed that my own spiritual training was insufficient. In particular, was I not proud that I thought I understood how the painting *should* be viewed as a painting? This pride is something that the Buddha and St. Francis both strictly forbade. Christ humbled himself – was not his end by crucifixion done first and foremost to kill this pride? I was truly ashamed that I had come here on this Friday and stood before the image of the saint and had such a heart, so I rectified my thoughts. Happy that I had learned this lesson, I did not mind when another person came along; rather I just stood before the painting and worshipped the saint upon his deathbed.

By and by the interior of the church became dim. I bade farewell to the image of the saint and left the chapel. I sat in a chair placed in front of the chapel and gazed at the main fresco in the distance. I could see dark figures against the gold-gilt background, and behind that were the shapes of Saints Catharine and Clare shining in the darkness. I sat there for a while, then said a last prayer and left the church. Outside, the remains of the sunlight shone cleanly on the white stones in front of the church and the cross at the top of the triangle reached austerely toward the clouds.

From there I went through the city where tourists and holiday makers had gathered in small groups in the twilight. I tried my best not to look at those people or the scenery of the city, and instead stood at the side of the cathedral and looked at the creation of man and the beginning of cultivation in the relief carving by Giotto. I returned to my inn without looking at anything else.

At my inn I closed my eyes and saw once again images of St. Francis. My soul dallied in a time seven hundred years earlier on this Friday, before Giotto's painting was created, in St. Francis's Santa Croce, with a joy to end all joys.

After dinner I read a book about Giotto, and also a chapter in the life of St. Francis, plus, in preparation for tomorrow, I took a look at a book about San Marco. Lost in thought about these subjects, my heart could not but be taken over by the beautiful art of the Renaissance in this city of flowers, the hometown of poetry, and the center of the Renaissance. I resolved then and there that, as I went through Assisi and to Rome, I had to devote myself to St. Francis, Giotto, and Fra Angelico. I would not turn my eye toward Raphael or any other such painter, but rather would concentrate on the two saints of painting. Coming to Florence and not seeing Raphael was like refusing to eat at a feast, but resolutely I would refuse to eat. The Renaissance feast was a delicacy of the profane world. No matter how much Raphael painted the Virgin Mary, it was an object of this world. And to taste the Buddha's excellent teachings, I had to fast in the profane world. Giotto's faith and the rapture in Fra Angelico's paintings give us a taste of heavenly immortality. Those and those alone were the means of religious austerities. Thus I was resolved. No matter what I saw, and no matter what I myself suffered, I would not look at other Renaissance art, with the exception of the works of Lippi and Masaccio[6] (who produced works like Angelico), and also the Brancacci Chapel.[7] With this revelation I decided that from tomorrow on I would not sightsee but rather be a pilgrim. The two hours I spent at dusk today provided a lesson for which I was truly grateful.

April 18
San Marco; A Painter Blessed by God

SINCE COMING to Florence and being enraptured by paintings – thinking about the painting I looked at for one whole day – I have been sunk in thought for hours at a time. Although I want to write intriguing sentences and words, my pen cannot capture the things which I have seen with my eyes, so keeping a journal and writing articles has become distasteful. When I came here before I did not keep a diary either, but this time I want to make the strenuous effort necessary to keep one. As I recalled what I had seen in the afternoon, I lost myself in the pleasure of it in such a way that could continue on forever, and so it is with great effort now that I pick up my pen.

I spent the first half of the day at San Marco.[8] When I woke up the sun was shining. After breakfast I rested a bit, then went to the Piazza San Marco to take a look around. The sun shone on the old monastery walls and the green cedars and pines in the piazza. In the shadows of the trees, the grass grew thickly and the flowers bloomed in a profusion of red and purple. Angelico, whose paintings I would surely see in this church, must have seen a similarly beautiful spring morn, and taken up his brush to paint the power and wisdom of the Lord that he saw. The monastery has become a museum which opens at ten o'clock so there were still thirty minutes to wait. I sat down in a chair in the piazza and gazed at the scene of the spring morning while I ventured into the past of this monastery. Inside those unremarkable walls had lived countless monks for hundreds of years, passing the days of their faithful lives. Among them came such virtuous monks as St. Antonine,[9] and through their virtue the aristocratic families of the time changed their attitude. With a compassionate spirit the monks pitied the poor and the sick, and saved tens of thousands of the city's people. There were also fervent monks like Savonarola[10] who came out of this monastery and captured the hearts of tens of thousands of Florentines through his eloquent teaching. His fervor was so strong that he took up arms, and did not fear being burned at the stake.[11] He never gave up. I took out a book [I had on his work] and when I came to the last sermon I really felt as if my blood were boiling. As a leader of the monastery he preached to the monks:

"My beloved children, in the presence of God, in the presence of the consecrated wafer, with our enemies already in the convent, I confirm the truth of my doctrines. All that I have said hath come to me from God, and He is my witness in heaven that I speak no lie. I had not foreseen that all the city would so quickly turn against me; nevertheless, may the Lord's will be done. My last exhortation to ye is this: let faith, prayer, and patience be your weapons. I leave ye with anguish and grief, to give myself into my enemies' hands. I know not whether they will take my life, but certain am I that, once dead, I shall be able to succour ye in heaven, far better than it hath been granted me to help ye on earth. Take comfort, embrace the cross, and by it shall ye find the way of salvation."[12]

This great tragedy took place within those walls. And, within these same walls that nurtured such a fervent person there was also an artist-monk who walked the realm between heaven and earth, sang the praises of heavenly virtue, and received divine revelation. I was going to see the marks of his faithful brush. I passed the thirty minutes I had to wait lost a daydream of times past. The museum door opened. I went inside with many other tourists.[13]

Upon entering I went into a garden surrounded by a cloister. The usually green trees were a darker color, and the silence of the old monastery was broken by the sound of the tourist's shoes. On one side of the hall was buried the coffin of an ascetic over which everyone walked; I stood before a painting of the cross on the wall directly in front of us.[14] The artist [Fra Angelico] painted not for wealth and honor, not for pleasure, but rather simply out of faith; he painted what he took to be divine revelation from God. Before putting down his brush he prayed and worshipped. When he painted Christ he cried tears of joy. Angelico painted the front arcade of the monastery where he wanted to live, and worshipped Christ on the cross every day with his brethren. Christ's body here is bleeding, but he shows no signs of suffering or agony; instead his head, hanging down in death, shows a great peace and tranquility. His body too looks like that which has been transformed into a spirit and has begun to leave this world. St. Dominic, who kneels below the cross and embraces it with both arms, looking upwards, has an expression of great lamentation but at the same time one can see that his body and soul are clinging to Christ.

To the side, above a doorway is a painting of the Dominican martyr Peter. Blood flows from an injury on his head, and it gushes from a sword cut on his right shoulder; despite this, the martyr carries a book in his left hand, and a finger of his stabbed right arm touches his lips, as if in silent thought.[15] He is protecting the most valued virtue of the Dominicans: silence. His eyes are fixed on something above him. It is almost a frightening painting. It would be best to say that this painting shows a figure of composure, silence, and faith all manifested in one monk.

Similarly, above a door on the south side of the arcade there is an image of St. Thomas.[16] He was a scholar monk of the Dominicans who was a great philosopher of the Roman Church, and his wisdom is expressed in his full-cheeked countenance. Like Angelico he was a faithful man who delved into the scholarly questions of wisdom unique to the Dominicans. Angelico did his best to paint this greatest representative of the Dominicans, and his fervency is clearly visible in the painting.

Next I came to another doorway – that of a special guest room – and above the doorway was the image of Christ the pilgrim in coarse robes with a walking stick. Two Dominican ascetics reach out to him with clenched hands.[17] The two monks' greeting eyes, and the arrangement of the colors between Christ's light brown robe and the monks' black and white robes, cause there to be a passion in the quietude, a strange harmony in the calmness.

Besides this painting there was another of Christ's resurrection, which was significantly different from the others in its palette and the way that Christ is shown coming out of his coffin.[18] Maybe the reason that I find this painting incomprehensible is because in Japan we do not have the idea of someone being physically resurrected. There was also a painting that had a sample of St. Dominic's handwriting, but it had largely peeled away and I could hardly make it out.

Along one of the hallways there was the monastery chapter house.[19] On one wall was a fresco by Angelico of the crucifixion.[20] It is famous both for its [large] size and for its artistry.

In contrast to the crucifix in the arcade, which has a sky-blue background, this painting has a ruddy reddish color. Christ is in the center, and there are two criminals crucified on either side of him. Beneath them is a line of various saints either looking up at Christ or with their heads bowed in grief. Many aspects of this painting make it a masterpiece among masterpieces: the unity of the painting across its breadth, the arrangement that reflects the brown sky, the cruelty of crucifixion, and the halos of the saints below. Blood flows from Christ's flesh and his body is dying, yet one can see a great joy in that body. Of the two criminals on both sides of Christ, the one on the left shows an ease in death that comes with the gradual growth of faith. The one on the right shows a heart that died while still in the throes of burning [passion]. Amidst the saints weeping for Christ, the Virgin Mary has lost her senses and her whole body has collapsed into the arms of the saints. Mary Magdalene kneels before her and St. John and another Maria grabs her arms from behind. The face of the Virgin Mary, her unconscious head bent, and the faces of the two who support her from behind are all filled with grief. At the same time, they express a great humanity as they console the Virgin. Moreover, the composition of colors of Mary Magdalene's light red robes and the other Maria's yellow undergarments, and the blackish-brown of the Virgin's clothes and the light brown of St. John's clothes, in and of themselves comprise a great painting. To the left of these four figures John the Baptist and St. Mark stand, half-kneeling. At the edge of the painting there are three saints associated with Florence gathered together.[21]

In contrast, there are also in this painting various teachers of the order. The one closest to the cross, Dominic, is kneeling and looking up at the cross. St. Jerome has placed his tall red hat on the ground, and in the form of a white-clad beggar he kneels with his two hands in prayer. St. Francis wears his rope belt on his wool habit, and holds his right hand to his cheek. In his left hand he holds a crucifix and without looking up he worships Christ, the stigmata of legend shining on his hands and feet. ("Stigmata" means a sign, and in this case, because Francis was always thinking about Christ's hands and feet being nailed to the cross, it is said that in the end he, too, had the these signs appear on his hands.) Between these three men stand St. Augustine and St. Albert, one of the patriarchs of the Carmelite Order.[22] The two men wear tall priest's hats and have countenances full of deep wisdom. They do not grieve for Christ, but rather they gaze at the cross as if there were a deep, important meaning to be gleaned from it. Behind Francis, St. Bernard holds a book and stares silently at the crucifix from the side. St. Guaberto has a look of sadness and shock. Last, the figures of St. Peter (the virtuous representative of the Dominican Order) and Thomas (who represents the academy) stand together to complete the painting. There are also separate portraits of these two in the arcade: in comparison, the arcade Peter seems to bear his suffering and guard his silence with a strong face, whereas the Peter in this fresco cries for Christ and in bearing Christ's death he shows a need for other's help. The Thomas in the arcade shows the wisdom of learning, but the Thomas in the fresco has a full face and a keen eye, never losing sight of wisdom. In his eyes, which are gazing slightly upwards, there is a feeling of vehemence, and with the power that comes from that vehemence is mixed deep thought, both of which lend a complete strength to the man.

Angelico's ability to express people's personalities, their thoughts, and their feelings through one brush is truly shown in this painting in a most satisfactory way. He is able to draw not just a person's countenance but also his entire body and thus his spirit. He concentrates on the attitude of the person and his expression (especially the look in his eyes), and is able to capture in his painting the inside of a person's spirit through his outside appearance. This is an ability that has remained unmatched throughout time. There have been many masters to appear on the scene in recent times, but none of them have the power of Angelico. The power of faith is truly frightening indeed.

I set down a chair before this painting to take a long look at it and as I did so the sunlight and shadows danced over it. And with those changes in light the whole painting came alive. As I examined each of the saints one by one they each seemed to be alive, and I wondered if I had seen them move. After sitting there in contemplation for about an hour I left the room and went to the second floor.

On the second floor there is the famous fresco called the *Anunziazione* in the front of the arcade. It gives one the feeling of having discovered the paradise of heaven's springtime in the dark hall of a monastery. The quiet break of dawn in the springtime at a convent. Outside the monastery the flowers grow in profusion, and inside the cloister there is not a soul to be seen. There is not a speck of dust from the secular world, there is not a voice. In this setting a single maiden, a lissome figure with a pure, unsullied heart, sits on a chair. An angel with rainbow-colored wings descends from the heavens. The angel stoops down toward the maiden, whose palms are joined in prayer. The angel puts her two hands to her bosom in reply. The profile of the angel shows an incomparable happy auspicion, and speaks of something so great as to be above all else. She is full of joy, and the maiden's two eyes are filled with half surprise and half joy. But she barely shows those feelings, and instead accepts the news, letting it fill her heart. In this landscape are the remnants of the mysteries of the Christian faith, and of the mysteries of the immaculate conception, both expressed in their entirety. There are certainly many arguments and discussions among academicians and religious scholars about this, but if, in the world, there was a mother who gave up her lusts and desires, and dedicated herself entirely to her child, and if that mother knew that she carried in her womb a lovely child who was pure of heart, and she knew that that child would save the world of mankind by bringing men together, how great would her joy, surprise, and thankfulness be? Angelico represents this Holy Virgin fully. And if, in this world, an angel was chosen to bring the congratulatory news, what shape would that angel's countenance take? Angelico shows us in this painting through his brush, which takes on the angel's expression. If there is, among the debaters of the world, one who does not understand the argument for these mysteries [of Christianity] and chooses to attack them instead, then that person cannot admire the strict rules of the church and its teaching. Surely it was the case that Angelico simply believed in these mysteries and feelings, and expressed the content of that faith here in his paintings. One should look at the message of these paintings without trying to apply an argument or agenda.

Opposite this work is another crucifix. It is almost exactly the same as the one in the arcade (the only difference is that Dominic is on the left in this one and on the right in the other). There are also many paintings throughout the monastery by Angelico's disciples. These paintings sufficiently convey to the viewer of today the weight of Christ's death on the cross. But [it is important to note that] Angelico, like Luther, viewed the crucifixion not as some legal compensation but rather as the spreading of empathy for Christ's suffering and his death.

Along the hallways ahead were countless small monk's cells, and in each one of them was a painting. Among them were paintings of Christ's birth, transfiguration, forgiveness, resurrection, and the crowning of the Holy Virgin. In the painting of the transfiguration, Christ appears divine. Christ's floating figure at the coronation with the Holy Virgin seems jewel-like or cloud-like. In the face of derision, Christ was submissive – even without defiance – and one can see the dignity in his eyes. All of this is beyond my power to describe. I am only able to write this much after gazing at the paintings for a very long time.

On these walls and in the cells there were paintings of the Holy Virgin and the baby Jesus. This infant, the so-called Bambino, has an expression of unsullied innocence that could rule the world. The Holy Virgin, who embraces him, cares for the lovely child with a love that cares for no other. It is said that Raphael's Holy Virgin in the Sistine Chapel has an air of sublimity and dignity and that the baby Jesus has a power in his eyes that could dominate the world, but it also has an air of ambition. Angelico's Bambino has not the slightest air of ambition, yet in his loveliness there is an indescribable air of dignity. Raphael's Holy Virgin's face has an attitude which seems to insist that one look at her child, but Angelico's Holy Virgin simply loves her child without any insistence. Angelico has painted the concept of "altruism." The Bambino's eyes look straight out at the viewer, and behind him the Holy Virgin bends her neck slightly toward the Bambino. The painting is a trove of the unlimited human spirit. The eight saints to the left and the right are the same ones as appear in the chapter house painting, and they all stand with full admiration for the Bambino and the Holy Virgin. Their faces are close to portraits, and one who has seen them in the chapter house painting will soon recognize who is who. The exception is St. Thomas, who here appears as a youth, not the older man he is in the chapter house painting or the portrait in the arcade. Perhaps Angelico, or even St. Thomas, when expressing his admiration and affection for the Bambino, lost his wisdom and wits and took on the feeling of a youth, and thus St. Thomas has that outward appearance in the painting.

In another cell there was a famous detailed altar painting of the Holy Virgin. Next to it was a painting of the coronation of the Virgin and the adoration of the Magi. Both were no more than two *shaku* high, but on the small altars were drawn many people and angels. Upon close inspection I saw that the brushwork was truly fine – indeed, that one brush had exhausted the possibilities of expression. When I looked closely at the fresco in the cell I could see it all. Angelico never painted an outline, then painted in the colors, then painted over them; rather, as is done in a Japanese painting, he completed his painting in one set of brushstrokes. One cannot help but acknowledge that he was very talented. In the early modern period Japanese painters who made Western style paintings by smearing oils on the canvas were simply fooling the viewer. Those painters should have looked at Angelico's paintings and responded in kind.

I spent the better part of the day enveloped in Angelico's faith, and was left understanding how this master came to be a *"Beato"* (one who is blessed by God) and had become one with the other *Beati*. I returned to my inn and could still see all the images of Christ, the Holy Virgin, and the saints. Just looking at those paintings – the impression I got, or perhaps it was the expression – inspired me. I cannot imagine how the artists themselves must have felt painting them – seeing the image of God before their eyes. In Avignon I had seen a painting titled *Angelico's Vision* and I thought what interesting work the artist had, for he titled the piece after the fact that Angelico had visions of the saints and Holy Spirit while he was painting. The painting in Avignon is a little bit too realistic, but it could have its equivalent in Japan if there were a painting with Eshin Shōzu's[23] meditation as a subject.

In the afternoon I wrote a letter to a friend about all the feelings I had experienced in the past day, then I read a book about Angelico and went for a walk in the twilight. I went out across an old bridge in front of the Signoria (the old government office). The river was swollen with rain water, and the current was muddy. The scenery near the Ponte Santa Trinità was just like the painting of when Dante finally met Beatrice. I went into a bookstore to buy pictures of Angelico's works and some landscape paintings of Florence, and when I came back out of the store it began to rain again. There were groups of people who had gone out for a walk in the Saturday sunset, and occasionally a horse cart with a broad canopy would pass by.

After dinner I read again, wrote letters, and sat in quiet contemplation. The light that I had in my mind from Raphael's paintings was lost when I thought of Angelico's paintings, and I took joy in my resolve as the sun set. I was sure that this resolve would not falter.

April 19
Easter; Santa Maria del Carmine; the Medici Gardens

UPON AWAKENING I could hear rain falling outside, but when I opened the window to look I discovered that it was the sound of cart axles. I washed my face and began the day by reading Francis's *Cantica del sole*.[24]

> *Altissimu, onnipotente, bon signore,*
> *tue so le laude la Gloria e l'onnere et onne benedictione.*

Most high, omnipotent, good Lord,
to you be praise, glory, honor and all blessing

I greeted Easter day with thoughts of a saint 700 years in the past.

A little while after breakfast the bells of San Lorenzo, immediately behind me, rang, followed by the sound of the bells of the cathedral. I found it odd how the sound of these bells resembled the sound of the bells of Senbon, the claim to fame of my home town.[25] I went toward Santa Croce to get out of the rain. On the way, the bells of the cathedral rang above my head, calming the rain and resounding through the empty sky. I went to Santa Croce and sat in a chair in front of the Cappella Bardi where I meditated. Soon the Santa Croce bells rang through the heavens. An officiating priest came out and began his work before an image of Francis in the Cappella Bardi. The sound of his voice reading the scriptures rhythmically started and stopped, resounding throughout the church. The voices of the men and women kneeling in prayer were audible only as a whisper. After the service the bells rang again. After my silent meditation I went into the nave where the service had ended and first I prayed before the image of Francis, and on this day again I looked at the painting of Francis on his sickbed.[26] I stood before the painting, looking at the saint who appeared holy. He was gazing into the void with a look on his face that seemed to be wondering, for the first time, about who all the saints gathered around him were. Presently I left the church.

It was raining heavily when I went outside. While I waited for the rain to let up, I gazed at Santa Croce. At the top of the church in the pouring rain were two angels, embracing the cross. Above the three entranceways the relief sculptures of the "Power of the Cross" were distanced from the rain and appeared to float mysteriously within.[27] While I waited for the rain to stop I went through narrow streets to the *duomo*. Here the day's festivities were still on, and the organ was playing, harmonizing with the choir, as I entered. The faithful parishioners and the sightseers milled about, causing a bit of a ruckus, but I stopped to sit in a chair, closed my eyes, and listened to the music of today's Easter celebration. At first the commotion of the crowds disturbed me, but as the music progressed I was able to concentrate my mind in that direction. A rich, broad bass voice resounded in the distance, and then after a moment of silence the voices of the choir began lightly and the sound of the alto came down from the ceiling. Then came the officiating priest's mass, followed by the recitation of the litany, then another piece from the organ. It occurred to me that the spring had been ushered in by the midnight mass Christmas music at St. Eustace in Paris, and I was coming to its end with the Easter Mass here in the cathedral in Florence.

Today, although I was in middle of a crowd, I sat alone in meditation and listened to the music. What caused this intriguing experience was not only the power of the music, but also the ascetic practice rooted in the teaching of the Buddha. The sūtra that states, "One must first empty one's dwelling; then one must empty the forests; then one must empty the earth; and then one is able to penetrate the immeasurable emptiness"[28] is a necessary one for those of us who live in today's harsh world. Our spirits are tangled in the chaos of the world, pulled by useless issues, and attacked by evils. Here in this cathedral there are countless people, and they bustle about with absolutely no connection to me, yet I am drawn by them. For my ability to control the cacophony and harmonize it I must thank the teachings of the Buddha. I continued thinking in this vein as I left the church and went into the village crowds. I went back to my inn and sat quietly in my room, letting sink into my soul the events of the day, from the sound of the morning bells to the mass at Santa Croce, to the music I heard in the *duomo*. Yesterday I was a *looker* by the end of the day, but today I became a *listener* by midday.

As I sat quietly, deep in my thoughts, the lunch bell rang. Is it time to eat again? How hard mankind toils for his food! I thought about how good it would be if we could devise a way to live with less food.

I was sleepy because I was up late last night writing letters. After lunch I took a nap and awoke at three o'clock. The morning sky had changed and now it was clear, the sun shining. I went across the river to Santa Maria del Carmine. There in the Cappella Brancacci there are frescoes by Masaccio and Lippi, and I exempted them from my current fasting from paintings. In the words of one art historian, the paintings in this church are the keys to the Renaissance. Not only that, I have often enjoyed looking at photographs of them, so I wanted to see them in person once.[29] On the right-hand pillar, like in the painting in which the saints are helping Peter escape from prison, here a kind of heavenly strength above the angels is shown in the shape of his mouth, and Peter's stance is not that of one fleeing. The inner painting, of Peter walking among the poor of Rome distributing alms, is dignified, and shows a precise brushwork technique.[30]

Although the paintings are large, in the depiction of the cross-examination by Nero, or the resurrection of the dead amid a crowd of people, the artists preserve the distinctiveness of the figures , with no shortcomings in the composition of those figures against the surrounding background. The people who surround Peter and are startled by his resurrection of the dead are distinguished not only by their countenances but by their overall appearances, done by a brush that clearly delineated each of them within a coherent whole. If one counts the figures there are twenty-some, but upon a glance they are simply a group. Masaccio's brush had a type of magic in it that was able to bring composition and blending to a harmonious result. Looking at these paintings after having looked at those of Fra Angelico, one does get the feeling of having seen it all before. Aside from the fact that the colors seemed blended together into one, the brushstrokes and the lines, and the types of colors, too, at a glance seemed undifferentiated, yet somehow they looked dissimilar. I found it fascinating and I determined to sit in observation until I could solve the problem, but I could not put my finger on it. Setting aside the complexity of composition, I decided to focus on something simple and compare it to the paintings of Fra Angelico. As I mentioned before, I was very familiar with other depictions of Adam and Eve, and after looking at this particular one [by Masaccio] for over an hour I decided that maybe the difference lay in the blending of shadow. At first it occurred to me that Masaccio and Lippi had made their shadows dark, that they had placed individual shadows where they were, or rather where they should be. In comparison, Giotto and later Fra Angelico differentiated shades of light, and rather than using shadows in their work they represented light and darkness through the use of shades of colors and the angle of their brush. It is thus that they painted cleanly piercing beams of light. In contrast to that, this painting in the Cappella Brancacci used dark shadows and was tedious as a result. I thought that it began to show the tendency toward too much of materialistic or photo-graphic qualities. I wondered if Raphael had also had this fault in his paintings (I searched my memory), but I felt for certain here in the Cappella Brancacci that Correggio[31] and Pinturicchio[32] had this fault to some extent. Those who would change Japanese painting to have more shadows would do well to reflect on this point.

I would certainly say this in comparison to Fra Angelico, but also in comparison to Raphael and those who followed him: these two expert artisans truly painted St. Peter well.[33] A man becomes immortal with such truth and talent alone.

While I sat lost in my thoughts an old British man who was also sitting there began speaking to me in Italian. He spoke about comparing these paintings to Japanese paintings, and other such topics, so I wished I could respond in Italian, but I simply could not. I was flustered, and asked him if he could speak in English; he said that English would be fine, replying, "Oh, well, actually I am more comfortable in English, too." He was an interesting old man who spoke of paintings and travel, and after we left the church together we bid our farewells.

Away from the church I went by myself to the Palazzo Pitti.[34] One still gets a feeling of its powerful majesty. It looks as if it had been built by Toyotomi Hideyoshi.[35] In Japanese art history, the Muromachi and Momoyama were the periods of Renaissance.[36] But the Renaissance of the Muromachi was thrown into chaos by war, and the Renaissance of the Momoyama was destroyed by Tokugawa vulgarization. Looking at the Palazzo Pitti I am put in mind of Toyotomi Hideyoshi, and of the Renaissance here in Florence, all of which makes me regret the waning days of the Momoyama period (but, in my current stay in Florence, I am fasting from the Renaissance, so I will go no further).

I went along the Palazzo Pitti and entered the Boboli Gardens.[37] I sat at the top of some stone stairs that provided a good prospect, from which I could see, sandwiched between the majestic Pitti Palace and a row of cypress trees, the city of Florence and its cathedral steeple soaring above it. In the foreground were the hills of Fiesole. The most appropriate sketch of Florence is had from this spot. The Arno valley with its cypress trees, the nature of the hills in Fiesole, the Pitti Palace, which was a seminal force in the Renaissance, Giotto's bell tower of the cathedral, which represents faith and devotion; all of these are brought together in this place into a fitting picture scroll.

I walked about the gardens, among the trees and rivulets, and came to the front of a stone statue. I climbed a tower that rose above a corner of the palace wall and looked all about, then walked along a row of cypress by an olive grove.[38] There, I found a paradise of villa after villa, all the way to the white marble walls of San Minato. In the foreground was the city of Florence, and below that was the Arno, flowing into the distance through the western hills, reflecting the setting sun. No matter how much I write, I cannot capture the scene completely. The sight is similar to that of the hills and rivers of Kyoto, but it transcends it to a higher level.

Although all one can see now of the grandeur of the Medici family, who built a palace wall around this expansive garden, is the palace and the church, one can still imagine fully their prominence. The seal of the lily and the seven-orbed Medici family crest[39] that remain not only on the Pitti Palace but also here and there around Florence, speak of its antiquity. But the House of Medici is now gone. Their palaces are merely places for hanging paintings, and the crests are simply commemorative. Upon this thought, I left the garden. In the green fields along the roadside, white marguerite flowers bloomed in profusion.

> The brilliance of the seven-orbed crest
> Time passes and the world moves on
> An ancient spring arrives
> And in the garden bloom heavenly flowers.

I left the garden, crossed the river, and returned to Florence. I gazed at the Arno from the Ponte Vecchio. The eternal current was crimson, colored by the setting sun in the western sky, which was just going behind some storm clouds. The light that came through the wild clouds had an odd sort of sparkle.

April 20
The Hills and Cross of Fiesole

TODAY IS Easter Sunday, the day on which it is said that Christ and his disciples went to Emmaus. I had planned on getting up early and climbing the hills of Fiesole, but of course I did not get up early and it was nine o'clock when I left the inn. I headed toward Fiesole by train. My car moved slowly through the city, so I had the chance to take in the palace eaves and the carved church façades at my leisure. Once out of the city center, the track gradually climbed through olive groves in the hills. The cathedral and bell tower that had been hidden by the houses earlier now appeared in the center of Florence, and the palace, the villas, and monasteries on the hill south of the river formed a pattern amid the rows of trees. The sight is the same no matter from which prospect one views it, but it is a scene of which one never tires. If one climbs the hills and has the houses of Fiesole right ahead, there is a particular group of houses there. Most of those houses are Dominican monasteries, as this area was once a Dominican stronghold. Fra Angelico lived here in one of these monasteries[40] for eighteen years before he moved to Florence. I rang the bell, and the door opened. Passing through a dark corridor, I was greeted by a monk who wore the Dominican habit, and who asked if I had come to see the paintings. I was guided in and entered the meeting room of the monastery. He intended to show me all sorts of paintings, but when I told him that just the paintings of Fra Angelico would suffice, he took me to a small hall where his work was on display. Fra Angelico lived here and for eighteen years barely had contact with the outside world. Instead, he practiced his devotions, meditated, and painted the scenes that that he believed God instructed him to paint. There were many such paintings, but many have been moved or lost, and now there is just one scroll left. Still, that one scroll expresses the saintly artist's faith, and his brushwork, even though it has been restored, is preserved.[41] First I entered the hall and sat down at a pew, my elbows on the edge of the pew in front of me as if I were in prayer, and looked up at the Holy Virgin.[42] There she was, a mother looking intently upon her child with eyes of pure love, offering him the red and white flower in her hand. The adorable child was held by his mother, and reached with both hands to take the flower.

There are six angels behind her, and two kneeling in front of her, offering flowers. Their wings are all colors of the rainbow, and they express all reverence, admiration, praise, and respect. On the sides there are four saints, who strike solemn and serene figures of respect, their eyes full of faith. In the background are two open windows, and in the distance one can see hills and verdant fields, between which copses are reflected in the water. The emptiness of the landscape is juxtaposed with the halos of the saints, thus harmonizing perfectly the pure azure of the world with the gold of heaven, all of which surround the Holy Virgin and Child. The artist's brush expresses through color and form the spirituality of his gaze, one that shows the harmony of the unification of the Buddhist paradise and the Christian heaven. It is no wonder that he was called one who "mingled with the angels." I had seen how he was close to divinity when I was in San Marco, but this painting brought anew a deeper appreciation of his merits. That Fra Angelico not only painted religious paintings and portraits, but also occupied a fundamental position in the realm of Italian landscape art was made clear to me when I looked at this painting. Looking up at it I was struck with a feeling of awe. Around me there was not a sound, only the silence of the monastery; this, together with the surrounding nature of the hills, created a separate realm. Living in this paradise of faith made it possible for Fra Angelico to create such a work for the first time.

I stood up from the pew in front of the altar and looked behind me to see my guide, the monk, waiting in boredom. I felt sorry for him and said, "Please let me be here for a time," at which he replied that that was fine with him and left, jingling his keys. I was left all alone to look upon the painting from the side and from the front; the sincerity of mother and child, the angels' countenance, the harmony of their heavenly robes, the figures of the four saints, their expressions, their eyes... as I looked, I saw something new. Each of the angels' faces and expressions had a special characteristic. Moreover, when one put them all together they had a unified divine virtue that praised God. Of the saints, St. Peter especially had eyes that showed great depth and a sharp expression. I was drawn by the stance of the martyr Peter, who practiced great humility and gave up his own self to worship Christ, and also drawn by the positioning of the fourteen halos. I wanted to change the lighting, so I lowered the far curtain. The monk, who I thought had returned to the monastery, heard the noise and came out to see what it was. I felt sorry that he had been waiting all this time for me, but he asked kindly who the saint was in a painting beside this one. I replied that I knew it was by Giotto, but I did not know who the saint was. The light was different now, and I stood before the painting. The monk lowered the cross that had been in front of the painting so that I could see it without any obstruction. It was kind enough of him to do so, but he took the cross down without the slightest reverence, and by placing it aside destroyed the excitement I felt.

I shut my eyes to bring back the impression, and then opened them to take another look, and pray. I left the chapel, gave an offering to the monk, and left the church. Outside, I was once again surrounded by beautiful nature, endless olive groves, and a cobblestone road through the stone fences of the country villas that lead up to the hills. Up at a bend in the road there was a vista below a row of cypress trees. Although I felt it a bit sad to take my eyes away from the paintings on which I had concentrated, it was also difficult to dismiss the view of this expanse of nature. Five hundred years ago, Fra Angelico too looked out over this evening scene of flower beds in the copses and in the fields, and the wide Arno. He saw God's glory in these single flowers, then would return to the monastery and take up his easel and brush to paint that same God's glory. When I thought of it this way, I realized that nature and paintings were not two separate items, but rather the way of looking at them and the spirit of the observer were one and the same; in both nature and paintings there is the same beauty, and the same teaching.

Who lives now in the old villa of the Medici family? It has good prospects, and is a noble house with statues of lions at the gate and a refined air. I climbed and climbed, and finally came to the village of Fiesole. At the end of the cobblestone road there are two cypress trees, and below them there is a stone seat from which the view of Florence is exceptional. It is the same sight as I saw from the road, but here one can see a much broader spread. Hills upon hills butt against the Arno into a unified whole. Not only the soaring cathedral, and its bell tower, and the governmental office towers, but even the clusters of red tile roofs below constitute the precious treasures of this world. Hundreds of years ago this one city was the center of culture and beneath those roofs the various great men of the ages, who governed the nature of the world's millions of people, passed their days and nights. The view of the city in the Arno valley, surrounded on all sides by mountains and fields, is not simply a view of nature, but actually it is a view that encompasses the glory of mankind. When I thought about the fact that, gathered in front of my eyes, I had seen the town of Fiora, the home of flowers, and the vestiges of the flowering of mankind itself, I realized that it was not something that anyone should take carelessly as I had done, simply standing on top of the hills and letting the western wind blow over me, feeling dejected and lost.

From that spot I climbed a little further to a Franciscan monastery at the top of the hill.[43] I sat down in the yard in front and looked out at the mountains to the northeast. Below the town of Fiesole and built up against the cliffs I could see the ruins of the stone stairway and stone arch of an old Roman theater. The theater was not the only remnant of the Romans: this monastery, too, was once a place where in ancient Roman times there was a capitol and they worshipped Jupiter. I was imbued with thoughts of the vicissitudes of mankind through the ages. When I entered the main chapter house of the monastery, I found two monks deep in their prayers. I quietly laid down my hat and walking stick, and I too took a seat along with the Franciscans in their robes in silent reverie in the hall. Absorbed in the quiet of the mountaintop monastery, I was able to forget this world. When it comes to man's life, quiet contemplation and Zen meditation[44] are extremely powerful, important religious practices. When I was in Japan, I missed the opportunity to do them, but here in Italy St. Francis has given me the gift of being able to meditate. It is my wish that people living in today's world of advancing civilization and competition do not neglect doing these practices themselves.

I do not know how long I spent in quiet contemplation, but eventually I returned to the world and left the monastery. In front, a profusion of various flowers bloomed among the green grasses, just like the painting on display of the spring field that Fra Angelico painted. The flowers that St. Francis praised as "the flowers that bloomed in the multitudes of grasses, in countless colors" were none other than these flowers.[45] I gathered a number of them as mementos of Fiesole and, pressing them in my notebook, returned to the town of Fiesole on the main road. I ate lunch at an inn that commanded a good view, and after the meal I took some coffee outside while gazing at the many houses of Florence, various deep emotions welling up inside me. The world is vast, and there are many cities within it, but somehow the flowers of painting and poetry flourished especially here. There are not such people today as there were in Florence or Fiesole in the olden days. Of course, there were evil men in ancient times, and there were also impoverished people, but why is it that the fourteenth and fifteenth centuries produced men of greatness such that we have not seen again? How odd that their names are not lost in today's evil world, and even Americans come here to see the treasures of those times. Even if we attribute it to Heaven's dispensation, it is still mysterious.

I descended the hill by a train that left from in front of the inn. It went past the Medici villa, and a Dominican monastery. I decided to take a nap, and fell asleep, waking when the walls of the cathedral rose outside the train window.

I went directly to Santa Croce, this time going to see the paintings of the two Saints John by Giotto next to the Cappella Bardi.[46] The birth of John the Baptist, his father's joy and surprise, his mother's death, and finally Salome jumping at John's head being presented to her father on a platter.[47] One can see the drama in Giotto's composition, and how it differs from that of Fra Angelico. The colors are not bright, as Fra Angelico's are, and the figures and their expressions are not of some wonderful realm like Angelico's, but the skill of their positioning and how they express movement makes it folly to try to determine which is superior or inferior.

Salome's dance is particularly dramatic in this painting. King Herod, who did not want to destroy his majesty as the king, appears disconcerted when faced with the head on a platter. Juxtaposed with the shock of the old man to the side, a young boy plays a musical instrument innocently. Standing opposite is Salome, who holds a lilac, and who concentrates on her father's face with burning emotion. Behind her there are two servant women, hand in hand, who have lost their nerve in the face of this scene, and who glare at the head, and at the king's face. That this is all captured in one painting, without the loss of a single point, is truly a sign of the genius of Giotto's composition.

On the wall opposite the paintings of John the Baptist is the story of John the Evangelist. At the top is the Revelation to John, in the middle is the miracle of the resurrection of John, and at the bottom is the ascension of John after his death.[48] I concluded, after seeing these works, that the artists of the Cappella Brancacci owed something to these predecessors. Giotto displays here a splendid model for the composition of groups of figures.

In the *Ascension of John,* Giotto painted well the faith that welcomed the adoption of Christianity. In the house that held John's coffin, on the one hand a group of people look at the emptiness of the open coffin, but on the other hand, although they are under the same roof, another group stares in wonder at the emptiness. The attitude, form, and composition of expression of those two groups of people defy detailed description. In the middle of the two groups, John's body floats up into the air, his two hands raised toward the Heavens. Christ grips his left hand, and reaches to take his right hand and welcome him to the Heavens. Here John's left hand, grasped by Christ, seems somehow to rise up to the position where it is grasped, his fingertips lightly and softly suspended, with no need any more for strength. In contrast, his right hand is quite raised, as if it will not reach Christ's left hand, and the fingertips show strength and the intent to grasp hold. His left hand seems to be taking on another power, and the right hand is making the transition from its own power to another power.[49] In contrast, Christ floats in the air facing forward, both hands extended tirelessly, his fingers on both hands showing strength, and he welcomes John. One can see here fully the power of acceptance and the compassion of connection. Behind Christ are row upon row of saints, and they all want to welcome John to their holy group. John's body is enveloped by Christ's light, and his feet depart from the ground, his faithful eyes turned toward the heavens. There are many welcoming Buddhist saints[50] in Japanese Buddhist paintings, particularly the famous paintings in the Genshin[51] School, and that Buddha is one who has a quiet, calm draw. Giotto expressed this same faith with an extreme, active stance without losing any of the saintliness. The welcoming depicted by Genshin is centered on the Buddha; in Giotto's case, John, who has been accepted by Christ, is the source of the faith. In his work there is a quiet determination, and in this he shows a fervent joyous faith; it is a work that cannot be dismissed. One cannot help but be surprised by how he joins in one painting both this acceptance and this faith.

I particularly value the way in which Giotto showed Christ and the saint coming together in the air. His arrangement here is intriguing. Against the azure sky light yellow clouds blend into an obscure mass, from which Christ and the saints emerge half-way. It is as if the blue sky had cracked, and the pure radiance of heaven can be seen through the fissures. Giotto did not, however, make the blue sky thick. Although it is not the only point on which they differ, this is clearly a departure in Giotto's work from Raphael's *St. Cecilia.* I had seen Raphael's painting in the museum in Bologna earlier, and due to the thickness of the sky, the fissures somehow *look* like fissures, and the heavens thus are put at a distance. In other words, because in Raphael's painting the blue sky of the heavens is given a material quality, likewise the heavens also take on that material quality. Giotto instead made his sky a limitless azure, and painted the world of the saints floating within it. Even if Raphael was the more talented painter, Giotto was the one who was able to see the ideal.

After viewing these paintings and taking their image with me as a keepsake, I left Santa Croce. I turned and bid farewell to the white marble façade.

From there I went up a hill to the Piazzale Michelangelo, then up to San Miniato al Monte and looked out over the city of Florence. The sight of the city center with its cathedral and bell tower always demands a bow of respect, but when I looked upon the walls and roof of Santa Croce, I was further struck by the idea that within that little building were not only vestiges of Giotto, but also the beginnings of Angelo's great works.

As dusk fell I walked along the hill in front of San Miniato in the breeze, returning to my inn as the darkness fell on the surrounding mountains and groves. Today too was a day of much learning for me.

April 21
Images of the Holy Virgin

I SPENT the day today in the exhibition rooms of the art school (Accademia).[52] But before the exhibition doors opened, I went to see the famous Crucifixion by Giotto in the church of San Marco. I did not look at it long enough to form any thoughts, but instead rushed through the gallery, where there were many works done in the style of the master Cimabue,[53] as well as works done in the Byzantine style which I felt I should see.

At the Accademia, I went directly to the Fra Angelico rooms. There were many fine paintings lined up on the wall, and the famous *Last Judgment* dazzled my eyes, but there were many people crowding about so I began with the *Holy Virgin* in an inner room. Painted on a wooden board (in this age, paintings were painted on boards as well as walls), it was more than ten *shaku* square and although the damage was so great that one could not see the original beauty, I could see the Holy Virgin and Child seated on a brocade chair and surrounded by eight angels and eight saints. In the background was a vast grove of summery trees, and between the trees and the saints hung a curtain. The effect was largely the same as with the *Holy Virgin* in Fiesole, but this painting was more open, and there was more movement. The angels, unlike as in other paintings, were not gathered in faithful praise but rather were drawn each with an individual stance. Fra Angelico's brush is compact and austere, but it also shows a change here toward broadening. In the background grove of trees we see a consistency to the summer sky, and we can also see a wreath of roses set as if a celebratory decoration. To distinguish this painting from the others (although it is given the number of painting #281), I have labeled this painting "The Holy Virgin in May" (I will refrain here from describing the shadows and other features of the painting).[54]

Turning from "The Holy Virgin in May" I moved on to two paintings of the Holy Virgin in the next room. I was struck by the difference in brushwork, which must have been the result of the development of Fra Angelico's skill. These were paintings #227 and #265, and although they were different enough, neither omitted detail; however, they did not have the power of the San Marco fresco. They were well preserved and I could see the colors clearly, but at the same time the colors floated in a way. The clothing of the saint in painting #227 seemed limited to the surface, with little depth, and the red of the Holy Virgin and Child's cheeks seemed to be applied superficially, and not to come from within. It would seem that even Angelico, in his early years, maintained something of the earlier styles, and could not shake the influence of his predecessors, especially Cimabue, but he did improve his own fine style of brushwork.

The Holy Child in this painting holds a pomegranate in his hand so I shall call it "The Holy Virgin with a Pomegranate." Like painting #265, "Holy Virgin by a Stone Wall" (this too is a name that I have given it), it shows signs of development. The ruddy cheeks look like natural skin and the faith of the two angels along with the attitude of the six saints are well focused. The complexion of the Holy Virgin is done in the same fashion as the Fiesole painting – one can see both a motherly expression and a virgin purity. Not only the posture of the Holy Child held in his mother's arms, but also his countenance are simply naïve and adorable, without the solemnity of the Bambino in the hallway at San Marco. But one must really view this as the special characteristic of this painting. If the trees that grow in front of the stone wall in the landscape were in bloom, it would look like "The Holy Virgin in May." When I consider it, if "Pomegranate," "Stone Wall," and "May" show the different aspects of the ages, then it would be safe to say that the Holy Virgin in Fiesole is the culmination of them all. But, I do not have time to study the opinions of art historians on this matter.

Between "Stone Wall" and "Pomegranate" there is a painting called "Holy Virgin in Brocade" (another name of my invention – its real number is #240). Not only is the cloth on the chair brocade, the Holy Virgin's clothing and the Bambino's clothing are also made with a brocade border. The Holy Virgin's eyes show strength as they focus on the Holy Child, and the Holy Child stands gravely, the light of wisdom spreading from his gaze and blending with the glory of his attire. I believe that here Angelico succeeded in painting a Holy Virgin with dignity. It is a work that shows not love but rather majesty; more than being deep, it is magnificent. One cannot help but think that Angelico took the authority of the church to heart and expressed his faith through the Holy Virgin and Child. Comparing this painting to the famous fine Holy Virgin and Child in cell #31 at San Marco, one finds that the latter has no other significance beyond the expression of the love between mother and child; but the former contains the great self awareness and self-respect held between mother and child. And it is not just the mother and child, but all the other saints and angels as well who do not have this characteristic. But on this point the two paintings pose an interesting comparison. In contrast to the San Marco painting that has adorable angels painted along the gold-gilt edges, above the painting of the Holy Virgin in brocade there is a smaller painting that contains the Lord as the father – the upper half of his body appears to bring congratulations to the mother and child. But even with the disparity of the attached painting, I think it is correct to interpret one painting as the expression of love and the other as the expression of dignity.

In any event, Angelico painted many works of the Holy Virgin and Child and in each one he was able to express every aspect of the Holy Virgin's faith with various backgrounds and in various stances toward her Child. In painting each work, the artist himself must have analyzed the differences of each, and arranged them in some comparative fashion. Certainly it must be the case that his constant faith was the result of Angelico's concentrating on one particular faith in some divine revelation grasped at one instant after examining each kind of faith included in the ideals of the Holy Virgin, and his paintings show the result of that process. As the master progressed in his skill the concentration of his faith likewise was expressed through his brush and in this way he was able to give each portrait of the Holy Virgin its own special characteristic. This was Angelico's genius. Different from the typical Holy Virgins that Giotto and Cimabue painted, Angelico's Holy Virgins were brought to life from his ideal in faith. From the standpoint of faith, one can see that he had total trust in the church, especially the Dominican order, and that he had no doubts in divinity or ideology. But because he maintained the strength brought to him by an active faith above and beyond ideology and logic, he did not simply reproduce the typical paintings of the Holy Virgin but rather used the inexhaustible material brought to him by his own faith to transform – but not debauch – his artistic expression. Given this, one can see that the painter-priest Angelico was a great man of the spiritual world, a man of independent action. The inexhaustible wellspring of faith flowed with virtue and produced St. Francis, and the spirit of beauty likewise produced Angelico.

In this room there was a scene of Christ having been taken down from the cross. The colors were more beautiful than anything I had seen before, but it was not just the colors that were striking. When I looked closely I saw that each one of the people had a different expression, and that the expressions blended with the brilliant hues. Each of the figures had a different, distinct deportment: there was one person who was simply sad (the woman on the far right), there was one person who had composed herself a little in her grief (the next woman), there were two people who looked at Christ's wounds with eyes that showed a surrender to their faith (the Holy Virgin in the center and the old woman to the left), there was a woman who looked both bereft and yet full of yearning, and there were two men who seemed to be speaking of the mysteries of the cross. Because this painting was painted in the so-called "brilliant coloring" style, it was lacking in strength. Moreover, in the style of fine painting it told of an event; there were figures of people arranged from Christ's head down to his feet, and each took on a different attitude. In this sense, the painting of Christ taken down from the cross in Cell #2 in San Marco is slightly more set, and has a little more strength to it.

There was also the famous painting of the Final Judgment in this room, as well as a detailed work of Christ's life, but because I went to see them during the lunch hour when there would not be many people about, I did not have time to look at them carefully. And so, although many thoughts came to mind as I glanced at the detailed paintings, I will refrain from writing about them here.

Next I went to the Rooms of the Tuscan School where there was a large painting by Angelico, also of Christ taken down from the cross. This painting, even more so than the first, was a painting meant to explain the event, so although it was detailed and beautiful, I felt that it was inappropriate for such a large scale painting. It is best looked at one section at a time. The saints along the edge of the painting are truly well done. These saints, all of whom surround the Holy Virgin in the larger painting, each appear in detail and we are afforded a splendid portrait of them. Of special note is that there are probably only two or three paintings (none in Fiesole) by Angelico that do not include Francis accompanying the Dominicans. This suffices to tell us how much he adored Francis.

The Accademia was established for the study of history and is set up to facilitate that, so when I entered it, the way in which I looked at and thought about the paintings tended toward the critical and the analytical – this was different from the reverent way in which I looked at the frescoes in San Marco or the altar in Fiesole. Oh, Angelico certainly did not paint his paintings to be analyzed by a historian like this! But in research one cannot but analyze, and so as I analyzed and criticized, I tried not to forget the overall emotion of the works, not just in looking at the works of Angelico but also in all aspects of my research.

In the rooms of the Tuscan School, Giotto's painting of the Holy Virgin was hung next to other works of the master. It had a Byzantine air to it, and seemed like a painting that had not been smoothed. Giotto's touch, after all, I thought, is in painting the life of movement.

I returned to the room of the Beato Angelico, and looked again at the paintings as if reviewing them. I left the Accademia at half past three o'clock. Today I forwent lunch and instead filled my stomach with the pleasures of looking at the paintings. I think it would be a good arrangement to do this every day.

In the evening I went to buy photographs along the banks of the Arno again. Of special pleasure was an old copy of Francis's *Fioretti* with a worn leather cover that I bought at a used bookshop. In that shop they designed individual books for disciples to use. I have Ruskin to thank for my liking this sort of thing.[55]

April 22
The Monastery Fresco; the Setting Sun from the Piazzale

I DECIDED to spend the day at San Marco and so I set off directly after breakfast. The weather had improved somewhat – the sun had begun to shine in the garden of the old monastery, and the smell of blooming marguerite flowers wafted through the air. I stopped to glance at the cross and St. Peter in the arcade and then went directly up the stairs and entered the monk's cells where I stood before the painting *The Mockery of Christ* in cell #7.[56] The figure of Christ, dressed in snow-white clothing and seated on a dark red dais against a yellow single-screen background, seems to hold a great weight, even at first glance. The white robes draped on his shoulders, the sleeve of his left arm, which holds a globe, the white hems that are spread broadly beneath his waist, all have an unwavering, graceful dignity. Not only that, but one could see the determined majesty in the still robes. Looking from below, I could just see through the folds in the white blindfold that Christ's face and closed eyes showed an accepting yet resolute spirit. The noble nose that does not yield to the blindfold and the remarkable red lips between his noble, thick beard and moustache both show an unbending forbearance. His blond head, wearing a crown of thorns, has a bright halo behind it with a red cross upon it, and surrounding the halo are various hands meant to mock the patient man and upset his spirit. One hand holds a stick as if to strike down the halo, another seems to want to pull his ear, and yet another holds a threatening pose above Christ's shoulder. Next to these hands is the head of a black man and from his lips blow harassments toward Christ. Christ's white-clad figure that does not flinch at these mockeries holds a staff in his right hand to rule the world; in his left hand he holds the globe, displaying a nobility above all other nobilities. But this nobility is not a nobility of arrogance; Christ turns his head slightly to the right in acceptance, without resistance, and sits calmly in the midst of the mockery. In this way, his nobility is truly entirely different from the typical nobility of the secular world. It is the majesty and dignity of a person who eliminates his own self in order to spread the true word, of a person who advocates, "If one strike thee on thy right cheek, turn to him also the other" [57] and "the meek shall possess the world." [58]

Many people find the hands and the head floating in mid air around Christ's head strange. Having hands unattached to arms or bodies heaping abuses on the yellow single-fold background, and having a bodiless head appear to blow abuses toward its victim are both unthinkable among artists that subscribe to realism. Those who paint only that which they see with their own eyes find this odd indeed. But surely Angelico did not think that real hands would appear in mid-air, or that, objectively, a head could fly in the midst of nothingness. The proof lies in the fact that a similar scene of the mockery appears in the detailed life of Christ in the Accademia, and in that painting the complete bodies of the mockers are depicted, from head to toe. But his ideas extended beyond this, as did his skill, and there is no doubt that, due to his faith, he felt some dissatisfaction at envisioning Christ tolerating the abuse in a simple corporeal form. And so, instead of painting the abuse objectively, he chose to show the violence that Christ suffered with a silent heart, and how the derision affected him subjectively. Moreover, even in the artist's masterly eyes, it would be wrong to concentrate on a group of derisive figures milling about instead of focusing on the essential

Christ figure. I have no doubt that he expressed, here in this painting, Christ's inner and outer feelings as he bore the mockery. Since ancient times many people have painted this same subject, but each has faithfully depicted the group of people and thus their paintings ended up being, more than about Christ, about the drama of those who mocked him. In other words, more than being about Christ bearing abuse, the paintings have been about those who abused him. The result is that Christ as a great figure himself is slighted, and he appears not as a forbearing, impassive figure but rather one who is put upon by mockery and who suffered violence. Correggio's piece in Paris[59] and the recent Hofmann[60] piece both, in this way, make Christ a small figure. Christ's forbearance, like his conquering of temptation, was something that he practiced his entire life. And so, depicting Christ's difficulties at this important moment is painting the real Christ, yet not painting the true Christ. Angelico's mature faith and his mind's eye came together in this painting to capture the true, stoic Christ, the Christ who triumphed even at the brink of death.

There are two saints who sit before the majestic, mocked Christ. One of them is St. Catharine. She, being a typical woman, feels pain in her heart in the face of this derision and cannot stand to see it. Her eyes look slightly upward, and her right hand is raised slightly as if to show her trying to ward off the derision in some way. Opposite of her is St. Dominic who, being a founder of an order and a scholar-priest of the church, sits in a state of slight composure, evident from the pose of his hands, and looks down at a book that he has opened before him. The mocked Prince is in the middle, sitting above the two opposing saints. When we look at the composition of this painting we realize that Fra Angelico did not arrange his paintings accidentally. (Further, the striking arrangement of the colors – the red cross, the yellow background and Christ's white robes, the light brown of Catharine's robes and Dominic's black and white robes – merits comment, but my pen is not up to the task here).

Half of Christ's face in this painting is covered with white gauze, but his eyes and his nose can be seen through the fabric so that one can see his calm, forbearing face; this work has the best likeness of Christ. Although Leonardo's Christ in his painting of the Last Supper (located in Brera[61] in Milan) is unprecedented as an image, there is too much in the way of sadness in it and thus it has a sort of weak air about it. (I have an anecdote about that: I had had occasion to send a picture of this painting [along with an article] to the printers of a magazine, and when it was being proofread I was asked where the "picture of the sleeping woman with washed hair" should be placed. This question was due not only to the typesetter's view of Christ, but also because Leonardo made Christ's face too weak.) Angelico's Christ shows an enduring forbearance and a solemn majesty, which makes me think that this must be the true face of Christ at that distressing time.

I stored this image of Christ in my heart and went to the next cell (#8) where I saw the painting of Christ's ascension to the heavens.[62] Above the crowd of onlookers shocked at the empty coffin that had held the body floats Christ, ascending into the sunlit clouds, his spirit rising into the heavens. His face here is the exact opposite from his face in the *Mockery*; his eyes face upward slightly and it seems as if his hair blows gently in the breeze. As in the *Mockery* painting, he wears white robes (unfortunately the color is soiled), but unlike the heavy draped sleeves of the former, here his sleeves seem lost in the clouds, lightly and naturally floating among them.

With these two images of Christ in my head, I went to cell #6 to see the painting of Christ there.[63] Here Christ's face is that of an angel, but his eyes gaze austerely down upon those gathered below him, showing them the image of his spirit. Both his feet are on the ground, but his arms are raised wide. His outstretched arms and body, both clad in white robes, look like a transparent gem.

Seeing these three paintings in succession and then considering them all together, I realized that they are the best set of images of Christ. The first shows a master with a bright countenance; the second a Lord of unmovable forbearance; the last the spirit ascending into the heavens. The fusion of God and man is expressed in the three paintings, and if one looks at the human figures they seem to be moving, as if they were drawn from the actual person himself. Angelico did not always see the same face on Christ (as I will explain below). But the person in these three paintings is the same person, and the same image, and each place and emotion is brought together in such a way that each maintains its own expression. At first when I had only looked briefly at them I thought that each face was different, but then after I looked carefully I realized that although they have the same likeness, each one is very different in terms of the expression of place. If one looks at the paintings in this way, Angelico's surprising skill – even if one thinks of him merely as a portrait painter – is clear. Painters such as Lenbach[64] who always drew Bismarck with the same eyes can hardly be called portrait painters when compared with Angelico.

I went back to cell #8 to see the ascension, and to see the people gathered below Christ.

The figure of the angel, seated lightly on the edge of the coffin and pointing upwards at the ascending figure of Christ, has a wise, innocent expression, and although she seems to be on the verge of saying something, she is silent. Next to the coffin and looking down into it stands Mary. Silently bending over the coffin to peer in in silence is the Holy Virgin, and next to her stand two women with knitted brows. The three women's expressions and stances contrast the lamentations of the three women in the chapter house – they are three different types of people. The profile of St. Dominic who peeks out from behind the angel is the same as that on the face of the Dominic at the base of the crucifix in the hall, but his eyes and his cheeks and the set of his mouth show an expression of deep joy and adoration.

The painting in cell #9 of the Holy Virgin's Coronation brings the white-clad Christ of the first three paintings and the white-clad Holy Virgin together in their ascension.[65] I had seen this painting before, but now I took a very good look at it and saw that the realm of heaven is well drawn. Within a halo that looks like a solid rainbow is a world of white clouds and pure light. And within that world, Christ places a crown upon the Holy Virgin's head. Mary holds her two arms close to her bosom and reverently wears the crown. The saints who, beneath the clouds, kneel on the ground and praise the events in the heavenly realm include St. Francis in the front, facing St. Dominic. Behind Francis are the martyrs St. Peter and St. Marco, and accompanying them are St. Benedict and the scholar-monk Thomas. The faces of these monks are so different from the faces on the painting below the crucifix in the chapter house as to be unrecognizable. But the wonder in their eyes is not regrettable.

The figure of Christ in this painting is the same as the figure of the pilgrim Christ in the hallway, but different in its own way from the figures of Christ in the other three cell paintings. Although it seems doubtful, no matter how much I look at the two different faces I cannot reconcile the two as the same person. I wonder if Angelico always saw the same Christ from start to finish.

As far as the Holy Virgin's countenance is concerned, although it had its differences in expression, it was the same as the one in the Annunciation in the hallway. But when I really compared the two different images, it was clear that there were differences. The Annunciation image was of the Holy Virgin at the start of her life, and the coronation image was of her at the end of her life. From the point of view of the faithful, Mary cannot age and cannot die, but one of these paintings is of her entering her spiritual life, and one of them is of her having entered it. The Annunciation Mary shows feelings of surprise along with joy and obedience. And not only are these emotions expressed through her eyes, they are also expressed through the way her mouth is opened slightly as if wanting something, and the way that her arms are raised softly to her bosom. The crowned Mary's eyes show a splendid calm, a gratitude in the midst of reverence, filling the entire painting with respect and majesty. That attitude – of the closed mouth and the arms held close to the body – complements the expression of her eyes and shows that she is the mother of God and the ruler of women. This immortal woman who has assumed her crown is given expression through [Angelico's] brush. The hallway Maria is a pristine virgin, and this crowned Holy Virgin is an eternal ruler. I went between the cell and the hallway, and this was how I felt in my reveries.

In the afternoon the crowd thinned and the hallway, which usually had a constant stream of people, was now empty. I sat in front of the fresco of the Mother and Child in the hallway and continued my reveries. Here was the loving Holy Virgin, and her innocent and dignified child. More than showing their divinity, the painting showed, to the extent it could on the wall, the ultimate purity of human emotion. The saints on either side each had their own special characteristics, but the central figures of the Holy Virgin and child were all that the painting needed. I momentarily set aside these figures of the saints with their fresh color palette and concentrated on the main figures. The color of the Virgin's blue robes and the pink of the lovely Bambino's robes were ample enough. I recalled the Buddha's words, "Even though a flame is small, one should not resent it; even though a king is young, one should not disregard his majesty," and I found myself wanting to call this painting, "The Virgin Mother of Kings."

When three o'clock approached people began coming back so I left the hallway and went into cell #1. Here was a painting of the morning of the resurrection.[66] It showed a spring morning on which the trees were thick with leaves and on a garden lawn surrounded by a fence red and white flowers bloomed in profusion. Christ walks out lightly from the door of the cave. Behind him is Mary, who kneels in surprise and adoration, and who looks as if she is begging him to stop walking. The pink sleeves of her robe are spread lightly on the green grass and her hands look as if they are grasping at the robes of the one who walks before her. Her eyes gaze upon her master who is half man, half ghost. Christ's figure is paused in mid-step, and the upper part of his body is slightly turned toward the person behind him. In his eyes there is the light of compassion. It seems to be saying that one should not chase after Christ the man but rather look to Christ the spirit. The composition of lively nature on a verdant spring morning and the human emotion between these two suggests the merging of religion and lyric poetry. But the Christ here resembles the Christ of the Coronation more than the Christ of the Ascension, and I still do not understand why he looks a little bit old.

In the next cell (#2) is a painting of Christ after being taken down from the cross.[67] In terms of its feeling it does not differ from the painting of Christ off the cross in the gallery; the people all exhibit their grief as they care for Christ's body. The color palette is simple and the brushwork is not fine but rather shows a power and strength, causing the entire painting to have a feeling of calm. To the right there is a cave opening in the cliff. To the left there are mountains and from them emerges St. Dominic, looking upon the other people with sympathy. His standing figure is as pure as the white lily he holds in his hands. Here Angelico shows his skill as a painter of landscapes.

The painting of the Annunciation in the neighboring cell #3 has its own special qualities.[68]

The angel Gabriel stands with dignity surrounded by light yellow and rounded monastery walls, and before him kneels a slight figure. Besides the martyr Peter, who partially appears behind the angel's wing, there are no other figures in the painting. Compared to the kneeling Gabriel in the hallway painting, this Gabriel stands properly. His wings are not multi-colored but rather a simple, strong color, and rather than being spread they are strongly poised. The hallway angel is filled with joy, but this one is filled with solemnity and casts his eyes downward. The Mary who kneels before him is not virginal here, nor is she masculine, nor is she overcome with joy as she is in hallway; rather, she is austerely obedient and simply silently shows her reverence. Her figure is slight and her light red robe is draped over her body in such a way that it seems to pull her body forward. Looking from top to bottom she has a dignity that cannot be described. Her arms are close against her bosom and her mouth is closed, showing almost exactly the same motion as the Holy Virgin in the Coronation painting. Her profile shows the fierce determination of someone who has undertaken a great task. Upon reflection, I suppose that Angelico painted this picture out of conviction when he imagined the great compassion that the Holy Virgin must have felt at the time of the Annunciation, when she took on the greatest event of her life. The Annunciation in the hallway shows her joyful at becoming a mother, but this Annunciation shows her taking on this great task, and her total submission to the revelation, and her total determination. That is one side of the Annunciation; this is another side of it. Thus one can see that Angelico's determination was not set on only one interpretation of the truth.

As I looked at the paintings, going back and forth between the cell and the hallway and comparing them, my feelings became much deeper. If there were in this world a supernatural person, a so-called "super man" who was not a man or a woman but a pure being, like Wagner's *reinmenschlich*, who had unsullied emotions, and if that person abandoned himself and took on a great command, then that person's feelings would be the same as those expressed by this Mary here. Purity, greatness, and solemnity can only be expressed through a great person or history; it cannot be simply expressed in a great painting.

The closing of the gallery at four o'clock grew near and my eyes were tired. I committed the vision of the Mary in this Annunciation to memory and with my eyes half closed I left the gallery and returned to my inn. The faces of the people I saw on the street, compared to those that Angelico had drawn, were in some way vulgar. But I tried not to look at them and instead returned to my inn and closed my eyes, lost in thought.

I went for a walk before dusk to the Piazzale Michelangelo on the hill. The azure of the sky was piercing, and the blue color grew lighter down along the sky until it reached a white mist, through which the green cypress treetops pointed up at the heavens. The fields below were covered in green grass beneath the dark green of the olive trees. Beyond the grasses were the hills upon which the palace looked down. The mountains which lie beyond the hills were dyed magenta in the setting sun and beyond them extended peaks shrouded in white clouds as far as the eye could see. Between the mountains meandered the Arno, sparkling in the sun, and on the water was the city of Florence, its cathedral dome soaring solemnly overhead. The view on a clear day brought an equally clear and lively feeling.

The purple and blue of the distant mountains gradually encompassed hues of red and the nearby hills also took on the color of dusk. The light crossed over the cypress trees by the Church of San Miniato al Monte and by the time it reached the western mountains there was nothing left but dark shadows. I descended the hill and walked home along the Arno. The iron fences of the palatial houses built along the river bank were full of blooming wisteria. The harmonization of the Renaissance with the ancient court and military came down to the artists, and it was a natural experiment. The sun sank behind the arch of an ancient colonnaded bridge, the deep red pierced by the golden rays of light. The color and the light were ultimately impossible for man to capture with his brush. They were the realm of Nature's living landscape alone.

I returned to the inn and after my meal I reminisced about the day. Various

forms of Christ, as drawn by Angelico after he saw the spirit of God; the view
from the Piazzale Michelangelo; the color of the sky; the fields and mountains.
They all came together to form a pure heavenly playground for my buoyant
heart. There has never been another painter like Angelico. His landscapes, his
Arno valley, Tuscan mountains – were they not just as he had painted them?
Angelico was also a loyal painter of reality. But his spirits are not empty or
shadowy – truly, they also existed.

April 23
Fiesole; the Monastery; and the Holy Virgin

TODAY I wanted to spend the day bathed in the last of the springtime's sunshine.
I thought that spending today in Fiesole would be a fitting memento of my stay
in Florence.

Today, as yesterday, brought clear skies, so I headed up the hill toward Fiesole
as soon as I had finished my breakfast. The young leaves on the trees had sprouted in the warmth of yesterday's sun, and the grasses and flowers too had begun
to grow and bloom in profusion: the yellow dandelions, marguerites waving as
if snow-capped, thistles blooming amidst them all, dotting the space here and
there with a dark red. The thought occurred to me that Angelico too must have
walked along this path and seen the footsteps of the angels in these flowers.

> In the hills where myriad grasses and flowers bloom
> Still live the angels of our Lord [69]

I passed by the Dominican monastery[70] and came out on a mountain road
with good views. When I looked up I saw rows of cypress trees like layers of
mountains above which the white clouds floated in the azure sky, poking from
behind the dark green of the trees. I climbed a stone stairway to the front of
the Franciscan monastery[71] and gazed down at the Arno. They were the same
mountains and the same river, but they appeared differently than they had the
other day under the clouds; now the verdant landscape was illuminated by the
bright sunlight and the houses of Florence were clustered within it. I sat down
on a stone and gazed absent-mindedly for goodness knows how long.

My meditation on the landscape was broken by an army signal corps' fatigue
duty, as the soldiers came and went and the signals rang. I left the view and took

a look at the Roman ruins that I had seen in the yard in front of the monastery, then I knocked on the monastery door and a monk dressed in wool robes with a rope belt greeted me. I glimpsed the simplicity of the monks' lives in the cloister which encircled a garden in the middle of which was a well. I passed by a field of irises, then cypress trees, and in front of me, by a mountain cliff where the view was broad, was a field of small dew flowers that bloomed like small stars, just like in Angelico's painting of the heavens. In that painting, the rays of sunlight shine and glitter to create a separate realm of spring light. The red flowers which grew amidst the profusion of white flowers are a variety of the flowers called *fūrosō* in Japan, but their Italian name is *gersomino*.[72] It was entirely different from the usual jasmine, but I simply took it to be the *gersomino* of this place. The light blue flowers that bloomed hidden amidst the red and white flowers were forgettable. Here and there were superior crocuses, as well as other flowers of these hues throughout the field.

> Amidst the red and white *gersomino* blooms
> Do not lose yourself in the violet dew

I asked if I could be allowed to rest here briefly, so the monk left and returned to the monastery. Here, alone on this bed of flowers, I bathed in the spring sunlight. Occasionally a light breeze caressed my cheek and the grass. In the peaceful, soft breezes, lay flowers covered with dew – or were they gems? – I gazed at them with grass as my pillow, and the world was fully a heaven of wind and flowers.

> In the spring breeze beside my pillow of grass
> The white dew on gently fluttering flowers

At precisely noon the church bells rang through the mountains, far and near through the villages, all the way to the azure heavens. Then the quiet world of spring sunshine returned. It brought to mind St. Francis's praise of the mountain winds and flowers of Tuscany and Umbria, and his thankfulness for God's grace.

> Blessed with the grasses and trees
> Glory be to God; spring comes
> To meet the memories of the ancient sage
> Thousands of flowers, blooming

I must have been there an hour or so, and when I got up from the grass, stood and looked back, I saw that the flowers and leaves where I had been were all flattened on the ground. I felt sorry for them, but it did leave a quiet impression of my lovely repose. I plucked a good many flowers and made a bouquet, sadly leaving that place and returning to the monastery.

> Here in our world
> We see vestiges of the angels
> One glimpse
> Is in the flowers gathered
> In Florence

When I returned to the monastery there was no sign of the monk. I went in search of him and headed down a quiet hallway to a window with a western view. It was a landscape that countless ascetics over hundreds of years must have seen, gazing out at the secular world. I happened upon another monk to whom I bowed in reverence, and when I left the monastery that monk took me as far as the door, saying *arrivederci* when we parted.

I headed down the hillside, the impression of the monastery indelible in my mind. The cobblestone walkway between stone walls and the rows of cypress trees made me feel exactly as if I were living in a painting. At about the half-way point I went to visit San Domenico [di Fiesole] and the same monk I had seen earlier came out, rattling the key noisily in the door. He showed me to the Fra Angelico fresco of the Holy Virgin. He knew me from before, so he left, his keys and rosary jingling. I was deep in thought in the quietude of the desolate hall, standing in front of the Holy Virgin. I looked back and forth at the Mother's – or should I say woman's – shape, and the robes of the surrounding angels, the beauty of their colorful wings, the countenance of the saints, and the natural background. This image of the Holy Virgin is superior to others in that the artist perfectly harmonizes the purity of the virgin with a Mother's love. In the normal realm it is not possible to blend the qualifications of being a mother with the virtues of being a virgin, but the artist's ability to bring these together truly shows the divinity of Fra Angelico's brush. Nowadays in the West there are many wives who prefer to go on vacations with their husbands rather than raise their children, and in Japan too, this trend is also catching on. The consequence of this is the practice of birth control; in France this has become a big societal problem.[73] As humans, women cannot bear children without a husband, but I wish that women, as mothers, would dedicate themselves to their children. A woman's greatest duty toward her husband is the care of her children, and I wish that women would enjoy that themselves without exchanging it for their own selves. The virtue of the Virgin is to have a motive without bias, to love unconditionally, to accept the beauty of the world meekly, and to experience mankind's love as pure, unsullied sincerity. In Japan, this virtue is only hinted at in Chūjōhime[74] and Fusehime.[75] The virtue of a virgin gains power through her devotion, and if later she is sincere toward her children then she shows hints of the Holy Virgin. These two virtues do not stand together in the flesh, but rather they transcend the limitations of the flesh. And if there is a woman who is endowed by God with virtue, then that woman will show signs of the Holy Virgin and will transmit her virtues to those around her. I think of my own mother when I look at various images of the Holy Virgin – that is, there are many of these images that have the same countenance as my compassionate mother. I have seen the stone images of the Holy Virgin in the church in Toulouse, but Fra Angelico's Holy Virgin somehow makes me think of my compassionate mother's beautiful days when she was younger. There are those who would criticize the doctrine of the church and who would disdain the worship of the Holy Virgin, but I for one hear a joyful sound in the prayers to her in the church.

After more than an hour the monk came back. I took one flower from the bouquet I had collected in the hills and put it in front of the image of the Holy Virgin, then gave the monk an offering for a candle, and left the church.

> As a written memento
> Of one who saw the gods
> In Fiesole,
> I offer a flower
> To the Holy Virgin

> A votive candle
> Does not suffice
> As an offering to God
> The Mother's image
> In my illuminated soul

I caught a train in front of the church and went blindly back to my inn in Florence, lost in my thoughts of Fiesole's flowers and the image of the Dominican Holy Virgin. My soul felt as if it were playing in a kind of enlightened world.

I had thought of going to the Uffizi museum,[76] if I had the time, to see more of Angelico and Giotto, but if I went I would see other paintings too, like those by Raphael, and because I wanted the image of the Holy Virgin in Fiesole to be last in my mind I ended my sightseeing in Florence here.

Tomorrow I will go to Perugia, and then on to Assisi. In place of the ideal of the Holy Virgin, in two days I would stand in the footsteps of a true saint who had appeared in the world. My seven days in Florence were unforgettable, and my five days in Assisi would, I hoped, bring an eternal inspiration.

⌒ CHAPTER FIVE ⌒

ASSISI, BIRTHPLACE OF A SAINT

ILLUSTRATION BY VITTORIO GRASSI

Intra Tupino e l'acqua che discende
   del colle eletto del beato Ubaldo,
   fertile costa d'alto monte pende,
onde Perugia sente freddo e caldo
   da Porta Sole; e diretro le piange
   per grave giogo Nocera con Gualdo.
Di questa costa, là dov'ella frange
   più sua rattezza, nacque al mondo un sole,
   come fa questo talvolta di Gange;
però chi d'esso loco fa parole
   non dica Ascesi, chè direbbe corto;
   ma Oriente, se proprio dir vuole.

Between Tupino and the stream that falls
   Down from the hill elect of blessed Ubald,
   A fertile slope of lofty mountain hangs,
From which Perugia feels the cold and heat
   Through Porta Sole, and behind it weep
   Gualdo and Nocera their grievous yoke.
From out that slope, there where it breaketh most
   Its steepness, rose upon the world a sun
   As this one does sometimes from out the Ganges;
Therefore let him who speaketh of that place,
   Say not Ascesi, for he would say little,
   But Orient, if he properly would speak.[1]
                                   – Dante, *Paradiso*

April 24
The Land of Flowers to the Land of the Sunrise;
Before the Saint's Sarcophagus[2]

I AM writing this letter as I gaze at a church steeple, not more than a block from where Francis's sarcophagus lies. The setting sun colors the hills to the west a lively color, and the distant mountains appear as shadows, surrounding the fields of Umbria which I can see below. In Assisi, where there is naught a sound save an occasional church bell, I am brought to mind of a world separate from the world of men. Fulfilling the wish that I have had for some years now of coming to the home town of the saint, and of being where his remains are laid to rest, has made me happy beyond words.

I left Florence at about nine-thirty in the morning. The city was behind me under clear skies and a spring mist, and I gazed at the cathedral to hold it in my memory.

> It will remain a mark
> A keepsake
> Of the town of *fiora*
> Wrapped in the mist
> The cathedral tower

We headed east, up along the Arno and through the mountains.

> Even God
> May be seen; the normal realm
> Disappears
> The *Beato*'s house[3]
> Hidden in the hills

> Look at the sky
> Green grass grows on
> The mountainside

How clear it appears
A poppy flower

I could no longer see Beato Angelico's house or the hills of Fiesole as we headed through the valley fields. The land gradually rose in elevation, and soon I could see the white snow of a tall mountain plateau close by.

In the spring fields
The smoldering green
Are its sleeves
The snow its head
A mountain plateau

Wheat fields
The sun shines and darts behind shadows
In the springtime meadows
The grape vines
Wait for summer

The fields are high
Here are the signs
Of early spring
Blooming proudly
The plums

I could see the towns of Arezzo and Cortona in the mountains, and at the top of the mountain I could see a castle enclosed by walls. These towns and castles showed evidence of past wars and scenes of carnage.

In the rocky mountains
Moss grows
On the scarred walls
The mark of men's blood
From many ages past

We came to the edge of a lake in the mountains. We could see the volcanoes of Amiata[4] and Cetona[5] in the distance, and on an island in the middle of the lake there was the place where Francis had fasted for forty days. Going up further into the mountains we came to Perugia where there was an ancient town. The next train would not come for another hour, so I did some sight-seeing in that time.[6] I had planned to spend the night in Perugia, but instead I decided to hurry on to Assisi, taking the train directly to the mountaintop town. The whole town of Perugia – not just the churches and the city hall – comprised buildings that looked for all the world like they were built hundreds of years ago. The streets were narrow and winding, leading one along under the house eaves. It was an odd place.[7] I looked at the ancient Roman city gate,[8] then went to a high prospect where I could view the eastern mountains and a good half of the city. The city was built on the mountain ridge, and is furrowed as a result. The walls that encircle it are next to cliffs, and make a fine fortress. When I looked from one corner of the castle down into the valley below and out to the distant mountains I could not help but think of this town's difficult past. I did not have time to dally, so I pulled myself away and went to the southern prospect to find that this too offered a view of a valley and mountains. The electric tram which I thought I could take from here back to the station did not come. I was pressed for time so I hurriedly walked down the hill. I thought it would take me about twenty minutes to walk to the station visible directly below me, but I was quite wrong and when twenty minutes had lapsed I was not but half way there. The train's departure was imminent, but even if I hurried there was nothing I could do to catch it. Realizing that if the train were late then the time would not matter, I finally reached the station. The train was quite late, and owing to that I made it in time, leaving for Assisi at just past two o'clock. I felt it somehow strange that I managed to make the train.

> Of I, who would visit
> The master's grave
> In Assisi,
> The train was aware
> And waited for me to board

The train headed east, down the mountains toward the plains around the Tiber River. Ahead was a tall mountain, and at its foot was a town that I could see shone brightly in the sun. When I looked closely I realized that it was the same image I had seen in a painting of Assisi, and the mountain behind it was Monte Subasio. I felt upon this occasion a different sort of happiness than that I had felt upon entering Florence – I felt as if I had discovered an ideal world.

I have come close
To the city of Assisi
Beloved be thy name
At the base of a lofty peak
A village of one family

Although I could see it, it was still distant. The Umbrian fields were surrounded by gray mountains in the distance, between which ran many rivers.
We passed through this area and arrived at Assisi Station at three o'clock. Looking from the station I could see that one point jutted out from the cliffs, and on
it was San Francesco.[9] From below, it looked like a painting of Trāyastrimśa.[10]
Next to the station there was also a church with which Francis had deep ties,
but I saved that for later and went up the mountain road in a horse cart provided by the inn. The wheat fields, flower beds, and olive groves along the way
were the same scenery I had seen all along, but I felt reverence for the fields and
trees when I thought about how Francis had spent time here. I wonder what the
townsfolk, cutting grass, thought of the ancient saint.

Oh Townsfolk!
Gather your field grasses
With care
The traces of the saint
Who sojourned here

The road gradually became steep and ran along a castle wall. A group of
villagers were gathered in front of the castle gate drinking. It was like a painting – the bottles were wrapped in something like a wicker basket (all the wine
bottles in this area are treated this way) and red paper was affixed at the mouth
of the bottles, then they were loaded in two or three carts that were pulled by
long-eared donkeys and stopped below the city gate. The driver on top of the
cart had on a big red tie, and wore light green trousers; beside the cart was a
woman who wore black clothes with a reddish yellow hat, and there was also a
man with a reddish yellow tie; the three of them poured red wine from the small
bottles and had their own wine party at the side of the road, laughing gaily all
the while. Seven hundred years ago, just such a wine party must have been the
scene beside the gate.[11] At the next gate we entered, and passing along a narrow
cobblestone street I soon arrived at the inn. This inn is right next to the Basilica,

and it is a house that commands a good view along the cliffs, but the views were all obscured, so instead I was shown to a room that faced the town. Looking out from my window, I felt that the house in front was close enough for me to reach out and touch it, and to the left I could see the church steeple, across the square. I would pass the next few days hearing the bells of this steeple morning and evening.

> St. Francis—
> How many days must he have passed
> The church bells ringing
> Day and night
> His congregation

I had become thirsty on the express train from Perugia so I went out onto the veranda at the inn to drink some tea. From here I was afforded with good views of the fields and the hills, and the monastery directly beside the inn.

After tea I went to the church. I passed through a small stone gate and came into the square in front of the main hall. On each side was an arched walkway. Made only of stone, these show charmingly the ideal of the "honest poverty" of St. Francis. The main hall likewise had a simple entrance. Upon entering I was in a dark space like a dugout storehouse, and I could hear from within voices reciting the scriptures. I forewent the last of the prescribed tour and sat down near the altar to listen to the scripture. The recitation was not like that in other churches where it is sung like a song; it was chanted, almost like in Buddhism. After praying with my eyes closed, I opened them to see, dimly and magically in front of me, a fresco on which Giotto had expended the skill of a lifetime. The church ceiling was built in a bow-shaped arch, and the four so-called vaults that supported it on each side were not tall arches but still looked somehow quite wide. Sunlight came in through the western window, and flickered with the passing of the clouds bringing the frescoes in and out of the light as if by some divine or ghostly spirit. The voices reciting the scripture permeated the hall with a cadence like waves, first growing louder, then softer, stopping and then starting again. Finally they intoned "Amen" and the monks prayed silently. At this point I too closed my eyes and prayed to the Saint and the Buddha. After the silent prayers and another short recitation of the scriptures, the five monks went to the side chapel to continue their recitation. Finally they knelt before the altar – that is, the sarcophagus of Francis – prayed, and took their leave. I too knelt with them, and after the monks left I approached the altar where I could see tiny beams of light coming through the stone steps and falling on the ground. It occurred to me that I was standing in front of the sarcophagus that contained the relics of Francis, and I found myself endeared by the thought of seven hundred years in the past. The inner chamber of the Okunoin temple on Mt. Kōya may have been ghostly quiet, but even standing before Kōbō Daishi would not give me the feeling of reverence and trust that I had here.[12] Not even the Yoshimizu hermitage of Hōnen was such a splendid place as this.[13] If Hōnen's remains were put in a place such as Okunoin, then I am sure my soul would feel as it did in front of the sarcophagus of the Saint of Assisi. The Japanese equivalent of standing in front of Francis's sarcophagus would be to be in the temple of Dengyō Daishi on Mt. Hiei.[14] The sound of the water in front of the Dengyō Daishi temple would be like the light underground in this church. In the face of either one, I would be inundated with a reverence like tears of gratitude, and I would be able to worship the bliss of the dharma, thus experiencing the greatest happiness in the world. The spring in front of the Dengyō Daishi temple has flowed continuously since antiquity, and the light in front of Francis's sarcophagus shines day and night. There are still some in this world who remain disciples of Dengyō Daishi, partaking of the waters, and some who are illuminated by that light. The spring of truth, the lamp of faith – they will not dry up or be extinguished just like that. Rather, somewhere there is a Second Saint who will yet pour those waters and shine that light upon mankind. After finishing my prayers at the altar, I looked at the monks in their woolen robes with rope belts and I too found myself wishing to enter their order.

There were people in the church who were loitering about to view Giotto's painting, but I had no need to view paintings today. Lighting one votive candle before the saint's sarcophagus was enough. I left the church and went back to my inn, looking back at the steeple from the square.

Back at the inn I spoke briefly with the author of a Francis biography, Mr. Sabatier.[15] In the evening I went to the church and then up the hill, where at the old wall gate there were yellow flowers blooming between the stones. I passed by there, and went down to the town cemetery. The view from the cemetery and the road leading to it was different from that from the cliff-side inn. The background hills, the valley below the cliffs, the river that flowed between the mountains and San Francesco and its monastery on the outcropping all came together in one scene, and in the distance the volcano Monte Amiata seemed like it could be either a mountain or a cloud. The sun had gone down behind the western mountains and the plains were enveloped with the colors of dusk.

I went back to my inn and began writing this letter from a library room that looks out and down over the square in front of the church; later, after my meal, I finished writing in that room. I looked out of the window at the moment the clock tower bells struck the half-hour past ten, and saw that the vague light at the entrance to the church looked forlorn in the darkness. That same light was surely still burning in front of the saint's sarcophagus inside the hall.

> Night has fallen
> There is a light
> Before the saint
> The eternal lamp of dharma [16]
> Illuminates the darkness of the world

April 25
Fresco; Sarcophagus; Arousal of Mind at Porta Nuova; Vestiges; Ancient City

I WOKE to the sound of church bells, which rang again while I was washing my face and getting dressed. I ate my breakfast to the sound of that music. My room has no decoration in it at all, not even an electric light. Blowing out a candle before going to sleep and waking to church bells makes this no different from being in a monastery.

After breakfast I went directly to Francis's sarcophagus to contemplate the light from below it and to view the fresco. This church has three levels:[17] the middle one has the altar before the sarcophagus, and the upper one has a fresco by Giotto of Francis's life that has been so severely damaged in the center that one can barely glimpse the original images. Here and there attempts have been made at restoration, thus damaging the painting. Nonetheless, Giotto's composition brings together many human figures and aligns many visages, creating a splendid painting overall. A result of his skill and faith, the piece contains twenty-eight panels over two walls, and is on the scale of the *Hōnen Shōnin Eden*.[18] I did not look at every detail, but I could see clearly that the scenery was inferior to that in the painting in Santa Croce in Florence. I thought that the other aspects of the painting were classic Giotto.

The most striking to the eye were the painting to the right at the end of the hall[19] (of Francis preaching to the birds) and the painting to the left[20] (which shows his giving water from a cliff spring to the thirsty). In the painting of his preaching to the birds, the spring sky is clear blue and the elderly saint ministers to the birds, who are all gathered beneath a thicket of trees. In contrast to this, the cliff spring painting shows only Francis kneeling before the mountain cliff, praying. Below him the spring emerges from the ground, and a single peasant lies there, looking quite thirsty, receiving the waters of the valley.[21] The two paintings face each other and it makes for an interesting contrast.

The story of Francis preaching to the birds is in chapter sixteen of his biography *Fioretti*. One day Francis, along with two disciples, was walking along in the fields and saw many birds, to whom he began to preach. The birds gathered around and listed quietly to his words. That sermon is interesting:

> My little sisters the birds, ye owe much to God, your Creator, and ye ought to sing his praise at all times and in all places, because he has given you liberty to fly about into all places; and though ye neither spin nor sew, he has given you a twofold and a threefold clothing for yourselves and for your offspring... he feeds you, though ye neither sow nor reap. He has given you fountains and rivers to quench your thirst, mountains and valleys in which to take refuge and trees in which to build your nests; so that your Creator loves you much, having thus favoured you with such bounties. Beware, my little sisters, of the sin of ingratitude, and study always to give praise to God.[22]

This sermon should be reverently listened to not only by the birds but also by mankind. In Buddhism, the concept of "Rejoicing in Divine Protection"[23] is essentially the same teaching; praising God is like reciting the *nembutsu* or sitting in Zen meditation. In today's educational system, the concept of "Divine Protection" is nowhere to be found, and there are many broken or troubled homes that ravish human emotions and know of no "Divine Protection." One should give proper consideration to this in children's education, too. Praising God's virtue or Repaying the Kindness of the Four Virtues are all one in the same with "Knowing Divine Protection." In order to know Divine Protection, one must first love Nature, to feel sorry for one trampled flower, or to look at a puppy and think that it, too, could someday become a Buddha. To view a single grain of rice as a bodhisattva, realizing that that grain was tied to one's own life, and being thankful for it, would also encompass this emotion. If, in this way, one knows Divine Protection in all things, one will see the beauty in human emotions and nature, and one will be able to see the light all around. Francis not only conveyed this teaching well in his sermon to the birds, he also showed this same compassion to all animals, birds and wolves alike. Giotto showed this in his painting with simplicity and depth, just as we see in the ancient paintings of the Sumiyoshi or Tosa Schools.[24]

I looked carefully at the upper level fresco, and then I went from the center level down the stairs which led to the basement. Here I found the small chapel that held Francis's sarcophagus in the center. There were many decorations in front of the sarcophagus, as well as many candles. There were also people kneeling in prayer before it. More than by the brilliance of the gold decorations, though, my feelings were deeply stirred by the thought that the saint's remains were interred here, where a blessed light shone upon it in contrast to the darkness of the center level. I worshipped in front of the sarcophagus and then returned to the center level where I took a quick look at the frescoes before going to the eastern part of town to do some sightseeing. The houses of the aristocracy had long ago mostly become the dwellings of the poor, with decrepit walls and slanting roofs. The arched entryways are blocked with stones and have simply become dumping grounds. However, the gardens surrounded by stone walls and the stone pillared balconies built around the upper stories still remained, the vestiges of observation platforms of long ago. Below them were small windows, but above there was a good view, making them resemble in some way the houses of the wealthy in India. The people I saw on those upper levels had dark complexions and wore bright red and green clothing, like the Indians do. At the top of one stone staircase in town there were three chickens at the entrance to a house, and I was yet again reminded of India.

I went up and up through the town to the market. In that area there is a church that was converted from an ancient Roman temple.[25] Further ahead and to the east was a gate in the city wall. I went past it and then further ahead I could see another gate; the scene, with houses, the gate, and womenfolk wearing those red and green clothes made for a very interesting composition. Above that the houses and the gates were just like those that Giotto had painted, and I disabused myself of the notion, developed after I had seen modern western architecture, that Giotto had painted unrealistically. Giotto had painted these houses and the city walls just as he had seen them. Between these two city gates was the church of Santa Chiara. It is the church of the very first Franciscan nun, St.Clare, and her remains are interred there.[26] I could not enter the church, so I went ahead and past the second gate, to where I could see a third gate. Matching my place with the map, I found that it was the "New Gate" (Porta Nuova) where the young Francis had gone out, looked all around him, and first entered the path of Christ.[27] I was overjoyed to be so close to the place that had the greatest significance in the life of the saint, so I left the second gate behind as I drew near the Porta Nuova. In the middle of the gate's arch I saw framed, as if in a fresco, the mountains beyond. The one whose foothills were close was Subasio, and in front of it Monte Seretto sat snow-capped in the blue sky. I wonder what Francis thought when he headed out the city gate, haunted by his illness, and saw this sight.

If I do not give the history here my reader will not understand. When Assisi was at war with Perugia (the town which I saw yesterday), Francis was twenty years old. He joined the fighting, but Assisi was defeated. At the base of the Perugian hills, at St. Giovanni's Bridge (nearby where I first laid eyes on Assisi yesterday from the train), he was captured and spent a year in a Perugian jail. After a year Assisi and Perugia reconciled and the prisoners, including Francis, were returned to Assisi. Francis subsequently fell ill and was bedridden the entire winter, but with the coming of spring he gradually improved, and reached the point where he could walk around a bit. Then, one day, he went out to see the world outside, walking with a cane, and came to Porta Nuova. It was the year 1204, three years before Hōnen was exiled.[28] The time was probably just about as it is now in the springtime. From the age of sixteen or seventeen, Francis, in the style of the aristocracy of the time, spent his time with other youths of the village drinking, singing, and parading about the streets playing drums and flutes and waving banners. That same youth, within the course of a year and due to his having been captured and imprisoned, had a complete change of heart. If he had been an average person, he simply would have been worn down and that period would have hardened his heart, but Francis had not the slightest difficulty; he said that he would become someone honored in the world in the future, and his frankness surprised even the prison guards. "Someone honored in the world" at that time had a set vernacular meaning – that one dreamed of having the honor, power, and influence of one who belonged to an aristocratic family. That youth, full of vigor, managed to escape the fate of imprisonment only to return home and fall ill. Just as he began to recover, after spending a long winter bedridden, he ventured out of this gate and bathed in the rays of the springtime sun. Many factors came together to bring about his extreme change of spirit. Francis, who had this change of spirit and entered the path of Christ, was, after all, a saint.

I traced Francis's footsteps and went out the Porta Nuova. Only a wall separated its two sides, but there was an entirely different world beyond the gate. The town, made of walls and stone fences, disappeared as if it were a dream, and I was in a world of completely natural green. The mountains were tall, the trees thick, and the fields were one solid surface of flowers. Looking up I saw that the little river that ran through the city wall formed a waterfall, and its pure waters roiled along the road. Especially in Francis's time, this city was not a town of the poor, but rather it was a place where there were rows of houses decorated with frescoes, a town that flourished thanks to the wealth of the aristocracy. There were no houses in the fields, so the contrast of the mountains and thick trees – it surely was one vast field of green – must have been strong. Standing in that spot, Francis's spirit must have had something like a revelation of nature; his previous life of dissipation must have been like a dream.

> Out of the city walls
> Away from others
> Here he was alone
> In the realm of nature
> One can see God
>
> The beginnings of
> The light of doctrine
> Illuminating the world
> Here I see the traces
> Of my beloved saint

As I lay in the grassy field and envisioned the past, I looked toward the city gate to see a woman dressed in a red and brown kerchief and carrying a large basket coming toward me, speaking in a loud voice. Behind her was a white ox pulling a cart loaded with wine. A Franciscan clad in a woolen habit was coming up the hill. It was like a painting. It resembled India, especially with the woman carrying something on her head and the white oxcart, and a man singing in the fields as he cut the grass. As I thought of Francis, I also thought of the four distresses observed during the Buddha's wanderings when he was a prince – birth, age, disease, death.[29] The walled town of Kapilavastu[30] was certainly, in its feudal past, like Assisi, encircled by a wall in which the families were grouped together. Outside there must have been a beautiful view of nature at the foot of

APRIL 25 · ASSISI

the snowy mountains. It was absolutely not coincidence that the two of them went out of their respective city gates in the same mind-set and similarly came upon the beginnings of their arousals of the mind.[31] Although I am not sure whether Francis left the city, saw the elderly, sick and dying, and was moved as the Buddha was, it was perfectly natural for him to leave the city, look back upon his life there, and decide to discard it.

> Awakened to dissipation in the city
> One who would awaken and rescue the world
> The master of Assisi, the Buddha
> East and west, one and the same

Occasionally someone or something would emerge from the city gate, and among those who emerged was a cart pulled by a donkey. The cart had a colored pattern painted on the side, and in the middle of it was written "This day comes but once" (*Oggi non si rimette*). It was an odd coincidence that I should read this proverb on the cart at the same time that I was thinking about the two saints. If people always think, "This day comes but once," and thus put emphasis on each action and thought, remembering that they will only be done once today, they will avoid carelessness, but it is not such a simple thing to do. A town girl came through the gate to get some spring water.

> Oh child, fetching water
> Gushing from the stream
> Do you know the taste
> That has not changed since days of old
> Of the doctrinal waters?

This is a question that everyone must ask of themselves.

I returned to the town and ate lunch. Thus after not eating lunch for three or four days I began again. An Englishman was at the table, and we had an engaging conversation about St. Francis and painting. The meal was very enjoyable, and for the first time since Lugano I had a real conversation in which I had some interest.

After the meal Mr. Sabatier took me up to the roof of the inn and told me about all the places we could see around us that had some connection with St. Francis. First, the mountain in the east was the peak of Subasio, which long ago was thickly covered with vegetation. In Francis's time the road that led into Assisi was that road through the fields, and on this side of the road that intersects with it at a right angle is a place where religious pilgrims stop. That place over there where the cypress trees stood was the place where Francis first preached to the little birds, and where he preached to them thereafter. The sermon of the Little Birds that is in Francis's biography was delivered between the villages there in the mountains. The big house visible below the town of Perugia on the hill to the west was once long ago a place that took in the ill, and Francis had slept there. And there in the distance I could just see a bluish mountain, which was the Monte Alverne, where Francis saw a vision of Christ. We talked much of Francis as we looked at each place. Hearing all this from Mr. Sabatier, who had dedicated his life to the study of Francis and had practically become a resident of Assisi, I felt like I had gone back seven hundred years into the past. We really need more people like this who can study Dengyō Daishi or Hōnen, Eshin or Jichin.[32] The Buddhist faith in Japan comes from those men. Truly Mr. Sabatier, in following Francis's footsteps and initiating all sorts of philanthropic work in the area, has become an unsurpassable might on this Franciscan hill.

We walked around, looking here and there in the town. We looked at the old castle, the remains of churches, pilgrims' inns, etc., then we climbed the hill to the top of the fort. On the mountaintop, the walls built of stone in the green fields and the steeples seemed to touch the sky. This whole town is surrounded by a city wall, but especially because the citadel is built on the hilltop, the people of this fort call it the "Great Boulder" (*Rocca Maggiore*). The drawbridge and the gate, the turrets – I looked at them all as I would any other, then we passed through a dark passageway and before us was another tower. From its top the view was really very good, much more encompassing than that I had had from the cemetery yesterday, and I looked in all directions for quite a while. There is no way to describe the grand scale of each scene. When I asked what the yellow flowers growing along the stone gate were called, I was told they were the "violets of the wall" (*violetta di muro*). I could not turn my back on such a name, for the flowers bloomed everyone along the stone walls, and I had also seen them on a church wall in Bordeaux. I picked some of the flowers and we descended the tower, this time taking a rest in the mountain fields and gazing at the scenery. The wind was strong, but the sun warmed me as I lay in the grass. The grasses and flowers that waved in the wind seemed to form a carpet upon which the city walls and the distant mountains sat. Of course the scene above was interesting, but also below me in the fields I could see mountains and the town beyond the two cedar trees and the monastery that had been described to me earlier. In the midst of those mountains and the town, Francis's Basilica was magnificent. Francis himself must have climbed these walls, and these flowers were surely grandchildren of the flowers that he saw. As was my wont, I picked some flowers and we headed down.

After dinner I joined the English guests and we spoke largely of painting, then I finished writing this letter. Now I will take my bath and sleep, the light from the church flickering in the darkness outside my window.

April 26
Santa Maria degli Angeli; the Sermon Crossroads; Sunday services

TODAY I was told that some pilgrims would be coming to the lower church, and so I headed there after breakfast. The lower church is called Santa Maria degli Angeli, and it is in the fields about half a *ri* from the town. After Francis passed through Porta Nuova and had his revelation, he experienced many hardships and although his father disinherited him he did not despair but instead gathered all his charitable feelings and set to work repairing churches. After the cathedral was repaired, while he was praying here, he renounced himself and refused to keep even one cent, instead saying that he had received an order from Christ to travel about the world, spreading the gospel. This was five years after his revelation, and it was how his solitary journey in asceticism in the world began. A large church stands as a reminder of this, and now it stands tall in the fields, visible directly below this inn.

I went out of a gate and down a mountain path along the main road in the fields. Some of the townspeople had wandered out to see the pilgrims who were to come on this Sunday. Although simple, they wore their formal clothes, with the men in bright red or yellow collars, and the women wearing embroidered silk kerchiefs on their heads, all the while frolicking as they walked. As we walked along the road the bells of the hilltop churches and also of the cathedral ahead of us rang out, giving the spring fields a somewhat airy feel. As I drew close to the church the crowd became thicker and I could see rows of red and blue flags. When I went alongside I could see that these were rows of pilgrims; the sunburned peasants wore white robes under which they wore trousers that looked like elephants' legs. In their hands they had candles, walking sticks, and crosses that looked like a flag or banner. They had lined up in rows and were about to enter the church. I could hear the pilgrims' singing from inside the church, but on the outside in the square there were hawkers selling clothing, food, balloons, and all manner of things, all lined up. The villagers wandered about, watching the pilgrims and shopping. To the side under a tree a man had set down a tall platform on which he stood and played a mandolin (like a *biwa*) while he told a story. Such storytelling was like the telling of the *Ramayana* in India, or the telling of *The Tale of the Heike* in Japan.[33] The way in which he stood, raised his voice and put power into it was different, but it was still something that we could perhaps call an Italian Satsuma *biwa* performance. Inside the church the crowd was equally dense and chaotic; there were people dallying about, there were some kneeling in prayer, and some were at confession. A row of male pilgrims and a row of female pilgrims mingled with the sacristan at the altar, and they were all mixed in with those who were there just to give thanks or as tourists – it was a chaotic scene.

The church is a fairly large building with a main hall done in the Renaissance style with various paintings hung on the pure white walls. It is completely different from the solemnity and profundity of the Franciscan Basilica on top of the hill. There is a small hut-like chapel in the center of the main hall – this is the Holy Virgin chapel that provided the source of Francis's great arousal of vows.[34] Its length was no more than five or six *ken*. Francis would come here occasionally during his life to pray, and when he was dying he purposely had his death bed brought alongside this chapel before his life ended. His dying hours were on October 3, 1226, a day on which the sun set west of the mountains and the twinkling stars began shining on the fields of Umbria. The bells of the hilltop church rang about seven or eight o'clock (or, as they say around here, around one or two o'clock)[35] across the fields. After having his arousal of vows at the age of twenty-seven in this church, until his death at the age of forty-four, the saint came regularly to this precious spot to pray. It is said that in Francis's time the fields here were thick with trees, so one imagines that this little chapel was also situated in a quiet place in the forest. At least the church is still located in the fields, and by its side today there is a cypress grove remaining, reminding us of the saint's past. More than three hundred years after Francis's time the current church was built, enclosing the original charming memento beneath its roof. The stars that shone when Francis entered eternal peace would not be able ever again to shine on the chapel roof. There was dust on the roof, and dust on the stone walls. Pilgrims would enter the chapel, and then be trained in the church. The pure spirit of the saint was disrupted by the large crowd in the uninspiring church, and by the ritual. Feeling oppressed by the crowd and also sad at these thoughts, I hurried out of the church. Outside a group of pilgrims playing raucous music came along. Along with the hawkers' voices it all made for quite a cacophony. Looking at this scene I was reminded of when Christ went to the temple in Jerusalem and scolded the merchants in front of it. There are some who say that Christ was mad or that he was impatient, but when I see this sort of scene on the sacred site of the saint I feel sympathy with Christ, and I think that it really is at the limit of what one can bear.

I left the church and went back a short distance on the same road on which I had come, then I headed down a road through the fields and turned to look at Assisi. The scene of the houses on the hilltops and the St. Francis Basilica perched on the western mountain struck my eye as if it were one large canvas. I had been told that the white walled house I saw on the plain had long ago been a clinic for lepers. When Francis had his ill body moved to the Santa Maria degli Angeli chapel he had his palanquin stop briefly before this place so that he could turn to look back at the town of Assisi, and raise his hand in one last farewell to the place of his birth. Although the view of Assisi now is certainly different from what it was back then, when I thought that these were the same mountains and the same village that the saint saw when he returned to his home town during his lifetime, I realized that it was not simply another view.

I headed east on the plain and came to the place that Mr. Sabatier had told me about where two cypress trees grew. Long ago it was a main road, but now it was bumpy with stones. At a place where this road forked with another there was a slight rise and nearby there were a few trees. I sat down in the field to think; no one came, and it was quiet all around, with just the sound of birds twittering.

> Long ago
> The voice of the law
> Heard from the master
> Chirping birds,
> Repeat it!

I thought about Francis preaching to the birds, and about hearing of God's blessing.

> Gathering together
> Dressed only in feathers

Hearing from the Father
Of blessings
The little birds chirp

The teaching
That the birds
Turn their ears toward
The wonderful law
The dharma nature of itself[36]

With that I picked some flowers and headed up the ancient road. How many times had Francis walked up this road?

A myriad times
The saint's footsteps
Left their mark
Although they are invisible
Still I look for them

Alongside the road a horse had been let out to graze in the pasture.

Pitiful horse
Go with your rider
Even now
If the master came
With blood flowing from his feet

It is said that Francis developed the stigmata on his hands and feet when he contemplated a vision of Christ.[37] When I thought about the fact that his bare feet had walked along this stone road I realized that the corns I had developed between my toes were nothing at all.

I was struck with an overall feeling of nostalgia for antiquity when I climbed up the hill, got close to the city gate, and looked up at it.

Returning home
And looking up
At the city gate

I long deeply
For my father

By the time I had left the city gate and gone back to my inn in town, the clouds had gathered on the far mountains and it had begun to rain lightly.

I took a brief rest after lunch then went to the Basilica to see the frescoes. The light was dim today so I could not see them well, but they were occasionally illuminated by the sunlight that reached inside the church. I admired Giotto's skill not only in painting the frescoes, but also in the composition of the arches and how he was able to separate the paintings on the arches, ceilings, and walls. At four o'clock the evening services began and the voices reciting the scriptures echoed around the vault. I listened to the voices and looked at the paintings; I looked at the paintings while listening to the scriptures.

At five o'clock the steeple bells rang out in great, united tones. Then the sacristan put away the Eucharist (the main object of veneration[38]) and lined up the children who were carrying incense and candles. The services proper began with a piece for organ and cello, then a chorus of four people from the village began to sing. The smoke from the incense filled the arches, the music resounded under the ceiling, the lantern light shone on us and I could see, divinely in the middle of the ceiling, the fresco "St. Francis in Heaven."[39] I did not think that I would hear music – especially not four beautifully harmonized voices – in this church. I was especially drawn by the architecture, the paintings, the music, and above all the fact that the service was held above the saint's sarcophagus. I spent a pleasant Sunday today. About the time that I returned to my inn, the sun was heading down in the western sky, Santa Maria degli Angeli stood towering on the plain, and the two cypress trees looked darkly dejected.

After dinner I spoke again with the British guests about painting. Among them I was introduced to a Miss Stoddart[40] who had written a biography of Francis, and I spoke a little to her about Hōnen. She had thought that there must have been someone in Japanese history who was like Francis, but she had not been able to discern much from the books she had and so was very happy to speak with me. I showed her the painting of Hōnen's life (*Hōnen eden*), then we talked again about Western painting and the cause of its corruption after Raphael, about how Giotto's painting of Francis was not necessarily a true likeness but rather a reflection of people's spirits at that time – it was an interesting and beneficial conversation, after which we parted and went to our respective rooms. I certainly have found many things to speak about with the British.

April 27
Carceri's Hermitage; the Wolf of Gubbio

THE WEATHER today was overall much better than yesterday. The sun shone brightly from the morning on, and it seemed very spring-like even on top of the mountain. In the morning I headed toward Carceri, where Francis spent his seclusion. I went up to the east side of the town to the square behind the cathedral. This is where the town's children called Francis, "Madman! Madman!" but Francis, assaulted, nonetheless pushed on to this spot.[41] Ahead the road sloped upward and at the head of the street there was a gate. Monte Subasio soared above the roofs of the ramshackle houses, and the snow that still sat on its peak was white, in the shape of a floating half moon. Outside the gate to which I had ascended, the scene was different from that outside of the Porta Nuova. I somehow found myself in mountains where olive groves covered the rocks and the mountains were a solid mass of green. The previous view of Monte Subasio was all but gone. I went up the mountain road and took in the vista of the plain below from above the olive groves. As I ascended, the green grass grew less and the olive groves disappeared, leaving a field of gray stones across the mountain. I sat down on a boulder on the roadside to rest and indulged in the view. A dark olive grove rose from the foot of the mountain, and at its near edge a wheat field spread across the plain. The clouds made speckled shadows on the green buds of wheat that grew scattered in the field, and the shadows looked like little dark, faint islands floating in a sea of green. There were no trees nearby, nor was there the twittering of birds; occasionally I could hear the *baa baa* sound of the sheep, and their bells, as they were herded among the boulders of the rocky peaks above me. I rested and climbed; climbed and rested. The road gradually became rough stones and the sunlight on the gray rocks shone brilliantly, making me feel like I was climbing Kirarazaka on Mt. Hiei.[42]

> In the sun of his hometown
> On the mountain of branches
> I crawl along[43]
> On this mountain road
> Along the master's footprints

As it does along Kirarazaka, the road forked occasionally, leaving me at a loss about which way to go. I went in the direction in which I had seen a cross earlier.

This way or that
My guide on the road
On which I waver
Is the cross
Standing before me

I turned a corner around an outcropping and in the valley below there was a thick forest in which I could see the church grounds of the Carceri cells [Eremo delle Carceri] which held mementos of the saint.[44] The road ended in the valley where the entrance to the hermitage is, like a cave. I knocked on the door, and the sound of wooden clogs came rattling, whereupon a monk opened the door and bid me enter. Another older monk came out from the chapter house and showed me about with a smiling countenance. First he showed me a chamber which had been a part of the old monastery but had been made into the chapel. It is said that the image of the Holy Virgin at the front of the room dates to Francis's time. The monks' quarters above that had walls made of rocky cliff on one side and on the other, from a small window, one could look down upon the valley.[45] We passed through a doorway that was like a small fox hole and descended. In a cave no bigger than three *tatami* mats, there was a stone bed, on which a wooden pillow lay in a slight depression. This is where it is said that Francis came to sleep. In Japan's *yamabushi* ascetic tradition[46] there is the expression, "sleep in the mountains with a stone for a pillow," but Francis took these austerities for granted and did not consider them a hardship. Francis, who fervently prayed day and night with nothing more than bread and water for nourishment in that rocky cell, has many similarities with Hōnen, who withdrew from society to the Yoshimizu meditation cell and with undivided attention invoked the name of Amida. Seclusion in the mountains by people in the early-modern period is usually directly ridiculed, or dismissed as Hinayana practice, or something that a weakling would do, but those who say such things do not know the character of the secluded saint.

Hōnen did not seek the Pure Land because he was weak in Hinayana austerities[47] or the difficult practices of enlightenment,[48] but rather he knew the difficulty of taking vows based on the strength of others while in the midst of austerities focused on the noble path of one's own power. Hōnen was able to gain the power to ferry sentient beings across the sea of reincarnation to the shore of nirvāna from within a type of Zen reclusive *nembutsu samadhi* akin to Hinayana practices.[49] Likewise, Francis retreated to this rocky valley cave, prayed to God, and then stored up the intrepid spirit that he gained from this state of medita-tion[50] and went out into the world to engage in the salvation of the masses. He had a pure heart that had been cleansed in the waters of this valley, and he went into the world to heal the wounds of the injured. He spread the teachings of Christ, rooted in the signs that he had received from God while in this cave, to the people. The strength that came from a life of bravery and hard struggles was truly nurtured on this stone bed, sleeping upon this wooden pillow.

> In ceaseless prayers
> On this stone bed
> God's name
> Has the power
> Of the lion's roar[51]

In the rocky chamber above the cave was placed the crucifix that Francis would not part with his entire life. The carved wooden image of Christ looked sadly faded but if one remembers that this was the chief object of the saint's rev-erent worship then one realizes that even a gold-gilt and bejeweled figure would lose its brilliance. Coming out of a winding passageway from the room with the crucifix one looks down to a deep valley below. The monks today call this the "Devil's Abyss." The saint, too, must have prayed regularly to the cross that he would not fall into the abyss.[52]

> The depths so deep
> That they are invisible
> To those in this world
> The Devil's Abyss
> Filled

> Even the master
> At Devil's Abyss
> Is warned
> By the valley shadows
> All around

From there we went across a bridge and along a mountain path surrounded by trees. The old monk told me to open the gate up ahead and go into the garden, after which he left. I walked through the shadows of the trees alone, and when I opened one gate I found a garden road that, although it was along the same mountain, was covered with green grass. On either side were rows of cypress trees and within them there was a church with pink marguerites blooming and the smell of violets wafting among the rocks – it was a different world from that of the monks' cells in the cliffs. I went to the church and lay down in a sunny place in the grass, taking in the quietude of the valley and bathing in the sunshine. Flowers bloomed in profusion about my head, and among them small insects danced.

> Lying amidst the rocks
> When set against
> The master's bed
> This mat of grass
> Is a brocade

Occasionally I heard a bird – something like a nightingale – singing in the grove, then a cuckoo would chime in, then the sound of sheep's bells from the distant hills. It gave me a glimpse of the spirit that moved those who chose this quiet valley as the sight for their meditation.

> Distanced from the world
> Their hearts deep
> In the valley
> A memorial service of admiration
> All the birds are singing.

For a long time I lay there on the grass, then I returned to the monastery, paid my respects one more time before the saint's stone bed, then went into the garden. In the middle there was a well, one that is said to flow thanks to a miracle worked by Francis. How many mendicant monks had tasted these well waters since Francis had, passing their days in meditation? I drank some of the water, and put some of the flowers I had gathered into it.

> I draw from
> The constant stream
> That flows from above

The taste of sweet dew
Slakes my thirst

I thanked the monks and left the monastery, looking back at the gate one more time. Monte Subasio seemed to be split in two from this angle, leaving this valley cut off from the world, a true mountain retreat. Even though it was a high elevation, there were still mountains on all sides. When the saint established these cave-cells, his thoughts must have been like those of the Indian Buddhist priests who carried out the commands of the Buddha about purifying their hearts. The wisps of smoke that came from the roofs of the monastery were from the fires used to boil simple grains. The sound of the plows beyond the stone pasture walls was that of the work of monks who are blessed by God. Today's Buddhism and Christianity have begun to forget the preciousness of a simple life, and this is surely the largest cause of their corruption. The actual expression of faith surely comes from the beginning of practical austerities. No matter what monks are like today, the laymen, like us, of today have not one ten-thousandth the true character of the saints of old.

I went back down the valley road. The monastery rooftops quickly disappeared, as did the trees in the valley. I went around an outcropping of rocks and came upon a tall cliff from which I could look down upon the broad plains below. The city of Assisi, its steeple, and its houses appeared at my feet, as if I could reach out and pluck them with my hand. I wonder how Francis felt when he left the Carceri valley after completing his prayers, went into the town to preach, came to this corner, and gazed down upon the walls and houses of the town.

On the mountain, out of the valley
In the eyes of the saint
Who looks at the worldly houses of the village
The light of salvation glitters

I descended slowly, eventually reaching the olive grove and fields of flowers. I went through the city gate and in the square where Francis had met with violence there was not a soul to be seen. From the steeple came bells ringing the quarter hour past six (that is, the quarter past twelve noon). In front of the church the bronze statue of Francis glittered brightly in the sun, standing alone and silent on the paving stones.[53]

The guests were dining when I returned to the inn. I divided up the flowers I had gathered at the Carceri monastery, putting one on my desk and giving one to Miss Stoddart. Those who would similarly adorn their desks asked if they were flowers from Carceri, and they each took the flowers in their hands to smell them. Miss Stoddart was very pleased, saying that she would dry the flower as a keepsake. These British love and admire Francis and thus treated the Carceri flowers with importance. Even though our countries are separated by a great distance, sympathy ties our hearts together.

I spent the afternoon in the inn's reading room, resting. I gazed at San Francesco and the plains below as I read. Among my books was one that claimed the story of Francis preaching to a wolf and taming it was not a myth but a true event. About ten *ri* north of Assisi is a town called Gubbio where a wolf once appeared outside the city walls, killing many of the residents. Francis felt pity for it, and went to the wolf's den to preach to him. The wolf became attached to Francis and in the end it became like a tame dog, and was kept by the villagers in a cave. This story is in the old biographies, and I had heard that the wolf's grave was in Gubbio, as was a stela that had been carved in memory of the wolf. I thought to myself that it certainly sounded like a myth, but recently the area had been dug up and they discovered a wolf's skeleton. The wolf had lived there and been kept there, and they made that grave when it died. If we take the grave marker and the bones as proof, then certainly the story was true and the wolf really was kept like a dog.

At dinner we discussed many things, and when we discussed the concept of *bodai ekō*[54] a British woman said that she did not know Japan had had such advanced concepts since ancient times. The women who had a close connection with the Roman Catholic Church were particularly keen in the conversation.

April 28
The Saint's Birthplace; the Saint's Statue; the Lord's Birds; the Hermitage at Damiano; the Eulogy of the Sun; St. Clare; the Education of Girls

THE WEATHER was clear, the sky a pure blue with hints of deep green. The steeple and walls of San Francesco glittered in the sunlight and the skyline was fresh in the azure sky, just as in Giotto's painting. The inside of the church was dark compared to the sunshine outside and in the faint light of the lanterns I could hear voices performing the early morning service. I knelt before the altar, closed my eyes and prayed, then opened my eyes and looked up at the fresco on the ceiling, which appeared divine, the image of Francis clearly visible in the center.

I left the church and went east on the main road to the central square. As I walked up the slope I could see, between the steeple and the bell tower, Monte Subasio towering above, the half moon of snow on its peak solid white against the pure blue sky. I went along the side road of the square, toward the church that was built over Francis's birthplace. The church is new, but this is the place where Francis uttered his first cry.[55] It is the place where his mother cried tears of kindness, where he did not yield to his father's rebuke, and where he decided to leave home to practice austerities. He did not look back at the fortune or houses of the wealthy men who lived close by in the center of town, but rather he took "poverty" as his ideal, and Christ as his master, living here for a time.

I went back up the hill to the cathedral.[56] In contrast to the charming Byzantine façade, the inside is done in a Baroque style. Inside there is a marble statue of Francis carved by Dupré.[57] The bronze statue in front of the church resembles this stone statue, with hollow cheeks that show the fervor for redemption of mankind and an upturned face that shows the merits of submission to one's faith. The life-size stone image gave a glimpse of the real man's stature.

I went, again, past the place where Francis had been called a madman by the town children. I looked up at Subasio's snow-covered peak, and down briefly at the park that had recently been completed through the great efforts of the empress,[58] then I went out through Porta Nuova. Lying down in the grass at this charming site, I looked up at the clear sky of the deepest blue without one speck of cloud, a sky that was full of lightless and silent illumination.[59] The swallows flying in the sky went so high up in the blueness as to become indiscriminate shapes, then they would fly back down right before my eyes. Giotto's painting, in which the angels came from just such a blue sky, was brought to mind. I also recalled that Dante had called angels "the birds of God". Swallows just as these must have flown about here when Francis had his revelation.

God's angels
Watched
Over him
Like the swallows
Swimming in the blue sky

I went down the road. The wheat grew green between the olive groves, and the poppies were deep red fissures in the greenery. After I had descended a considerable distance, I reached the hermitage of San Damiano. I knocked on the door, and was led in by a monk who guided me through the interior.

The monastery of San Damiano is a place of deep significance in the life of Francis. After his revelation at Porta Nuova, he occasionally assisted the poor, and went to leper colonies. His father did not like this, and scolded him for it. One day Francis came to this church and before the crucifix, while he was praying to Christ, he heard Christ's command to repair the church, which had fallen into disrepair under the stewardship of only a single monk. He eschewed help from others and, by himself, brought stones cut from the mountains and finished the repairs. Francis came here to pray often, but one day when his father commanded him to go out to sell silk, he sold the silk and his horse, came back to the church and tried to give the money to the monk, but the monk feared Francis's father's wrath and would not take it. So Francis tossed the money outside the window, and took up residence in the church.[60] His father came to get the money, but at that moment the walls mysteriously hid Francis. Some time afterwards, when Francis was disinherited by his father and became a totally free man, he repaired other churches, cared for lepers, and for a while lived here, reaching maturity in this church. Later Francis took on disciples in his work, and he established a retreat in another church, Santa Maria degli Angeli. In the year 1212, when a young, well-to-do woman named Clare left her family and became one of his disciples, Francis established a nunnery in San Damiano where Clare and the other nuns could live. Then, after dozens of years had passed, Francis fell ill and eventually lost the use of his eyes. He knew that his death was near, and so, in order to bid farewell to Clare and the other nuns before departing on his journey, he came once more to this retreat. He had intended to leave immediately, but his fever flared and in the end he spent two weeks in the retreat, being cared for by the nuns. But of course it was improper for a monk to stay in a nunnery, and so they built a hut out of reeds and bamboo and it was there that he lay. The famous *Cantica del sole*, a hymn, was composed in this little hut outside the retreat.[61] In autumn of that year Francis died in the degli Angeli Church[62] and when his corpse was returned to Assisi, Francis one again returned to Damiano and in death bid farewell for eternity to the nuns. The importance that this monastery played in his life, and the connection that it had with the first female disciple, Clare, makes it a place of great significance.

My tour of the grounds began by entering the church. There were many small objects of reverence in the church, such as rustic decorations, and the simple room itself had a low wall with a round ceiling. On the left is Clare's votive image, and the bread from the Holy Supper,[63] and other such relics. In the middle were small chimes, like a bell, that Clare would strike to tell the nuns that it was time for services. When I ventured to strike it, it made a small but very pure sound, and the resounding notes went on forever.

> The sound of the chime
> When I struck it
> Resounded purely
> It is the spirit
> Of the mistress Clare

On the right-hand wall was the relic of an old window. This is the window niche where Francis threw the money.

> The spirit
> That tossed gold
> Out the window
> Unattached to the world
> Or to treasures

Past the front altar in the back of the church, there was a place where the monks gathered. In Francis's time the altar had been here, and there is a hole there where it is said the crucifix once stood, from which Francis received the command to repair the church. However, today that crucifix is kept in the Basilica di Santa Chiara in the middle of town. After Clare's death the nuns of the church received a new church in the city center, and when they moved there the crucifix, too, went with them.

There is a small chapel to the side of the main church. This is where Clare's sarcophagus was originally placed, and from that sarcophagus a constant scent wafts, causing a marvelous perfume throughout the room.[64]

> The lingering scent
> Of her worldly shell
> Even in the passing years

The remaining perfume
Imbues my soul

The little room next to this is currently used as the church office, but it was the place where Francis's reed hut once stood, and where he composed the hymn to the sun, moon, water, and fire that said [in part], "O most high Lord, Praise be to thee" and "Our revered brother, the bright Sun, O most high Sun in the Lord's shape."[65] The room has one window, but one can see the blue sky through it, and on this day the sunshine was particularly warming. However, there is no doubt that Francis's reed hut was, it goes without saying, a humble, wretched affair. There he was constantly assaulted by rats, but he did not suffer.[66] Even after his eyes had grown progressively worse and he could barely see at all, he still praised the Lord's light and embraced a spirit of repaying kindnesses and being thankful for goodness by singing the *Cantica del sole*. That disposition was not born of the usual courage or faith. Even though Francis's physical eyes could not see, his spiritual eyes were filled with the Lord's light and the light of compassion. When I think about that, it reminds me of Hōnen's poem, "Although there is not|a moment when it does not shine|the moon|resides in the spirit|of one's gaze."[67]

Straining his eyes
Extolling
The merits of the sun
That spirit
Is made of sunlight

I looked at all the other places in the monastery, missing not a thing, including the prayer room, the dining hall, the sleeping quarters, and all the other rooms that the nuns (and now the monks of the monastery) used, thinking all the while of the past. I was especially struck by the thought of the small flower gardens on the roof between the walls of the monastery, as it is said that this was Clare's flower garden. Dirt has been piled up on the roof where fragrant yellow and purple flowers are planted, and there is a stone bench along the wall.[68] The monk who guided me ceased his tour and sat down on the bench, silently bathing in the warm sunlight. In this tiny space between the walls I crossed over the flowers growing above the laundry poles and came to a place where I could see two or three dark green cypress trees soaring tall. In the distance I could see the green fields and the mountains on the other side of the valley. The blue sky was deep azure as far as the eye could see, growing misty with the distance, and a bright lapis lazuli color floated at the edge of the mountains. The world was full of light, from the various flowers to the color of the mountains, the green of the cypress trees, and the azure of the sky. The insects were quiet around me.

> Full of fragrance
> Bright silence
> In this park
> I catch a glimpse of the shape
> Of the nuns

As I watched, small clouds would occasionally appear along the mountain ridge, illuminated by the sunlight and shining white, then briefly disappearing, only to reappear again.

> It makes me think
> Of the pure shape
> Up above
> The white, bright clouds
> In the pure blue sky

I passed the time sitting lazily in the warmth of the sun. When it was time to leave I plucked some flowers and pressed them in my notebook.

> Pressed
> The scent in my sleeves
> Of plucked flowers
> A memento
> Of St. Clare

Once again, I went to the incense room and after sitting in quiet contemplation of Francis's hut, I left the hermitage.

In front of the hermitage I lay down in the grassy field and bathed again in the sunlight, taking in the surrounding landscape. There was a little building with an old wall in among the olive trees. The view long ago for Francis was likely such a one. I felt like I could see his visage, the poor nobleman, who had repaired the church with stone cut from the mountains I could see towering on my left.

> On this wall
> Just one stone
> Praise-worthy through the ages
> The saint's hand touched
> This memento

I climbed the hill and turned toward the city gate. The sunshine at high noon shone on the cobblestones, as well as the sand. The deep red of the poppies beneath the olive trees swayed in the wind. Suddenly summer was upon us, with the whiteness of the stone against the blue sky, and the circles of lonely poppies among the trees' leaves. It was no coincidence that this phenomenal, sharp, deep contrast was expressed in Italian painting and poetry. Japanese poetry has the spring mists, Italian poetry has the azure sky. Japanese painting has cherry-blossom clouds, Italian painting has stands of cypress. Bashō was a quintessential Japanese Buddhist poet when he silently composed, "Flowery clouds | Is the bell in Ueno? | Or is it in Asakusa?" [69] Dante was the quintessential Italian Christian poet when he saw the Holy Virgin and wrote, "The eternal Rose who fragrantly praises the sun of the eternal spring." [70] Similarly, although each one had his own special characteristics, one can see traces of Hōnen in St. Francis.

Just as I went through Porta Nuova the bells of the Basilica of St. Clare rang noon.

> The sound of the bells
> Ringing out
> In the blue sky
> Share Clare's
> Pureness of voice

In the afternoon I went to St. Clare's (or, in current Italian, the "Chiara") Basilica. This church has a deep association with both Francis and Clare, and today there is both a church and a nunnery here. St. Clare was the eldest daughter of a powerful count in Assisi named Favorino. [71] This count had a castle on a slope of Subasio, but in the winter he lived in his mansion in Assisi. It is said that the stone walls below the Clare nunnery were once a part of that mansion. Clare was the beautiful, renowned eldest daughter of this count, and she had two younger sisters but no brothers, and therefore was in a position to inherit all of her father's wealth. Nonetheless, since childhood she had a deeply compassionate spirit, and she often cared for the poor. When she was eighteen years old, there were arrangements made for her marriage, but the groom that her father had in mind was simply not to Clare's tastes; he was a typical aristocratic prodigal son. Then Clare heard that Francis was teaching in a church in Assisi about honorable poverty and about Christ's love, influencing people, so one day she went to hear his sermon and Clare was inspired, like Francis, to leave her home and practice religious austerities. Right next to Clare's mansion, where the Basilica of Clare is located today, there was a church called San Giorgio where Francis delivered his first sermon, and where he delivered many subsequent sermons. Clare was influenced by Francis's sermons; the Basilica of Clare was established on this spot. When Clare got it in her mind to leave home, she did not consult with her mother, but rather spoke only with her aunt and then asked Francis for the tonsure. Just as the Buddha did, Francis at first was hesitant to take a woman from her home and into his order, but even after hearing about the hardships she would face, Clare refused to change her conviction. So, she was granted permission to leave her home and enter the order, and it was arranged that she would be allowed to come to Santa Maria degli Angeli on the eve of the Easter celebration. That day, March 18, 1212 (just three months after the passing of Hōnen), Clare, accompanied by her aunt and one other woman, left her house and went out through the Moiano gate, through the fields, to Santa Maria degli Angeli. There they performed the ceremony in which she took her vows, and she became the first nun in Francis's order. Afterwards, Clare's younger sister Agnes and Clare's aunt both became nuns, as did others, and so Francis took Damiano, where he had been staying himself, and made it into a nunnery, with Clare as its leader. After Clare's death the dangers outside the city walls were too great, so a different nunnery – the Basilica of Clare – was built, and Clare's remains, along with the crucifix that awoke Francis, were moved to this church.

The interior is very simple, and has almost nothing to it. There are paintings on the ceiling, but they cannot be seen through the scaffolding that has been set up for restoration purposes. In the basement is the splendid hall of marble where Clare's sarcophagus is placed. It is said that if one lights a lamp and takes a look, one can see the remains of Clare, but it is better to be in the hall in the dim light, so I extinguished the lantern and sat silently for a while in the darkness.

I left that hall and had them open the door on the side of main hall, within which was a small chapel decorated with rather good portraits of the Franciscan saints (done by artists such as Lorenzo), including Clare and her younger sister Agnes.[72] As the bell of that hall rang, a window in the wall was opened, and a nun came forth to the window to show me the original crucifix that had been in Damiano. In the window there were iron bars, and the crucifix did not appear as I had imagined it would. In the candlelight as I looked up at the crucifix against the curtains, the craftsmanship was better than I had expected. It was in the Byzantine style, and the expression on Christ's face looked as though He were alive. It was not without reason that Francis, raised in the faith of the twelfth century, and suffering spiritually, prayed before this crucifix in the quiet, rural hermitage and had the vision that he had. The crucifix had been kept well in the rural hermitage. The merits and demerits of the piece as an image are a different issue; more than just being the image that led Francis to God, it is the image which expressed the Christ that was in Francis's soul.

> If it were not you
> Who would speak
> Through this image
> In my spirit
> God's voice must speak

In the morning I visited Damiano, in the afternoon I saw the Basilica of Clare, such that I saw in one day all the major traces of Francis and Clare. I felt that, more than seeing some other churches, I would rather spend the rest of the day taking in the view of the fields, so I climbed one of the watchtowers above the cliffs and lay down in the grass there, lazily taking in the view all around, as was my wont. Although they were the same fields and the same mountains, today the fields and mountains looked clearer in the pure air of the sky. Lying down and looking only up at the sky, the deep, dark blue emitted a light that seemed to have no end. The bells of the churches below seemed like voices from some faraway world.

I walked through the peaceful fields and headed down the mountain, then went along a new narrow road and through an olive grove, all the while gazing down on the town. There was a monastery where I entered the town, and opposite it there was a house with a sign out front indicating that it was a school for poor girls. As I was standing there in front of the school, a British man named Mr. Goad,[73] who was staying at the same inn as I, came by. Upon asking him,

I found out that this was the school for the poor that he had worked so hard to establish, where they taught girls how to read and write, and how to do manual labor. That being the case, I asked if he would show it to me, and the two of us knocked on the door. A nun came out from within, and led us to the work area on the second floor. There were other nuns there, and about twenty girls who were doing various types of work. They all rose happily when they saw that Mr. Goad had come, and greeted him with "Good day!" They were busy with all sorts of work, such as sewing, lace-making, and crocheting. The children, at a glance, seemed hardly like the children of Assisi; they were clean and even their countenances were gently refined. The nuns who looked after them cared for them as if they were their own children, and showed us their work. Mr. Goad also seemed like he was with his own children and younger sisters, and he chatted with the children. From there I was shown other rooms, such as the dining hall, the kitchen, and the gardens. I was surprised that such a clean place could be found in Italy. The children's dining table was made of marble, and on it their cups and plates were beautifully arranged. The children did not sleep there, but they received their board and clothing from this school, and were educated here, and so they felt closer to the school than they did to their own dirty houses. We returned to the room where we first entered the school and bid farewell to the children, then Mr. Goad and I left the school together. We happened upon two British women who were making their way along the street and so Mr. Goad took them back to the school to show them around, and I went to San Frances-co. As I turned around I saw the evening sun reflecting on the school windows, giving off the appearance of a happy, pure life therein.

I went to the church and looked at the frescoes. The sunlight shone just through the western window, illuminating Giotto's painting of the crucifix straight on. The blue sky in the background was the same as today's azure sky, and the sleeves of the angels in flight were just like clouds, the clouds that I had seen from Clare's garden. Beneath the crucifix, the Holy Virgin and disciples, grieving Christ's death, were to the left, and to the right Francis led those disciples in tears before the crucifix, and to the right of them the Jews, surprised at the arrival of angels on the wing, stood poised to flee. The representation seemed to come alive, and one could easily see the special skill of a Giotto who had come into his own. I continued to look about the main hall at the frescoes in contemplation, and then returned to my inn at dinner time.

After dinner, I spoke with Stoddart and Goad about various things, such as the paintings I had seen during the day, the school, and then the conversation turned to Hōnen. I showed them a picture of the *Chokushūgoden* and told them of the priest's life and faith, which the two were very happy to hear, and they agreed that there were many similarities between the Buddhist priest and Francis. At that moment the three women who had gone on an outing to Perugia that day returned to the inn with some sweets, and the six of us spoke merrily into the evening until we parted at half past ten.

Today was truly a happy day – I saw two churches, went to a school and had a nice evening conversation. I have hardly spoken Japanese in a month, but in speaking English without restraint I felt as if I had returned to my home town, and was speaking freely with the people there. That I have met and spoken with these British people here is thanks to the merit of Francis, and that these people have listened to my talk about Hōnen is thanks to Francis. The idea that Orientals and Occidentals have a different core emotion is held by those who do not understand human emotion; I think that considering Christianity and Buddhism as two separate entities is the same as building a fence around oneself and standing encircled inside it.

April 29
Santa Maria degli Angeli; the Saint's Last Moments; a Thornless Rose

IT WAS cloudy this morning, as it was yesterday. I read for a while then went to San Francesco at eleven o'clock. The middle level was very dark, so I went to the upper level to see the story of Francis's life, and remained there until lunch time. Giotto's brush captured the splendid drama of Francis's power in single handedly stemming the collapse of the Roman Catholic Church, the interment of Francis's remains in front of the Damiano, and the kindness of Clare's farewell kiss when she left to become the first nun.

After lunch I went to Santa Maria degli Angeli in the fields below. The morning clouds had all disappeared and in the perfectly clear sky the sunlight shone down brightly on the plain. I sat down on the stone where Francis took his last look at Assisi, then looked up at the town on the hill. The towers and walls that soared into the blue sky and the houses in the sunlight were so clear as to seem translucent. Francis had bid farewell to his hometown in October, and in the clear autumn sky the view of these hills must have been as it was today. I wonder how he felt, looking up at his hometown with his misty eyes that had lost all but a little sight. It must have been a sad farewell, and as he looked at the faint scene he must have been joyous to see clearly in his heart his true home in the heavens.

I went along the main road, bathed in sunlight. It was quite warm and I found it difficult to bear the dust that covered my head, but the sun shone gently on the wheat in the fields and occasionally the wheat would sway in the wind.

> Sunlit
> The heads of wheat
> Blow in the wind
> Summer has come
> To the fields of Umbria

I arrived at Santa Maria degli Angeli and washed my hands in the nearby stream. When I rinsed out my mouth I felt rested. When I entered the church the guide opened the inner chapel[74] and told me to wait there. In this church there is a Franciscan priest who can speak English and French, and I found out later that one of the British men at my inn had spoken to him about me and consequently the father had told the men working at the church to keep an eye out for a Japanese. Sitting in the inner chapel, which I had only viewed from the outside on my previous visit, I realized that it was smaller than the Damiano chapel and was originally just a wayside chapel of sorts. This was not only the first chapel where Francis had lived, its stones had been carried here by Francis when he repaired the church, and pilgrims came to touch and kiss these stones, making them highly polished from all the places where hands and heads had caressed them. The interior of the chapel had no decoration, just an altar in the very middle, and that was a simple affair, reflective of the past. Before this altar Francis had opened his Bible and read the passage, "Spread the good news to all the world," and was driven to espouse the teaching of honorable poverty, and this was where he first preached the happy news of [Christ's] love.[75] Also before this altar, Clare took the tonsure and her vows. As I reflected silently on these events, the priest came to greet me and shake my hand. This priest's name was Father Bernardo, and he was originally from Germany. He began speaking in English, but then when a German tourist came he switched to German and explained all about this church. Behind the church there was a small chapel which also had been subsumed inside the larger main hall. This was where Francis died, and in its center was a statue that wore the death mask of Francis; on the surrounding walls were images of his disciples. Upon close inspection, the statue of Francis had a face that looked drawn, as if he were consumptive, and in it I saw a kind of benevolence and dignity that is hard to describe. In merely sixteen or seventeen years, this ailing man began a truly immense movement, the strength of which came from faith.

> Skin and bones
> Even in this ailing body
> Was the faith
> That moved
> The world and its people

When his illness became especially grave, Francis did not hope for recovery, but rather, when he knew his end was near, he had his disciple Leo sing his *Cantica del sole* with a part of his "Eulogy of Death" appended to it. That part means, "Death can be avoided by no one, we must simply pity those who die in a state of sin; Those who follow the will of God will not suffer this death" [76] and contains the feeling of the *gata* in Buddhism about the will of the gods, "Whatever is phenomenal is impermanent." [77] Just as Hōnen passed away as if falling asleep while reciting the *nembutsu*, the saint's end brought East and West together. Coming here and seeing his death mask, silently contemplating it in the darkness of the church, I felt like I had traveled back in time.

> His spirit
> Returns to the Father
> His earthly remains
> Left behind in this state
> Are still pure

In the wall of the hall there remains a hole. That is where Saint Francis would leave medicine for the lepers, and where today is kept the rope that he used as a belt. On that belt remains some blood from his chest wound (the wound that appeared on Saint Francis's chest as it had appeared on Christ's chest). I do not know whether the blood from his chest wound was coughed up through his throat, but it was probably the last blood to come from a body that had endured the privations of life.

The rope belt
of he who gave himself
to the Lord —
Untie it, oh bodhisattvas
and welcome his spirit

Even from a mouth of blood
came praise
for the Lord
The remains of an era
have come to rest here

I left the main hall and went past the sacristan's room, down a corridor to a flower garden and chapter house. The roses had not bloomed in the flower garden yet, but the leaves were beautifully verdant. This was the rose from which Francis removed the thorns, and it is said that to this day there are still no thorns.[78] The chapel in front of it is called the Chapel of the Roses, and is where Francis, after taking on four disciples, created living quarters for them alongside Santa Maria degli Angeli. It is said that the storage place beneath the altar was where Francis slept at that time. Although it is not quite like his cell at Carceri, there is still there, as a memento, a little stone bed and a wooden pillow. One cannot help but be surprised at his bravery in providing for his disciples; just as Christ, he thought nothing of the difficulties of his austerities. There is no doubt that Francis would have found sleeping on a brocade bed a hardship, rather than a comfort. Francis carried out difficult holy austerities in the same manner as one might follow the easy path of an entrusting mind through other power.[79] Hōnen, too, rejected difficult austerities, distancing himself and abandoning the practices of "knowledge of things and realization of truth"[80] and instead joyfully sought the Pure Land through crying out the name of the Buddha. This spirit is nothing like that of some bad monk who fails on the path of austerities and who borrows his name from others, indulging in ease and idleness. Hōnen was enveloped in the true spirit of saintly austerities within the realm of the easy path of practicing the *nembutsu*.[81] It is not that Hōnen was buying his way into his own paradise through the wisdom and merit of his own power; rather, the two men [Francis and Hōnen] had the spirit of men who entrusted themselves to the salvation provided by the other power, embracing the compassionate light of the Buddha toward other sentient beings. Both the transfer of merit of the *nembutsu* and the giving of oneself over to the deep joy of one's innermost heart are expressions of this spirit. The spirit of the transfer of merit is the teaching of the easy path of recommending the *nembutsu* to the masses; in the giving of deep joy, one does not have time to reflect on one's own difficulties and privations, but rather, for the sake of mankind, and for the sake of Jesus Christ, one dedicates oneself to charitable acts. Although the way in which the men did these things was different, the two saints' faith was one in the same.

I left the Rose Chapel and met a priest named P. Robinson.[82] The priest had heard that I was here, and he had come to meet with me before heading off on a journey of his own. We stood for a while in the Rose Garden and spoke briefly about our studies of Francis before parting. When I returned to where I had been before, I saw that Father Bernardo was now leading a group of French tourists. I joined them in their tour, and after they left, I left the meditation hall and Santa Maria with not a little regret.

On my way home the setting sun shone upon the town of Assisi. The sun, as it headed into dusk, dyed the clouds a myriad colors, showing off a sky of deep reds and purples. I went up on the roof of the inn to take a look at the last rays of sunlight striking the hills and fields, and the setting sun sank down, much to my regret.

> How precious
> The last of the setting sun
> Dyes the sky
> The residual light
> And thoughts of the master

After dinner I spent a gay evening in the reading room with the British guests. In particular a Miss Dove was headed to Rome, and two others were going to leave for their own country the next morning, and so we spoke at length in our parting, promising to meet again, and everyone returned to their rooms at ten thirty, leaving me by myself to finish writing in this diary.

April 30
Nature in Early Summer; Reminiscences of the Saint

GOOD WEATHER ensued, and I felt like the sky's blue became a gradually deeper hue. When I went up on the inn's roof early in the morning, the sun was rising above Monte Subasio and was shining directly upon San Francesco. The hermitage in the valley at Carceri was also probably fully bathed in sunshine. After reading for a bit, I headed along a road that led through the fields outside the city walls and along the mountain cliffs. The world was full of flowers, and among them were poppies of a dark red hue, which grew in abundance in this area. The deep red, shining out from the dark green shadows of the olive trees, seemed very lively.

> The shadows of the olives are dark
> The scent of the poppies among the grasses
> If it is not red, then it must be green
> The colors are fickle!

The marguerite flowers, much like wild chrysanthemums in Japan, are particularly common close to the town walls. I lay down on the grass and looked at the valley landscape, thinking about the past. These stone walls were the foundation of Count Favorino's mansion – I wonder what the princess Clare looked like as she appeared in the garden. That princess one morning left her home and took nun's vows. And the castle lord's mansion became a nunnery, and has remained such until today. I wonder how Clare's father, who was angered that she was unfilial, would feel if he were to come here today. Through these thoughts, I was inspired to compose a poem or two about Clare's life. In the end, I only managed a few stanzas.

> The graceful maiden, purer than a flower
> Looked up at the dais on the hill
> The brash figure of the Count
> Sent countless love letters
> But the letters in Clare's eyes
> Were the words and teaching of the Lord
> And the verse from her tongue was not of love
> But praise of the kingdom of heaven

The poor listen
To the teaching of the happy master
A wealthy lifestyle becomes trial by fire
Brocade robes become clothing made of needles

Loath to turn her back on her father
She entrusts herself to our Heavenly Father

At the daybreak of her heart's awakening
Holy austerities are not harsh
Leaving one's home and saving the world
Francis, leading the way
At the city gate where he crawled forth
The olive trees cast dark evening shadows
A white-clad figure travels the road
In the light of the heavens
In the church, still dark before dawn
Led by the beckoning saint
The holy altar where her hair fell down
Is still today a place of sacred journeys

On the morning of the Lord's resurrection, full of light
She is brave at the beginning of a difficult life [83]

I wanted to write a biographical poem of Clare that would describe how she was awakened and left her family, and how, in the face of her father's anger, she entered the nunnery at Damiano, and how she stood by the master Francis in his last hours, but then after I had left there the memories could not be readily recalled. Tomorrow I will go to the church again and see if I can continue.

I walked past St. Clare's basilica and the Porta Nuova, then went from the gate to the front of the church and home to my inn, by which time it was time for lunch.

In the afternoon, first I went to San Francesco to view the frescoes. The walls have such a complicated collection of many works that no matter how many times I look at them I always see something new. Today I focused on the four paintings that are located directly in the middle of the ceiling. [84] Francis in heaven surrounded by the angels; [85] the angels and the saint praying before the virtue of Obedience;[86] Francis's marriage to the queen of Poverty;[87] and the angels offering books and flowers to the virtue of chastity, beneath which a soldier protects a monk being purified.[88] Through their symbolism and arrangement, these paintings all show the ideals of the Franciscans, and they also show the skill of Giotto.

I left the church and went out the Giacomo gate down the road into the valley. As I went down the hill, I looked up at San Francesco, soaring above on the hilltop cliff, and down at the olive groves in the valley; the nearby hills were beautifully verdant. The songs of the children who were cutting grass in the valley came wafting with the wind, and I found the tunes charming. The view from the outcropping just before the bottom of the road had the Tescio river valley in the foreground, then on one side a thick grove along the church cliff and on the other side an olive grove along the gentle slope at the foot of the mountain. The hills in front of that, closer to me, were dark and the distant hills seemed layered one upon another, gradually leading to Monte Amiata, jutting high into the sky. It was a scene that seemed somehow separate from the realm of mankind, a mountain and field landscape in a pure state of nature, one about which the poets would compose pastorals. I went down to the end of the road and crossed an old stone bridge. Alongside the bridge the stream waters flowed blue along the bank, and a row of birch trees in the sun swayed in the breeze. On this side of it, there was a farmer's house. Some children had made a cross out of olive leaves on the tip of a small pole, and had stood it in the field. Tomorrow is the first of May, and I saw signs of the beginning of summer in the form of people making blessings in the fields.

> The cross of olives
> Here before
> Standing in the field
> How joyous!
> We too rejoice

I went along the river on the cobblestone road, past the olive groves. The songs of the maids herding them calmed the bleating voices of the sheep.

> Hearing the songs
> Of the shepherdesses
> By the mountain

I do not feel as if
I were floating in another realm

I went around the base of the church and came out on the road. There are many birch trees here, too, and the view of the fields between the rows of trees is different from that of the valleys in that it is calm and pleasant. I climbed the road bathed in the western sun, and back at my inn I slaked my thirst with a cup of tea, the flavor of which reminded me of the sweet taste of dew. As dusk came the mountains to the west became clear in the setting sun, their outlines layered starkly against the sky until eventually they too fell into dark shadow. For the first time since I came here, dinner time was accompanied by a slight darkness, but in the past week the length of the days has increased, and the verdancy of the fields shone brilliantly in the evening sun.

As usual, I engaged in conversation after dinner. We were seven here at the inn until last night, but today we are a lonely three who nonetheless were able to carry on a good conversation. This evening our discussion was led mostly by Miss Stoddart, who spoke of St. Clare. However, because the Church is loath to show written records about St. Clare to outsiders, there is much that we do not know. All we do know is that she survived her teacher Francis by about twenty years. In that time she managed the nunnery at Damiano and rebuffed various interventions in her guidance of her disciples, thus proving herself to be a solid woman who could stand up to a man. She was a woman like Dante's "A perfect life and high in deed in heaven" (*Perfetta vita e alto merto inciela*),[89] and it is a pity that we cannot know more detail of her life.

May 1
Olive Groves; Rare Book Rooms; The Shining Fresco; The Setting Sun's Light

THE MONTH of May has come again. The church bells ringing in the early morning light let me know that the May 1st holiday had arrived.[90] It was too early for me, and so I went back to sleep; when I awoke again the sun was already coming through my window. I arose and went directly to the church. The sky was a beautiful color today again, and the stones of the main basilica in the sun against the deep blue were a delightful, crisp sight, of which I would never tire. Inside the basilica it was still dark. The sounds of someone saying mass in one of the side chapels were just audible. I stood in front of the paintings of St. Martin in the Cappella di San Martino,[91] then returned to the inn to have my morning tea.

At ten o'clock, thinking that the festivities of the day must have started, I went to the church to see, but there was no activity and so I went outside the city walls again and rambled about in the olive groves as I had yesterday. The sky was a little foggy today and it made me think of the spring mists. The red of the poppies in the wheat fields was remarkably deep, and white peonies covered the edge of the fields. In one day, the appearance of the fields had changed. From the foot of the mountain I headed down to the crossroads of the "Sermon of the Birds," and as usual I lay down in the field briefly before continuing on my way. I spent a long time lying down outside of San Damiano, thinking about Clare, and managed to continue composing the poem I had begun yesterday.

> Yesterday she was a princess in a castle
> Today she is a mendicant nun
> Raising medicinals in the hermitage garden
> Her sewing, merely rough robes of poverty
> From the hermitage window she sees
> The world of mankind, and those who pray
> In her ears comes a voice, "The fields are golden
> Now is the time to harvest!"
> Redolent of virtue the four winds blow
> The sister who spreads the scent of prayer
> Adds her aunt and mother to their numbers[92]
> They are now friends on the road of conduct
>
> In the twilight the evening bells ring to gather the sisters
> Let us thank the Lord for today's blessing

This is the point where the "Hermitage of Damiano" appears [in Clare's life], but the words would not come to me. I was only able in the end to come up with a verse about her last hours.

> Sixty years of blessed life are over today
> Tomorrow she shall see the saints and the Holy Father

As the last verse of St. Clare's life this is rather wretched, so I will have to give it more thought. I went from Damiano up the hill along the usual road bathed in sunlight, and returned to my inn. I was told, upon asking, that there had been a service already this morning in which the participants formed lines and surrounded the church.

In the afternoon I sat in the reading room soaking up the sun, reading, and thinking. In the midst of my reverie, I looked out the window toward Santa Maria degli Angeli and I was able to compose another part of my biography of Clare.

> At the master's abode
> The madder red of the evening sun on the church
> In the Lord's light Clare
> Sheds jewel-like tears of reverence
> Happily the master permits
> And the Lord in the evening
> In respect and obeisance
> A scrap of bread soaked in tears
> His illness abates not, the hymns continue
> The master's voice consecrated by God
> Praying before the Father
> Take this body in exchange for his!
>
> Until we meet again in the heavens
> She embraced at their parting, for her lord was lost

I went once more to San Francesco, and walked along the path through the cemetery then to Francis's study, where I found Father Robinson sitting alone, studying in the big room. Among the books and maps that he was looking at were some that the priest had received to take home with him to other libraries. These items which had originally been the property of the monastery of San Francesco were now protected by the town of Assisi, and were managed by an old scholar named Alessandri. The old man had an assistant who very kindly showed me around. In four or five rooms were bookshelves filled with old books that had white leather bindings. Here were collected the writings of the monks of San Francesco for more than the past six hundred years. This library truly spoke of all the wisdom of the Franciscan order. Of the rare books I was permitted to look at were the large Bible that Francis himself used, a splendid copy-book with its letters written carefully on sheepskin, a pardon sent to San Francesco from the Vatican, and other sorts of records. These too were written on sheepskin, and most of them were quite old. Francis's poems and letters were gathered together in one splendid, red and gold volume and were well preserved, the characters written five hundred years previously no different from those written yesterday. Only the place in the book which held the *Cantica del sole* was dirtied, because so many people had made a point to look at it. Also of interest was a fifteenth-century copy book of the *Fioretti*, a wood-block print collection of ancient texts collected by the Bollandists.[93] A separate room where musical scores were stored was full of musical manuscripts written by monks over the ages, including the musical score that was used in the main church. They had such poems as one by Petrarch,[94] and they also had a few musical instruments. I could tell that the residents of the monastery held music to be of great importance by the fact that they had filled two rooms with the scores.

At six o'clock the church bells rang. The evening services associated with today's holiday were beginning, so I went into the church.[95] On the altar was a veritable forest of candles, shining like stars in the clouds beneath the vaulted ceiling; the paintings on the ceiling of the vault shone in the candlelight. Mr. Goad came out of one of the side chapels near the altar, and the two of us stood in silent awe, looking at the ceiling. The recitation of the service began, and singing accompanied the organ; prayers, song, and voices resounded off the ceiling, and the scent of incense filled the hall. The paintings on the ceiling cast a golden light through the music and the incense smoke. Francis, surrounded by angels, the old soldier protecting Chastity, and Christ, extending his hand of honorable poverty to Francis – they all seemed divine, and I admired all the saints in the heavens. When the service was finished the monks stood, raised a relic (much like a relic in Buddhism) in the air and gave a benediction (providing the blessing of God) to the parishioners. The only sound came from the organ, the echoing sound of which was like the cooing of doves reflecting off the ceiling. Being church music, this benediction has a special rhythm, like what Wagner put in *Parsifal*,[96] but in any event it gave one the feeling of having one's spirit float up into the heavens. It was natural for the monks, who were accustomed to this music, to hear it coming from above as if it were the music of the saints at one's dying moment. Especially here, in this eerie, divine space below the ceiling that arches over Francis's sarcophagus, listening to the music I felt as if I were in a different realm from the world of man.

With the benediction the service ended and the monks departed, as did the parishioners. Mr. Goad and I were left alone gazing at the frescoes, and as we did so the sacristan put out the candles one by one. The images of Francis in golden light, and the white-robed angels gradually became dimly visible. The frescoes on the side walls also faded into the darkness, until all that could be seen was the golden halo above the saint. In the slight remaining candlelight the appearance of the divine paintings looked shadowy, and then the last light was extinguished. The ceiling and walls were in total darkness, a trail of candle smoke wafting by them.

There was still some evening light when I left the church, and the sky sparkled with it. Mr. Goad and I went up to the roof of the inn. It was at the very moment that the last of the sunlight was disappearing behind the western hills. In its remnants the clouds formed golden threads, odd remainders of light. Then in the golden light a reddish color gradually grew until the sky in all directions contained clouds, each responding in kind, in all the colors: maroon, purple, and yellow, the faint light being cast all about. As the light slowly faded, the color of the clouds drew darker and the distant mountains turned various shades of dark green in the setting sun. The nearby fields also took on a greenish gray color, and the river bed and banks had a strange gray hue. Mr. Goad said that this color was purple, but I thought that it was rather more like a kind of blue light amidst gray. The light of the sky, the color of the clouds, the twilight over the fields – this type of splendid dusk is rare even in Italy. The two of us let out an occasional sigh and stood on the roof for a long time, gazing at the scene, at a loss for words and struck with admiration. Looking back over our shoulders we saw the top of Monte Subasio still slightly visible in the light, the chilly wind coming down from it. The distant mountains appeared as faint shadows, and light that seeped out of the house windows sparkled in the fields below.

Upon leaving the roof and descending to the dining hall I found the other guests in the midst of their meal. Beginning with the midday meal today, I have had an old Russian woman seated next to me on one side, and on the other side has been a woman from Denmark. Mr. Goad was kind to these ladies, too, and showed them around Assisi. In this fashion we have found ourselves a merry party around the table, with everyone talking and enjoying their meal.

May 2
Image of the Saint; Plucked Flowers; a Tea Party; an Old Country Church

I HAD intended to leave Assisi today and head for Rome, but Miss Stoddart has invited some guests for tea this afternoon, and she insisted that I stay and join them. Other friends, also, have requested my presence, so I decided to stay yet one more day in Assisi. The weather was, as usual, clear; today there was a little morning mist, and the snow on Monte Amiato looked like it was floating on top of it. Religious pilgrims have been thronging the church since morning. I went to the church after they were all done, and there was still some candlelight left to accompany the organ playing for services in the side chapels. My gaze moved from the ceiling frescoes reflected in the candlelight to the portraits of the saints in the side chapels. Among those (many of which are attributed to Lorenzetti) I found a portrait of St. Clare and another image of Clare (by Martini) that showed not only her kindness, but also her gentle fortitude, which was depicted with particular reverence.[97]

I went out the Giacomo gate and walked along the cemetery road, and then I lay down on the green grass. I thought then about Clare's life and compared those thoughts to the images I had just seen in the church, whereupon I tried to compose the last stanza of my poem. The saints that Clare saw welcoming her to the heavens were a group of radiant heavenly beings, but I was unable to clearly express that.[98]

> Surviving her master by twenty years
> Visiting the mementos yesterday and today
> The days pass by in the hermitage
> The end of an era draws near
> The clouds hindering her from salvation gone[99]
> She walked along the pure path
> Saving others and herself
> Through the blessings of God and the master's teaching
>
> At this moment she goes to her heavenly Father
> Follow behind me! My younger sisters of the doctrine
>
> Light shines in all directions

Look up at the Heavens in hope
The myriad joys offered man
For which we should thank the Lord

The bright clouds falling from the heavens that greet our spirits
Are the blessed saints, let us go to them!

On my way home I went to the photograph shop and looked for a picture of
the image of Clare, but to no avail. I went back to my inn on the sunny road and
ate lunch.

In the afternoon I arranged the all the flowers that I had picked so far. Their
colors were bright, and even though some of them had withered leaves they were
happy mementos of my journey. Even though I was not taking home a splendid
souvenir, I was satisfied with these flowers. Remembrances of one's hometown
need not be utilitarian or precious items.

They are not gems
The plucked flowers
That I take home
But they speak
Of the fields that I passed

At Miss Stoddart's tea I met Mrs. Sabatier for the first time. There were about
ten guests from Assisi and Britain, and we all went out on the big balustrade of
the inn to look out and praise the view of the fields. We spoke of many things
as we drank our tea. The sun was warm, and as the breeze blew we could hear
the church bells ringing. I did not feel at all out of place as I conversed with the
other guests.

After the tea I went for a walk with three or four others along the same road I
had been on before, through the fields outside the town. The familiar road was
bathed in the evening sun, enveloping the grass and the trees in a golden color.
The red clover was especially bright in the sun, and along with the poppies they
made the plain appear as if it were on fire. We went to a farm house, which was
actually a chapel that dated from the twelfth century that had old Romanesque
pillars and simple carvings. But now the church from eight hundred years earlier had become a peasant's house, and the image of the Holy Virgin was placed
right in the center. At the next house, we found that part of a seven or eight-

hundred year old steeple was being used in a storehouse. I had passed by these houses before once or twice, but I had never noticed this before. When I was shown around, I found that the fields in the vicinity also had many remnants of the past. Ancient countries have many points of interest to them that one does not notice initially. After taking a look around there we went back to the road and climbed up the hill. The evening was gradually falling, and the green grass and the gray stones all appeared red in the setting sun. The last of the sunlight coming through the leaves of the trees in the olive grove disappeared. Lingering at the base of the city wall, I saw that the sky was steeped in a dark red and a sliver of the new moon was already shining in the sky.

After sunset we gathered again to talk. This evening the talk turned to ghost stories, and there were some additional ladies who joined us. The ghost stories filled my being. This was my last night in Assisi. I bid farewell to everyone, and from my window I looked at the lantern light coming from the lower church of San Francesco. To this too I bid farewell, and returned to my room.

CHAPTER SIX

THE ETERNAL CITY;
THE POPE'S THRONE

VIEW OF THE FORUM, ROME, ITALY

May 3
Lodging in Rome; St. Peter's

I LEFT Assisi and came to Rome. It gave me an unpleasant feeling to leave an old-fashioned quiet town in the mountains and come to a raucous and chaotic city.

The weather was clear as usual. I gave Assisi, up on its hill, a parting gaze, and this brought to mind the feeling that Francis must have had when he bid farewell to his home town before he died. The train left Assisi a little before ten o'clock. The fields were covered with flowers, a brocade of red clover and peonies that I had not seen much of these past ten days. "No matter where one goes in Italy there are fields of flowers."[1] Within that landscape Assisi grew distant, so that only the boulders on the mountain were visible. The hermitage at Carceri was hidden in the hills, and only the stark Monte Subasio remained visible.

The fields and mountains that I will remember forever
Become so precious as they grow distant

The cities of Spello and Spoleto are both in the mountains. The road went up the hills, through many tunnels, and came out by the Tiber River. Here was the majestic walled city of Orute, which, like Assisi, was situated on top of a hill. The surrounding fields had the usual flowers.

At the base of the mountain fort a brocade
Flowers along the fields

The land flattened out gradually onto the Tiber River plain, where cows and horses gamboled in the fields. I thought that I would be able to see the steeple of St. Peter's before we were close to Rome, but I took a short nap and when I awoke the train had already entered the city walls and was close to the station.

I got off the train at about two-thirty. I went by horse cart to the inn I had chosen. It was a fair-weather Sunday so there were many people out for a walk, many of whom were clothed in whites making it feel like full summer. I passed by various churches, rivulets, and towns that were fairly familiar, but when I went to the inns in front of the Pantheon they were all full and had not a room to rent. All the other inns were likewise full. After inquiring at five or six and finding them all the same, I decided that there was no way for me to stay in the city center so I went to the bluff in the northern quarter, but the inns there too were full. The manager of the Britannia Hotel told me that if I dined there three times it would put me in good offices for a room, and if one opened up then I would be invited to stay. There was nothing else for me to do, so I decided on this and was guided to another house. It seemed to be the house of a young couple who worked as record-keepers, and they rented me a room. The house was dirty, but the people did not seem to be of a bad sort and they quickly brought out soap and water, saying they would clean the room. However, two cockroaches leaped out of their cleaning water which made me a bit dumbstruck, and so, recognizing that the room was solely for sleeping at night, I unpacked my luggage and went out sight-seeing.

I had no inn, and my rented room was dirty. I felt that circumstances for me so far were straitened, but I did not take umbrage at it and thought that at least I would be able to sleep *somewhere*; then I was completely at peace with it all. This was all due to the influence of Francis, who, I felt, had made my spirit entirely more generous.

I left the house and headed down the stone staircase knows as the Scala [di] Spagna.[2] I waited for a tram that would take me to St. Peter's, but they were all full. As I stood there waiting by a stream, I looked around and noticed some tourists with *Baedeker's* in their hands and the mark of pilgrims on their chests – they were being guided by a boy. There were also some Dominican monks dressed in black and white habits. I found the traffic of people rather interesting. But, because every tram was full, in the end I decided to walk. Presently I came to the Tiber River bank and found the courthouse looming before me among the other buildings. Compared to six years ago, the amount of this new architecture has really increased. Then I saw, in front of the famous Castel S. Angelo, which is Hadrian's tomb, the large round tower of St. Peter's. I had a beer in the café out front, then went to see the church. I had been disappointed in the façade of this church before, and this time, having just seen the ancient interior of the church in Assisi I found it absolutely uninteresting. It was a design for small architecture that was big for the sake of being big, and I did not get the feeling of it really being big. The only way that I knew how large it was was that the people walking past it looked like ants in comparison. The inside of the church was the same, boasting of being bigger than any other church in the world, filling one's eyes, and showing how other churches measured up to itself.[3] It is so big that even the biggest churches would not be two-thirds the size of St. Peter's. And even though there are plenty of decorations in marble and gold gilding, it doesn't have a glorious feel but rather is full of a vulgar air. The country bumpkin pilgrims may be surprised by it, but anyone with eyes can see that it is awful.

The front façade of the church has a pointless palace façade over the original design of Bramante that obscures the prominent large round steeple.[4] The colonnades in front of the church have stone statuary on top of them that look like play dolls.[5] It is best simply to view the round steeple of this church from a distance. Although the basilica of San Francesco [in Assisi] is good enough to enter, this church is the opposite.

I ate dinner at the inn. Until yesterday evening I had had interesting conversations over my dinner, but now I was by myself and once again I felt as if I had embarked on a trip to a foreign land. But our lives themselves are journeys – Francis and his kind lived lives of itinerant priests with no home in any realm. When I think of him and other similar respected Buddhist monks, this sort of problem [that I face] is really nothing at all.

I returned to the house where I had rented a room, where the missus was gazing out the window in a rather proper form; carrying a candle for me, she came down and opened the door. For the first time in quite a while I was with a kind-hearted person. It is like they all say, there is kindness everywhere in the world.

May 4
The Park; a Message from Home; the Church of Baths

I SLEPT in, then went to the inn for breakfast, after which, on my way toward the embassy, I went to Pincio Park. From atop a small hill in the park I could see St. Peter's, the Vatican, and the various steeples of churches in the city center.[6] A large plain spread out before it toward the sea, and mist gathered above it. The sunshine in the clear sky shone brightly, and I was grateful for the coolness in the shade of the trees. The sun shone so strongly on the world, but the Pope was shut up in the Vatican on the hill, never setting foot outside of this little walled fortress. It really is incredible that he is heir to Christ, who walked across the hot fields of Judea to save mankind. That the Pope has come to strictly protect this walled city is the product of a very narrow world-view, one that came from the fact that in the Middle Ages Rome was, more than a political entity, a territory of the Vatican. After the unification of Italy the royal family made Rome a municipality, and chased the Pope from the palace on the Quirinal Hill to the Vatican. Consequently, all territory outside the Vatican was occupied by the Pope's enemies, and he was not allowed to set foot in his enemies' territory. It really is incredible that, despite the fact that the territory of the heir of Christ should not be some tiny territory in Rome but rather the territory of spirits throughout the wide world, this stubbornness borne from a narrow point of view persists. Fogazzaro, in his novel, recommended that the Pope should be kind and be in contact with the people, but the current government did not accept this and banned his book.[7] When I saw that the sun shone on St. Peter's and the Vatican in the same way as it shone on all other places, this thought became all the more salient.

> Although he claims he will save the world, shut up in the Vatican
> He cannot take one step outside

The saying that the Pope is the "prisoner of the Vatican" was not some severe criticism but rather the words of the previous Pope, Pius IX. In recent times many pilgrims from various countries have gathered here and every day the Pope holds audience for them, but although he can hold audience with them, at the same time he himself cannot leave. One cannot but feel pity when one looks at the Vatican.

I left the park and headed down to the church called Santa Maria del Popolo, where I looked at three or four paintings by Pinturicchio.[8] His work shows signs of the early Renaissance, and he seems a bit held-back; his colors are not pure like Angelico's or Giotto's, and his expression is not strong like Perugino's. Looking at the work of a great painter like Pinturicchio with the same eyes that viewed the work of Angelico, I am dissatisfied – nay, I am too satisfied, I have seen too many paintings.

When I got to the address of the embassy, I found that it had moved, so I went by horse cart to the new location where I waited briefly to be seen in. The office was in a fine old palace that was finely appointed with many paintings from the seventeenth century. I met with Secretary Kameyama, received several pieces of mail, and took a look at a Japanese newspaper.

They had papers up to April 9, so I could not find the results of the Boat Race.[9]

I read of various news items, but was truly pained to hear of young Prince Arisugawa's passing.[10] There is no need for me to write of each of the other items.

I went out in the afternoon about four o'clock, and first I went to Santa Maria degli Angeli, which is a church that was converted from an old Roman bath.[11] The large church building was one room in the center of the ancient bath; the other parts of the bath are being used for a hospital and a museum. All these together still do not constitute the entire bath house – there is still part of the remaining walls. It is almost impossible to imagine how big the Romans made their bath houses. If one includes all the exterior walls, the total area is 110,000 *tsubo*.[12] Therefore, a large part of the bath has become the square in front of the station. There are many frescoes in the church, but none of them are remarkable – they are simply surprisingly large. There are many ancient temples dedicated to the gods that have been converted into churches, but a bath being converted into a church is unusual.

I left the church and went to the station to pick up my luggage but after being made to wait for a while, I was told that the customs office was closed today and I should come back tomorrow. I put in a request with an agent and on my way home I walked through a lively part of the city center. At a café that had tables out on the sidewalk I drank a glass of lemonade and watched the activity of the city. There was a shoe shine in front and he was napping on the job. A customer walked up to get his shoes shined and stuck his foot out, causing the shoe shine man to wake in surprise. It was so funny that I tried my hand at composing a rhyme about "being awoke by a shoe's poke."

From April through early May the tourists flock to Rome, and there had been horse races scheduled these past four or five days.[13] Rome was full of pilgrims who had come to see the churches, officials from every country who had come to the horse races, and tourists from the countryside, all of whom enjoyed clement weather every day. People got around on foot, by horse cart, bicycle, or whatever. They would get covered with the dusk kicked up in the sunshine of the clear days, and it reminded me of the cherry-blossom-viewing season in Tokyo. The men wore loud outfits, but the women wore more somber ones, especially those of a light red and the purple that had been prevalent in Paris that winter, in contrast to the blue that Italian peasants normally wore. Many Italian women have black hair, but there are also pure redheads and when one mixes their hair color with the color of their clothes the street scene becomes an exhibition of pastel colors.

In the evening I thought that I would like to take in the view of the moon, but the houses were all so tall that I could not get a glimpse of it. Behind the inn the tall stone fence of the palace enclosed the area, leaving it gloomy. The mountains of Assisi became all the more endearing.

May 5
Ruins of the Forum; Gianicolo Hill

CLEAR SKIES and a strong wind. After sending various letters to people to whom I had received a letter of introduction, I decided to spend the rest of the morning at the ruins of the Forum, so I caught a horse cart in that direction. The sunshine was bright on the stone pillars and cobblestones of the ruins, up between which bloomed various flowers – the irises stood out as especially beautiful. Today is the 5th of May, the [Japanese] Boys' Festival. Seven years ago on this day I passed this festival pleasantly on the Indian Ocean. When I recalled Otowa's play at that time, and thought about how he had since been lost, it gave me an odd feeling.[14] I wondered how my two sons were passing this holiday, and I also recalled the decorative soldier dolls from my own childhood. Passing the Japanese Boys' Festival at the two-thousand-year-old Roman ruins was an odd turn of events.

> A glimpse of the sky over my home town
> The irises bloom behind the palace

I went down the stairs to the ruins of the Foro Romano and stood between the stone columns. This was the place where, in the glory days of Rome, the emperor had the seat of his government. The pillars of the palaces of the gods were lined up, their tiles vying against one another, and amongst it all were meetings and forums of all sorts. This, over the course of two thousand years, up until the fifteen or sixteen hundreds, eventually deteriorated, was burnt, and the remaining pillars and stone stairs were buried for eternity. These ruins are what has been dug out. Emperor Severus's arch of triumph is still standing, and next to it the temple of the god of war, Saturn, remains as six or seven pillars. Otherwise, there are just pillars, walls, and a random stone here and there, and splendid statuary, broken into pieces, is common.

The skies were clear, but the wind kicked up the dust in this weather, and the stones took on the color of the dust to make it a solidly dead landscape. Nonetheless, here and there flowers the color of violets blossomed on the stone walls and on the pillars. There were also some charming light purple flowers on an ivy, the name of which I do not know, that bloomed in between the rocks, as well as many other kinds of plants that blossomed in the cracks between the stones. This was the place where, in Rome's heyday, the senators, politicians, and priests would gather and the soldiers would come decked out in different types of armor and line up between the great halls. The spring of the Roman Empire may never come again, but the small flowering grasses bloom every spring, as they have since time immemorial.

> It has lost its charm—
> Thousands of flowers bloom
> as if to ridicule
> the acts of man
> amongst the palace ruins

There were various chapels in the small valley area, but there is no need to recount each one's history. Now there are only piles of rubble and half fallen walls left. Among them, there are the remains of a round wall, the inside of which is shaped like a shallow crypt. This is where the fire of the gods was kept and guarded carefully; there were also many people who were slaughtered here. It is a sacred yet frightening memorial. In front of it is the place where the virgins protected the fire of Vesta and offered up the festival flames. Girls ten years old or younger were taken in here as female priests, and they would live here for thirty years. There is water yet in the garden pond of this house, and next to it there are many red roses blooming. The walls of the Vestal virgins' rooms remain, but of their beds nothing is left but the underlying stones. Among the virgins, those with particular merit had marble statues carved of them, but only one of those statues still has its head intact. The others are missing hands and heads, and some are broken off half-way down the torso. Some of those that were buried in the ground have been stood up now. On the edge of the pond I thought of the past as I gazed at the statues:

> Thousands of virgins guard the fires
> The mementos of where the gods were served
> Their heads of stone have broken
> Next to them the roses bloom

In addition to the Temple of Vesta, the stone ceilings of the emperor Constantine's palace,[15] the Triumphal Arch of Titus commemorating his defeat of Jerusalem, and other such sites all spoke of the heyday of Rome. In front of the triumphal arch there is some excavation going on now, and more than ten *shaku* down there is nothing but stone and concrete before one reaches an earthen floor. I am not sure what ruins each is, but they are all large work sites. Toward the east from the arch there are the stone steps of a viewing box of the ancient horse-racing site called the Colosseum, and Constantine's triumphal arch is also clearly visible. In the opposite direction, apart from the many ruins that I had just passed, was the ancient hill of the Capitol, where I could see the tower of the Senate. Each and every one brought back memories of the olden days.

I climbed the hill of the Temple of Vesta. This area was where the goldsmiths' houses were, but now there was nothing left but their walls, inside which the flowers bloomed in profusion, and a stream babbled.

> Those who would come to draw water have gone
> But the stream continues to flow through countless ages

The temple walls at the foot of the hill were tall, and some passageways remained. I passed through these, and below a cold, stone passageway I came upon a church, the Santa Maria Antica, that had been built where once a library had stood. The church had been excavated to reveal frescoes on the walls. The frescoes were damaged, but one could clearly see that they were from the fourth or fifth century and done in a Byzantine style. The figures of Christ and the saints all had large, startled eyes. The style of painting, when compared to that of Cimabue, had many similarities. For six or seven hundred years the paintings of Christianity did not change much, but with Cimabue's disciple, Giotto, the changes were so great as to be shocking. Giotto's fluid style breathed new life into the stiff style of those early paintings, and the way in which the figures looked liked dolls.

I walked on through the ruins, picking flowers here and there as I went. I left the Forum and went straight toward the Capitoline Hill. Once, when the Romans were confined to the Palatine Hill in the distance, this hill was home to the Sabines, with whom the Romans were at war.[16] Once these two tribes merged and exerted the power of Rome, the major gods of the Roman tradition were venerated on this hill. When the temple was built, a severed head was excavated from the earth, and this was taken to be an omen that Rome was superior in the world. Therefore, the hill was named Capitoline, or "head" hill. Before the Forum became the center of Rome during the imperial era, this "Head Hill" was the center of Rome, and all the government celebrations in the age of the Republic were held here. Today there is a museum and the original Senate here, and between the two is a plaza (although it is very small for a plaza) where the sun shines on the cobblestones and the wind kicks up the dust to make it all very unpleasantly hot. Behind the museum is a church called Santa Maria in Aracœli. Upon entering the church I was somehow comforted by the cool air in the chapel. From behind the altar I could hear the familiar voices of Franciscans reciting the office. The contrast between outside and indoors made me feel clearly the change between ancient Rome and the Christian world. It is said that Gibbon, the historian who wrote of the fall of the Roman Empire, went from the Forum ruins to this church, and was put in mind of the change from the olden days to today, and it was this that caused him to think of writing his great history.[17] I am sure that anyone would have reacted in the same way. Especially because my ears had heard sermons every day in San Francesco in Assisi and then heard them again in this church after being at the Roman ruins, I was naturally drawn deeper into thought, giving me the feeling that I had entered another realm.

This building was originally dedicated to the god of the capitol, and the temple (dedicated to his wife, Juno) was made as it was into a church and so it is called "Altar of Heaven [Aracœli]."[18] The cobblestones and the stone stairs outside the building hold the history of that age, and mark the place where many people were killed. The pillars and paving stones inside the building too are mementos of the past. Santa Maria became Franciscan, and in a small chapel inside the church there is a painting of Francis. Next to the monks in woolen robes with rope belts who amble about are housewives knelt in prayer. In one of the little chapels is a painting by Pinturicchio[19] that could be the work of his lifetime. There is also a landscape done in the style of Angelico, one that shows the beginnings of the spirit of the Renaissance. In the chapel opposite this there is a doll of Christ at his birth; I was told that children gather here in the week after Christmas, but it was closed now.[20]

On the ancient marble floor, I stood between the pillars made of stone brought from Egypt, but I felt a chill and so I went outside through the main entrance. The stone steps, numbering over one hundred, shone brightly in the sunshine and below the stairs the traffic of horses and carts was so fierce that I felt as if I had come back to the real world. I stood in the middle of the stairway and turned back to look at what was once the temple of Juno, with its flat tile façade, free of decoration. It stood out shining in the sunshine, and to its left they were in the midst of constructing a monument dedicated to an earlier king of Italy. Many of the white stone pillars of the monument had been stood up between scaffolding. The place where the current monument is being erected had been a monastery connected to Santa Maria in Aracœli, and had been where the head of that order had lived. Long ago the monastery had a steeple and a spring, and many mendicant monks had lived there, but the current monarchy confiscated it and decided to erect the monument to the previous king.[21] Once, during a time of economic difficulties, the building was postponed, but now one can see that there are plentiful funds and three or four years ago the building began in earnest. The large stone pillared colonnades glare out at the ancient city center of Rome, and the remains of the medieval Franciscan monastery. The locale has gone from a Roman imperial temple, to a Christian monastery, then to a monument to what could be called the enemy of the church, the monarchy. Over two thousand years of history are on display here.

The sunlight was hot and the wind strong so I spent the afternoon resting at the inn, then before the sun set I went for a walk on Gianicolo hill. This hill was where, originally, the Roman god Janus (the guardian god of soldiers) was revered. The hill is on the far side of the Tiber River, and it curves around the western end of the city of Rome. From the top of the hill one can see all of the "Seven Hills of Rome" at a glance.[22] When I had come here before I went directly to St. Peter's and climbed this hill. Today I had come up from the opposite direction, and had climbed the hill first. On the edge of the hill is a church called S. Pietro in Montorio. Standing in front of the church one sees first the seven hills [to the east], and then the broad plains of the Campagna skirted by the sea in the distance [to the west], plus the snow-capped Appenine mountains [in the opposite direction].[23]

The Palatine Hill is where Rome originated. From between the rows of dark green cypress trees the gray color of the ancient palace ruins seem like something from the lonely world of the dead. The rows of construction of the monument on the Capitoline Hill, in contrast, speak of the glory and flourishing of the current monarchy in the way that they soar upwards. To the west, the Palace on the Quirinal Hill[24] is done in the style of a military house, with its thick groves of trees in the garden. The building flaunts the power and influence of the monarchy, glaring harshly in all directions.[25] Between these hills and the Tiber there are thousands of rooftops. And, among them, there are church steeples and the houses of the aristocracy soaring high, speaking of the prosperity of Rome in the Middle Ages. Away from the city toward the west is the Pincio Hill,[26] which, with the pine and cypress trees of the Borghese forest, looks like a painting. Even further beyond that lie more hills and plains which extend into the misty mountains. Turning left, I saw the great dome of St. Peter's rising from among the trees, its cross atop pointing loftily toward the heavens, indicating the glory of the church in a stand-off with its enemy, the Quirinal Palace. These views hold their own interest as single landscapes, but in addition to that the hills, buildings, and trees each speak of their own histories, providing a souvenir of more than two thousand years, during which the fate of the world was controlled in the area encompassed by this view.

While I was gazing around at the sights a number of peddlers came selling their wares. When I ignored them and tossed their wares aside, there was one young man among them who conferred with the others about something, then approached me and said something incomprehensible. When I asked him what he was saying, it turned out that he was saying "*rao tse, rao tse.*" That is to say, the result of the young man's consult with the other peddlers was the resolution that I was Chinese, and he had decided to try to say something to me in Chinese. Somehow he had come to know the name of Laozi, and I discerned that that was what he was saying. It is doubtful that the youth knew anything about Laozi, and it was quite strange to hear Laozi's name coming from the mouth of an Italian youth while I was gazing at Rome's Seven Hills. In Germany, there were often people who would call out Li Hongzhang's[27] name, "*li han chan, li han chan,*" and throw rocks at me, but here they called me "Laozi."

I left the hilltop and its view and went into S. Pietro in Montorio. This church was built by the King of Spain, so there is still a school here for Spanish monks.[28] There are Franciscan monks in the church, and there is a portrait of Francis in a small side chapel, but it is nothing remarkable. Legend has it that it was there that St. Peter was crucified, and there is a place marking the spot in the monastery. Another legend holds that Noah landed his ark here after the Flood, and that St. Peter was killed on the same rock where Noah had tied his boat. No matter where one goes there are old stories connected with a place, but in Rome these stories are especially numerous. When in Rome, one finds that the people are always thinking of past history, of mementos of the past that mark the locales here and there of important events. Many folk tales are born from this.

I headed north from the hilltop and went walking in a grove of trees. Flowers bloomed in the green grass of the park, there were red flowers alongside the cypress trees, and there were purple flowers blooming there, too, that resembled wisteria, reflecting the purplish-red of the setting sun. Standing by a memorial to Garibaldi,[29] I looked out toward the Seven Hills of Rome, and across the fields of the Campagna where there were forests of pine trees and beautiful flower gardens by the country houses. On Vatican Hill there is an astronomical observatory (associated with the Vatican), and there is another observatory on Monte Mario.[30] Even in their observatories, the Pope and the government compete.

At the point where one begins to descend from the top of the hill is the Church of Onoforio, the last place that Petrarch ever was.[31] I was unable to enter and so headed down the hill, arriving just below the city wall. The stone of Porta S. Spirito was black and dirty, and showed only a tiny bit of the past, but the houses of the poor folk nearby were bathed in sunlight, and the green of the willow trees, which I could see through the gate, was beautiful.

> The green willow fronds
> Next to the sooty
> Stone gate
> Are green threads
> To the past

Passing by the houses of the poor, I saw children playing in the cobblestone streets, covered with dirt. There was an orange vendor who had stopped his cart and was selling his wares. The color of the oranges, contrasted with the dirty children and the dirty houses, was beautiful – the oranges looked like out-of-season mangoes that had fallen from heaven. The children ate every bit of the oranges, right down to the peel.

I came to the front of St. Peter's, where I caught a tram and went back to my rented room. The road went through the Porta del Popolo – it seemed that today was the fifth and last day of the horse races, and there was a steady stream of people coming through the gate.

When I returned to the inn I was surprised to find that Mr. Shinmura[32] had arrived from Germany and had left his calling card. After my meal I went to call on him at his inn and for the first time in quite a while had a long conversation in Japanese. On my way home, I found that the afternoon heat had dissipated and there was a cool evening breeze which cleared the sky of clouds and left the stars twinkling.

May 6
Farnesina's Painting; Palazzo del Laterano; a Privy Councilor; a Musician

AFTER BREAKFAST I went with Shinmura to the Villa Farnesina on the other side of the river. This villa was built in the beginning of the sixteenth century, at the height of Renaissance art, by a wealthy Roman family,[33] and has a fresco by Raphael in it. It is located on the banks of the Tiber River, at the foot of Giancolo Hill and has a garden full of trees, in the center of which stands the house, the extreme of all luxury under the sun. The building is old and the garden is almost entirely in ruins. In addition to the two or three old trees, there is a dead-land-scape lawn, surrounded by a brick fence, all the result of renovations being done in the city.[34] In the large entryway Raphael and his disciples painted the old story of Amore and Psyche on the ceiling.[35] The human figures and their coun-tenances, and the composure of the painting are really very well done, extraor-dinarily beautiful and brilliant. The painting as a whole is, however, nothing more than a display of naked young men and women, displaying the spirit of the Renaissance at that time. It really is nothing more than a palace decoration made by throwing together beautiful naked bodies from Greek myths. As a decoration it is splendid, but the painting is too realistic and as decorative art it fails to stimulate the imagination. That this trend in art progressed into the degradation [of today's] crude photographs shows the power of Nature. The Baroque and Rococo decorative paintings of the seventeenth and eighteenth centuries ended up being much like color photographs; the beginnings of that can all be seen here.

In the next room, in addition to the ceiling, on the four walls there are simi-lar paintings, mixing landscapes with Greek myths. Surrounded by those walls and ceiling the wealthy men and ladies danced and slept, drank and conversed. Even in such a luxurious lifestyle mankind cannot forget his love of Nature, and consequently he most certainly enjoyed looking at the landscapes painted on the walls. However, these too fell into corruption and as we see in seventeenth century French painting and tapestries, people were no longer satisfied with simple landscapes – these paintings depict young noblemen who rode white horses with gilt saddles into the forests to drink; noble ladies are shown wearing white wigs and wide sleeves, and dancing in the hills. Mankind's spirit began at this point to depart from Nature, and to rejoice in thoughts that were not natu-ral, thus leading to the beginning of corruption. In Japan we love the serenity of mind that comes with a bright moon after a storm, and we love the contrast of red flowers with the dark green of a willow tree. In the case of Zen, even in the early Zen paintings, there is a vitality that is not distanced from nature. But the Kanō school of painting in the Tokugawa period – the school that protected this form – died. The corruption of the arts in the Tokugawa period came about because they did not connect with nature the way that they did in the Muromachi or Momoyama periods.[36] It was the result of the domination of all things under the shackles of a restrained society. The paintings here by Raphael were not really all that corrupt – the goddesses born from the sea and surrounded by sea nymphs were lively and charming. But, the charm is all in the color and form on the outside; on the inside there is no deeply seeded charm. Böcklin[37] painted many similar paintings, but in those there is a kind of weirdness, a charm that is not simply the color and the shape. Raphael was a painter; Böcklin was a poet. No matter how renowned Raphael was, his works do nothing more than show the floating spirit of the Renaissance.

In contrast to Raphael's paintings, the one work by Michelangelo that is also in this room proves very interesting.[38] It is a simple painting of one human head done in dark colors, but the brushwork shows strength, and it overshadows the other paintings. The dark colors seem to be ridiculing the other beautiful colors.

I left the villa and took a horse cart to Laterano. I went past small, dirty blocks, the foot of Capitolo Hill, and the front of the Colosseum, then entered the Laterano Church from the square. The Laterano, for a long time, was the seat of the Pope. After the first Christian emperor, Constantine, consecrated the Roman Bishop here it became the most important church in Rome, and later it was the head church of the Roman Catholic Church, in a position above St. Peter's in the Vatican.[39] The mosaic, done with fine craftsmanship on the ceiling vault, is a restored inlay based on an older work. Christ and many saints are drawn with Byzantine lines, their large eyes looking strange, yet very charming in their simplicity.

The tomb of Pope Leo XIII[40] is located at the entrance of the sacristan's quarters. The marble image retains the brash carving in the style of the eighteenth century, but the dais shows much quiet design in its black stones and in comparison to the pointless decorations on other Pope's graves this one is quite tomb-like. Going round beneath this and through the hallway, I came upon a small inner chapel where there was an old, refined painting. Next I entered the monks' garden cloisters (*chiostro*). These cloisters are Rome's most important *chiostro* architecture. The sunshine shone brightly on the green leaves surrounding the garden, and the designs on the various pillars were cold and quiet. These pillars, which spoke of the ancient monastery, were greatly decorated with fine inlay, some directly, some enveloped [by the design] as if wrapped in vines.[41] Although any monastery anywhere has the air of being separated from the outside world, this one was particularly graceful. Standing within it my spirit was naturally put at ease and I was able to return to myself from the [distractions of the] outside world. The passageways that lead from the entrance of a Zen temple to the library have the same design, which is the natural result of the monastic lifestyle, and this is why we have developed the same kind of architecture in both the East and the West. I went out into the garden and picked some flowers, then went back to the cloisters and the artless carving outside, thinking of the world seven or eight hundred years ago. Presently I returned to the main hall. Going from the monks' cloisters to the gold gilt main hall with its tall columns presented me with the stench of the vulgar world. But the decorations there were not like the sparkling decorations of St. Peter's; they had the special characteristics of basilica architecture – the stone columns, the marble chapels, etc. – and were relatively understated. On one of the columns was a painting said to be by Giotto, but someone had later taken his own brush and added color to it.

Although vestiges of the past are no longer in the architecture and decoration of today, this basilica was the central church in Rome, and hundreds of years ago it was where the church held five great sessions.[42] Also, it was at the entrance to this church that St. Dominic and St. Francis first met and embraced each other, crying tears of deep emotion.[43]

I went out through the north entrance and went around the building. There were fragrant white roses in the garden behind the church, bathed in sunlight, and in the middle of the roses there was a large white marble statue of a laborer. This statue was built with donations from laborers because Pope Leo XIII was their protector, and the statue expresses thanks to him. From the neighboring platform I could look out over the city wall at the Campagna and the Alban hills.[44] Ruins of a wall stood in the green fields, and beyond the fields was the sea. In the sunshine of early summer the bright scene was a happy view.

Next to the garden was a small baptistery, and inside it was a baptismal font that was surrounded by pillars that had been erected in the fifteenth century. It was small, but it was a nicely arranged building.[45] The two chapels connected to this baptistery were for celebrating John the Baptist and John of the Gospels. One of the doors was made of bronze and made a strange noise when it was opened and closed, as if performing a song. It is said that this door was from the baths of emperor Caracalla,[46] but in any event it had an ancient patina to it and was quite interesting. It was said to weigh close to two thousand pounds, and it was due to the weight that it made music when it opened and closed.

In the other direction from the Baptistery is the famous church of Scala Santa. The architecture of the façade is disagreeable, but inside there are two white stone statues of Christ on each side. One Christ has a cross, and one is with Judas; both speak of Christ's hardships, and are rather well done.[47] Between those two white stone statues is a staircase that climbs up into the tall building. These are said to be the steps that Christ climbed when he went to be interrogated at [the palace of] Pilate, and they are venerated as holy objects. One is not permitted to climb these on one's feet; rather, one climbs on one's knees.[48] The faithful kneel and climb these steps, praying as they go, turned toward the lantern light in the darkness that begins half-way up the stairs. When I had come here before it had been at dusk, and then it was so dark that I could only see the small light at the front of the stairs. There was a woman there climbing the stairs in the dark, and she wore black clothing and a black kerchief on her head. All I could hear was a praying voice as the dark figure crawled silently up the staircase in the dark as the light gave me a feeling of lonely grace. But today the sun was brightly shining in and even the staircase was illuminated. The people milled about, destroying my earlier memory of Scala Santa.

It was time for lunch, so I returned to the inn and ate with Shinmura, who later went out on his own sightseeing.

I had promised Signor Luzzatti[49] that I would meet with him in the afternoon, so I set out in his direction before four o'clock. Mr. Luzzatti was once the Finance Minister and been the meritorious retainer who arranged the Italian economy, but now he was a Privy Councilor. The road that led to his house was the Borghese Park Road and today there was a flower competition in the park so there were crowds of people who had come out to see it. There were many noblemen and women who filled horse carts in their bid to view the flowers. Their parasols had flowers on them, the women's hats had flowers on them, the carts had flowers, and most of the spectators wore a flower in their hats or on their lapels. It was as if the god of flowers had come down to earth. But, of course, in this earthly realm there is flying dust and sand, and the sun is hot. Despite this, the spectators were strolling about easily among the flower-decked horse carts. A military police officer in splendid dress not short of full court attire stood in the middle of it all, becoming a decoration all of his own.

I went into Luzzatti's home and was shown to the library. In this simple room there were books scattered about and in the middle of them a fat, red-faced, half-gray old man stood, greeting my arrival. I knew that I was supposed to address this man as "your excellency," but he had a simple manner and was very familiar and so in no time I left off using "your excellency" and we set to talking. Italy, just like Germany, uses these bothersome addresses and formalities, but there are also men like this, who behave like commoners. I asked him about a few things concerning Italy, and we spoke about the relationship between the church and education. Luzzatti stormed, "In Italy the monks are still strong, and Christianity truly lacks a tolerant spirituality." [50] More than answering my questions, he spoke eloquently (if not dramatically) at great length, praising Buddhism, and the fact that in Japan and India we have not had any religious wars. I had already learned of his contention by reading one of his lectures, and when I told him, "I have read your excellency's lecture on this topic and already introduced it to Japan," he became more pleased and spoke even more about the issue. I lost all opportunity to ask him what I wanted to ask him, and in the end too much time passed and I had to take my leave.

On my way home I found the streets filled with crowds of people and I was unable to see the beautiful setting sun in the sky through all the dust and dirt that had been kicked up. I passed through the dust clouds and went back to the inn to wash my face and catch my breath.

In doing so, I found that the musician Maestro Costa had come to call. [51] This man is a musician, but he dislikes popular music; I had heard that he particularly liked Bach's compositions. Although I really should have been the one calling on him, he came to me. Italians are a uniquely relaxed and modest people, and they make conversation with ease – we spoke of many things. He asked me, "What is your view of Western civilization?" to which I answered, "There are many movements – too many movements." Mr. Costa said, "I, too, am dissatisfied with this society. It is not just the society – today in Europe people's thoughts and emotions are too quixotic, and I wish that they would have deeper interests. That is why I wanted to know more about your opinion – I am practically a Buddhist myself, so please do not hesitate to criticize the West!" We proceeded in our conversation from there, speaking of how Western thought was too attached to the individual, and how Westerners want to be praised by God even after they have died and been resurrected. I think that this is the cause of the current movements, competition, and the fighting between the capitalists and the laborers. The current Christian faith – that of the Protestants of course, and the Catholics, too – lacks contemplation and meditation, and the reverent faith that prayed for the avoidance of calamities in the middle ages.[52] Therefore, as the attachment to individualism develops, man fails to order his sympathies with the masses, and to think of others. The individual turns in toward himself and abandons the pursuit of knowledge, and this seems to cause a kind of inequality among people. We spoke of such fathomless issues at length. Mr. Costa said, "I often think these things myself, and at the level of fundamentals I think that Christianity and Buddhism differ in some way, and that is why this difference [between the two] has emerged." I said, "Actually, Buddhism – even Buddhism in Japan – has gradually become impoverished in terms of this self discipline of one's thoughts." The two of us fully exchanged our mutual thoughts on the same difficulties in the East and West. Then the conversation turned to our thoughts of spirituality, music, etc., and we spoke until dusk fell. When I speak with the British, especially ones like Mr. Goad whom I met in Assisi, I inhale information about beauties that are solidly set in British thought. But my conversation today with Mr. Costa was entirely different. He has tendencies that are different from the general Italian of today, he enriches his spirit through the lofty and elegant music of Bach, and he listens to those who are opposed to the current tide of selfishness. I, too, find myself caught up fighting this same whirlpool, and so we saw eye to eye and had an enjoyable conversation. But whereas I was ultimately consoled by Mr. Goad, I was troubled by Mr. Costa. I admire Mr. Goad; I sympathize with Mr. Costa.

May 7
The Vatican; the Villa Borghese; the Via del Corso; Moonlit Night

TODAY I met Cardinal Merry del Val of the Vatican.[53] When I arrived at the Vatican, I passed through throngs of the sightseers at the museum and the pilgrims who had come to have an audience with the Pope. I climbed up the wide gentle stone steps to find the large inner garden of the palace. I passed through a group of soldiers wearing red, yellow, and black uniforms to the second floor, where I asked to be shown in. Another man in a splendid uniform took me through two or three formidable palace rooms to the secretary's room. I was told to wait momentarily, so I sat down in a large chair in the room. The walls in this room of the great palace were all covered with red wallpaper, and chairs upholstered in the same red with gold arms were lined up together. On the transom there was an old painting, and above it the ceiling had been re-papered to have the current Pope's seal written majestically in the center. In the center of the room next to the wall was a black lacquer desk with a gold cross on its center, and on either side of it were gold-colored candle sticks in the shape of angels. In the same room there was a secretary at the secretary's desk; two or three women, who seemed to be American, and an Italian man were waiting. There were no sounds, and no other sign of any other people – the palatial room was quiet, and all I could see were the bright papered walls. After a while, a monk who looked high-ranking came out from the inner room, fastening his white robe. The people kneeled before him and kissed his hand. Thinking back on it now, I realize that his face looked like the Pope's, but I thought that the Pope would absolutely not walk in by himself. The robes beneath his white robes were black, so I thought he was not the Pope. All the high-ranking priests of the Church have similar countenances. After a little while, from some offices somewhere in the front, came a monk who accompanied two or three people and went into the inner rooms. Next came a graying man who seemed to be a noble – he had many medals hanging from his full court dress – with his wife and three children, all of whom went into the inner room. The sight of his daughters' pale faces and pure white clothes, and his wife dressed in black with a red sash, all filing past me into the room, seemed a fitting scene in an Italian palace. The chair consumed me, and I dozed off while I waited a long time. Then, near the secretary, a bell rang. The secretary went into the inner room, came out again, and approached me. He showed me into the next room and told me to wait briefly in a chair there. This room was decorated in the same way, but it was larger, and had a large desk in the middle which was surrounded by twelve or thirteen large chairs. It seemed to be the cardinal's meeting room. I waited there while a bishop and monks stood speaking. I was not really listening, but I could tell they were speaking in German… "up until now the Pope… audiences… increase his authority…" and other such snippets of words came my way. It seemed to me that there was much discord. The bishop came out, and the accompanying monks left with him. After a few minutes the family of nobles also came out and left together. I was led by the monk on duty into the next room. The decoration here was also the same, but the room was smaller than the secretary's room, and on the desk there were perhaps over fifty documents. There was one graceful person there. That person was Cardinal Merry del Val, and he greeted me warmly, speaking of Archbishop O'Connell of Boston[54] and then shifting the topic to Japan. I had heard that Cardinal Merry del Val could speak English, but I was surprised at how good his English really was.[55] He did not have an assistant, but occupied his office all by himself, and by himself he received all manner of people. Truly his French, his German, even his Spanish were equally fluent, and I imagined that it made no difference who came to speak with him. We spoke at length about Japan and then I requested to see the workings of operations of the Church. I bid him farewell and he saw me to the entrance of the room, and he promised again that everything would be at my disposal. Before we had met, I had imagined this man to be various things. Some people, and the newspapers, had said that he was a villain, and that he surrounded the Pope in such a way that the Vatican was his own. Some others said that he was a fool who was just a puppet of the Jesuits. Although I cannot say definitively after just one meeting, my feeling from our twenty-minute interview was that he was not a villain or a fool. I do not know about his resources, but as a person he is a splendid man who appeared very serious. I felt that his reception of me in the studied manner of a diplomat was the natural result of his having much experience as a cardinal, not simply a matter of him making pointless flattery.

I left the Vatican and returned to the inn. Even as I left there, and on the way back to the inn, I thought about my visit to the Vatican this morning, and realized that this was a new experience that I had never had until today. I, who had never seen a royal palace, or, for that matter, had never met a cabinet minister in Japan, had today for the first time seen life in a palace. And I had met the prime minister of the Vatican who, although his power was weak in matters of government, held great sway in the hearts of people all over the world. Our type of middle-class life would be like the wretchedness of the slums to him. In contrast, his life in the palace has wealth and power at his command. Although there is discord among the poor in today's society, there is also discord among the wealthy and powerful. We do not suffer the wretchedness of the poor, and so we must, through the power of education and compassion, rescue the indigent. We have a duty to interpret between the lower classes and the upper classes, and to create harmony. We have no need to fight with the powerful and wealthy. We are in the position of rescuing the people in the upper class by promoting the spirit of a peaceful and harmonious life. Those in the lower classes who live in a family of discord become anarchists and try to topple the palace life, and those in the upper classes do not sympathize with the poor, and so they necessarily tread on them. We, the middle class who stand between the two, have a big job that we must do. This is something that we all know and speak about, but today when I saw it directly at the palace I felt it keenly.

One issue is the relationship between the Pope and the faithful. Those who support Catholicism hope that the Pope will be close to all his followers. The Protestants criticize the Pope, saying that he is enveloped in his own eminence and has lost the meaning of Christ. There is some truth to what they say. If one looks at the Vatican today, one cannot help but think that these hopes and charges are unavoidable given the present position and attitude of the Pope. Today there are thousands of pilgrims who come to Rome and they all want to meet at least once with the Pope. If they were all permitted to do so freely the Pope would not be able to accommodate them. And so it has become necessary to set a time for a public audience, when tens or hundreds of people can meet with him. Most people have their audience with the Pope in this way, and do not have the opportunity to speak individually with him. The Pope is haughty and does not speak to them, and comes to these meetings out of necessity. Of course there is a need for a system to accommodate this organization, and with the system comes the officials. When there is a difference of opinion, a monk may wish to have a direct consultation with the Pope, but the monk is not permitted to speak with him individually. Although the Pope is meant to follow in Christ's footsteps, he cannot follow his every move. When I think about these issues, I understand that the current system in the Vatican arose out of a number of necessities. But, when I look at the grandeur of the Vatican palace and think that Christ would never have lived in such a palace, I am full of severe criticism. That said, the fact that the Pope cannot step foot in the Italian king's territory because he has lost his own territory is nothing short of narrow-minded. I cannot help but be sympathetic with Fogazzaro[56] and others who went to great pains to bring peace between the Pope and the government. The government was reckless, but if the Pope would just have serenity of mind then I think that the people of Italy would be much happier.

In the afternoon I went out about four o'clock, and called on Miss Dove. Her niece and the niece's husband, a Mr. Landrum, were also visiting and we spoke briefly over tea. This Mr. Landrum had met Mr. Yokoi[57] in the United States. We also spoke of hometown churches. I have traveled far in the world and met many people, only to discover that the world may be large but it is still small. I left Miss Dove's house and went to Mr. Goad's mother's inn, but she was out so I did not see her.

I went out of one of the city gates and entered Borghese Park. The many children playing on the green grass in the shade of the pine trees were truly charming. Unlike Paris, they were not playing with tops by themselves, but rather the little black and red-haired children chattered on in peaceful Italian, jumping and skipping. I sat on the grass and watched the children and then got up to walk further. At the edge of a pine grove there was a white stone monument to Goethe.[58] I do not know who made it, but the fierce look in Goethe's eyes made it look like a military statue. Goethe, who is depicted as a thirty-four-year-old man here in Rome, looks almost like a Greek god. But this Goethe has the eyes of a thief. It seems that this monument was sent as a gift from Germany to Rome, but if Germans saw this frightening Goethe today they would surely be surprised.

In the afternoon there were many people who came to walk on the tree-shaded path. There were many of the popular pinks and purples in the ladies' clothing, but the complexions of the pale Italian ladies looked a little blue under pink hats and red parasols. Among the fashionable, gaudy clothes were also the dark red, black, and green kerchiefs of those who came from the countryside; there were also many men wearing red and orange neckties. And, in the crowd, there were some seminary students ambling along in their black uniforms with blue, red, and green accents and wearing black hats. In the spring and early summer this park becomes an exhibition of Roman style.

Toward the west from the pine grove there is a small, old horse racing track, and the stone gallery around it looks like an ancient ruin. There were some young men and women sitting on the lawn, playing some sort of game. There were cypress and pine trees all around the gallery, which formed it into its own little world. Beyond it, the shores of the lake were the same. Wherever I went there were groves and lawns, and splendid looking men and women, both young and old, plus seminary students in their distinctive uniforms, and of course there were also the typical military police in full formal dress. As Wagner said, wherever one goes in Rome one finds a world of color, a feast for the eyes. From the race track to the shores of the lake, to the imitation Egyptian stone gate, to the road lined with trees, I was reminded of each place that I had seen six years earlier. While I felt transported back to the past, at the same time the sadness of the autumn sky then was the exact opposite of the liveliness that I saw today.

I left the park and went back into the city through the Popolo Gate, walking along the Via del Corso. This too provided an exhibit of style. There were lines of people showing themselves off, and there were also people walking about with no other business but to watch the other people, horse carts, and automobiles. Although I was on a large boulevard, it was narrowed by the people and the carts; I wondered if all the people of Rome had been gathered here between the tall houses on either side. It is said that Romans enjoy nothing better than walking along the Via del Corso, but really it is nothing special. Every day the horse carts run in the same way up and down the street, and the people come to watch and be watched; it is unfathomable how this can be the ultimate entertainment. This trend is a remnant from the days of old Rome. Then, the daughters of the wealthy would don their best hats and frocks and be seen on this road; the young gentlemen would do up their beards and throng about, dressed to the nines. This was the place for Rome's high society to meet each other, and they came here every day to make acquaintances, many of whom later married. Many emotions gathered on the narrow Via del Corso: pride, flamboyancy, desire, and so on.

After dinner Mr. Shinmura came to see me and we went out together for a walk to Piazza di Venezia where we drank some beer and gazed at the moon. In the sky the moon looks the same no matter which country you are in. Similarly, the old stone palace roofs and the monument being built right now both have stone pillars. All around there was nothing but the square and the moon, and when I looked at them, they seemed to have become hard somehow. The moon, when seen through the pine trees from the window of a rustic abode, has a poetic look, but the moon here seems sad for having been captured by proud human souls. Stone houses have their convenient aspects, such as the fact that they are safe, but at the same time they increase the tenacity with which we remain attached to this world. I could not help but think that the difference between tenacious, proud, and jealous Westerners and insouciant Japanese, who live in houses made of wood or bamboo, gathered from the fields and bundled together, was evident in how their houses are built. From ancient Roman times to today, when they build a big memorial, the people from this area want others to surrender to them. They have an all-encompassing desire and need to make others bend to their aspirations, whether it makes others miserable or even kills them. This history started in the Palatine, and remains in the stone palace, the stone monuments, the stone pillars, and the stone staircases. This feeling of mine became especially strong as I stood, surrounded by piled, angularly cut stones, and gazed at the moon.

Mr. Shinmura will be leaving Rome tomorrow. We promised to meet again in Leipzig and I returned to my inn to climb up to the roof and gaze once more at the moon. Here too, there was a high stone castle wall behind me, and a stone palace in front of me. But if I looked up I could see the moon shining gracefully and quietly in the large, clear sky.

May 8
The American School; the Via Ostiense;
San Paolo Outside of the City;
the Poet's Grave; Monte Testaccio

I HAD an appointment to meet the principal of the American School, Monsignor Kennedy, so I headed in that direction before eleven o'clock. On one side of the road that ran beneath the high palace walls was a stone fence that reached to the heavens; on the other side were the slums. In a small vegetable garden a horse had collapsed and above it all I could just see the heads of the people looking down from the palace windows at the ensuing chaos. This was the type of world where the Fontana di Trevi overflowed with clean waters in the middle of the hustle and bustle of the city, but still the dust was kicked up into clouds. Italians' normal speaking voice is raucous and loud, and they speak in tones that sound like fighting whether they are inside or outside of their homes. This discord mixes with the dust of Rome and adds to the unpleasantness. In the form of poetry Italian is beautiful; in the form of song it is gentle, but in speech the words are vulgar, and naturally so is the cacophony of the street.

It was a different world inside of the school, where the sun shone softly on the trees in the courtyard. I was shown in and met with the principal, and asked a few questions about the school and the church. In the midst of my doing so, the monk who had shown me around the Vatican, Don Pieri, came to the school, and so after visiting the classrooms I left and went home. The road home took me past the front of the palace. The reddish walls of the palace and the cobblestones were hot in the full mid-day sun. The excessive heat caused an unpleasant dry wind, and so I decided to take a rest in the afternoon, leaving the city shortly after four o'clock.

I went out of the San Paolo gate, just below the Aventine Hill on the banks of the Tiber. Since time immemorial, the two sides of the Via Ostiense have been lined with trees into the distance, and in between them have been wine shops; the landscape in all the outlying towns around Rome is generally the same as this. On the roadside where there was a little hillock there was a large church in a ravaged landscape. The pillars and windows lining the walls made it look like a railroad station to me. This was the S. Paolo fuori le mura, and it had been erected as a memorial to the martyrdom of Saint Paul. According to legend, St. Paul was killed to the east of this church, where three springs roiled up from a small hill. There is still a monastery there today, and his bones are buried alongside the Via Ostiense nearby – thus the church was built here. The origins of the Church are old, but the original structure was more recently burned down and rebuilt, and one part is still under construction.[59] The inside is like a basilica, with dozens of large stone pillars in rows, above which is a gold gilt ceiling. In a place like a *ranma*[60] there were relief images carved in stone of all the important people in the church. It was big and elaborate, yet unremarkable and not interesting. In front of the building there had been two open, rectangular holes dug for the purposes of having springs on both sides of the church, and around them were erected the same sort of stone pillars, still very much under construction. Looking at this architecture sunk me into the same very deep thoughts I had had the night before about stone houses. In building something that would convey the legacy of the martyr St. Paul, one should make a design that represented his devotion and faith. But this building simply used much gold and was nothing but an immense structure with stone columns all built in a row. The innermost feelings behind this design were the same as those held by the Roman emperors in ancient times who built their basilicas, temples, and palaces to display their authority and influence. Looking at the large walls on the exterior, and the rows of cold columns in the interior, I was in no way brought to mind of St. Paul even though there was a stone statue of Paul inside the building, in addition to countless other images of popes and scholars lined up between the stones.

There was an ancient stone relief image of Christ inside the church, done in a rather Byzantine style. The monastery courtyard and the little chapel next to it had been spared by the [recent] fire. The courtyard was rather nice, but the barren landscape of the main hall was unpleasant, and I left half-heartedly with mixed feelings.

I walked along the tree-lined road toward the city gate, [the Porta San Paolo]. At the entrance of a small road-side chapel two small stone images of Paul and Peter embraced each other. It is said that the moment depicted here is the moment when each of the saints realized their own mortality and embraced each other in tears to bid farewell. When I think of the past, I think of the scene of the Via Ostiense. No matter what area a ship comes from in the Mediterranean Sea, at some point they all sail out of the Port of Ostia. The prosperity of the road that leads between this port and Rome is beyond imagination. People in the southern half of the Roman Empire traveled this route on their way to and from the capital. Soldiers, merchants, officials, all manner of mankind traveled this road in countless numbers. St. Paul, too, when he first came to Rome, traveled on this road, and when in the end he was killed, it was after he went out of the city gate and was captured on this road.

When I drew close to the city gate I saw that there was a stone pyramid[61] near it and the top of the city wall afforded an interesting view of a row of cypress trees. It is said that long ago the view outside of this city gate was truly magnificent, but now the poor have built houses in the area and all one can see along the road is the pyramid and the city wall. But even that is quite reminiscent of the past. When Paul came to Rome and was captured and sent to prison, he went out of this gate and must have looked up to see this pyramid. The gate and the tower are left today, landmarks of the entrance to Rome from the Via Ostiense.

Inside the gate, where one side of the pyramid faces the city wall, there is a cypress grove. This is where there is a Protestant cemetery for people from England and others like them who died in Rome, or who loved Rome and who left a testament requesting that they be buried there. The poet Shelley lies in the shade of the city wall, and Keats and his artist friend Severn are buried a little way from the pyramid, beneath a stand of two pine trees.[62] Long ago the graves were in a dense growth of trees, and there was a flavor of antiquity about the pyramid and the city wall that was appropriate for a cemetery, but now a good part of the city wall has been relieved of its surrounding foliage, and it has largely lost its ancient air. That said, the trees at the base of the pyramid and the gravestones nearby stand quietly, befitting the world of the dead. When I had come here before it had been on a gloomy autumn evening. Today it was springtime but still evening, and the setting sun shone on the pyramid with fragrant flowers underneath the trees. On Keats's grave is the epitaph, "This Grave contains all that was Mortal of a young English poet" and on Shelley's grave is the epitaph, "Nothing of him that doth fade | But doth suffer a sea-change | Into something rich and strange";[63] the gravestones and the setting both bring the poets to mind. While I stood passing time at the gravesides in silent thought, an English woman who had been sketching nearby packed up her implements and left. The caretaker wanted to close the door, so I left the gravesites and turned back to look at the grove of trees from outside the wall.[64]

A little ways beyond the cemetery is Monte Testaccio. It is about 150 *shaku* high, but from the summit, where there is a cross erected, the view in all directions is truly vast. While I stood there looking at the landscape, many clamorous beggar boys came by. When I tried to shoo them away, they pulled out a blood-soaked swallow and insisted that I buy it from them. I waved my walking stick at them to chase them away and when I looked to see what they were doing, I saw that the boys had been on the hill all day, catching swallows by tying a string to a bamboo pole. This cruelty on the part of the impoverished youths was really quite pitiful. After the boys left I was able to see the last of the setting sun. The view encompassed the Tiber River flowing at the base of the hill, its undulations carrying it through the Campagna. San Paolo soared up from the middle of the fields, and I could not tell if the mists beyond it in the direction of Ostia were actually sea or sky. To the east were the Monti Albani, and beyond those the snow-covered Apennines. To the north, I could see from the monastery on top of the Aventine, to the stone statue on top of the Laterano church, to the clusters of thousands of Roman houses. Turning toward the west, the steeple of St. Peter's towered especially high above the surrounding little hills. All of these were dyed a light shade of purple by the madder red of the setting sun as the church bells rang out in the evening sky.

This hill was not made of earth, but rather it was made of pottery shards, which were from broken wine bottles brought into ancient Rome. These shards were proof that there was a tax at that time. The pottery shards, over the course of hundreds of years, became a little hill from which there is a good prospect. It is a strange bit of history.[65]

As I descended the hill to return to the city center, the lights of the city began to twinkle here and there. Along the banks of the Tiber there were the remains of Rienzi's house walls[66] and the Temple of Vesta.

I returned to my inn to find that a letter had arrived from Mr. Matsunaga. I opened it in haste to find a newspaper clipping that included the words "Faculty of Humanities" – and at this moment I first learned the results of the Boat Race. The worries of the past month were wiped clear in this moment. There were more details, most notably that the Faculty of Humanities and the Faculty of Law were both victorious, presenting such a favorable outcome for the first time in four years. I was so happy I could not bear it, but I had no one with whom to speak and so I read the newspaper and the mail, and wrote some letters, then went out after my meal for a walk and to drink a beer before returning to the inn. Back at the inn I climbed up to the roof where the pure moon in the clear sky put me in high spirits. I began thinking about next year's Boat Race.

May 9
Hadrian's Villa; Tivoli

THE MORNING brought a bright, sunny day. Today I decided to go to Tivoli, and I headed out of the Lorenzo Gate. At the city train station there were many people bound for Tivoli. Presently the train departed. We pulled out of the city and into the grassy world of the sunny Campagna. The red, white, yellow, and purple flowers all blooming in profusion were spread across the green expanse of the fields. We embarked into Nature – "Who laid it out? | The flower brocade | of the Campagna." The flowers on the embankment stood tall against the azure sky. "Raise the flowers | in the azure sky | embankment flowers." [67]

The fields opened up before us and the mountains grew closer. Looking back, the sky over Rome was enveloped with smoke and dust in contrast to the clear blue sky over the fields. No matter where one goes, the cities are dusty, and the fields have flowers. After about one hour the train stopped in a place called Terme.[68] Sulfur springs rose up from the fields, making the river water a sulfurous color. And all around was the smell of sulfur. If one walked just a bit, one could find the remains of an ancient palace in the fields. The next stop on the train line was close to emperor Hadrian's Villa (Villa Adriana).

I disembarked from the train and went along a road through the fields toward the villa. The entrance to the villa was where the flowers grew thick and there was a grove of cypress trees. I went through the cool shade of the trees to the top of a hill where nothing but the walls remain of the ancient palace. When they had been built the walls had been decorated with all sorts of marble, but now there was nothing but a brick skeleton left standing, with fragments of the sculpture that had decorated the pillars scattered here and there. Whether the building had been a rotunda, a philosopher's den, a library, or a military office, all that remained was a name – all of it was now part of the same bed of rubble around a brick wall. Between the walls and the colonnades, no matter where I went, I found the same ruins. They were enhanced by the silhouette of a pine, or made more pitiful by the shadow of a cypress, and among them all the flowers bloomed in profusion.

Here Hadrian built a large mansion on top of the hill which afforded a grand view of the Campagna and environs of Rome. He used it as a seasonal resort to which he invited the wealthy for meetings, and scholarly conferences. He gathered in his garden all the landscapes of the world's famous places, and it was here that he strolled with the literati. Sitting among the many stone statues in the palace (today there are many masterpieces that have been excavated from here in such places as the Vatican), Hadrian, who had compared himself to the gods, was, along with the first emperor of China and Japan's own Kiyomori,[69] the type of man about whom ballads are sung. The vast palace ruins on top of this hill, and the boundless remnants of the garden, make this the sort of place about which great poets could write lengthy poems.

I dawdled in the shade of a wall in one spot, and sat on a stone pillar in another, and lay down in the grass to pick flowers. Looking through a window in the crumbling wall, I could see a cypress against the blue sky; it looked like a wonderful painting, as if someone had spread a brocade of flowers on the remains of the rotunda.

Looking back on the past
The blue sky
Through the crack in the wall
Looks like something in a painting
The stands of cypress

Only the old walls
Remain of the palace
A brocade of flowers
Decorates the floor

Summer grasses
Thick and quiet in
The palace ruins
Birds, too, walk through the dream realm
Chirping on the path

The early summer sun shone across the nearby crumbling walls all the way to the distant mountains and fields, and I lay down in the grass to look up at the sky – it was like I was dreaming of a world of hidden truth.

I walked along the road lined with cypress trees and went out the gate to where a horse cart picked me up and took me toward Tivoli, about a mile away on a hilltop. There was an olive grove on one side of the hill, along a gentle sloping road, and the prospect from the top of the Campagna fields was good, including the nearby town of Tivoli. A little further in the distance on top of a mountain was the village of Montecelio standing on its own. Further in the distance beyond the fields the city of Rome appeared as a mass in which the houses and the hills were indistinguishable. In the midst of the mass was the great dome of St. Peter's, soaring grandly toward the heavens.

Our ascent up the hill completed, we arrived in Tivoli. I got down out of the horse cart and entered the Villa d'Este.[70] I descended the mansion staircase and came out on a veranda that afforded a good view. The garden immediately below had large cypress trees that shot up toward the sky and interspersed among them I could see waterfalls and fountains. Beyond the trees the view opened up to the mountains and the fields. This was not a ruin, but looking at the large garden of this palace where no one resided made me reflect on the extravagances of four hundred years earlier.

I went down into the garden, down the steps one by one like descending a mountain. A stream flowed through the copse and there were various stone statues nearby – the sound of the waterfall briefly took me away from this vulgar world. But gardens constructed under the overly proper rules of the Renaissance are contrived and not all that interesting. Seeing the garden, of which the nobles were so proud, in disarray with the statues shattered made me realize the transient nature of glorious dreams. Among it all, only the old cypress trees maintained their natural shape, pointing toward the azure sky.

I left the Villa d'Este and walked through the small, dirty town. In the plaza I saw a group of children in front of a restaurant jostling to see something. They gathered to see, sitting at a table that had been placed outside the door there, a negro. He was wearing a red necktie in a fashionable way, and with him was an older, comely woman with a white powdered face, gaudily dressed. The two were taking a meal together. Perhaps she was a lady from America who had brought her negro servant with her. The contrast of black and white was too distracting, yet I felt sorry for having stared at them. But they themselves did not seem ashamed. Although one would think that this negro, taken on a world tour with his mistress, would not want to be seen, it was I who turned away.

The town consisted entirely of slums. I finally made my way through them, exited the town and came to a place where there were waterfalls, despite the lack of a river flowing below. I crossed over a bridge and went into a garden of waterfalls,[71] where I came upon one at the base of the hill. A tunnel had been dug out of the hill and the large waterfall came out of it, throwing up spray that made a beautiful rainbow. Below that there were other waterfalls, all of which came out of holes dug in the hill. This mountain was formed by stalactites[72] and the water then comes through the rocks, creates a hole, and spills downward into a waterfall. I passed through the shaft in the rocks and climbed the hill on the opposite side of the waterfall to where there were the remains of two temples. This area, where the shaft and waterfall are, is said to be where the Sibyls and the Sirens lived, and the ruins there were relics of the temples where they were worshipped.[73] Going around the temples I came upon a restaurant that had put out tables by the cliff. I sat down and looked out over the valley from the cliff top. Here and there waterfalls appeared from holes in the rocks. It was an odd landscape, and really was not so noteworthy – rather, it gave the impression of being a toy valley-scape.

The train left Tivoli at half past four o'clock. The tracks ran along the cliffs, on the opposite bank from Tivoli. I could see numerous waterfalls in a glance from the train window. Once we left the valley and began our ascent, the view opened up to a solid line of olive trees from the foothills into the Campagna. Once again down onto the plains, the flowering fields and the herds of sheep grazing in the pastures presented a charming country scene.

I returned to the inn at about six o'clock. I had been invited to dine with Miss Dove, so I set out toward her house. The Landrums were there, as well as a female painter named Weld, and a French earl – we guests spoke of many topics. I spoke with Miss Dove about art, and I found her opinions engaging as she expressed many of the points that I myself had felt. We agreed that in architecture and painting, Byzantine and Romanesque art had a kind of artless naïveté. There was evidence that the artists had some sort of satisfaction in their work. And, thusly, when we looked at their work, we too were swayed to their temperament, and we too felt a kind of quiet satisfaction. Gothic art held active elevation as an ideal, and consequently they often produced surprising works. When one looks up at them from below, one is struck by their height. But this limitless height does not provide the viewer with satisfaction. The Renaissance works are mostly done in this sort of style, the most extreme of which show off the artist's pride and are not in the least interesting. I beheld these works of art with all this in mind. The number of people who felt the way this English lady did was growing. The British are the most appreciative of the Japanese sense of Zen quietude, refinement, and *shibui*.

The sole topic of conversation during dinner was that of mysteries, and after the meal we repaired to Miss Weld's studio to see her paintings. There were many different Italian landscapes, beginning with one of Rome. Because the artist had gone to each place and painted her work, these pictures were quite different from those that one sees for sale in front of stores. Nature in Italy – the flowers of the Campagna, the Venezia River, the monasteries of Assisi – was beautiful, but the Italy found in paintings was also beautiful.

Later I spoke with Mr. Landrum about Japanese religion; it was past eleven o'clock when I returned to my room. This was the most enjoyable evening I had spent since leaving Assisi.

May 10
Church on Sunday; a Concert

TODAY IS Sunday, but in Rome from the break of dawn Sunday is in no way peaceful. Moreover, the weather was humid and most unpleasant.

I went to Santa Maria Maggiore[74] sometime after ten o'clock. The service in the main church was finished, and from a side chapel I could hear voices reciting scripture. There were many people who were standing and kneeling before the altar. I had walked here in the heat, so I leaned against a cool stone pillar and gazed at the scene inside the church.

The origins of this church are ancient, but the architecture has been added to over the ages and so there are many parts that are new.[75] According to its history, in the fourth century the Holy Virgin appeared here, and the church was built where snow had fallen in the heat of August. And so, as it is said, this church was built.[76] Every year on August 5 there is a festival to commemorate this event, and they scatter white roses in place of snow in the church. The building is in the style of a basilica; there were rows of stone columns up to the square ceiling. It was not austere and uninteresting, like San Paolo outside the city gates was; rather, it looked like the Church of Santa Maria. On the altar there is a stone relief carving like the one in Laterano, and the craftsmanship is quite good.[77] The side chapels are also splendid.[78]

Amidst the many worshipers a priest entered one of the confessionals and put out front of it a flag on a pole that was six or seven *shaku* long. The worshipers knelt before it and prayed, and the priest would touch them lightly on the head with the pole. This was his benediction. This monk, who raised and lowered his pole mechanically and with dead seriousness, was playing an absurd role, but the faithful who stretched out their heads in prayer were also put to shame. However I am sure that for the faithful, this was something for which they were thankful.

On my way back I went to a Dominican church called San Carlo.[79] It was nothing special, but it had a statue of Saint Dominic and also one of Antonio of Padua, and the faithful prayed incessantly. For Antonio they had varied requests, and from Dominic, I do not think the faithful were praying for wisdom. For the scholar-monk Dominic, it must have been a nuisance to receive varied requests.

There was a concert scheduled at four o'clock to which I went because Mr. Costa had invited me. The concert hall had originally been the tomb of the emperor Augustus, and was a large, round building constructed of bricks.[80] It had been restored, and had become the city concert hall. I listened to Beethoven's *Coriolan Overture*, then we moved on to Berlioz' *Symphonie Fantastique*. I had heard this once before in Paris, and did not appreciate it well, as it was like a dreamy fantasy, music of the dream of love. Mr. Costa said that this piece had been entangled in the trend of "program music" (*programmusik*) and he hated it.[81] Besides the shepherd's piping and the formulaic "confession and absolution" of it, it had an odd harmony – one that went beyond the usual bounds – and I could not truly understand it even though I read the explanation of the piece.

Next after Berlioz was the "Tristan Prelude" along with the last part of "Inside Tristan's Fortress."[82] The prelude contains Isolde's agony and determination. We see her last breaths, as she has been drawn in by the taste of love in her yearning heart. The music truly portrays the inner voice of the soul. I closed my eyes and listened, and in the end Mr. Costa said, "Now *this* is real music." The last piece was the overture to *Tannhäuser*.[83] I enjoyed this piece, too, because I was familiar with it, but I did get a feeling that it was a bit shallow in contrast to *Tristan*.

I left the symphony hall and climbed the Scala di Spagna with Mr. Costa to view the sunset from a good prospect. The setting sun in Assisi was pure and bright; the sun here has a hot hue. The steeple of St. Peter's stands extremely tall in that bright, impassioned, hot sky. The Roman sunset reflects the pride of her people, and it seems to me that the steeple of St. Peter's represents the authority of the Catholic Church.

May 11
Congregazione della Propaganda; Schools; Abbeys

EARLY IN the morning Don Pieri from the Vatican came to be my guide, and we went walking to see various schools. The first place to which we went was the central proselytizing unit for the Roman Catholic Church, the [Collegio di] Propaganda di Fide, which has been the medium for missionary work since the seventeenth century.[84] The head is a cardinal (a councilor of the Vatican) who manages the school, the dormitory, and the training of the missionaries. He also administers the secretariat and accounting. The Congregazione della Propaganda comprises the cardinal and over ten other people.

We went to an academy and observed the students in session. They wore various uniforms, which indicated their group (for example, the American College, or a dormer in the missionary group). They had gathered together from various countries in the world, and there was even one Japanese in their midst. Although they came from various countries and each spoke his own language, in the academy they spoke only Latin, and so there was not even the slightest inconvenience. However, at the time the curriculum had been mostly set since the Middle Ages, and did not touch on the modern. They study philosophy, literature, history, physics, etc., and then finish with a focus on theology. At Jesuit universities in the United States they teach philosophical history in English, but here they do not teach philosophical history per se. Psychology and other such subjects are taught under the rubric of Philosophy. In the Philosophy lecture hall the lecture had not started. I took a look at the Physics lecture hall, but here their regular Physics instruction focuses not on academic inquiry but rather the methods for conducting missionary work. In newer missionary schools they teach some medical arts, but here there is none of that. Beneath the school there is a printing office where they publish materials in languages from around the world.[85]

The secretariat divides the world into regions and manages the business of each; written records since the seventeenth century fill a large room. If one were to examine these records, one would surely discover an interesting history of propaganda. At the end of the tour we went to a meeting room where we met with two or three instructors, then we left the building. Recently there was a heretic among the instructors at this academy and it seems he had caused a disturbance, but he has been removed from office and the matter ended.[86]

After taking a look this place, I felt that as a school it had nothing special to offer, and that it was similar to other seminaries. It was nothing more than a Catholic seminary that educated religious scholars and sent them out as missionaries. However, this school is the central missionary school in the world, and the Sacred Congregation of Propaganda controls all the other congregations (for example, those in Paris or Lyons) and collects contributions from all over the world – the mechanism is really quite large.

Next we went to a nearby school called San Guiseppe. This school was started by the Frenchman Jean-Baptiste Lazare, and it is a school of the Lazarist tradition, where children are educated in arts and crafts and also the usual curricula of other schools. The Lazarist school originated in France as a place where monks would educate the children of commoners, but now the school there has been ordered closed, and so it no longer exists in France. At the entrance in a small garden there is a statue of the Holy Virgin among many flowers. I felt as if I had entered a monastery. The principal was an elderly Frenchman who welcomed us gaily and spoke freely with us. Past the central garden at the entrance there was another garden which, along with broad colonnades, formed a play area for the children. There are three hundred students, ranging in age from seven or eight to sixteen or seventeen years old. About half of them lived at the school and were afforded clothing and board by the school. The expenses averaged a thousand francs per student per year. There were also others who commuted from their homes, and they did not have to pay tuition, receiving books and other materials all from the school. The students gather in the chapter house at eight o'clock for prayer, eat all together at twelve o'clock, and at three-thirty when classes are finished, the faculty take the students for a walk. At six o'clock the students review their lessons. In addition to the regular teachers in the classrooms, there are also regular attendant teachers who answer students' questions and accompany them on their walks – they take care of them exactly as if they were the students' fathers. In Japan the Gyōsei School[87] also has this sort of organization. For a true education, the instructors must have this sort of arrangement in which they watch over the students, in effect substituting for parents and older siblings. On this point, Catholic schools are superior to secular schools and have better relations between the students and the instructors. The teachers give selflessly of themselves for the sake of the students, not for the sake of a salary. I visited one or two different classrooms and saw that the teachers and teachers' assistants all were monks in the Lazare order, and wore black robes with white collars. They were as friends to the students. In the ten minutes of recess between classes, one of the teachers' assistants took the students out to the garden where they lined up and then were permitted to frolic as they pleased. Even the elderly principal mingled with them; when I saw him playing with the children it gave me a truly pleasing feeling.

The chapter house was fairly typical, with a painting on the front wall of St. Joseph embracing Christ. There was also an image of Christ appearing as a child to St. Antonio, and one of the founders of this order, Lazare, as well as other saintly images that were associated with Christianity and children. The dining hall was truly beautiful with its white marble tables. Behind the building there was a large garden with a grove of trees, through which a road wound its way along the foot of Monte Pincio. Looking upward beyond the copse in the garden, I saw that the trees around the Medici Villa on top of the hill were emerald green against the azure of the sky. Even if the children did not leave the grounds, they could still play amidst the summer trees and spring flowers in the school garden. We really should build many such gardens in Japanese schools, too. And it is not simply a matter of building the gardens – we must also instill in the children the idea that the garden is the same as their own home. In order to make the children feel at home, the teachers must be kind to them. This does not only apply to the Japanese Buddhist schools that comply with the dictates of the Ministry of Education [and thus lessen the quality of their work]; would that we could provide an education with faith, one that treated children with kindness! We must learn from the Catholic monks who give of themselves selflessly and who provide a kind, gentle education.

I looked at the student compositions in the design and planning classroom, and saw that the room afforded a truly good view of the garden and the hills. The principal smiled, and said that they had purposely made it such that the view of God's blessings would be good in this room where they would teach the arts. He seemed refined in comparison to those Japanese school principals who say that students should not gaze at the flowers, and who remove the cherry blossoms from the school grounds. The room near the exit had been made into a meeting place for the teachers and the alumni. There were billiards and other such amusements, books to read, and also portraits of the Holy Virgin and other people who were connected to the school in some fashion. Those who graduate from this school progress to other schools (particularly the governmental industrial school) but do not forget their alma mater, taking special care not to lose their religious influence. British universities have changed their curriculum from seminary training to gentleman's training, but this school supported the spirit of seminary education, and resisted secular teaching that went counter to religious teaching. For the British, it is a natural evolution; for the Italians, it is a source of strife.

We left the school and walked a bit together, after which time Don Pieri and I parted and I returned to the inn. The horse cart drivers went on strike today, so there was not a passenger horse cart to be seen in the city, and it looked very quiet. I thought it might be good if the automobile drivers also went on strike.

In the afternoon I went again with Don Pieri to a Franciscan nunnery near Laterano. This Franciscan nunnery belongs to the order of Mary (Les Franciscaines Missionaires de Marie).[88] It is a Gothic building of pure white stone, situated amidst the houses of the poor on the outskirts of town. When we rang the bell at the little side door, a young nun clad in pure white robes with a pure white habit emerged. When we told her that we were there to meet the "mother superior" (the head nun is called "mother" [mère], and the nuns are all called "sister" [soeur]), we were shown to the reception room. Besides two or three portraits, there was no decoration in the room. After a short while the mother superior came in with two nuns to greet us. The elder head nun was French, and was about fifty-six or fifty-seven years old. Her face was wrinkled, showing the hardships of her life, but her countenance showed a confidence and a kindness, and she seemed like a virtuous and good person. The two nuns who came with her were both about thirty years old; one was British, and we began speaking in English. She was not as peaceful as the elder nun, but she was solid and rather keen, and her health seemed good. The other nun was Italian, but she spoke French well. She was mature, and had the countenance of St. Clare in the painting by Martini in Assisi.[89] All three of them were dressed the same as the nun who had showed me in: in pure, snow-white clothing from the top of their heads to the tips of their toes. On their bosoms they wore ivory crucifixes which rustled against their clothes and looked absolutely pure. The elder nun spoke first. "Because the fulfillment of St. Francis's compassion is paramount in our faith, we cannot separate our missionary work from charity. Charity is, first and foremost, the work that our nuns and other women must take on. Half of this nunnery is a place of work." She then guided us through the nunnery, up stone steps to a room on the third floor. That room was the painting and sketch room, and there were three or four nuns there, along with two women from the outside, and they were all working on a painting or a sketch. They were not paintings done from their own design, but they were done in oils and pastels and the skill displayed was rather good. Completed works were displayed on the walls. There were paintings of the Holy Virgin, and of Raphael's St. Cecilia, and other sketches. There were many sketches done in an old-fashioned style on sheepskin with old-fashioned lettering, all piled in a box. They were all works that had been sent to the mother superior at the main mission by the sisters who had traveled to various locales as missionaries. Some of them had prayers written on them, and some expressed thanks to the mother superior. The next room was where they made lace, and here too the nuns wore pure white work clothes and wove exquisite lace. Weaving a square inch takes a day or two of total effort; this lace is entirely different from that which one buys in a store. The fine, beautiful lace is as white as the nuns' habits, and the entire room is one pure white world. While Don Pieri moved about observing the work, the mother superior explained in detail the spirit behind the work.

She said, "In today's society there is inequality, and Socialism and Anarchism commit outrages; the source of these problems stems from indolence and wastefulness. Men's issues aside, women do not know the first thing about home economics. They are miserly and throw their homes into chaos. That is to say, they play about not working, and lose all interest in working, becoming indolent and considering only various issues of pride, wishing for a life that is unsuited to their station. And, wishing for a life above one's station naturally causes inequalities, and those inequalities fan the flames of economic disorder. Social problems are economic problems, but they are moral problems, too, and those moral problems are consequently problems of faith. The spirit of St. Francis was dedicated to the belief in God; he was thankful for His blessings, and that thankful spirit drives each person in his or her work. Therefore, in this mission, if they love anything, the nuns and lay women love doing work, and they are guided by that joy that they take in their work. If one enjoys one's work, one can find faith in it, and inequalities will not arise, and one's household will be economical. A woman's greatest virtue, modesty, is born from this diligence, and along with the womanly virtues and chastity, she will progress and come to have a heart filled with benevolence. Our work is not limited to the nunnery; our main mission is to promote this diligence among lay women, too." I listened to her explanation, given with a gentle yet strong countenance, one that showed her fervor. I watched the nuns in the room all working diligently weaving their lace. And, before my eyes, the chastity and womanly virtues of the mother superior and all the nuns in their pure habits were displayed. When I heard that this order of nuns spread their integrity, diligence, and benevolent works, and established leper clinics all over the world, and took care of the unfortunate ill, I felt deeply the strong faith and burning spirit of benevolence maintained by these seemingly frail nuns dressed in white.

The next room was where the sewing work was done; the nuns created images of flowers and of the Saints one stitch of embroidery thread at a time. Among the finished pieces were ceremonial vestments, as well as tapestries. Compared to the white lace in the previous room, here they were creating splendid pieces of gold and blue. The mother superior said, "According to the reports of our sisters who have gone to Japan, the Japanese girls are skilled at this sort of embroidery, and in our Kurume Mission they do much of this sort of work." This order maintains missions in Kurume and Sapporo; in Kurume they care for forty or fifty lepers.

The next room was for leather work. I opened up a leather-bound book on one of the desks to find, collected within, photographs of this order's missions, including the sight of three-thousand sisters in countries all over the world doing benevolent missionary work. The leather cover of the book was made here, and the photographs were all taken by the sisters. The embroidered pictures in the previous room, too, were all done by the sisters – without help from others. The leather work was different from the sort of machine-embossed leather produced in the stores. Each line was traced by a needle and on the leather appeared various pictures and patterns.

This is work that would be impossible were it not for the joy the women found in their work, and the patience that came with faith. The next room was the printmaking room where one nun, her sleeves tucked up, printed images of the Holy Virgin using a copper plate. The etching on the copper plate was also done entirely by hand. She looked happy as she printed one sheet after the other. She enjoyed this work; it brought her pleasure to print something etched in copper of her own design. These days manufacturing is divided up such that a different person does the design, another the carving, and another the printing, and so the workers do not do the work themselves from start to finish and consequently it comes as no surprise that they do not find the work appealing.[90]

Next we went downstairs where lay people from outside the mission kneeled at the door and the nuns from inside the convent kneeled at the altar in prayer. I was told that the main hall of worship was built with outside help, but the windows, decorations, and holy images were all done by the nuns, and I was quite surprised at their skill. It made me think of the olden days in Japan, when a high priest would paint paintings and carve images. This is a special characteristic of the Franciscans.

Just as I was about to leave the main worship hall, several nuns dressed in white came in to the hall single file for the evening services. The sight of them was just like *Lohengrin* when Eliza appears, but this sight was not a play – it was real life.[91] From there I went out into the garden. There was a large central courtyard, surrounded by long colonnades that were supported by Gothic vaults. White flowers grew in profusion amidst thick stands of citrus trees. The colonnades were two-tiered, and on each tier flower pots of all sorts were lined up; an image of the Holy Virgin was surrounded by white flowers that looked like wild chrysanthemums. The white chrysanthemums in the white stone halls and the visage of the white-clad nuns swaying down the halls were like some sort of avatar of the Pure Land. The mother superior explained that these halls were where the nuns could take a turn, and she continued, "In the secular world, people think of a nunnery as some dark, shadowy place, but here the flowers bloom, God's light shines upon us, and the sisters happily perform their work, receiving all the blessings of nature when they walk the halls or go out into the garden. This is the Franciscan spirit." Truly, as she had said, the spirit of St. Francis was alive and filled every corner of the nunnery. The nuns in pure white walked the halls, and the way in which they kneeled before the Holy Virgin of white blossoms made them seem particularly pure in comparison to the soiled outside world from which they were separated by a simple wall. Moreover, the nuns' cheerfulness, from the mother superior on down, brought a happy feeling to those with whom it came in contact. This hall commemorated the founder of the order, and her birth and death dates were carved in the wall. Her name was Hélène de Chappotin, and she was born on May 21, 1839 in Neuville, and died on November 15, 1904 in Italy. She began her vocation on January 6, 1887 (when she was forty-eight years old), and she received permission from both the Franciscans and the Roman Catholic Church to begin the order nine years after that (on May 11, 1896). Materials for her biography have been gathered and are currently being edited, and when the biography is finished I am sure it will be quite interesting. In any event, since its founding twenty years ago, there have been three thousand sisters in the order who have gone all over the world to pursue their vocation, which is a surprising number of people who have been called to a vocation [by God]. I do not know the details of their faith, but I have no doubt that their faith is deep, given that they are practicing in the spirit of St. Francis, seven hundred years after his time.

As I passed through the corridors I could hear the songs of evening services from within the house. After I took a look at the meeting rooms behind the chapter house, I bid farewell, gave my thanks, and left.

Not far from this nunnery was a Franciscan monastery, which served as the head monk's (the Minister General's) residence and the center of the academy. Once inside the monastery I could hear the monks laughing on the second floor. Compared to the cleanliness of the wide open nunnery, here things were haphazard. In the hallway that led to the monks' quarters, there were no flowers and no decoration; it was truly a simple arrangement. If the nunnery represented

Francis's ideal of morals and integrity, this monastery represented honorable poverty. The Minister General was not in, so a representative of his plus three or four of the other priests came to shake our hands and greet us as if we were old friends. Among them was Father Robinson, whom I had met at Assisi, and we were both happy to see one another again. Passing through the hallways in the dark of the evening we found them full of rope-belted monks because it was the time when the novices of the academy were all going out to take a walk.

I passed through the monks' quarters – the second story, the third story, the fourth story and beyond – and came out on to the roof. The setting sun reached the horizon in the west and the steeple of St. Peter's stood squarely in the bright light like embers from a fire. All of Rome was collected within one view – to the north was the Pincio Hill, to the west was the Gianicolo Hill where the pine trees were ink paintings against the evening sky, to the east past the nearby Laterano I could see across the Campagna fields to the Alban hills. Directly below us the monastery fields of beans and other vegetables grew verdantly, and white flowers formed the fringe between the green leaves of the trees. When they were not outside of the monastery, the monks would come to this rooftop for their walks; it was where those who had forsaken the world could look down upon it. Father Robinson pointed toward the commemorative stela that had been erected to the earlier Italian king on the Capitoline Hill and said, "That is where we lived long ago, but the government forced us to move here. But our spirit remains the same no matter where we are." There is no doubt that a quiet old monastery on top of the Capitoline would be better than this new house in the city. However, Francesco held the ideal of having no abode in this world, so it really does not matter where the monastery is. But, it is certainly a pity for Rome that where once there was a monastery garden filled with trees and a graceful steeple, now there is only a stone stela with a typical horrid statue of someone mounted on a horse.

I came down from the room and took a look at one or two of the classrooms, but besides a few simple desks and chairs, there was nothing particularly of note. There was a collection of many different items that had been sent from all over the world by Franciscan missionaries, making a museum of missionary work. This, too, was nothing special. The library room was truly exceptional; it was really twenty some rooms strung together, and each division was nicely arranged. The original monastery had materials going back hundreds of years, but they were all confiscated by the government and now all they have are materials from the past ten or so years. The Franciscan movement did not intend to become a scholarly group originally, but rather to be the Gospel for the common man. Just as Jōdoshū or Shinshū Buddhism gradually became the study of religious tenets and gave rise to numerous debates, as well as scholarly issues, this monastery had become a place of academic inquiry such that for a while materials had been collected here. The academy in this monastery also serves such a purpose; the students who come here from all over the world become priests in this order. Downstairs from the library is the debate room where twice a week the students gather and debate doctrine (the language they use is, of course, Latin). On all four walls of this room are paintings of St. Bonaventure, who belonged to this sect, and portraits by Leonardo. These paintings are all done by the hands of the students at the monastery.

Further downstairs there is a large kitchen and dining hall. Disciples clad in aprons worked in the kitchen. The air was like that of a Zen temple. The bread, the wine, and the cheese were all made by the disciples. In addition, all the clothes and even the shoes are made within the monastery. The dining hall was divided into two groups – the priest instructors and the students – but both had seating along the four walls with the meals lined up on wooden tables in front of the chairs. On one side there is a lectern where the disciples go up in rotation to recite scripture during the meal. This is as it is at any monastery. Just as I was about to take my leave, I was ordered to drink a cup of wine which had been prepared for me on the table. When asked what I would like to accompany my wine, I replied that the most enjoyable food to receive at a Franciscan church would be bread. They all smiled, and said that they would give me some bread with some cheese. The wine was poured, and they gave me bread and cheese. I was waited upon by the apron-clad disciples in the dark dining hall and enjoyed my wine and bread as I spoke with the priests. It reminded me of eating in a college dining hall at Oxford. Just as the British spirit is expressed at Oxford by their custom of eating after grace is said in a dignified manner, here I was able to sample the ideal of Franciscan honorable poverty as I nibbled on my bread and drank my wine. (In Japan, having wine would be a sign of luxury, but here it is drunk like tea.)

Finally I went into the chapter house. The ceiling above the altar had Christ in the center, surrounded by Francis and saints from this sect all carved in stone relief. The style was of a modern bent, and I was told that this too was done by the disciples. The other paintings and decorations within the hall were all hand-made, just as the work that I had seen previously at the nunnery. Franciscans, in whatever context, love nature and the arts and fulfill the spirit of their religion through them. The disciples who grow vegetables in the fields, make shoes and rope belts, and cook meals are the same disciples who paint pictures and carve reliefs in stone. In America this spirit is seen in the schools, and that is the special aspect of their schools of which Americans are proud, but the Franciscans have been doing this in their monasteries for hundreds of years.

In the chapter house I could see the dark shadows of the worshipers in the candlelight. When I exited from the hall the remnants of the setting sun were still in the sky, sending out rays of dark crimson light. I thanked the priests and bid them farewell, as well as Don Pieri, and returned to my inn. As I walked along the road I looked up at the steeple of Santa Maria Maggiore and saw the pure light of the moon in the eastern sky. If one compares the remnants of the hot sun that shine in the sunset to the activities and scholarship of the Franciscan monks, then one can compare the color of the pure moon to the chastity of the nuns.

May 12
Academy of an Order of Nuns

TODAY, AS yesterday, I had an enjoyable experience. I left the city through the Porta Pinciana and was led to a splendid palace that flanked the Borghese Park outside the city walls. I was told that this was the house of the order of nuns called the Assomptionistes,[92] and I was surprised at how luxurious it was. In front of the entranceway was an ancient Roman stone statue, and the stairs that led all the way to the reception room were made of white marble, as were the pillars alongside. As I waited in the reception room I looked about to see that, aside from the crucifix on the wall, everything was palatial. Presently the head nun came into the room with another nun and began by saying, "I am English," continuing with her explanation entirely in English. I came to understand the origins of this house from her explanation: The house had been that of an aristocratic family originally, and was not suited to be a nunnery or a school, but its location outside the city walls was close to the park and had clean air and so they had rented the house and made considerable renovations to it to make a nunnery and a school. The school was intended to provide an education to upper-class girls, so four languages were compulsory, in addition to music, painting, and history. The nuns came from various countries, and taught the languages of those countries as well as whatever skills they had. Other required subjects were taught by outside teachers. The students all lived in dormitories, and the nuns became their mothers and sisters, taking care of their every need. After these prefatory remarks by the head nun, we went to see the classrooms.

The habit of the Assomptionistes is, like the Franciscans, brown; the head-dress is white, and the crucifix they wear on their bosom is white. It does not look as divine as the all-white habits of the nuns that I saw yesterday, but the crucifix looks as if it were ancient armor, and imparts a military flavor. There is little difference between their classrooms and classes and those of other schools. Music and language are especially promoted but painting and design are not very advanced. The bedrooms are splendid palatial affairs – there are three rooms that could each sleep perhaps thirty people, but there are two nuns per room. The other nuns sleep in a basement room; they say that they give the finest rooms to the children.

Next I went to the kindergarten that is affiliated with the school. This is a kindergarten for poor children, and they are thus provided with clothing and food. The children are divided into two classes, but both learn singing and drama, which they showed me, after which I was asked to give them treats and so the Japanese uncle divided up the treats among the poor Italian children. Because they were poor, the children snatched the treats and many of them forgot to say thank you.

In the afternoon I went to the nuns' school outside of the Porta Pia. As we passed through the gate, Don Pieri told me that the Italian army had entered Rome through this gate. Sixty years ago the royal family had unified Italy but Rome was still under papal rule and would not surrender to the royal family. The royals and the people both saw in Rome the vestiges of the ancient Roman Empire, and in the end they attacked Rome. On September 20, 1871[93] they crashed this gate and invaded the city, and bombarded the current royal palace (what was at the time the Pope's castle). The Pope escaped to the Vatican, and the Pope and the royal family became the enemies that they are today. Those from the Vatican call this the Gate of Enmity.

Outside the gate but still close to the city there is a large, dreary house. This is the main church of the nuns' order of Saint Ursula, where there is a nunnery and school. This sect was founded by a French nun named Angela, and their purpose is to educate.[94] At this nunnery they train nuns and they also educate girls between the ages of seven or eight until the ages of seventeen or eighteen. They include all classes; one-third of their students pay tuition and stay at the nunnery. The mother superior is French; she is more than sixty years old, and quite plump, and she served as our guide. There are Americans in the order, as well as Germans. We watched the children play in the large pine-shaded garden, then we went into the house where we were shown the nun's rooms, the mother superior's office, and the chapter house. The mother superior's reception room had a wooden lattice that separated her from her visitors as they spoke. When I thought about it, I realized that usually men cannot enter a nunnery, but our visit here was accomplished through special permission from the Pope; I did not realize this yesterday, and for the first time became aware of it after coming here today. I thanked the mother superior for giving us this special reception, and asked her to convey our thanks to the Vatican, which seemed only right. Next we went to see the classrooms where we were treated to some music. Afterward we went out onto the roof where we could see the entire northeastern countryside, from Tivoli to Albano in one sweep. I felt sorry for the plump mother superior, for whom the climb up the stairs seemed quite difficult, and told her so. She smiled and said that she had not climbed up to the roof for many years, and that even walking about the house was something she did not do normally.

I stopped at Mr. Goad's mother's house on my way home, but it was time for her evening walk and she was not at home.

May 13
San Isidoro; the University; Franciscan Shoes

EARLY IN the morning the Franciscan priest P. Robinson and another priest (by the name of Baldwin) came together and we all went to the monastery of San Isidoro. This church has produced many monks in the Franciscan order, and the famous philosopher Duns Scotus[95] also did some of his writing here. Wadding[96] died and was buried in this church. There were portraits of these people hanging on the walls in the sermon room. There were many old books in the library, and such interesting pieces as a wood-block print of Duns Scotus and a compendium of Wadding's works. We viewed the courtyard and the monks' quarters, and took in the view from the rooftop, after which we were invited to eat in the dining hall. The fare was the usual wine and bread, and the three of us had an interesting conversation while enjoying this one aspect of monastery life. In the dining hall there was a painting of Franciscans being killed in Japan – it gave me an odd feeling to compare the past with the present.[97]

We left San Isidoro and went to Santa Maria in Aracœli. We went inside the metal railing to view the painting by Pinturicchio that we had only viewed from outside before. We also heard much of the church's past history. I had an appointment to meet Mr. Luzzatti at the university at eleven o'clock, so I bid farewell to the two priests and took my leave for the university. Once there, I went up the stone staircase of a palatial house and was shown in. A group of students gathered together and looked at me as if I were some spectacle. Mr. Luzzatti came forth and greeted me in his usual informal manner, taking my arm in his and walking me down the hall while he spoke. The man who put Italy's finances in order and who was an important minister in his country took a young foreign scholar by the arm and spoke with him. It is no wonder that the students were surprised.

I returned to the inn and after lunch I sat in the reading room, which two Franciscan novices presently entered. One of them was German and one was Belgian. Because I had been speaking with Father Robinson that morning about Franciscan shoes, they had come to measure my feet in order to make a pair for me. My foot measurements having been taken by the Franciscan novices, I recalled the story of about how Christ had washed his disciple's feet. Our foot-business finished, I served the two of them tea and we chatted. The two of them were truly unsullied men, with the naïveté of children. I fell into thought about how the spirit of Francis was alive even today in these monks who would make shoes for me, and I thought about the age when the saints were here on earth.

Before dusk Secretary Kameyama came and invited me to dine with him at a restaurant. On the rooftop with a bank of roses below us we had a truly pleasant meal while we conversed in Japanese. After the meal we went for a walk and drank beer outside of a café, where we continued our conversation at length before parting. The moon was clear on the way home.

May 14
The Sirocco; A Meal at the Academy; the Park

THE HOT sirocco has been blowing since morning. It is dry and hot and gritty, the sands coming sometimes from as far as the African Sahara. Since I first visited to Rome I have experienced the sirocco from time to time, but never to such a degree as I did today. In my room it was hot; outdoors it was also hot and the air was filled with debris. In my inn there was a woman who had very strong under-arm perfume, and the smell of it filled the hot hallways in a most unpleasant manner.

I passed the morning reading in my room. I went to the American school at noon as Monsignor Kennedy had invited me. The sky was as if it had been covered in ash. At the school everyone dined together in the dining hall, including the principal. The dining hall was long and narrow as it is at Oxford, and there were portraits of graduates lining the walls on both sides. At the far end was the principal's desk, and facing it were the student's desks all lined up along the wall. The three hundred students in their red and black uniforms filed into the dining hall and stood before their desks before the meal began. One of them stood on a platform and read grace in Latin, during which everyone was silent. When he was finished the meal began, and he continued to read from the Bible in English. I sat between the principal and the director for my meal. After the students had said a last prayer, sang a hymn, and left the dining hall, I retired to the principal's room where we took coffee and spoke of Rome and Japan, after which time I left to return home.

The wind died down a bit after five o'clock. I went out to San Vittoria[98] to see the famous stone sculpture there. The white marble statue glittered like ivory with indescribable beauty; however, I found it so beautiful as to be disagreeable.[99] The statue is of St. Teresa, who, rising to the clouds of the heavens upon her death, is greeted by an angel who points an arrow of love at her bosom. The charming countenance of the angel and the way in which it holds the arrow is just like a Greek myth – it is not a product of Christian thought. It is representative of the decadence of the late Renaissance. That, plus the other interior decorations and sculpture, were all done in an overly Baroque style. I felt that, more than being elated by the light I was filled with a totally disagreeable feeling.

I went from Mr. Goad's mother's house to Pincio Park which is situated alongside the hill. The view of the city of Rome from the hilltop was the same [as it had been before],[100] but due to the sirocco the entirety of Rome was enveloped in mist, as if smothered in smoke, and the Campagna was a complete sea of ash. The sky was entirely dark – it was unclear whether from clouds or smoke or sand – as if there were a conflagration nearby. Yet the swallows flew this way and that chirping in the sky, as they always did. Their shadows, though, were dark, and they looked as if they were black sesame seeds dancing in the sky. The evening church bells sounded like alarm bells. I do not know how many times in Rome's past there have been disturbances or riots of one sort or another. Whether it be battles between the aristocracy and the commoners, or battles within the aristocracy, or as in this summer a disturbance caused by strikes, Rome repeatedly has been a center of bloodbaths. The skies today somehow look as though they are from that realm of bloodbaths. In addition to their preternaturally strong emotions, the people of Rome are cold-blooded and selfish; inequalities are *de rigueur* and they are ambitious. Today's weather made me fretful, and I imagined that the city could explode at any moment.

Despite the weather, I was calmed somewhat by taking a walk beneath the green leaves in the park. Seeing the flowers and grasses also calmed my soul. In the park there were elegant people competing in their extravagance, lines of horse carts, ladies exhibiting themselves, and among it all an orchestra was performing and children were playing. Living as they do in houses built of nothing but stone and enduring the sirocco, I wonder if they could live at all if it were not for this sort of park. The Japanese – even the poor – all have their own gardens in their own houses – and have not had the need for this sort of park. But, as they build more and more houses closely together, the need for parks will increase. Although it is fine and well to imitate the parks, I feel it would be best not to imitate the Romans' fierce battles in the environs of Hibiya.[101]

The evening was much cooler and I felt revived. I went out for a walk to the flower garden in front of the royal palace.[102] Although enveloped in mist, the moon was bright, and the green leaves looked cool in the electric lights of the evening.

May 15
Angelico's Painting, once again; Half a Day on the Palatine

I WENT to the Vatican in the morning. I went past the people thronged in front of the Raphael painting and continued on to the Cappella di Niccolò V, which was alongside. There were many tourists here, too. But I paid them no mind and looked at the drawing by Angelico that hung on the wall of the chapel. Fra Angelico had drawn happy countenances full of faith, in pure colors, presenting the biography of Sts. Stephen and Lawrence.[103] Standing in front of the paintings I felt a deep, quiet happiness, much like that of the figures in the painting. In Rome, where, walking through the city I saw nothing but stone buildings and churches crowded together, and people whose faces exhibited wildness and avarice and disorder, I felt a longing in my heart, but here I felt as if I had come upon a pure stream. These frescoes depicted the lives of Saints, so their arrangement was complicated and active. As with other paintings by Angelico they were not solely composed of quiet figures. Perhaps for the purposes of painting such a topic, or perhaps because he had left his monastic life in Florence and come to Rome, Angelico here painted a rather lively arrangement of varied human figures. In the end, Angelico, who had seen angels and been touched by the light of God, did not draw evil men, and so in his painting the men who burn Lawrence to death [in the *Martyrdom of St. Lawrence* on the east wall of the Cappella Niccolina] and the Jews who stone Stephen [in the *Stoning of St. Stephen*, also on the east wall] do not show expressions of anger and rage. In the painting [*Condemnation of St Lawrence by the Emperor Valerian*], the countenance of the magistrate who is examining Lawrence is too tame. And the faces of the hungry beggars and those accepting alms from Lawrence [in *St Lawrence Distributing Alms*, on the north wall] do not show want, but rather a kind of gratitude. This is especially true of a blind man, who, although he cannot see, is overcome with joy and is grateful from the bottom of his heart. Angelico could not envision a sinister or vulgar countenance, and thus his brush cannot draw such expressions. Surely, in the eyes of a "*Beato*," one who has been blessed by God, even in the eyes of a beggar there is a blessed gratitude, and it was this that he expressed. A group of women who are shown sitting on the ground listening to St. Stephen's sermon [in *The Sermon of St Stephen* on the north wall] are clearly in the earthly realm, but their faces – faces that show trust, reverence, bliss and praise – are just like those of angels. In the face of Stephen's sermon, all people become angels, and I could not help but think that these women resembled the Holy Virgin. Of the eleven paintings hanging in this hall,[104] Stephen's *Sermon* and Lawrence's *Alms* best expressed the particular characteristics of Angelico's paintings. Not only were Lawrence's inquisitors [in *Condemnation of St. Lawrence by the Emperor Valerian*] portrayed with beautiful colors, their arrangement and expressions were also rich. Of particular deep interest, when viewed in contrast to the warm compassion that is seen elsewhere, is Lawrence's profile here which shows conviction and courage. The magistrate may appear too kind, but the other people in the painting are pitiful, doubtful, and perhaps a bit scornful, and it is because of this that there is merit in saying that this painting is superior to Lippi's painting in the Brancacci Chapel. It is said that the fountainhead of Renaissance art is in the frescoes of the Brancacci Chapel,[105] but *their* origin lies in the art of Angelico. Not only did Angelico come before Perugino and Raphael, it is safe to say that he was their teacher. Although the skills of those who came after Raphael did progress, and they were capable of good use of color and arrangement, they did not have Angelico's gentle spirit – that is, his pure faith. Therefore, their works turned toward ancient arts, and away from Christian art, and in the end those who came after Raphael fell into a state of corruption.

Besides the biographies of Saints Stephen and Lawrence, there were images of other saints in all four corners of the room. The saints beneath the crucifix of St. Marco carried the same air here in Rome as they displayed elsewhere. Only Thomas was entirely different, and I could not understand why his image was so inferior to the rest.[106]

Spending half a day among the paintings of Angelico revived me in some way. No matter what I looked at, all the paintings and sculptures seemed to call attention to themselves. Even here in Rome, in a tiny corner chapel of the Vatican, I felt like I was in a different realm. I returned to my inn, blind to the many people crowded around Raphael's work – even blind to the work itself. Upon my return, I wanted to write about the feelings I had that morning, of the emotion that I felt standing before the paintings, but outside there was the sound of automobiles and inside there was the sound of electric chimes. On the street people spoke in angry voices, and it was very raucous. I thought about how Rome was not the sort of place for the saintly, pure paintings of Angelico.

It was cloudy and humid, but I thought I would spend the evening on the Palatine Hill so I left the inn and headed in that direction before four o'clock. This place shows the remnants of past glory. This small village on a hilltop was the original center of Italy, and it became the place where the Roman emperors – men who made the Mediterranean their own garden pond – gathered. Here on this hill there are the remnants of an original Roman stone wall from over two thousand years ago, as well as the remains of the great imperial palaces where the emperors lived. The first emperor of the Roman Empire, Augustus, who was also the head priest of his religion, had a large, tall colonnade built in the Forum through which he could pass on his way from his palace to the Temple of Vesta, and the remnants of that colonnade are on top of the hill. Below, the ruins of the Forum stand gathered together; to the left are the ruins of the old city wall leading from the Capitoline, and to the right the ruins run from Constantine's triumphal arch to the Colosseum. This sweeping view of the world spoke wholly of the history of the Roman Empire. From the hilltop, I could see where, long ago, the Senate, temple, and government offices stood and where now the Forum ruins remain, their tile roofs side by side. This hilltop, which had been Roman headquarters since the age of the ancient kings, is where the great palaces that reached for the heavens were built; the place where the emperor exerted his authority over all the land is now in ruins. In the section that has been excavated, there is a thick, toppled wall that remains a broken bridge to the past. The view is no different from what Hadrian would have seen from his villa; here there are all manner of vicissitudes of history. The intrigue and duplicity of those who gathered power and authority to gain the position of monarch, and who expressed the authority of the emperor through their pride and arrogance, all happened at this place. This is where the banquets – the ultimate expression of the emperor's pride – took place, when the people ate and drank with abandon, and danced and sang raucously. This is where assassins lay in wait at the entrance to the colonnade to kill the emperor upon his return from abroad. Comedy, tragedy – all manner of human drama has been played out here. When I consider that, through those dramas, the fate of the world was decided, I realize that this hilltop is one of the most fascinating places on earth. While there are still walls and pillars from those palaces above ground, there are also items buried in the ground like some sort of subterranean warehouse – indeed, there is no knowing what still lays buried in the earth. Even though we know that there are undoubtedly palaces below us, now a stand of trees grows here and if one walks on it, it seems to be nothing more than a hill. When one begins to dig here, one finds that beneath the brick walls of the age of the Empire is the rubble from the age of the Republic, and beneath that is a layer from the old days of the monarchs which contains bits of building stones. This single wall speaks of all of Roman history, and shows the vicissitudes of over a thousand years. Four years ago I sat down on the altar of the temple of Jupiter,[107] next to the palace of Augustus[108] as the sun sank in the west. I looked at the steeple of St. Peter's soaring in the sunset and ruminated on the changes over the ages. When I sat in the same place today I found that the newly built Jewish synagogue[109] stood between me and St. Peter's and ruined the view. In the natural cycle of life and rebirth, as the buildings of the Roman Empire began to crumble, the Christian churches began to be built and the remnants of the past were buried. The churches that had adorned Rome for over four hundred years became things of the past and now there were things being built that competed with those churches. The synagogue before my eyes now, and the large courthouse in front of it, and also the stelae dedicated to the ancient kings that one finds all over the city were how twentieth century Romans adorned their city. When these disintegrate, I wonder what sort of things will take their place?

Next to Augustus's palace there is a garden attached to what was, until recently, a monastery.[110] Here cypress trees grow in abundance, and between them are thick patches of grass. It is not dilapidated yet, but it has become unkempt. When I came here before it was still a monastery and I was not permitted entry. A British man named Mills had bought it previously, but now it belongs to the Italian government. Below this garden is the place where the remains of

Tiberius's palace were discovered.[111] This house and its grove, too, will surely, as the years pass, fall into disrepair and be dug up from the earth as Roman ruins. Now it is overgrown, its grasses taller than a man, with roses from the old garden blooming wild in among the brush. Most of it, though, is covered over by the weeds. I sat down amidst all this and found myself enveloped in a world of grass. The occasional bird chirped among the trees, and the sound of their voices echoes off the walls of the abandoned houses. It was a silence that was more terrifying than lonely. And in the end, it held much more of interest than the ruins that had been dug from the ground.

From there, I turned toward where the hill jutted forth, to the ruins of the Circus and the Palace. Here the walls and the ceilings are still standing in many places; within the buildings there are places that are dark like cellars, but also countless rooms on the second and third stories that command a view. I wondered if one could become inextricably lost if one were careless. The roofs on these buildings were as one over a large garden, and they all looked out toward the southeast. The view was the same landscape of the Campagna as one usually sees, but I could also see emperor Caracalla's baths, which were huge and appeared like a mountain.[112] Beyond it I could just see the Via Appia running [southeast] through the fields, and the tombs[113] on either side looked like ant hills. The Romans truly loved display, so they built a mountainous building on top of the hill where people entered the city gates so that those who were entering from the southeast would see Caracalla's baths. And, although the tombs on the Via Appia appeared like anthills, when I drew close to it I found that, although they are relatively small, still they are about the size of a large house in Japan, the largest of the graves being big enough to be a fort. People would live here by the Palatine Palace, and when they died their graves would be large so that the people walking along the road would see them. This focus on the self was transmitted from the Romans to the Westerners of today, and it has begun to infect the Japanese, too. With the growth of this pride Rome suffered from strife between the classes, and in the same way Western civilization is suffering from social problems. I hope that Japan does not imitate this trend, but who knows what the future will bring?

Thoughts of Roman conceit are unpleasant, but it is truly pleasant to gaze at the countryside at sunset from the top of the ruins. The sun gradually grew dimmer, so I struck a match to light the path through the ruins and finally reaching the end I walked along the base of the hill. This is where there remain remnants of a palace wall that, it is said, was built by Romulus,[114] and soaring on top of that there were ruins from a palace of the Imperial era. The ruins of the Forum were gray in the dusk, and looked exactly like embers.

In the slums the workers returned to their homes, people walked at the roadside drinking wine, and beside them bare-footed children played while the women met at the side of the road. At first I feared walking in the slums at dusk, but now I do not fear it much. I could hear music emanating incessantly from the second floor of one of the houses. It sounded like the sort of song one hears from a woman in one of Japan's theaters. In front of the house, two dapper men stood looking up at the second story. This is one of the spectacles of the slums.

I went for a postprandial stroll to the Piazza delle Terme. Clouds covered the hazy moon on occasion, forming a rainbow around the moon. I thought how wonderful this view of the moon between the greenery on the Palatine Hill and the ruins was.

May 16
The steeple of St. Peter's; the Sistine Chapel

TODAY AGAIN it was already hot by morning. I hastened to St. Peter's and climbed the steeple tower. I climbed the leisurely stone staircase around the pillars, and came to the roof after hundreds of steps. The stone statues that look like tiny dolls from below were like large spirits now. On the [surrounding] roofs were dwellings for guards and stonemasons which had not only a water supply but also flowers decorating their windows.[115] Indeed, the rooftop was an entirely different realm. Seeing this, I could understand for the first time the ancient practice of building dwellings upon dwellings on the top of the Palatine Hill. I climbed the stone steps and entered the round steeple, then looked down upon the interior of the building from the round stairway. The throne, which I had only viewed from below before and which had seemed large, now seemed small below my feet, and all I could really see were the heads of the people below. The interior of the dome and its surrounding walls were completely covered in relief carving depicting Christ and the angels. These too, upon close viewing, seemed like immense spirits. I went up another flight and into the second arcade, from which the people in the hall below looked even smaller. Going up yet one more level to the highest place beneath the dome, I found that the relief carvings that seemed like immense spirits before appeared to be a normal size now when viewed from the first arcade. The entire hall was before my eyes, and the view was comparable to that from the top of the Eiffel Tower in Paris. However, the difference was that from the Eiffel Tower one can see far and wide, whereas here the view was limited to the height of one building. One cannot get a feeling for the size of the building by simply walking about below, but when one looks down at it from above like this one realizes just how huge a building it is. Moreover, the tall, large dome is built entirely of stone, and I was surprised that such a thick stone wall could be made. It is also worth noting that the stairway that has been built along the perimeter of the dome so that people can climb to the higher level has similarly thick stone walls. Constructing such a large dome of stone requires the support of tall stone pillars and walls that are two or three *ken* in height. The weight of it all is almost unimaginable. I climbed from the top hallway a little further up to the highest passageway in the dome, where I could go out and look down on the exterior. I had seen Rome from rooftops and hilltops, but now I looked down on the entire city from the top of the dome, from which the Campagna no longer looked flat. I could see the Alban hills and Tivoli, all part of the panorama of mountains and fields. The Vatican and its gardens were below immediately below me, and all of Rome looked like a map.[116]

I looked askance around me at the place where monarchs gazed proudly from their palaces on top of the Palatine Hill long ago. When Rome became the capital of Christendom and gained glory in the fifteenth and sixteenth centuries, they built the Vatican and established Rome as the capital of the world. That Church had now lost its authority in worldly matters, and its political power had been transferred to the Quirinal Hill that stood directly below me. But the Roman Catholic Church today still maintained power in the religious realm, and the people in the Vatican believed that the time would come when the entire world would surrender at the knees of those in the great dome. In the spring and summer of this year, when the current Pope celebrated the fiftieth anniversary of his salvation,[117] tens of thousands of pilgrims from around the world gathered at St. Peter's. From the outside, the Vatican suffered a severe blow from the French government; from the inside it was shattered by a stab by new directions in thought, but the denizens of the Vatican still have hopes for the future.[118] They believe that, as this great dome soars loftily into the sky and looks down in all directions, so too does the power of the Church extend to the heavens and envelop the earth. This faith is the same sort of faith that made the ancient Jews hold that their temple in Jerusalem was the central government of the world. It is the same as the skill that brought the Romans to rule the world. It is a tradition that has been passed on to the Roman Catholic Church. As the Jews, who have been dispersed in all directions, believe that someday Jerusalem will prevail, so too do the Roman Catholics believe that victory will come to the Church in the end, after difficulties and vicissitudes from within and without. The beliefs of these people, who normally stand beside this great church and look up at the dome, or who climb up into the dome and look down at the remnants of glory from the fifteenth and sixteenth centuries, are not unreasonable. But one must wonder whether the Roman Catholic might that looks down upon the land like the great dome is a thing of the past, or one of the future.

Within the Vatican grounds there are flower gardens and groves of trees interspersed with the roofs of churches. There is an astronomical observatory up on a hilltop and a chapel that looks like a small version of the Grotto of Our Lady of Lourdes. This is the realm of the Pope, and the Pope cannot set foot outside of the church or its grounds. All other large spaces are property of the Italian monarchy; the cardinals do not set foot within the city of Rome. Although the thought of being the head of a world religion is immense, the fact that the Pope has only this hilltop as his territory, and cannot set foot outside of it is a small thought indeed. This contradiction of big and small can be seen in various activities of the Church. A similar phenomenon took place when the wealthy and influential people of the past clung to their power and held the ideal of being extremely influential although they really only controlled many small issues.

I stood gazing all about for a long time in the hot sun, then I descended to the Cappella Sistina (Sistine Chapel) to look at the fresco there. Michelangelo's strong hand, which so skillfully painted this scene of the earth's creation and the end of the world on this large ceiling and walls, surprises me so much as to be vexing. Looking up I see God in the sky, in the likeness of man, creating all the world with one breath. It is hard to imagine one could capture with brush and paint the power that gave life to mankind with the touch of a finger. At the end of the world, in the dark, chaotic sky, Christ appears in the heavens, raises his hand and with the power of his outstretched arms he resurrects all of mankind, the good flying up into the Heavens and the sinners falling into the depths of Hell. The sky is full of human bodies as far as they eye can see, as if all the forces of nature in all directions had become humans. Michelangelo himself had heard tell of the creation of the earth and of its inevitable end, and believed these stories. Perhaps he felt that this was an important part of religious doctrine, and that is why he painted this painting. But even if this painting was not an expression of doctrine or of faith, it still shows a great power and a frightening might. When

I look at this painting, I do not think so much of the Church's doctrine of God's power of creation or Christ's judgment; rather, I am surprised by the frightening power of the artist, who with his two hands drew this frightening power. Haydn composed music about the Creation[119] and expressed through a full, rich rhythm the songs of the angels, equating the entire Creation with a beautiful spring dawn, giving one a feeling of a boundless light in the great sky. But in the creation of the world there was not such a beautiful melody; rather, there was just the omnipotent power of all creation. When Wagner wrote an opera about the end of the world and the obliteration of the gods and of mankind, the cessation of the world had a quiet flavor enveloped in pathos.[120] In Brünnhilde's last song when the waters of the Rhine rise, God and Man are united in love; hidden within it all is the theme of entering a state of nirvana. In contrast, the last judgment as depicted here gives the feeling that this is not the end of the world but rather a large change, a revolution, a rebellion – as if there were still something to come next. From Angelico on down to today painters have depicted the end of the world as a time when Good and Evil are eternally separated – the good go to a boundless heaven, where there is eternal light. But Michelangelo seems not to have thought of it in this way. In his painting he displays limitless strength and he is full of spiritual action, as if the end of the world is rather not really an end. Later painters often imitated his style, but they could only capture the forms without the spirit or strength. Michelangelo is thus without peers, a truly remarkable man.

On either side of me as I stood before this frightening painting were frescoes that were the exact opposite, showing beauty and brilliant hues. Expert Florentine artisans such as Perugino and Botticelli[121] were brought together to depict the life of Moses on the one hand, and on the opposite side the life of Christ.[122] The beauty of these paintings is of special note; the men and women have beautiful figures, their robes and arms are also of beautiful hues, and the arrangement of the human figures in the landscape is graceful and serene. They are entirely beautiful, and not gaudy like the paintings that came after Raphael. They do not have the naiveté of fourteenth century paintings, and they show skilled spirit. I wondered, as I compared these to Michelangelo's works, that there could be such a contrast in this world.

It was past noon so I parted from the Sistine Chapel and went to bid farewell to Cardinal Merry del Val of the Vatican. Today as before, there were many people coming and going. A German diplomat adorned with medals accompanied a soldier in full military attire. Their gait was strange – they put their feet forward and then their bodies bent forward also. In contrast, the high priests wore red and black stoles hanging over their coats and they threw their head and shoulders back slightly as they walked as if putting their weight into it. I saw quite a variety of sights in the short time I waited. I met with Cardinal Merry del Val and thanked him for showing me so many things, then took my leave and went back to my inn.

In the afternoon before dusk I went to the embassy and met with Mr. Kameyama, read a newspaper, then went to see the main Jesuit church[123] before going home. I ate dinner with Don Pieri, whom I had invited to dine with me.

Don Pieri went home after dinner and I had a conversation with a British man who was also staying at my inn. Eventually we came to the topic of labor disputes and the discussion went on at length. I returned to my room at close to midnight.

May 17
The Courtyard at Terme; the Great Service at St. Peter's

TODAY IS Sunday, and under continuing clear skies I went to the Museo delle Terme to sit down in the shade of the trees to enjoy the sight of the old monastery in summer.[124] A spring burbled among the cypress trees, and red and white roses set off their green color nicely. As the breeze blew, the falling spring water and the smell of the roses filled the courtyard with fragrance. Surrounding the courtyard there are arcades in which there are ancient stone statues. Sitting among them was exactly as if I were living in the ancient world. But on all sides of the arcades there have recently sprung up tall buildings that house the poor, and from their windows hangs dirty laundry. In another direction is the Finance Ministry building, whose façade is completely composed of windows and which has a military look. It is a strange contrast to put this modest courtyard with its ancient stone and classic style amidst high rise buildings for the poor and an office building that obliterates the landscape and which cost goodness knows how much money. I went into the courtyard and walked about looking at the sculpture and the flowers, the time passing without my realizing it until it was past noon.

In the afternoon there was to be a great service at St. Peter's at five o'clock, and I had received a ticket for entry to it. A French nun named Marie Madeleine had undertaken a number of projects since the revolution, and in the end she had founded an educational group.[125] She was to be elevated to the level of "Beata" (which means "blessed," and which is one level below being a "Santa") and today was the day of her beatification ceremony. The main part of the ceremony had been completed in the morning; in the afternoon the Pope would pay a visit to the place where she had become a Beata and worship her. The ceremony meant an appearance by the Pope, and so the number of pilgrims expected in attendance was thought to be forty or fifty thousand – therefore, I needed to go to the church a little bit early. I went to Don Pieri's house and the two of us entered the church at about four o'clock. The general audience of pilgrims had all entered through the front, and the hall was full of standing visitors. We had special admission tickets and thus we were able to enter through the side door. We showed our tickets countless times to the Swiss Guards[126] in their uniforms of red, yellow, and black, and to other assistants and finally we were led to our reserved seats. [Cardinal Merry del Val] was a Frenchman, so some people whose seats were in the front had given them to us. We were seated directly beside the altar, not far from the Pope's seat, in a high place that was like a reviewing stand, and that was already full of priests and nuns in black habits. Sitting there, we could see all the way from the altar to the far reviewing stand. In front of the altar were two rows of seats covered in red upholstery, and in the middle of them, facing the altar, was the Pope's chair, covered in a light brown brocade. In the far reviewing stand were the nun disciples of the day's Beata, Marie. Their families occupied the foremost stand, and behind them were the clergy in a sea of black clothing. The priest in whose parish Marie had been born wore a black robe and purple belt, and he walked here and there, making his rounds very happily and skillfully, speaking to the attendees. Besides the Swiss Guards who stood with their long spears at the side of the chairs and stools, there were also people in attendance who seemed to be attendants of the Pope and who were dressed in costumes that one only sees in the theater or in historical paintings (they had black robes and narrow pants , but I cannot remember what they are called). Above our heads the pillars of the hall were painted crimson and decorated with bits of gold on the edges. There was an electric chandelier decorated with glass balls that spanned the space from the altar to the throne. Behind the altar by the most recessed window, surrounded by angels and golden clouds, was a painting that showed the Beata receiving the angels' divine revelation (this is usually where one sees a painting of doves emerging from golden clouds). It was all more dramatic than the theater, and I thought to myself that they had decorated everything that could be decorated. In the hour that I waited I did not tire of the decorations and the conversations of the people who were coming and going. Presently five o'clock drew near. Groups of ambassadors to the Vatican from every country appeared and took their seats. The cardinals appeared by ones and twos, wearing fire-red robes and hats, and they kneeled in prayer before solemnly taking their red seats. The electric lights were turned on one by one and illuminated the whole hall and the altar. Even the painting of the Beata, deep in its alcove and hard to see, was brightly lit. Each time a light came on the sound of voices resounded through the hall. Then the people near the entrance began to lean to the side. I realized that to their left they could just get a glimpse of the Pope above the crowd. The graceful procession slowly advanced deeper into the hall. The Pope was seated on a chair on a high palanquin, and he lightly raised his right hand, giving the crowd of people his benediction (giving his blessing) as he drew close to them. As the group came closer, I could see the Pope's old visage, the red robes of the palanquin bearers, the gold uniforms of the guards on either side of them, the monks dressed in black habits to the front and rear, and finally a line of *protonotarii* (secretaries) dressed in crimson. The people in the crowd bowed their heads and kneeled, all of them making the sign of the cross on their bosoms as they paid homage to the Pope. The procession line progressed with the music, and finally they came before the viewing stand where we were sitting. Here the palanquin was lowered and the Pope stood up from his chair. He moved to a light brown chair before the altar where he sat again, facing the altar, and prayed. The Pope, clad in a pure white robe with crimson on the shoulders, stood out with a particularly divine visage in contrast to the red, black, crimson, vermilion, and gold that decorated all the people surrounding him. After the silent prayer was finished the sacristan advanced to the altar and lit incense. Next the organ played, accompanied by singers. The Pope returned to his seat, placed his arms down and turned toward the altar. The elder priest of the church intoned the name of the nun who was being beatified today, and noted her elevated holy status. Next there were songs in praise of the Beata. Again the Pope advanced to the altar, lit incense, returned to his seat, and with this the beatification ceremony by the Pope was finished. Next the priest from the hometown of the Beata came forward and offered a record of the Beata's life to the Pope and introduced the nuns from her order. The nuns showed the Pope some of the papers of the Beata that had been preserved in a holy vessel,[127] and they also offered him a bouquet of flowers. The vessel was to be returned to the nun's own church and celebrated at their altar, and so having the Pope view it indicated his approval of their worshiping this relic. Next, bound copies of the life of the Beata were presented to the various cardinals and secretaries, each its proper uniform color, and then the ceremony was completed. Accompanied by music, the Pope returned to his palanquin and the procession moved with the music, the Pope once again raising his hands to give the people his benediction. All the worshipers kneeled. As the Pope's procession grew distant on its way out of the church the music concluded and briefly the voices of the worshipers filled the hall with their chattering. I am sure that everyone was joyful at having seen the Pope, and they spoke about how splendid the ceremony was. As we rose to take our leave, we were swept up in the crowd of people who wanted to get a closer look at the altar. Later, after viewing the altar, one of the nuns from the nunnery I had visited earlier came to give her greetings. She said, "How was it? How did seeing the ceremony make you feel? It this not exactly as if Heaven had descended on this place?" I replied simply, "It was splendid." When she bid me farewell, she said, "We will see each other again in Heaven; I will pray with all my heart that we will be able to meet in Heaven." These nuns must think that for the faithful, seeing this grand ceremony was just like seeing the visage of Heaven, and that the Pope looked like God. Zola wrote that this ceremony was actually a horrid ceremony and that it was just a lot of superstition,[128] but on the other hand one cannot but sympathize with the feelings of happiness that the solemn faithful have in the joy of this ceremony. Today's scholars view the ceremonies at the main hall of Honganji as illegitimate. Similarly, collecting charity and decoration are also illegitimate. But it is not illegitimate; one cannot but sympathize with the feelings of respect that the faithful in Kaga had for the Buddha when he attained enlightenment.[129] Although Zola wrote that ceremonies such as the one that was held today were bad political maneuvering to get money out of pure avarice, there is an element of untruth in what he wrote. Moreover, even if the ceremony *is* done to collect money, at the same time it also plays an important role in educating and expressing compassion to those who have dedicated themselves to the religion. It is a way of praising those who set the example of doing deeds through faith. It is a commendable act in the world of man that gives a ceremonial form to the idea that God blesses those below from on high. This ceremony, in which the spirit of a nun is praised through the reverence of Pope is the same as the Japanese emperor making an imperial visit to the Yasukuni Shrine.[130]

The crowd broke up and I was finally able to exit the main doors, where I found a vast sea of humanity from the cobblestones in front of the church all the way into the city blocks beyond. I went to Don Pieri's house to rest for a while, but then on the way home there was not a horse cart or tram car to be found. I walked all the way back to my inn in the hot sun that struck me from the side as it blazed in the western sky.

I went to visit Mr. Goad's mother after my dinner, and this time she was in. We spoke of Assisi, of future travels, and also about Mr. Goad coming to Rome. She told me how happy he would be to see me again, and about how he wrote of me in each letter, and how overjoyed he had been when we had met unexpectedly in Assisi – the conversation made me feel as if I had known her for ten years. She gave me a copy of a play that Mr. Goad has written and I went home.[131]

May 18
Packing my bags; Bidding Farewell

I PACKED my bags in the morning; I'm always unpacking and packing... I wonder how many times I will do the same thing? Mankind owns material possessions, manages and disposes of them as he wishes, and leaves them behind when he dies – the process of packing and unpacking is the same.

In the afternoon I went to bid farewell to Miss Dove. The Landrums were also there and I spoke briefly with them, after which I went to St. Antonio's church. A disciple in that church, named Richard, had taken a measurement of my feet to make me a pair of Franciscan shoes, and I had gone to St. Antonio's to pick them up. Other disciples also came out to greet me, and I tried on the shoes. I said, "While we are at it, can you also make the robe and the rope belt?" to which he replied, "Would you not join our ranks and become a Franciscan?" all of which made me admire the constant light-heartedness of the Franciscans. The spirit of the Saint still lives today. When I was among those monks I felt exactly as if I were among Zen monks in Japan. Each of the monks told me where their home-towns were, and what the names of the priests in the churches there were, and said that if I went there I should make sure to go to the local church – they wrote down the locations of many churches for me. They would not take payment for the shoes and so I made an offering at the church and bid them all farewell and returned to my inn.

I invited Mr. Kameyama and Mr. Costa to dinner and we ate together. The three of us spoke of music, and after our meal we went to a café on the boulevard and stayed there past eleven o'clock in the cool outdoors, the three of us chatting, until we bid our farewells and went our separate ways. This was my final night in Rome.

Addendum

IN THIS Roman diary I wrote two or three times that the Pope never left his residence, but afterwards there was a great change in that the Pope's carriage ventured out of the Vatican. Pope Pius X was extremely moved by the news of a large earthquake in southern Italy this past January, and although it was said that he would go so far as to visit the disaster area, he was old and could not travel so far. However, he did visit the disaster victims in a Roman hospital. This was an important event for the Church – it was the first time in over forty years that the "Prisoner of the Vatican" had set foot on the Roman soil that was ruled by a monarchy. Whether this means that the papacy and the government will improve their relations is debatable, but at the very least it shows that the Vatican is not entirely composed of narrow-minded people. If this results in the Pope and the people becoming more intimate, it will be a happy occasion for both the Italian people and the Church.

April, 1909

CHAPTER SEVEN

FROM ROME TO VENICE

CLOCK TOWER, ST. MARK'S, AND DOGES' PALACE,
PIAZZETTA DI SAN MARCO, VENICE, ITALY

May 19
The Train Trip Leaving Rome

TODAY I left Rome and came here to Ravenna.

The train departed Rome after noon. In the end, I could not avoid leaving the Eternal City. Out of the city I headed to the vast Campagna. The bright sun shone on the green of the grass and the dark red of the flowers, making the fields and the mountains the perfect summer landscape. It was hot for May, but I felt compassion for how hot June would be. I followed the same route I had followed a fortnight earlier on my way to Forigno. The groves were thicker with trees; the birches and poplars that had been but sprouts before were now covered with dark green leaves.

I could see Monte Subasio as we drew close to Forigno. I could not see Assisi, but I could see the neighboring town of Spello which looked like a fortress on the hill. From Forigno we followed a new route, the train climbing the hill as it ran along the river valley. A cool breeze blew from the mountains, making me forget the Roman heat entirely and giving me a feeling of revival. At a place called Nocera they sold natural mineral water that came from the mountains. I had forgotten the heat, and slaked my thirst with the pure waters of Umbria, all of which cleansed my spirit. As I thought of Rome I could feel the horrid heat deep within me.

We passed through mountain pass after mountain pass. The fields below were beautiful brocades and the new leaves on the oak trees looked as cool as drops of water. We passed through a place called Fabriano which was a castle town nestled between the mountains and surrounded on all sides with highlands where the air was pure and the landscape quite appealing. Here two British women got off the train to take tea and, as a result of being a little late, they missed getting back on. I felt sorry for them, but there was nothing I could do to help. It would have been nice if they had held the train just a little longer, but in rule-based Italy they have not the slightest notion of such kindness. Even though the time is not properly set and the train does not usually run according to schedule, they still refuse to stop a train that has just set off. This is the result of the lazy being bound by rules.

From Fabriano on the mulberry trees grew thick. At the foot of the mountains the mulberry buds were a solid green, interrupted by the red clover flowers that bloomed like flames. The fields gradually opened up before us and the train descended out of the mountains, down to the coastal town of Falconara at about half past six. This is where I would change trains. The evening sky was slightly cloudy, and the surface of the sea was like a mirror that reflected the reds and purples. The water's surface, perhaps due to the clouds or the mist, was indistinguishable from the sky, the two of them blending into the same overcast color. And on that quiet surface floated boats that could not move despite having their sails raised. I was reminded of the summer seascape on the Indian Ocean, and I began then to think of the joys of the route home by sea. The train ran along the coastline. The port of Ancona seemed to float on top of the sea peacefully, and ahead of us the evening sun dyed the clouds and the water a crimson color.

An old man in the same car as I insisted on conversing with me. He spoke of the war with Russia,[1] and then asked me if I had not fought in the war against China;[2] he asked me if my father was still alive, and if so what he was doing – it was exactly like a police interrogation. Next he asked me how the weather was in Japan, whether we had many mulberry fields, if there was an import tax on wine and rice and if so how much it was, how much rice Japan produced, etc. He was vexing, but he seemed like a nice old man and so I answered his questions. In the end he said that Japan was great. The sun had dimmed considerably and we reached a place called Pesaro as darkness fell. The old man told me that this was the birthplace of the musician Rossini. He said that he would get off here, and bid me farewell cheerfully. Just as I thought it was over and done with, a young man who had overheard our conversation started it up again. Presently it was pitch dark outside, with fireflies flitting about and frogs croaking. I watched the fireflies and recalled my trip to Hakone the previous year, finding an urge to go there again.

I changed trains again at a place called Rimini, and had to wait there an hour. In the meantime, I sent postcards to various people. Rimini became famous in Dante's poem as the place where the tragedy of Paolo and Francesca took place.[3] Today it has a swimming area and is lively in the summer.

The train for Ravenna left in the dead of night. The young man from before sat briefly in the same car and chatted with me, but soon the two of us both fell asleep. I awoke when we arrived in Ravenna. Outside of the station I found a horse cart from the Grand Hotel Byron,[4] but there were no others because all the other hotels were full. Moreover, the cart from the Byron had come to meet a guest who had made a reservation, and only if that person did not appear would they have a vacant room. I stood before the station, wondering whether the guest would come. It was half past eleven o'clock and a cool evening breeze blew. The gas lights shone prettily through the green trees. I decided that, should the guest for the Byron appear, I would spend the night sleeping on the bench in front of the station. I waited a while, but the guest did not come and so finally the horse cart driver let me on and after passing through the quiet city streets we arrived at the hotel.

When I could not find an inn in Rome it had been daytime and I thought that something would work out so I was not concerned. When I think back on it, I realize that if it had been the middle of the night I am sure it would have inconvenienced me not a little. And today, indeed, I was inconvenienced. However, deciding that a rustic inn would be just fine, I was calm and did not feel put out in the least. That I was able to have such a good feeling was certainly due to the influence of Francis. Still, I wondered how it would have been had I been in the cold of winter – perhaps someday I will have the opportunity to experience such a situation.

The inn was an old palace, and I was shown to a splendid room on the second floor, off a large balcony. What I was sure would be a rustic inn turned out to be a palace in which I could sleep, and a spectacular one at that. Standing on the balcony and looking out I could see beautiful gaslights shining through the leaves of the trees. The night was quiet, with no other sound than the bells of the neighboring Francesco Church chiming on the hour.

May 20
The Churches of Ravenna; Ferrara

WHEN I arose in the morning a cool breeze blew through the trees and felt good to me. I took my tea at a table that had been placed in the garden. This was an entirely different world from Rome.

I went to S. Francesco which was directly beside the hotel, and visited Dante's tomb next to that. There was no caretaker so I was not able to enter and instead looked from outside. Nonetheless, when I thought about the fact that the remains of such a great poet were lain in this place now it seemed all the more precious and sacred. In the *duomo*[5] there were fourteenth century sculptures and some Byzantine mosaics. The mosaics expressed through animals the concepts of faith and immortality. The mosaics produced in that era have many animals in them, and I have seen many pieces in southern France and Italy that use animals or angels to represent the four Evangelists. Here, sheep were Charity, peacocks (ostriches?) were Immortality, deer were the Gospel, doves were the Holy Ghost, the *anatra* bird (?)[6] was Faith, and fish were Christ. To this day I still do not know why it has come to be this way. On the outside of the church there was an octagonal baptistery which, like the baptistery at Laterano, was very old.[7] The mosaics on the walls and ceiling were quite interesting; on the top of the ceiling was Christ's baptism, and below that were various saints, all done in the typical style with large, child-like eyes beautifully laid in stone.[8]

Next I went to the church of S. Vitale. This too was octagonal, its altar set on the outer side of the octagon and with the same stone mosaics on its ceiling. This mosaic showed the life of Moses and emperor Maximilian,[9] and also had some landscapes and portraits, all of which made for a complicated work. To the side of the church was the mausoleum of the fifteenth century queen Placidia, and this too was placed inside a chapel covered with a mosaic. The ceiling was blue with sparkling stars, and the walls shows Christ shepparding sheep, and Lawrence protecting the four Evangelists while he burned other heretical works;[10] in the darkness of the church the mosaics sparkled beautifully. Today's experience took me back fourteen or fifteen hundred years, as I looked solely at Byzantine mosaics.

On the way to the church of S. Giovanni I entered another church but it was nothing noteworthy. I merely made my way through lonely streets of old houses, reflecting that Dante probably walked along here, too, all of which gave me the feeling that I had left the twentieth century. After having the hot sun beat down on me I went into the church of Giovanni.[11] It was ever so slightly cool. On the ceiling Giotto had painted a picture of the four Evangelists.[12] Others later had added their own ruinous colors to the painting, but Giotto's arrangement could still be seen through it all. On the one hand, Giotto had long drawn movement with a kind of dramatic air, but here on the decoration of this ceiling he also showed his skill as an architect. After looking at many carvings and then looking at this style of decoration, I can clearly see that Giotto's paintings were a departure from Byzantine art. Beside this church there is a hospital that was once a monastery.[13] In front of it is a piazza where a monument depicts Dante donning a suit of armor and placing a crown of laurel on the head of a dying soldier.[14] It is as if, with the changes in the world, Dante is exhausting all effort for the army.

I went to take a look a little way outside the city walls, but there was nothing but mulberry fields so the scenery was nothing of note. I returned to the city and went to look at the sad remains of the façade of Emperor Theodoric's palace.[15] Next I went to see the mosaic on the wall of the church of S. Apollinari, which depicted the glory days of the palace. About nine hundred years earlier, when Ravenna was next to the sea, Theodoric built his palace here and flaunted his pride. That palace is now in ruins and the image of its past can be seen on the church walls. Lined up with the palace frescoes on what became the wall above the pillars is a solid surface of mosaic. In one scene is a line of saints before Christ; in another scene is a line of girls before the Holy Virgin, and above the two is the life of Christ.[16] The skill shown in the mosaic is more advanced than that of the fifth century, and the paintings are quite well done, but yet they have the naiveté of mosaics, with their special characteristic of childlike features. In Japan we cannot imagine the appeal of mosaics. How odd it was that the extravagance of ancient Rome, which required a certain fortitude in developing the skill [necessary to make mosaics] was passed on to the Christian tradition.

I returned to my hotel and ate lunch. I went to my palatial room and wrote in my diary as I gazed at the garden. Presently it was time to leave for the train. I walked along the now hot road which had afforded a breeze the night before when I arrived. But it was cool in the shade of the trees, and there were even people napping there. At three o'clock the train left, headed north. Directly next to the road the tomb of Theodoric stood like a little fortress. Outside the moving train were first flat fields filled with grape vines, next poplar trees interspersed with mulberries, then wheat fields, hemp fields – the whole world shone green in the strong light, and the hemp leaves were especially beautiful. These flat fields were formed from silt from the Reno and the Po rivers, and were Italy's largest and most fertile fields. According to some of my fellow passengers, there had been a strike of laborers the year before and all the fields had become one sea of weeds. This year near Parma the same sort of disturbance was starting up. The strikes were moving from manufacturing to agriculture.

We arrived at Ferrara at six o'clock. We had to wait for an hour and a half [before the next train left], so I went into the city to sight-see. Beyond the green trees of the park I could see four turrets. A moat surrounded the building on all four sides; this was where the warlords of Ferrara flaunted their power, the Castle of Este.[17] Inside the castle there were various remnants of the drama.[18] In all countries, warlord castles necessarily have seen the tragedy of massacre.[19] Not far from the castle was the *duomo* of the city.[20] On the façade, which was strange in that it had three triangles on top of each other, was a Romanesque sculpture.[21] Inside the church the artwork was all Renaissance – the sculpture, from the late Renaissance, was beautifully life-like.[22] I rested in front of the church and watched the business of the town, then turned to look at the church again. There were some mustachioed and dapper passers-by. The odd building façade and the houses nearby brought visions of a world seven or eight centuries previous, and I was put in mind of what the town was like at the heyday of the House of Este.

I returned to the front of the station, ate some pasta[23] for dinner and waited for the train. It was a little late, and left before eight o'clock, headed northward. Presently we crossed the wide Po River. More than a month after I had crossed this river heading southward, I now crossed it again, this time heading north. As this hot day came to its end, the moonlight shone red on the river. We continued north, across the plains. The gaslights of the village of Monselice at the foot of a little mountain twinkled in the night against the dark shadow of the mountain. It was here that the train broke down and was further delayed, causing our arrival in Padua to be close to ten o'clock. There were many people who sat drinking coffee or wine at open-air tables in the piazza in front of a hotel.

May 21, Morning
S. Antonio; Madonna dell' Arena

I SPENT the morning walking through Padua looking at churches. I went past the place that I had seen yesterday. The city blocks were made of colonnades, the same as in Bologna. To the south there was a park with a horse-racing track.[24] One of the palatial houses there was once the horse-racing office. On the front there was a statue of Giotto and one of Dante[25] – I found it odd indeed that the painter and poet had become overseers of a horse track. In the other direction was the church of S. Giustina,[26] whose face was solid brick piled up in such a way as to be quite barren, but inside there were large marble pillars. It was quite pleasant to sit all alone in the middle of the church, surrounded by the white stone and the quietude of early morning. After winding through the narrow streets I came upon a large piazza above which soared the church of S. Antonio with its round steeples layered one on top of the other.[27] The walls were Gothic, but the steeples were done in an Arabian style. I looked up at the large walls and tall steeples in their odd arrangement, and felt that although they were not impressive they were vast.[28] I went in to get a view from below. The inside of the domed steeple had a round ceiling, with what looked like a round hole at the top. Long ago there had been a fresco that extended all across the wall, covered with gold and azure hues, but at some point it was painted white. Later the white was removed and the colors of the old painting were restored.

This church of S. Antonio was built for Francis's disciple, Antonio. People worshipped Antonio as a living god because in his lifetime a number of miracles occurred. The church was built over his grave, and to this day there are many pilgrims who come here. There are many paintings in the church of Antonio holding a baby Jesus, and the people pray for all sorts of things. His sarcophagus is in a small chapel on one side of the church[29] where many candles were lit and where a monk dressed in red robes performed a service for the many worshipers in attendance. I am sure that they were each and every one of them praying for what they desired.

In the chapel opposite of Antonio's tomb there is a painting of the crucifixion on three panels done by the painter Altichiero of Verona.[30] To the side there is a painting of the life of Saint Giacomo (St. James). Altichiero was of the same generation as Angelico, but this was the first time I had ever seen his work. It had a Lorenzetti-like air that postdated Giotto, and brushwork that gave a feeling of great depth. His hues were not as beautiful as those of Angelico, but overall they were still truly good, and softer than those of Giotto. The face of the model saint had an elegant power within it, like that of Martini's saint in Assisi. How sad that not many other works of his survive, and so he is relatively unknown.

On the altar in the main hall was a bronze sculpture of the Holy Virgin and four saints by the famous Donatello,[31] and below were depicted child angels in bronze relief. The figure of the Holy Virgin appears somehow old-fashioned; Antonio, carrying flowers, strikes a kind figure, and Francis seems as if he is dedicating himself to the cross he carries. Although these figures lacked strength, they were still beautiful. Francis's countenance was not that of the compassionate saint, but rather that of one shedding tears out of reverent faith. All of Donatello's works are gentle and beautiful, their lines are elegant, and that is why people like them. They are comparable to the sculpture of the Kamakura period in Japan.

There is a chapel behind the main hall that has modern paintings, and behind Antonio's tomb there is a relief stone carving of his life.[32]

I left the church and turned toward the façade where I could look at the towers from the side. I wish I could ask the faithful of Antonio who come here on their pilgrimages how they feel when they look at this strange church. In front of the church is a statue by Donatello of a great general of Venice riding a horse.[33] It looks like the equestrian statue on the Capitoline Hill, but patterned in a later style.[34] The form of the general, mounted proudly on the horse, has clean lines and speaks of the work of Donatello. When I look at this statue and think of the statue of Kusunoki in Japan, I find that there is something displeasing about it all.[35] However, Japan is not the only country that should be ashamed of the fact that it has no good statues of its early monarchs that were made recently, despite the availability of such models as these in Italy.

Directly next to the church there is a museum which has been made out of an old church school.[36] It has old stone stelae from the Roman era, and old sarcophagi and stone carvings, plus works by various artists associated with Padua.[37]

In the afternoon I went to see the paintings by Giotto at the church of Madonna dell' Arena. The church sits inside of the remains of an old Roman stone reviewing stand. It looks unremarkable from outside, but in this small church there is a famous work by Giotto on the wall, one that has become the most famous work in Padua.[38] The painting is of the life of Christ, and the brushwork is the same as what I saw in Assisi, much as the content of the painting is also similar. But this painting's style of light was pleasant to look at and I found the different approach interesting. To wit, the people were well arranged and their postures showed movement, their countenances had lively expressions and the pure colors were beautiful without having the least bit of darkness in them. It was a harmonious composition. Compared to other works by Giotto, it was better. When I had seen this work in a photograph, the image of Christ receiving a kiss [in *The Arrest of Christ (Kiss of Judas)*] looked somehow troubled and I had wondered about that, but now, looking at the painting in person, it has no such quality. It is not as stately and dignified as the fresco by Angelico in S. Marco, which shows a submissive Christ, but it is distinct from the work of other painters in that it does not show agony but rather shows fully a sense of submission and tenacity in Christ's face. There were other scenes too numerous to recount entirely here – the expressions of the people at the site of Lazarus's resurrection; the floating figure of Christ, pointing up at the heavens as he ascends to them; the dignity of Christ at the final judgment, etc.

Three hours passed without my realizing it and it came time for the building to close. I went to the church of Eremitani next door and took a brief look at the frescoes by Mantegna. Mantegna is known for his reserved nature and arrangement, but his colors were not as pure as Giotto's.[39] My eyes, after having looked at Giotto's works, were not interested in others, so I took but a glance at this work then left to return to my inn.

The train left Padua at six o'clock, headed in a straight line north on the Po River plain.

⌣ CHAPTER EIGHT ⌣

FAREWELL TO ITALY;
TWO DAYS IN VENICE

INTERIOR OF ST. MARK'S, VENICE, ITALY

May 21, Evening
Arrival in Venice

I ARRIVED in Venice, a place that I had long held in my imagination as a world
of dreams but which had now become a reality. Although I knew it was reality, it still looked like a world of dreams and I felt as if I had entered a Dragon
Palace.[1]

After I had left Padua the sun had sunk in the west and was now coming
directly into the window making me hot and I found even my breathing was
uncomfortable. I was able to persevere, though, when I thought about the fact
that I would be in Venice by nightfall. The train stopped briefly in Mestre. A
little further on we would come to the sea and Venice would be on the opposite
shore. This was a place where the city sat in the middle of the sea, where palaces
sat on waterways, where one could hear gondoliers singing. Although I had read
of it in poetry and seen it in paintings, I still had all kinds of images of it in my
imagination. We would be there in ten or twenty minutes! Oh how long this five
or ten minute stop was!

The train began to move. The fields became paddies. I could see something
that looked like a coastal dike up ahead, and a city floating on the surface of the
water in the distance. On the water, just as I had seen in Turner's paintings,[2]
there were many yellow sails flying. I could see the windows of the houses along
the waterfront. The train arrived at the station. I collected my luggage, called out
for the man from the hotel, and soon boarded a gondola that was waiting at the
river's edge. I was not stepping foot into Venice from the train, but rather, I was
floating on the water.

The gondola was painted a pure black with black tassels hanging from it;
only the very tip of it that projected forward was polished metal and it glittered
brightly in the sun, reflected on the water. The boat glided forward quietly in
the water with only the sound of the oars to accompany it, which was very different from riding in a horse cart with the clattering sound of the cobblestones
beneath. The scenery was cool and in the light of dusk the red and blue images
of many houses were reflected on the surface of the water. In an instant I had
left the train and entered a different world of boats. We entered a side canal off

of the main one and the boat entered what seemed like the wrong route, as on both sides were doorways and stone steps, all of houses that soared up above the water. As we passed along the route the gondolier would make a sound like a lowing steer at each bend, and he moved his oar in rhythm with the sound. At what seemed to be houses of the wealthy, the main gates had family crests painted on them. Lacquered pillars were lined up on the water where one could tie up a boat, then climb the stairs into the house. In front of one of these houses we went through a narrow channel between walls, and then soon were out on the Grand Canal again. That area with houses on either side was where the notable families had lived since antiquity. A boat came into view which was rowed by oarsmen wearing white clothes with light yellow belts. My gondolier pointed to it and told me that that was a boat owned by a private family, and that the passenger was lord or lady such-and-such. A little distance ahead over the large river I could see the roofed Rialto stone bridge.[3] The colors of the curtains and walls of the houses mingled reflected in the water, and each arrangement of colors produced an interesting effect. We left the Grand Canal and went into a smaller one. When we returned to the Grand Canal again our objective, the inn, was along the bank. The gondolier called out in a strange voice and a boy came out and put down a gangplank covered in red damask across from the stone steps to the boat. I climbed onto it and went directly from the water to the sitting room of the inn. I felt in no way like I had made land, but rather felt like I had entered the sea palace of a Dragon King.

My room was settled upon and I went to the bathroom, having ordered a bath straight away. Words cannot describe how I felt in the solid white bathroom, washing away and the dirt and grime I had collected since Rome.

I got out of the water and went to have my meal. Everyone in the dining room was dressed in formal black. It had grown dark outside and the lights from the passing boats glittered in the night. After my meal I went out on the veranda, which was surrounded by stone blocks. Beneath me the water lapped at the floor and the occasional gondola would come, drawing up to the stone stairs. The shape of the gondolas is odd; both the bow and the stern are raised. The bowsprit is made in the shape of a bird's head and looks like a sword. There is also a golden metal piece that looks like a saw that stands up, and that piece shines darkly and brightly as the boat floats softly on the water. A field of lights float over the water, and in the distance, from boats with red and green lanterns, one can hear the songs of the gondoliers. The harmony of the cool soprano[4] and the strong tenor hits the water and gives one the feeling of hearing music from another realm. All of it seems to come from a world separate from this one. The palaces along the canal, the shape of the gondolas, the songs on the water – the sights that one usually sees in the theater or in a painting are here in reality before one's eyes, yet one still does not think that they are of this world. A dream that is not a dream; a reality that is not a reality. How is it that such a place can exist?

For a while I stood staring, taking in the sight, but finally I decided that I should set my feet down in Venice and so I went to see the night scene at the Piazza San Marco in the city center, leaving through the back door of the inn. Here there was a cobblestone road. I passed through the narrow streets lined with various shops selling paintings and glassworks, and came out upon the Piazza San Marco. The wide plaza is lined on three sides with palatial colonnades built of white stone that shine brightly even in the evening. Ahead of me the gaslights of the church of San Marco shone with golden hues. This, too, was another realm. On top of the cobblestones, which had not a grain of sand or a speck of dust on them, there were pedestrians – some stood still, some walked along (but not hurriedly), as if they had not a care in the world. There was not a horse cart to be seen in the city. There is no other word for it than uncanny.

I went to the coast from the church. The old palace of the Doge (the "Doge" was the president of the city) shone bluish-white with gaslight. Above the line of columns that were erected one next to the other, the heavy, palatial building stood spectacularly in the night. On the shore there was a concert underway, with some of the audience sitting in chairs and others milling about on the cobblestones. I crossed the canal on a tall, bow-shaped bridge between the streets. There were also many people who were listening to the music while enjoying the cool breeze afforded by the white marble columns of the bridges. If one were staging a play about the garden of a Dragon Palace, one would need to use a setting such as this.

I passed beside the church of San Marco on my way home. A lantern light came from a recess high in the wall. There was probably a picture there, too, of the Holy Virgin. It made me think about looking at the lantern of the altar at Itsukushima, which, similar to the Dragon Palaces, is close to the sea. There, one gets a feeling of mystery emanating from its deep inner reaches. This lantern of the Holy Virgin was faint, but along with its surroundings it expressed a sense of present joy.

I returned to my inn and went back to the veranda. It was the same seascape with song, even though the sun had set. The people of Venice are a people of pleasure, and this is a place of pleasure. Five or six hundred years ago aristocratic families made this into a powerful republic. It was this aquatic Dragon's Palace that spread its commercial might throughout the Mediterranean, extending its military hand, and enjoying the wealth of conquered territories, and they did it all from this locale. Using those they had conquered as slave labor, they built palaces for their nobility, and churches and steeples.[5] They used the slaves for their pleasure and work, and they had slaves row their extravagant ships. The people here, both the nobility and the commoners, lived lives that pursued happiness in this world, that maximized pride day after day, and declared one must get all the enjoyment one possibly can out of each day. That air remains today and it is why the nobility of old fell in their circumstance. Even if the palatial pillars fall, the gondolas are still painted black[6] and glitter with gold decorations, and the songs of the gondoliers can still be heard both on land and at sea. In the evening almost the entire city goes to play on ships along the coast. This sort of Dragon Palace, which is like something out of a poem or a painting, is the result of greedy competition, and has become a marketplace of pleasure and pride.

Although it too is the product of a similar pride, Itsukushima, built by Kiyomori,[7] has an entirely different flavor to it. This shrine is located at the foot of mountain and on the edge of the water, linked together by a hundred and eight colonnades with low roofs around the main worship hall. It has a quiet air about it, as if the entire shrine went about its business floating on the water. In the case of Venice (which has palaces with stone stairs and stone floors built in the sea, and tall tile roofs lined up next to one another with many windows below), looking down on the water, what we have are the vestiges of human attachment and pride. This is what remains when mankind is left to pursue pleasure freely. Itsukushima is the result of people taking as much prestige as they can out of the *demimonde* and trying to get as close as possible to the ideal of transcending this world.

May 22
The Venetian School of Painting; Ticiano;
The Church of San Marco;
The Lido; Sunset on the Sea

I BOARDED a boat after breakfast and went by canal to the Accademia.[8] This gallery was where the lauded paintings of the Venetian school were collected, and they showed the kernels of the early art of the seventeenth century.

First I viewed the most famous painter of the Venetian school, Ticiano's *Ascension of the Holy Virgin*.[9] At the top a green sleeved, red robed Holy Virgin floats up toward the clouds into the heavens, the angels surrounding her. At the bottom of the painting are amazed onlookers witnessing this miracle. This painting has a beauty that comprises the contrast between heaven and earth, the composition of beautiful hues, the peace of the clouds, and the folds of the clothing. This is clearly the work of the greatest member of the Venetian school. It is no wonder that Ticiano is loved by many people. But, after looking, I found myself more and more dissatisfied. The figure of the Holy Virgin ascending to heaven is bent at the waist, making her body seem short and consequently she looks not like a god rising into the sky so much as she looks like an earthbound woman dancing. Her arms are across her chest in a sign of reverence and thanks, but her face simply looks bewildered. Ticiano's painting does not have the flawless quality of Angelico's Holy Virgin's, nor does it show any of the faithful trust of the Holy Virgin at the Immaculate Conception in Murillo's painting.[10] In both the seventeenth century and today, there are such famous beauties in Venice who are thought to suddenly rise up into the clouds and when they commence this ascent it is thought that their expressions are just like the expression in this painting. It is all fine and well that they ascend to heaven, but one wonders whether they are surprised because they still have regrets rooted in the pleasures of life on earth. Ticiano did not paint the Holy Virgin; rather, he applied the story of Mary's ascension to the beauties of Venice. Then he made a painting of famous beauties that had beautiful hues and adorable angels flying in colorful clouds.

Next I viewed Paolo Veronese's[11] greatest work, Christ's Last Supper.[12] In this painting, the table is set in a palatial hallway between marble columns and Christ, with a halo, sits in the center. Surrounding him are members of the Venetian nobility of that age.[13] There is a cardinal dressed in red, fat noblemen, a thin soldier, and a black slave among them – even a dog takes part in the feast. The view between the pillars is exactly that of the contemporary Venice, and the setting sun in the sky behind Christ shines brightly in the sky. The scene is the same as what one would see at a high-class banquet in Venice at the time, from the palace structure to the guest's clothes, to the landscape and other buildings, right down to the meal laid out on the table and the cups and plates upon which it is placed. The colors are beautiful and the composition is skillful. If one goes to the doorway to the next room and looks at this large fresco from the side it is almost like a panorama. Christ is in the center, but that is simply to have a figure in the middle – any figure would have sufficed. That is to say, it is best to view this as a popular painting to which portraits of the nobility of the time have been added. Surely Christ, invited and treated to this feast, was put to great pains by it.[14]

Besides this painting, there were many works by disciples of Ticiano and his contemporaries. Among them, many had religious subjects, such the site of Christ's death, the Annunciation, the Coronation, etc. But not any of them were painted to express the artists' faith; they were simply beautiful works that met the tastes of the nobility and were done for that purpose, borrowing religion for subject matter. It may be impossible to paint a purely popular painting or landscape completely divorced from religion. One would have to depict the cows and pigs in the fields and mountains gamboling about, and the bystanders staring on indifferently after Christ was taken down from the cross and the people wept. Or depict dogs and mounted soldiers on a mountain road, loitering about after St. Francis received the stigmata – after his body took on the injuries of crucifixion. It would mean painting entirely for the purpose of joining colors together in a pleasing and beautiful way, without any other care. In Paolo Vernese's famous painting of the Annunciation, God comes flying out of the clouds and the archangel Gabriel rides a cloud down from the heavens, dancing as he descends. In contrast, Mary is strangely bent at the waist as if she is waiting pensively for something – she looks exactly like an acrobat. The painting is of nothing more than the noble sons and daughters of seventeenth century Venice performing their own acrobatics, taking on the name and form of the Holy Virgin. The Venetians are half-breeds in the realm of painting. The palette and the layout are a compromise on the palettes and layouts of Botticelli and Raphael, and simply pandered to the tastes of the nobility of the time. Making a complete change from this, the Dutch school of popular painting and landscapes is distanced from religion but the Venetian school was unable to create only popular paintings and landscapes in this way, so half of what they made were old-fashioned paintings of religious themes. In truth, this was none other than a greedy bid for power on the part of the Venetian nobility of the time, or a reflection of the artist's coquettish nature toward the churches and priesthood of the time.

Nonetheless, the Venetian school set the stage for the Dutch school, and one should not lose sight of the fact that they did develop special landscape characteristics in their popular paintings. In such paintings as Ticiano's depiction of the Holy Virgin in childhood, there is, at the bottom of the fresco, a splendid popular painting and a portrait, and even without the mountains in the background it is a very good landscape. But Ticiano's skill only progressed to this point; he never achieved the pure ideal of freely depicted man and nature. He has the same brushwork as Raphael and Pinturicchio, and his arrangement of colors is similar, but his works are entirely leaden, and leave one with a bad taste in one's mouth. Although he had tired of the church and the priesthood as subjects, still he could not break his bonds with them. He did not have the pure spirit he needed to return to the old subject of faith, and he lacked the courage he needed to strike out on his own to find his own voice. The result of his borrowing his style from various great masters and pandering to the tastes of the aristocracy was the creation of this half-breed. People are enchanted by his palette and praise Ticiano, but a half-breed is a half-breed no matter what. I cannot understand myself why everyone down to Ruskin[15] praises Ticiano.

There is only one Ticiano painting of note in this hall. In it, two or three figures stand in the dim evening light, embracing a deceased figure and mourning.[16] I am sure that the painting was supposed to be of the moment after Christ's death, but no one cares about that. Rather, it expresses the grief of survivors after a death against a wonderful background. Ticiano, who lived to the age of one hundred and who, in his lifetime, painted nothing but pretty paintings, was able, when his end was near, to leave behind this notable, wonderful painting as his legacy. One could even say that this one painting is the confession of his life. What must the Venetian nobility – those who had Ticiano paint so many pictures, who were proud of their beauty, who decorated the churches they built, who were so proud of their sitting rooms – have thought when they saw the master's last confessional painting? And the people today, who are so drawn to the beautiful colors of Ticiano's paintings, do they not realize the impermanence and inevitable decay of all life when they see this painting? There are still many Europeans who, clinging to their present reality, are unable to see clearly.

After noontime I left the hall and this time returned to my room by a land route. I went through the narrow winding streets and across tall bridges to rest at my inn. Afterwards, I went to the church of San Marco. The building is a loud mixture of Gothic and Eastern styles, and the façade is heavily decorated with gilt mosaics – it looks more like a reception hall than a church. Inside the pillars, dome, and archways come together in a complex of intersections and above, as far as the eye can see all around are golden mosaics. The gold glitters in the dim light and the sight of the arches and dome covered in stone paintings is beyond even what one sees at the most colorful Japanese halls.[17] This is what remains of the extreme pride of all the Venetian nobility gathered together in this one place at the height of Venice's glory. The entrance to the altar has a stone screen with stone pillars and the stone staircase of the entrance is made of layered stone crescent shapes. The interior of the altar is dark and elegant. I had once seen a picture of a wedding ceremony held in this church. The elegantly dressed newlyweds descended this stone staircase, and below them were many noble guests who waited to receive them while at the altar there were many people dressed in brocade. Now it looks like the backdrop in a theater; I wonder how many such grand ceremonies have taken place in this church? That is to say, this was not a church built out of faith; it was built so that the wealthy could have such ceremonies, complete with gold and lapis lazuli.

There were more recent, rather bad, mosaics [in the church], but there were also some purely Byzantine-style mosaics that were of note. Venetian culture contains much Mediterranean influence thanks to trade with her colonies. That Eastern influence mixed with the later Renaissance art and the result was this church of San Marco where even today the glass and mosaics (these too are made of glass) are the most notable characteristics of the building.

I left the building and my guide said that he would show me how they made the glass. I went to find that the factory was simply put together for display, and for selling their products to the tourists.

I passed by the front of the church again, turned to look at the interesting architecture of the Palace of the Doges next to it, and came to the waterfront. I boarded a gondola and set off for the Lido.[18] My route went along the seaside park and then I landed directly on the opposite shore. There was a long, narrow sandbar. I crossed over it to a road lined with trees where people rambled along on leisurely walks. The flowers of the birch trees fluttered in the breeze and looked like small wads of cotton. I walked along that road about four or five blocks until I came to the seaside. Along the pine grove of the harbor there was a hotel from whose garden music came wafting. There were tables set up in the garden where the tourists sat to have a drink. On the harbor beach there were small huts set up for use by swimmers in the summer – the whole beach was nothing but these huts. In front of the huts on the strand there were many people swimming. When I looked at the pure sea water I too felt like jumping in, but there was not time and so I went back whence I came.

The gondola next turned toward the center of the bay of Venice. In the north I could just see the Alps in the distance, and the houses of the city seemed to be floating on top of the water; between the two I could see a few steeples jutting up and the sounds of evening church bells came drifting over the water. In the past the pleasant visage of San Marco's tower could be seen in the center of this scene, but in recent years it had collapsed.[19] Nonetheless, it was still a charming view. Gray-colored clouds emerged in the western sky and the setting sun, instead of being a red globe, hid behind the clouds and tinged their edges with red; the reddish-purple hues reflected off the still waters. Wagner wrote in his letters that he had gone to the Lido every day at sunset.[20] This setting sun has been enjoyed by artists and poets since antiquity – it is definitely like something straight out of a painting.

After dinner, I could see lightning on occasion in the western sky. Soon the rain began to fall in big drops and the thunder rumbled. The sea, where I had until now enjoyed riding in gondolas and seeing the lanterns sway to the songs of the gondoliers, became suddenly dark. The flashes of lightning illuminated the shapes of the palaces and the white stone churches, and then suddenly the images would again disappear. The rain grew heavier and the thunder boomed. The visage of the churches in the rain – visible in the lightning flashes – took on a certain gloom. The change in scenery was like something one sees in the tropics, and I felt as if I were in a dream.

Eventually the lightning died down and there was nothing more to see so I returned to my room. I listened to the music coming from the distant houses as the rain continued.

May 23
The Grand Canal; the Palace; Farewell in the Rain

THE RAIN from last night had departed this morning but it was now cloudy and humid. I traveled the Grand Canal by steam launch. On either side were old palaces in the Gothic and Renaissance styles. The view of gondolas on the canal was surely the same as it had been even in the old days, but there were a number of stone palace walls that had shifted and many houses that had been renovated. There were no more than two or three aristocratic houses that still had pilings with family crests where boats could tie up. All the rest had become city offices, or schools, or businesses, or factories – all of which spoke of the decline of past pride. I left the launch close to the station and went through small canals along alleys and across bridges to a church called Orto.[21] There were many paintings here also. They had works by the likes of Tintoretto,[22] but I had seen enough of such things and did not want to see more. I went further through similar, winding streets and came out upon the north shore. On an island opposite the shore I could see a stand of cypress trees. A group of people were riding a boat, laden with a black casket, to that island. What an interesting place that island must be for a funeral, I thought. The idea for Böcklin's *The Isle of the Dead* must have come from this sort of island.[23]

The evidence of the reduced circumstances of this neighborhood could be seen in the poor slums. Laundry hung outside the windows of what used to be splendid mansions, and there were a number of places where the stones from the staircases that led down to the canals had been removed. Where there had been magnificent stone-relief carved doors there were now warped metal doors. Here was where poverty and filth met.[24] Nonetheless, the gondolas that plied these waters were decorated with flowers and floated gaily along the surface. In contrast to the dirtiness of the surrounding houses the red azaleas and white daisies looked all the more beautiful.

It began to rain. I left the Grand Canal and by small boat went back to the road where I had been before. I gazed at the Palace and then returned to my inn. The rain drizzled, making the view from the veranda of the churches and the bay seem like nature was crying. There was still much sight-seeing I wanted to do. I still had plenty of time to see the Palace of the Doges, but wherever I went I quickly grew tired of the sight of aristocratic architecture and paintings and mosaics. It was a place out of one's dreams, but it was a stifling dream and the feeling that the longer I was in it the more stifling it became only increased with time. I had also tired of Rome. Places like this became distasteful after a long stay. I had only been here for two days, but I decided today that I would leave. After lunch I packed my bags and then went to the sitting room of the inn to write letters and gaze at the sea.

Ah! My two months in Italy end today. They began with the spring flowers of Lugano and end with the summer rains of Venice. I received spiritual nourishment from Angelico's paintings, I shed tears of reverence in Francis's footsteps. But I also tasted the complicated life of Rome and the sweltering tastes of the aristocracy in Venice – I have learned much through all these varied experiences. The unification of the Roman Empire, Venice's conquering of the Mediterranean – Italy was the queen of the world when all there was to the world was the Mediterranean, but from now on there is no reason for such aspirations. Still, the Italians reminisce about the prosperity of ancient times and most have similar hopes for the future. The religion that gives expression to that dream is Roman Catholicism; the patriots of Italy today give political expression to the dream. However, those dreams are at odds internally between the Vatican and the Quirinal. What will happen to that dream? I find Italian art interesting, but equally interesting is the Italian dream for the future.

〜 * 〜

I went to the station by gondola in the rain. From beneath the canopy all I could see of the houses was their stone foundations and the stairs leading up to them; the water falling on the stone made a dripping sound. The charm of this city on the water in the gentle rain was the exact opposite of the muddy cities on land.

The train departed at seven o'clock and I turned to glance back at the city on the water. Once back on the mainland I found the rain-soaked foliage truly beautiful. More than the palaces on the water, the natural greenery was fresh, and it cooled the feeling I had of being in a sweltering dream. Although there was evidence of decay all over Venice, the wide-open fields and the rain-soaked foliage filled me with a feeling of steady growth.

VENEZIA

Fu il sospiro del mar, nè vide il mondo
Cosa che fosse di costei più bella;
E quando Italia lagrimava ancella,
Libera diffondea l'inno giocondo.
Ebbe mistiche nozze, ed it profondo
Flutto ricinse la fatal donzella,
E in mezzo al perversar della procella
La vittoria le aperse il sen fecondo.
Ma, poichè i tempestosi abbracciamenti,
Or le diniega il mar, franto l'amore,
E a nuove terre dà l'amplesso infido,
Sparsa l'algoso crine, e i rilucenti
Sguardi conversi alle fuggite prore,
Fende le braccia, e si congiunge al lido.
— Giuseppe Revere [25]

How Christianity Appeals to a Japanese Buddhist*

N O RELIGION, not even the most catholic or cosmopolitan in its character, can claim an absolute unity and homogeneity. Christ's teaching of the love of our Father in heaven and, as its consequence, of the brotherly love of men can in no way be an exception to this rule. This is too obvious a fact to need a demonstration. It is a well-known fact that even among the synoptists there are discrepancies as regards their respective views of Christ's person and teaching; still more is this the case with the relations between them and St John or St Paul. The Christ of the Roman Catholics is more the world-ruler than the High Priest of the Protestants. I never think that Christianity, because of the manifoldness of its historical developments and varieties of personal beliefs, is not a unified religion. The unity of Christianity must be fully recognised, so far as it is founded upon the teaching of Christ and so far as its religion consists in a belief in the person of Christ. Truth is one, but modes of its expression cannot be so. The essence of Christianity is universal, but its adaptation to various hearts and heads needs a certain flexibility. The function of each instrument in an orchestral performance consists in its harmonisation with the general concert, and at the same time in the playing of its own peculiar part. The whole concert cannot go on without respect to the characteristics of the different instruments; no instrument can enter into the harmony of the whole without consonance with the general theme. The question how the grand harmony of various Christian nations is to be accomplished awaits its perfect solution in the future.

But Christianity is not the sole religion in the world. Leaving many undeveloped forms of tribal religions out of account, there is at least one religion which is, or claims to be, as universal in its character as Christianity. A religion which

---

* Reprinted from *The Hibbert Journal: A Quarterly Review of Religion, Theology, and Philosophy.* Edited by L.P. Jacks and G. Dawes Hicks. Volume IV, October 1905–July 1906 (London: Williams and Norgate, 1906). "Impressions of Christianity from the Points of View of the Non-Christian Religions. II. How Christianity Appeals to a Japanese Buddhist."

intends, as its ideal, to lead every sentient and non-sentient being into the path of immortality, cannot but be universal. A religious community which is ideally in communion with the Buddhas, the Enlightened in Truth, of the past, present, and future, cannot but be catholic. If Christianity is an absolute religion, not in its actual visible condition, but owing to the universality of its Gospel, Buddhism may claim the same as possessing a similarly universal ideal. "Go ye into all the world, and preach the Gospel to the whole creation" – that was the message of Christ to his disciples after his resurrection. The same mission was given by Gotama, the Buddha, to his sixty disciples, *i.e.*: "Go forth on your journeys for the weal and the welfare of much people, out of compassion for the world, and for the wealth and the weal and the welfare of angels and mortals. Preach the Truth thoroughly glorious and proclaim a religious life wholly perfect and pure." I am not in a position to convince those who think that Buddhism is a mere diabolic imitation of God's religion of the truth of my statement. To the present writer, a student of religions bred in a Buddhist atmosphere, this striking similarity of the two creeds, at least in their formal aspects, is a grave problem to be considered. Is the harmony of these two absolute religions not as much a question of the future as is the harmony of various forms of Christianity? Speaking more concretely, should Buddhism wholly yield its claim and mission to Christianity? Can a Buddhist nation contribute nothing to the civilisation of the world and to the progress of humanity without being converted to Christianity? Might she not remain Buddhist and be Christianised in spirit, and, in this way, enter into the world-concert of the future civilisation? On the other side, is it impossible that the Christian nations and the Christian civilisation, adhering to Christianity, should keep harmony with the Buddhist nations and the Buddhist civilisation?

These questions lead us first to the consideration of the fundamental characters of these religions. The difference between these two, which calls our attention, is the intellectual character of Buddhism and the emotional one of Christianity. If we characterise the former as a religion of intellectual resignation, we may call the latter a religion of hope and love and faith. Many critics have found the difference between the two in the monotheism of Christianity and the pantheism or acosmism of Buddhism. Even admitting this kind of characterisation, we think it more scientific, in the study of religions, to look first to the main feature of a religion and to its actual influence upon the human mind. The fundamental teaching of Buddhism consists in the conviction of the pain and impermanency of every limited existence, and in the release from it. As a necessary step to this conviction it teaches the constituents of our bodily and mental life, and for the realisation of the ideal it practises meditation. The so-called Buddhist metaphysic, which mainly teaches these phenomenal aspects of our life, presupposes a long history of Vedic philosophy, which culminated in the contrast of the true universal self (*ātman*) and the sensuous life (*jīva*). The enlightenment of the pre-Buddhistic philosophy consisted in the abandonment of the empirical life and the realisation of the true ego or the absorption into the highest being (*Brahma-nirvāna*). The Buddhistic ideal of nirvana, the wisdom of the truth, the meditation leading to it, and the good conduct – all these teachings are founded upon the Brahmanic philosophy. Buddhism teaches the non-entity of the ego, and uses the very term *ātman* for the ego which is to be annihilated. But that means the transcendence of the empirical ego, which is made up of constituents, and after this extinction there remains the universal *Bodhi*, the highest, eternal life in Truth. (This point would require separate elucidation.) In this respect Buddhism is no heterodox branch of the Brahmanic philosophy and religion. Buddhism has grown out of the very philosophical soil of the Brahmanic wisdom. Though the powerful personality of the founder had given the religion a very strong impression of the faith in and the love of the Master, its enlightenment consisted in the intellectual conviction of the truth; and the calm resignation of all worldly interests by the Master has become typical of a Buddhist saint.

On the other side, Christ's religion is a necessary outgrowth of the fervent religion of the Jewish prophets. The idea of an almighty and omniscient Creator, the faith in Jahveh's love for the people of Israel, the expectation of the day of God in a future not very far off – all these intuitive and emotional religious experiences of the prophets have given the religion of Christ heat and vitality. Though not without the melancholy tone of a Jeremiah and of a suffering servant of God, Christ's religion, in its main feature, could not but be a religion of hope. Even his suffering shows no trait of weakness, but is predominant in its sublime and tragical character. In his last words, "My God, why hast thou forsaken me?" there sounds in the background an absolute trust in the God who delivered his forefathers, his God ever since he was in his mother's womb, whom he always praised and declared to his brethren. Christ's religion of love and trust is a natural outcome of his fathers' religion, and inherits the very essence of the Jewish monotheism.

Here lies an unmistakable difference between the religions of Buddha and Christ. The one has grown out of and completed the religion of a serene, intellectual release from the evil of this world, and the other has likewise grown out of and completed the enthusiastic love of the Father in heaven, each respectively in its most universal and complete form. The two religions, viewed in their respective historical sources, show two uncompromising, if not contradictory, aspects of the religious experience of mankind. But are they, each of them, nothing but a succession and continuation of the Brahmanic and Jewish religions respectively? Buddhism cannot be understood without reference to the idealistic philosophy of the Brahmins, but yet it is not a mere philosophical teaching of nirvāna. In the same way, Christianity is founded upon the Jewish monotheism; but no Christian will think his religion to be solely a religion of Jahveh, the Creator and Ruler of the world, and especially the protector of the sons of Jacob. There is something more in each of them, and there lies the keynote of each religion.

The Brahmins believed in the Highest Being revealed in the mind of a sage (*muni*), but their Highest Deity is a pure Being which is at the same time pure Thinking (*sac-cit*). Though it revealed itself in the mind of every thinking sage, there was lacking the faith in a man in whom the "Being-Thinking" was fully manifested. They aspired after the Logos, but the Logos in flesh was wanting. The weight of their religion falls on, to use Kant's language, the ontological argument; the living moral proof was lacking. What was sought for in the observance of ritual (*ṛta*) or in faithfulness to holy tradition (*satyam*) became all embodied in the idea of *dharma*, and the very source of the Dharma was found in the essence of ego, the macrocosmical and microcosmical *ātman*. Buddha appeared indeed as the personification of the *Dharma*, or, to use a more Buddhistic term, of *Bodhi*. He was Bodhisattva as a seeker after truth, and his enlightenment, Bodhi, was expounded in his teaching, Dharma. As a personification or incarnation of the Dharma he dared to teach that "he who sees Dharma sees me." What he saw he taught, what he was he revealed. His teaching and his wisdom were nothing but what he himself was in the quintessence of his personality. He is therefore called the Tathāgata, one who has appeared as he was in reality, or, speaking metaphysically, as the personal manifestation of eternal truth. If the doctrine of Buddha's *Dharmātman* or *Dharma-kāya* were not expounded fully in the primitive Buddhist faith, the necessary foundation of the doctrine was applied in the faith in his personality as Buddha or Tathāgata.

When we, conveying this idea, come to Christ, we cannot help noticing the same religious self-consciousness as implied in many sayings of his in the synoptic gospels, and more manifestly expressed in the Johannine representation of Christ, the incarnate Logos. Christ is the Son of God, not merely because he loved God as his Father, but because he was from eternity the very *Word of God*, by which God manifested Himself. He is not one who leads to the way, but himself the Way; not one who preaches truth, but himself the Truth, just as Buddha was the Way (Magga) and the Truth (Bodhi). Christ strengthened and completed the physico-teleological argument of God's existence in the Jewish religion by the moral evidence of his own personality.

Here we see in both cases personal moral evidence of religion in the persons of the founders. The Buddhist nirvana is the outcome of a long course of metaphysical thought, and the Christian God is the Creator of the world, the Father and the King. But in each case the centre of gravity in the religious consciousness falls on the personality of the founder, living among men and leading them to the One who has sent him, or to the ideal which he saw face to face. Faith in a person like this means becoming, through him, one with the Truth he represents and living with him in love. That all may be one, one with the Father, one with the Son, and one with them, is not only the kernel of Christian faith, but the very essence of Buddhist belief. The faith (*saddhā*) in and the love (*pema*) for Buddha, the Lord, lead to nirvāna and "pour forth into nirvāna." Not only the mind of Buddha, but the mind of everyone who has faith in him, who has become one with him in faith and love, pervades the four quarters of the world with thoughts of pity, of sympathy, of deep-felt love, and leaves no being outside. That is the sole way (*ekayāna*) by which every enlightened man, who is free from passion and egotism, goes and comes.[1]

I shall not minimise the differences existing between the two religions, but no one should overlook this cardinal affinity of faith in both, Christianity is certainly the absolute religion, *i.e.* the religion which requires for its existence no other assistance but its own truth, and the religion which teaches the only way to God by faith in Christ. Does this absoluteness necessarily exclude the truth and absoluteness of another? The existence of two absolute religions is seemingly a contradiction, and it seems that the claims of the one can only be established by the sacrifice of the other. Many a Christian of firm conviction has tried to explain the many apparent similarities of the ideas of other religions with those of Christianity by a theory of diabolic imitations. Here we must ask: Is the Satan who imitates God in His most important characteristics condemnable? Are these "imitations" of Christianity by other religions always insincere and of bad intention, as the disguise of a devil in a monk's garment? I shall not enter into polemic with these ardent believers in Christianity, but, as a student of the world's religions, I wish to find another explanation for these so-called imitations, and especially for what I might call the Christianity in Buddhism.

According to the Christian doctrine of the Trinity, the Father is God, the Son is God, and the Holy Spirit also. That God is absolute needs no remark. There are three absolutes in Christianity; but these neither exclude one another, nor melt into one. They are three in person but one in substance. Even among Christians there were and are many sceptics as regards this seeming arithmetical contradiction. This scepticism is merely a product of an over-rationalistic head which has no sympathy with the mystery of faith. Christ is the Son and God is the Father. Still, has not Christ taught that they are one, and that those who love God in the name of Christ are one with them? This oneness of different persons is neither physical nor individual unity, but union in faith and love. One who believes in Christ as the Son of God has communion with the Father of Christ by virtue of his faith. Christ's Father is our Father, and just as the glory of Christ is the glory of the Father, so is our perfection the perfection of God. I called this a mystery of faith, but in reality it is no mystery. In daily life, the true love of husband and wife or of two friends transcends the difference of personality and makes both lovers feel one in their life. And moreover, this feeling is no mere subjective illusion, but the source of many a human activity. Where there prevails love, harmony, or faith, there is participation, communion, or union; and this union is possible only by virtue of the oneness of essential character or substance. The consonance of two musical notes presupposes the difference of scale, but at the same time the communion of sound-waves. This communion is only possible by virtue of the fundamental affinity of wave-motions. When we admit that there is union in different persons, and that one substance is manifested in different personalities, not merely as a difference of attributes but as a participation of the substance in full, then nothing obstructs our belief in the full divinity of each of the three persons. In this belief we have a right to call ourselves children of God, who can participate and realise the divinity of the Father in full. This is the source of divine authority in Christ's ministry, and the foundation of a Christian's belief in Christ as truly man and truly God.

Viewed in this light, does the absoluteness of the Christian religion necessarily exclude the same claim of another religion, whose fundamental faith is belief in a divine master? Anyone who accepts Christ's personality as the true moral evidence of religious faith must admit, or at least sympathise with, the Buddhist faith in Buddha. One who sees Buddha sees the Dharma, the Logos, eternal Truth, unmade, unchangeable, and the source of immortality. If there were any difference between the Christian concept of God and the Buddhist Dharma, the fundamental and essential identity of the beliefs of both in the incarnate Divinity could not be left out of account. The differences are necessary consequences of the historical circumstances in which the two religions have grown up, and of the different demands of the peoples they were intended to lead; but the religious foundation of both is the same. If we call the Buddhist faith in Buddha's person the Christianity in Buddhism, we may, with the same right, see in the Christian doctrine of the Logos the Buddhism in Christianity.[2]

A time may come when all the world will accept the Christian religion, but this will never abolish the difference of tastes or modes of expression. Eastern peoples will hardly lose thoroughly their inheritance of serene meditative faith. Their Christianity will never be the Christianity of a Jew, fervent and sometimes very exclusive. The Greeks demand wisdom and the Jews a sign; the gifts are diverse, but the spirit the same. There are many paths and roads in forests and valleys, but those who have climbed up to the hilltop by any of these routes equally enjoy the same moonlight on the open summit. This is an old Buddhist proverb. Buddhists will never lose this spirit of toleration. There may grow in Japan a form of Christianity without Pope and without Holy Synod, but Buddhism will nevertheless hold its footing therein for ever.

In short, we Buddhists are ready to accept Christianity; nay, more, our faith in Buddha is faith in Christ. *We see Christ because we see Buddha.* The one has come to us in order to release us from the fetters of passion and avarice, and to convince us of an ideal higher than any worldly good. His gospel was that of resignation, attainable by meditation, yet never leaving one to the dreamy quietism of pantheistic or nihilistic philosophy, but purifying human activity by calm enlightenment, and pushing one to the love of all beings by faith in an incarnate Dharma. The other appeared in flesh as Son of Man, to redeem us from sin, to recover us to the love of our Father, from a covetous attachment to our own egotism. His gospel was that of love and hope, but never of fury and vanity. He preached no wisdom, but the wisdom of his believers is holy and leading to the Father, purified by faith and strengthened by hope.

The question of the future depends upon how fully the followers of the two Lords understand each other, and how the two streams of the civilisations nourished respectively by them in the West and the East can harmonise with each other and contribute conjointly to the future progress of humanity. The solution of this problem is no matter of merely abstract speculation, but of sympathy and faith. Just as at the fountain-heads of these two streams there appeared thy

Truth in flesh, the Faith in person, the realisation of this harmony in love and faith needs an incarnate person, representative of humanity. The person may be a powerful individual or a nation. If the appearance of Christ or Buddha has not been in vain, if the two streams of civilisation have been more than ephemeral, then we shall hope not in vain for the *second advent* of Christ or the appearance of the future *Buddha Metteya*.

Turning from this rather speculative side of our view of Christianity and the future of the world's religion, we shall enter into the more practical and historical aspects of the problem. The most visible and tangible product in which a religion manifests its actual influence upon human mind and civilisation is art. The one thing which strikes most the mind of an Asiatic in Europe is the grandeur of religious architecture. It has not the impressive but overwhelming grandeur of an Egyptian sepulchre, nor the gigantic but extravagant magnitude of a Mohammedan mosque, but grandeur in proportion, sublimity with harmony. The Gothic tower of a Strassburg or Rouen Cathedral, pointing imposingly to heaven, rising from among the roofs of human dwellings or along the undulating hillside, appeals to us as something grand and elevating. Standing among the pillars of a cloister like that of the Lateran, or sitting under the vault of a Cappella degli Spagnuoli, no one could restrain himself from uttering a prayer to Him, or singing in praise of Him, who has caused a pious architect to plan this or that impressive building in His service. God does not dwell in a temple built by human hands, but there is the Divine exhibited to us in these harmonious grandeurs or in these serene beauties. At the same time, while we are impressed and inspired by the sublimity and beauty of the Christian architecture, we cannot but admire the same power expressed before us in the graceful temple of Hōryūji or meditatively serene building of the Zen-Buddhism. I shall not enter into description of this Japanese Buddhist architecture, but the similar plan and idea, expressed, though on a smaller scale, in the Buddhist buildings, never fails to excite my wonder. Certainly there is a gap between the tastes of the West and the East, but it is not an unsurmountable one, when we examine into the very root of religious faith which has produced such similar grandeur and harmony.

Passing over to another category of Christian art, we find painting, especially that of the Quattrocento, remarkable in its depth and vitality. In this respect, the works of the Quattrocentisti appeal to our inner heart incomparably more than the later European art, excellent through this be in execution. There is in them nothing comparable to the gracefulness of a Raphaelian Madonna, but these earlier artists knew how to paint the deep store of faith or emotion, to attract the beholders and to assimilate their hearts to the inner hearts of the figures depicted. One expects in vain to see the skilful shadings and colourings of modern French painters in Lippi or Bellini, but their naive sincerity and sometimes childlike freshness are truly products of piety. I find no necessity of saying more on this subject to the English public, whose taste is now much influenced by Ruskin and who are true lovers of Italian art. What I wish to enforce is the wonderful similarity existing between the art of the Quattrocento and our old Buddhistic painting. My impressions when I first saw Angelico's Madonna in the National Gallery of London, and then in Florence, were simply the feelings I had when I looked at the old paintings of the Tak'ma school.[3] Not only in intention and depth, but in treatment and colouring, they show a striking similarity. They depicted their piety in figures and colours, and have appealed to the heart of the same emotion. Their paintings were not for the sake of amusement or of dilettantism but for worship. For them art was not a merry thing, but serious as life. It is a great misfortune for our Japanese painting that it is known in Europe only through the genre of an Utamaro or the caricature of a Hok'sai. But there will come the day when the European public will no more be merely amused with the genre, but will find the existence of deeply religious painting in Japan, and appreciate the sincerity of its intention. The stream of a similar faith will at last communicate through the inner heart, despite of differences of outward forms and materials.

I write this because I think that art is the universal language of the human heart, and through that channel the heart of religion may be communicated incomparably better than through that of dogmas or of reason. If the kernel of a religion consists in and is founded upon the moral evidence, as brought forth in the personality of its founder, its outward realisation is manifested in its religious art. It is much to be regretted that Christianity is now known in the East only by dogmas and creeds, and European art only in its modern secular form. If the Eastern peoples were shown the artistic side of Christianity, and began to talk with pious Christians heart to heart through Christian art, they would be found far more ready to appreciate Christianity than the experiences of missionaries have led them to expect.

As to Christian morality, I find nothing to add to Christ's saying: "*None is good save one, even God.*" Here is the inexhaustible fountain of Christian morality. All moralities flow out of this one and only source. No long sermon, no deliberate ethics can open all the secrets of human conduct without this one key. Anyone, though poor both in knowledge and in property, imbued once with this one thought, is the richest in heaven. Modern ethics endeavours to exclude the idea of God or of the *summum bonum* from its sphere. But the bankruptcy of an ethics without this idea is too clearly shown in utilitarianism to need elucidation. Ethics without the highest good is a mere *Lebensweisheit*, and finally a *Lebensklugheidt*. It justifies everything useful to the need of the hour, anything convenient to the *Stärkeren*. Modern European civilisation has too many riches and too great possessions to follow Him whom God has destined to die in order to live.

Buddhist ethics is blamed by its Christian critics as lacking the very foundation of morality, God. We do not use the expression God, never Jahveh; but there prevails in Buddhadom an unmistakably idealistic element of morality, *i.e.*, esteem for a higher than worldly happiness. "*Leaving the good and the evil* (or, merit and sin)," is the motto of Eastern morality, ever since the rhapsodists of the Mahābhārata sang the great epic in praise of virtuous warriors, ready to die for the sake of the *Dharma*. Their moral ideal consisted always in the highest good, transcending any merit or evil of human life. Buddha's teaching of resignation was nothing but the realisation of this highest ideal. "This idealism," said a Buddhist father,[4] "is the mother of all the holy men, and love (*karunā*) is her daughter." Though this morality of resignation has been much defiled in the course of its transmission through China, we Japanese Buddhists preserve, at last, an earnest aspiration after this ideal. "No evil," said Shinran (1178–1262), the apostle of the Jōdo Buddhism, "is to be feared, except disbelief in Amita's grace; no good is to be esteemed, but faith in our Tathagata's promise (*pranidhāna*)." A saying of another Buddhist sage, Nichiren (1222–1282), the founder of the Hokke Buddhism, which exhorts his followers to sacrifice everything to the *Dharma*, reminds us again of Christ's teaching. And these were no mere teachings, but the morality inculcated by them has tuned the actual life so deeply that self-sacrifice for the sake of one's ideal has become the spirit of our national life. Applied to the morality of the warrior class it has caused many warriors to die gladly for the sake of their lord or of the nation. Parents as representatives of heaven and earth, as is taught usually, are the most prominent objects of the ideal of self-sacrifice. This spirit of self-sacrifice is the vital force of our morality, and has manifested its power during the present war most remarkably. Is this not a good soil for the plantation of Christian morality?

This remark leads me naturally to a problem, important for us, on the relation of Christianity to our national spirit, which has become a subject of controversy since the introduction of that religion into Japan. As is well known, filial piety is the cardinal virtue of Eastern morality in general, and loyalty to the sovereign was the chief point of Confucianistic teaching. These two were completely unified in Japan. A Mikado, or Emperor, as the patriarchal head of the people and the benevolent ruler of the country, has been, since the beginning of our history, the object of loyalty and of a kind of filial piety at the same time. This morality has been brought to a clear consciousness by Confucianism, and then universalised by Buddhism. On this ground, the present Emperor, when he issued an edict on the morality of the nation in 1890, expressed his reverence toward the manes of his ancestors, and appealed to his subjects to hold fast to the virtues their ancestors had cherished under his fathers. Here is expressed what critics, both foreign and indigenous, call the ancestor-worship of the Japanese. This view has led, in 1892, to a hot controversy between the conservative thinkers and the converted Christians. The points of the controversy were formulated by its propounder as follows: —

1. Christianity pretends to be a universal religion and does not recognise national differences, and this contradicts the fundamental teaching of the edict which is strongly national and patriotic.
2. Christian morality is founded upon a supernatural belief in Divinity, and this is contrary to the practical and naturalistic basis of our morality.
3. The love of Christianity is universal and does not admit special virtues toward ruler and parents, and this is diametrically opposed to the cardinal virtues, filial piety and loyalty, as insisted upon in the edict.

Christianity was accused in this way, and since that time both foreign missionaries and converted Christians have fostered a strong antipathy against these two virtues of filial piety and loyalty. That this representation of Christianity is a very erroneous and partial one, needs no remark; but at the same time I find myself obliged to express my regret as regards the attitude of Christians toward the controversy.

In order to make my position clear, I think it necessary to correct the misconceptions of many about the so-called ancestor-worship of the Japanese. We observe strictly the anniversaries of the deaths of relations, and these rituals are connected with the idea of family unity. Every clan in ancient times had its clandeity (*Uji-gami*), and this nomination is preserved in the worship of the protectors of villages and communities. One may call this cult ancestor-worship. But these family rituals are not observed in order to invoke the spirits of the dead, but rather to offer our homage toward them and to communicate our faith and merit to them. The expression *tsuijen* means just a communion, *i.e.* the communion of our spiritual gain to them, who partake in our faith and virtues in the all-embracing spiritual community. This is due to the influence of Buddhism, and not a primitive conception. But that is our actual idea, and it shows how a religion of universal salvation could, adopting the primitive ancestor-worship, sanctify, universalise, and spiritualise it. On the other hand, the worship of protecting clan or local deities was never exclusively that of the blood-related. Omitting many historical evidences for the support of this remark, I say simply it was something similar to the hero-worship of the Greeks, or not seldom to the saint-worship of the Catholics. In modern times this kind of cult has gone decidedly into the background, and is not so much in vogue as represented by Lafcadio Hearn. If not quite so ideal as Carlyle's, our hero-worship has been much elevated by Buddhism. Even among Shintoists, the adherents to the primitive religion, the spiritual unity of these worshipped manes of ancestors or of heroes is recognised. Some of them have even tried to establish, out of our traditional Shintoism, a monotheism much akin to that, of Zoroastrianism. The imperial edict itself states, at its close, that this morality of piety and loyalty transcends the distance of time and difference of nationalities. This point needs a minuter remark, but it lies now out of my scope. I must now content myself with saying that our primitive faith has been much elevated by Buddhism, and still has enough room to be purified by a more decidedly monotheistic religion such as Christianity.

It is rather singular that Christians have not tried this purification and elevation of the Japanese moral and religious ideas by their love of the Heavenly Father, which is the root of all piety, and absolute obedience toward the Lord of heaven and earth, which is the root of all loyalty. None is good save God; but does the oneness of God exclude all that is good, not beside Him, but within and under Him? The field is ripe, the harvest is truly plenteous. Where are the labourers who know how to burn the tares and to gather the wheat into the barn?

To express my personal conviction in short, it is enough to say: Where there is the faith in Buddha, there may grow the faith in Christ. The two religions may preserve their respective traits, but they must share in the deep root of religious faith. Japan may remain Buddhistic, or be converted to Christianity, but she will in either way keep her own tone of national spirit and civilisation, and in this way play a part in the grand concert of humanity.

This will be enough to state the cardinal points of my attitude toward Christianity. But as the editor of the Journal asks me to point out what I think to be the defects of Christian morality, I shall venture to respond to his request. What I wish to point out is certainly not the defects of Christianity itself; but there is one thing which strikes our minds as regards the actual tendency of Christians in Europe. It is the exclusiveness of their attitude toward non-Christian peoples. Apart from the theological or ecclesiastical exclusiveness, there is manifest a moral one, especially in recent years. Not only ignorant monks or farmers, but the educated classes and influential rulers, see in the rise of a Buddhist nation the incarnation of Antichrist or a diabolic power. Everything, however good and beautiful it may be, should be extinguished, if it is not Christian. These words were addressed by an Emperor to his soldiers going to the East, and they were stimulated to commit murder for revenge, so that the peoples of the East might remember for a thousand years the terrible vengeance of Christians. These and similar phenomena are by no means products of true Christianity, but only remains of Jewish bigotry. The harmony and concert of the world's religions and nations are made impossible by this un-Christian Christianity. If we should be threatened by a bigotry like this, we are ready to stand against it in the name not only of Buddha but of Christ Himself.

Notes

INTRODUCTION

1. "Principal Works by Masaharu Anesaki" in *Monumenta Nipponica* Vol. 6, No. 1/2. (1943), pp. vi–x.

2. In *Testugaku zasshi*, pp. 590–619.

3. In *Taiyō*, 14:10,11, pp. 13–12.

4. In *Taiyō*, 15:1, pp. 59–68.

5. In *Taiyō*, 15:10, p. 131.

6. See *Musashino in Tuscany* (Ann Arbor, MI: Center for Japanese Studies, 2004).

7. Anesaki's name (姉崎正治) would ordinarily be romanized as Anezaki Masaharu, but in light of his extensive body of work in English we have elected to preserve the form of his name that he himself preferred to use for his English-language publications.

8. *Waga shōgai: Anesaki Masaharu sensei no gyōseki* 我が生涯・姉崎正治先生の業績 (Tokyo: Ōzorasha 大空社, 1993), p. 11.

9. Ibid, pp. 25–6.

10. Although he does not specify, it was probably *Geschichte der Philosophie im Umriss: ein Leitfaden zur Ubersicht*.

11. *Waga shōgai: Anesaki Masaharu sensei no gyōseki* わが生涯・姉崎正治先生の業績, p. 5.

12. Masaharu Anesaki, *History of Japanese Religion* (London: Kegan Paul International, 1930), p. 378.

13. "Takayama Chogyū ni kotōru no sho," 高山樗牛に答ふるの書 reprinted in *Takayama Chogyū, Saitō Nonohito, Anesaki Chōfū, Tobari Chikufū shū* 高山樗牛・斉藤野の人・姉崎嘲風・登張竹風集 in *Meiji Bungaku Zenshū* 明治文学全集, vol. 40. Tokyo: Chikuma Shobō 筑摩書房, 1970, p. 211.

14. Ibid, p. 212.

15. "How Christianity Appeals to a Japanese Buddhist" in *The Hibbert Journal*, Vol. IV (1905–6), p. 9 (see also Appendix, p. 243).

16. Ibid, p. 10 (Appendix, p. 243).

17. Ibid, p. 5 (Appendix, p. 240).

18. Masaharu Anesaki, *History of Japanese Religion*, p. 387.

19. Later he turned his focus to Nichiren (1222–1282), the founder of Nichiren Buddhism.

20. Masaharu Anesaki, *History of Japanese Religion*, p. 170.

21. Masaharu Anesaki, *History of Japanese Religion*, p. 361.

22. A reviewer in *Science* concluded that the requirements imposed on scholars by the funds – visiting many countries over the course of a year or more – placed proper academic research "out of the question." He continues, "As matters stand, the aim [of the Foundation] is too nondescript to induce confidence." ("The Kahn Foundation" in *Science*, New Series, Vol. 37, No. 964. (June 20, 1913), p. 933.)

23. Ibid, p. 932.

24 "How Christianity Appeals to a Japanese Buddhist" in *The Hibbert Journal*, Vol. IV (1905–6), p. 13 (see also Appendix, p. 245).

25. Ibid, p. 12 (Appendix, pp. 244–245).

26. Ibid, pp. 11–12, (Appendix, p. 244).

27. John Ruskin, *Modern Painters* vol. IV. London: Smith, Elder, and Co., 1873, p. 408.

28. "Takayama Chogyū ni kotōru no sho," p. 218.

29. Anesaki's interest in art was more than an adult development. He was born the son of an *edokoro* (絵所) in the Bukkō Temple (仏光寺) in Kyoto. An *edokoro* was an atelier or group of ateliers affiliated with a temple and tasked with producing religious art. Although Anesaki was not an artist himself, the connection between spirituality and art was something he was exposed to early in life.

30. The early issues included such titles as "Il Cristianesimo e un Buddhismo rinnovato" by Raddaele Ottolenghi, "De Unite des religions" by Hudry-Menos, and "Il Buddhismo second un Buddhista" by C. Jinarajadasa.

31. Capsule review from *Chūō kōron* as reprinted in *Teiunshū* 停雲集 (Tokyo: Hakubunkan 博文館, 1911), p. 3 of appendix.

32. Capsule review from *Shin kōron* as reprinted in *Teiunshū* 停雲集 (Tokyo: Hakubunkan 博文館, 1911), p. 4 of appendix.

PREFACE

1. This title is an allusion to Takarai Kikaku's 宝井其角 *Hanatsumishū* 花摘
集 (Flower Gathering, 1690) and Yosa Buson's 与謝蕪村 *Shinhanatsumi* 新花摘み
(New Flower Gathering, 1777), both *haikai* collections dedicated to the authors'
mothers. It also alludes to the collection of biographical tales of Saint Francis
of Assisi, *Fioretti di San Francesco d'Assisi* (The Little Flowers of St. Francis of
Assisi). Anesaki included a title page here in Italian, *Il Fioretti*. The title *Flowers of Italy: Diaries of a Pilgrimage* is given by Anesaki himself in the list of his
works included in *History of Japanese Religion*.

2. From Paolo Rolli's (1687–1765) poem "La Primavera." These are six of the
total twenty-two stanzas in the poem. Rolli was the disciple of Gian Vincenzo
Gravina, one of the founders of the Arcadia. His literary nickname as an Arcadi-
an poet was Eulibio Berentiatico. A translation of the stanzas Anesaki chose is:

The Spring

You have returned, o Spring,
and the green grass, and the flowers,
and the youthful loves
have returned with you.

And my happy mood,
which was once born because of your presence,
with your sweet rebirth
returned sweeter to me.

On its native thorny stem
the rose is already waiting for
the dewy sunrise, which
makes its color more vivid.

The beautiful hyacinths have blossomed,
along with the colorful anemones,
the violets, the buttercups
along with all other lovely flowers.

· · · · · · · · · · · · ·

And in the sown, ploughed fields

> which are the farmers' hope
> the young crop's leaves
> start to turn green again.
>
> . . . .
>
> To compensate for the damage of the winter frost,
> the year becomes young again,
> and joyful pleasure returns.

The omitted stanzas of this poem describe trees, particularly cherry trees. Rolli writes about his love for the young girl Dori, a love which is not perishable as flowers are. Rolli continues, saying that he would like to go with his beloved to the countryside to admire the meadows, the hills, the spring fountain, the birds. The poem ends with praise of the simple, bucolic life versus the greed, the ambition, and the ostentatious luxury of cities.

3. Anesaki was abroad from March 1900 to May 1903, funded as a scholar by the Japanese government. The countries he visited included Germany, England, Italy, and India.

4. The friend is Takayama Chogyū 高山樗牛 (1871–1902), a Meiji scholar and critic who was particularly interested in religion and philosophy. Anesaki published a collection of Chogyū's letters in 1905, titled *Kiyomigata ni okeru Chogyū* 清見潟に於ける樗牛 (Chogyū at Kiyomigata), and this introductory essay was also written at Kiyomigata (see note 3 below for further information). Chogyū had been scheduled to travel abroad in 1902, but contracted a lung illness and never left Japan. He died while Anesaki was abroad. Chogyū was buried near Kiyomigata, at Udoyama 有渡山, which could be construed as "the mountain on the opposite shore" as viewed from where Anesaki was writing.

5. Kiyomigata, located in Shizuoka Prefecture is an *utamakura* 歌枕 associated with moonlight and waves.

6. Albert Kahn (1860–1940), not to be confused with the American architect Albert Kahn (1869–1942), was a French financier. He established "bourses Autour du Monde" (also known as "La Bourse du Tour du Monde") in 1898 with the purpose of increasing French knowledge of the world at large. The fund provided scholarships for scholars from various universities to tour the world and bring their knowledge home. In his autobiography, Anesaki credits Kahn with inspiring him to become a vegetarian. (*Waga shōgai*, p. 135)

7. The Japanese proverb he uses here is *seken ni oni wa nai* 世間に鬼はない,

which means that, although there are many thoughtless people in the world, when one is truly in need someone will appear and help.

THE SNOWS OF GOTTHARD

1. The opening sentence is reminiscent of an early sentence in Matsuo Bashō's 松尾芭蕉 *Kashima mōde* 鹿島詣 (A Visit to Kashima Shrine): "I thought I would like to see the moon over the mountains at Kashima this autumn," and an early sentence in Bashō's *Sarashina kikō* 更科紀行 (A Visit to Sarashina Village): "The autumn wind urged me to see the autumn moon from the village of Sarashina." The conceit of traveling to see the moon was stock, and it seems likely that Anesaki had Bashō in mind when he began his travelogue. It is also possible that he was thinking of countless other travelogues that begin by presenting the desire to see some famous sight as the incentive for a trip.

2. Göschenen is at one end of the Gotthard tunnel, which was completed in 1880. This tunnel, fifteen kilometers long, joins Göschenen and Airolo. It was passable by trains by the time Anesaki visited, making an easy journey through the 2,108 meter-high pass.

3. This cottage, near Zürich, was an early home of the composer Richard Wagner (1818–83). It was here in 1857 that he began work on *Parsifal*, the second act of which has been connected by some critics to events in the life of the historical Buddha. Although Anesaki does not tell us why he visited Wagner's home, one wonders if he was searching for Wagner's Buddhist inspiration. He mentions Wagner again, and appears to have read his autobiography (see entries for Venice).

4. This refers to the play *William Tell* (*Tellspiele*, 1805) by Friedrich von Schiller (1759–1805). This play is still performed today, on occasion in open-air theaters such as that in Interlaken.

5. Anesaki calls the steeple the pagoda of the temple (寺の塔). Throughout this travelogue, churches are referred to with the character that normally means "Buddhist temple" (寺).

6. This poem is in a 7-5-7-5 | 7-5-7-5 syllabic structure, which is a traditional form usually seen in theatrical works. It is unusual in the context of a travelogue.

7. This poetry was often written by soldiers who longed for home while they were stationed on the frontier.

8. Senjōgahara 戦場ヶ原, which literally means "battlefield," is a famous

locale near Nikkō 日光, north of Tokyo. The "battle" happened in mythical times between the gods (in this case, the surrounding mountains of the region). In any event, the geography of the area is similar to the landscape before Anesaki here, with a wide field and a lake sandwiched between soaring peaks.

9. Here Anesaki reverses a common poetic conceit in traditional Japanese literature, that of mistaking some object, usually the foam of a whitecap or the cherry blossoms of spring, for snow. This conceit begins in travel literature in the *Tosa Diary* 土佐日記 and is continued throughout the centuries. Three poems from *Tosa* that illustrate this are found in the entry for the eighteenth day of the first month:

> Snow falls constantly
> with no regard for season
>   on the wild seashore
> where great breakers thunder in
> to shatter against the rocks

> Forever blooming
> on rocky strands where the wind
>   drives home the wild waves:
> flowers unfamiliar
> to the warbler and to spring

> It seems to intend to deceive our human eyes —
> the wind blowing waves
>   forever toward the seashore
> to break like snow, like blossoms

(Translations by Helen McCullough in *Kokin Wakashū: the First Imperial Anthology of Japanese Poetry, with Tosa Nikki and Shinsen Waka*, p. 276.)

10. Antonio Rosmini (1797–1855) was an Italian priest and philosopher. Anesaki does not indicate which text he was reading, or the subject matter, but given that Rosmini wrote on both religious and political ideals it is not surprising that Anesaki would find his work interesting.

11. The reference here is to the Gotthard tunnel, mentioned earlier (see note 2 above). Anesaki uses the *ri* as his unit of measure (1 *ri* is approximately 3.927 kilometers [2.44 miles]).

SPRING ON THE LAKE

1. Sesshū 雪舟 (1420–1506) was a landscape painter in medieval Japan. His work is seen as representative of the late fifteenth century, and often evokes superlatives in terms of its execution and beauty.

2. Anesaki is still in Switzerland at this point, and will not cross the Italian border for two more days. His reference to arriving in Italy seems to mean that he is in the Italian-speaking region of Switzerland, so he is in Italy *culturally* if not *geographically*.

3. Nichiren 日蓮 (1222–1282) was the founder of the Nichiren school of Buddhism, unique to Japan. In the course of his career, Anesaki wrote a number of treatises on him. However, he is not mentioned again in *Hanatsumi nikki*.

4. Hōnen 法然 (1133–1212) predates Nichiren, and was also a seminal figure in Japanese Buddhism. He is best known for spreading Pure Land Buddhism 浄土宗, particularly among the non-elite. A contemporary of St. Francis of Assisi, who is also a focus of this travelogue, Hōnen occupies a referential center for Anesaki. In subsequent pages, we shall see Anesaki draw many parallels between the two charismatic religious leaders.

5. "Signor Bignami" is Enrico Bignami (1844–1921), a prominent socialist and pacifist. He was also the editor of the philosophical magazine *Cœnobium* in which Anesaki published often.

6. Anesaki had lived in Germany for an extended period, and it was his first major experience abroad. In theory, he should have been more comfortable with the Germans than anyone else, but because of Kaiser Wilhelm II's anti-Chinese / Japanese stance, Anesaki had taken a strong anti-German attitude.

7. 卯月八日. The eighth day of the fourth lunar month, called the "deutzia month" (deutzia being a shrub with white or pinkish flowers). The significance of this is fleshed out in subsequent entries.

8. This holiday falls on the eighth day of the fourth month in the lunar calendar, but when Japan adopted the solar calendar (in 1872, to take effect in 1873), they began celebrating many lunar holidays – including this one – according to the solar calendar.

9. Anesaki mentions reading this biography often, but does not specify the title. However, later in the travelogue, he meets Paul Sabatier, the author of what was then the definitive biography of St. Francis and they discuss Sabatier's book. Consequently, it seems likely that the biography Anesaki mentions here is Sabatier's.

10. The 1903 edition of Baedeker's guide book on *Northern Italy* comments, "Although the style of the composition strikes one as old-fashioned, the eye cannot fail to be gratified by the numerous beautiful details." (p. 10). Anesaki's comments echo these sentiments, which may suggest that he was familiar with the travel guide observation. There is also the following anecdote about John Ruskin's response to the fresco: "In June 1870 a party of English and American tourists met Ruskin in the Church of Sta. Maria degli Angioli at Lugano, and engaged him in conversation with regard to Luini's 'Passion of Christ,' painted on the wall of the screen. 'Luini's works,' said Ruskin, 'were relatively few, little known, and less understood. This was his chief and characteristic work, and he was thankful that it had not been meddled with by restorers. It was thoroughly genuine; and though dirty and dilapidated, those who had eyes to see and souls to appreciate could yet realise something of the grandeur and genius of the painter.' He went on to speak of 'the simple boldness and grandeur of the composition and the fire and feeling of execution.' One of the company dissented. 'Sir,' said Ruskin, 'Luini is an artist of such superlative excellence that I have never yet ventured to criticise him in detail.'" ("Ruskin on Luini at Lugano," by John Holmes, in the *Sheffield and Rotherham Independent*, May 1, 1886, Weekly Supplement, p. 5; reprinted in *Two Papers on Ruskin*, by John Holmes [Sheffield, 1886].)

11. Bernardino Luini (1480–1532), a noted Italian painter.

12. Anesaki's meaning becomes clear later in the travelogue, when he draws strong parallels between Buddhism, particularly Pure Land Buddhism, and the Franciscans.

13. Anesaki is referring to a popular piano setting of an aria from the third act of Wagner's opera *Tannhäuser*.

14. Anesaki gives the romanization of "Orio" but the town is called "Oria," and is located on the northern shore of Lake Lugano.

15. Antonio Fogazzaro (1842–1911), an Italian novelist and poet. Later, when Anesaki is in Rome, he mentions Fogazzaro again and implies that the novel to which he refers here and later is *Il santo* (*The Saint*). See the entry on May 4 (p. 152) for more details. Earlier, in September of 1907, Anesaki published an article titled "Zola's *Paris* and Fogazzaro's *The Saint*" (ゾラのパリとフォガッツァロの聖者と) in the magazine *Taiyō*. This is of note not only because it indicates Anesaki was reading *The Saint* right before his journey, but also because it shows he was reading Zola's *The Three Cities Trilogy*, which he alludes to much later in the context of traveling through Rome. See entry for May 17 (p. 208).

16. A *shaku* 尺 equals approximately 30.3 centimeters (about one foot).

17. On this holiday in Japan children traditionally go into the hills to pick flowers. Anesaki, as many Japanese do, conflates the holiday of flowers (*hana matsuri* 花祭り) with the birthday of the Buddha. Moreover, the traditional name of the lunar month ("deutzia month") refers to a flower.

18. The word Anesaki uses is *tegami* 手紙, which implies a letter, although it is more accurate to say he is writing a diary entry. This entry did not appear as a separate publication prior to the publication of the work as a whole.

19. Lake Lugano, not Como.

20. The shores of Lake Como, still renowned for their beauty, are lined with chestnut, walnut, and olive trees, plus oleander and laurel.

21. Camellias were introduced to Europe in the mid-eighteenth century. Sources disagree about the date of the introduction of camellias to Italy specifically, although they indicate it was probably the late eighteenth or early nineteenth century. (Stelvio Coggiatti, "An Introduction to Camellias in Italy," in *International Camellia Journal*, Vol. 1 (1973), pp. 68–70)

22. Steamboat and row boat tours of the lake were readily available at this time.

23. Most likely Anesaki is describing the Villa Arconati (now the Villa del Balbianello) although he does not identify it by name. *Baedeker's* notes, "On [Punta d'Avedo]'s extremity… glitters the Villa Arconati (visitors admitted; fine view)." (*Northern Italy*, p. 156)

24. *Baedeker's* notes:

The Cathedral, built entirely of marble, is one of the best in northern Italy. The nave was rebuilt in the Gothic style about 1396, the façade in 1457–86 (by Luchino da Milano); and in 1487–1526 the transepts, choir, and exterior of the nave were altered in the Renaissance style by Tommaso Rodari. The southern portal (1491) is built in Bramante's style by an unknown architect; the modern ornamentation is by Tomm. Rodari and his brother Jacopo. Over the magnificent western portal reliefs (*Adoration of the Magi*) and statuettes (*Mary with Sant' Abbondio and San Protus*, etc.); at the sides are statues of the two Plinys, erected in 1498. The overdecorated north portal (Porta della Rana) dates from 1505–9.

Interior. The heavy and gaudy vaulting, restored in 1838, destroys the effect of the fine proportions, which resemble those of the Certosa near Pavia. To the right of the entrance is the monument of Cardinal Tolomeo Gallio (1861). Farther on, to the right, second altar, with handsome wood-carving, and scenes from the life of St. Abondius (1514); adjoining *The Adoration of the*

Magi, by Bern. Luini, and *The Flight into Egypt,* by Gaud. Ferrari. Over the third altar, a Madonna by B. Luini. In the Choir, *The Apostles,* by Pompeo Marchesi. The Sacristy contains pictures by Guido Reni, Paolo Veronese, etc. Fine statue of St. Sebastian (1481) in the north transept. In the left aisle: at the first altar, *Entombment* by Tommaso Rodari (1498); at the second altar, G. Ferrari, *Nuptials of the Virgin,* B. Luini, *Nativity*; by the third altar, the busts of Pope Innocent XI (Odescalchi) and Carlo Rovelli, Bishop of Como. (*Northern Italy,* p. 149)

25. "Garnier" is Charles Marie Georges Garnier, a French educator and scholar of English literature who was born in 1869. He was one of the first friends that Anesaki made abroad. In his autobiography Anesaki mentions that he often dined at Garnier's house in Paris. During the war their correspondence was curtailed, but they were overjoyed to find, after the war, that both families had come through unscathed. Eveline was his daughter.

26. "Rensi" is Giuseppe Rensi (1871–1941), an Italian philosopher. He also published under the pseudonym Natanio il Savio. Rensi was a regular contributor to Bignami's magazine (see below).

27. This is the first of three instances in which Anesaki mentions "the magazine," although he does not specify its title. It is Bignami's *Cœnobium* (1906–1919), which carried a number of articles by Anesaki – including one in 1907 titled "Cenobio Laico nell' Estremo Oriente," (vol. 2) one in 1912 titled "La moderna civiltá dell'Europa" (vol. 6–8) and one in 1913 titled "Nichiren, il Profeta del Buddhism Giapponese" (7–7). (Source: *Waga shōgai: Anesaki Masaharu sensei no gyōseki* (second part), pp. 136–7)

28. The reference here is to Pietro Adolfo Tirindelli (1858–1937), a popular Italian composer who later faded into obscurity.

29. "Italian *udon*" is most likely spaghetti, as *udon* is a long, thin Japanese noodle.

30. Anesaki echoes here many passages in the *Tosa Diary* in which the author and his companions note a particular day and what people in the capital would be doing at the very moment that they are traveling far away. In his autobiography, Anesaki writes that, as a college student at the Imperial University (today's University of Tokyo) he cheered at the regatta races, and then when he became a professor he attended the races between the Faculty of Letters and the Faculty of Agriculture, but soon lost his interest in the sport. (*Waga shōgai,* p. 62) Here, in *Hanatsumi nikki,* he obsesses over the results of the race (he mentions it many times), perhaps simply as an affectation of the style of earlier travel writers.

31. Antonio Ciseri (1821–1891). His subject matter was often religious; his style is described as Raphaelite.

32. Anesaki is probably referring to Antonio Ciseri's *Trasporto di Cristo al Sepolcro* (1870).

33. "Signor Pioda" is Alfredo Pioda (1848–1909), a politician and student of religions. He also published in *Cœnobium*.

34. Anesaki is either confusing the layout of the building, or referring to the third story using the French style: ground floor, first floor, second floor.

35. Both Saigyō 西行 and Bashō, the most acclaimed travel writers of Japan, recount resting in the shade of a willow on their journeys. Indeed, Bashō sought out the very same willow tree in Ashino where Saigyō supposedly rested and composed his poem. Once there, of course, Bashō himself composed a poem, too. Saigyō's poem was included in the *Shinkokinshū* anthology (poem number 262), and is as follows: "In willow shade on the roadside where clear water flowed, I stopped, saying, 'Just for a while.'" (Translation by Hiroaki Sato in "Record of an Autumn Wind: The Travel Diary of Arii Shokyū" in *Monumenta Nipponica* 55:1. See *Narrow Road to the Deep North* for Bashō's account.) Later this poem became the inspiration for the Noh play *Yugyō yanagi* 遊行柳. Anesaki was likely familiar with this theme.

36. "Hōgai" is Kanō Hōgai 狩野芳崖 (1828–1888), a Japanese-style (as opposed to Western-style) painter. At a time when Western style painting was becoming popular, Hōgai stood out and maintained the Japanese-style tradition. Here Anesaki seems to referring to one of the paintings that Hōgai did of Avalokitesvara (Kannon 観音) "as merciful mother."

37. The deity Brahma-Deva.

38. The deity Asanga.

39. Part of the tradition associated with the Buddha's birthday involves surrounding a statue of the newborn Buddha with flowers. According to legend, the Buddha took seven steps immediately after birth, surrounded by flowers. Anesaki does not have the usual statue/image of the newborn Buddha, which would depict him standing with one arm extended up and one arm extended down.

40. "In the winter of 1909/1910, the German-born Theravāda monk Nyanatiloka sojourned in southern Switzerland, near Lugano. This stay and his plan to establish a *vihāra* (Pāli: a dwelling place for monks) mark the beginning of the history of institutionalized Buddhism in Switzerland. Nyanatiloka and his lay supporters from the German Pāli Society ambitiously intended to build a mon-

astery in which at least five monks could live according to the rules of the Vinaya (monastic codex) and work towards the spreading of Buddhist teachings within the German language area. The thirty-two year-old monk lived in an Alpine shepherd's chalet, dressed in a traditional Theravāda monk's robe and scanty sandals. Nyanatiloka wrote his Pāli grammar and translated texts from the Abhidhamma. He did, however, suffer from the snow and the 'unspeakable cold,' as he later wrote in his autobiographical notes…. In danger of succumbing to his illness, Nyanatiloka left for North Africa in order to found a monastic settlement near Tunis." Martin Baumann, "Buddhism in Switzerland." *Journal of Global Buddhism*, 1 (2000), pp. 154–5. Nyanatiloka also published in *Cœnobium*.

41. "Ishiyama in Ōmi" is in Ōtsu city, Shiga Prefecture. It is an *utamakura*, mentioned in many Heian period texts such as *The Tale of Genji* 源氏物語 and *Sarashina Diary*. It is known as a place where Heian noblewomen went on religious pilgrimages dedicated to the bodhisattva Kannon.

42. The article was published in *Cœnobium*, 2–4, titled "Il Buddhismo e i Suoi Critici."

43. Karl Seidenstücker organized the first German Buddhist Society in Leipzig in 1906; other Buddhist groups consequently were established. See Frank J. Korom, "A Review of Deutsche Buddhisten: Geschichte und Gemeinschaften" in the *Journal of Buddhist Ethics*, Vol. 5 (1998), pp. 433–435.

44. See Note 40 above.

45. "露の身はここかしこにて消えぬとも."

46. Here Anesaki uses a set expression: a four-character Chinese compound "會者定離."

47. This line comes from a poem by the Chinese travel writer Su Shi 蘇軾 (1037–1101). Su Shi sent this poem to a fellow-official, Qian Xie 錢勰 (1034–1097) while Su Shi was serving as Prefect of Hangzhou 杭州 (1089–1091) and Qian was serving as Prefect of Yuezhou 越州. In the poem, Su Shi comments on life as a traveling official, a life that was associated with hardship and distance from loved ones. The word that Anesaki uses for "inn" is a metaphor for the traveling life of an official.

48. This is Anesaki's first mention of Fra Angelico (Giovanni Angelico da Fiesole, 1387–1455). He will later dedicate days of his journey to viewing Angelico's work. Angelico is usually seen as a ground-breaking painter whose techniques led to the style of the Renaissance, but Anesaki sees him as the last respectable painter before the Renaissance brought a pointless decoration and decadence to the art world, particularly the art of Christianity.

49. "Right Vision" (*shōken* 正見) is one of the items of practice in the Buddhist "Eight-Fold Path" 八正道 which includes right vision, right thoughts, right speech, right acts, right living, right effort, right mindfulness or recollection, and right meditation. Faithfully following the Eight-Fold Path leads one to Nirvana. Anesaki's point here is that he would likely come back to Lugano with a holy monk who was close to attaining enlightenment.

50. This is apparently a reference to Nyanatiloka's work on a Pāli grammar. See Note 40 above on Nyanatiloka.

51. Andrea Maffei was born in Molina in Val di Ledro, Trentino Alto Adige (northern Italy) in 1798 and died in Milan in 1885. He was a poet and a novelist. He translated Gessner, Shakespeare, and Milton. He is considered a minor neoclassical poet. Neoclassicism was a literary Italian movement that flourished in the first decades of 1800 and tried to imitate the beauty and the simplicity of ancient Greek poetry. This is the first half of a poem titled "la Prima Viola"; Anesaki omits the last four stanzas. Here are the stanzas he does choose in English:

The First Violet

Scented messenger of April,
You were just born from the soil,
as quickly as the first thought of love
is born into the heart of a gentle woman.

Your blossom on the dry winter soil
is like the hope that gives courage to sad people,
It is like the smile that life sends when a sharp pain ceases.
Among the snows that the gentle breeze melts
I pick you up, hermit of the meadows,
I absorb from your most inner petals
Your supple vital scent.

And it displeases me that this arcane outpouring
of your blessed scent
cannot be transformed into human words.
Oh, what if it could resonate into my soul
as a note of a vocal spirit!

The omitted stanzas say that if the violet could talk he would be able to know about the homesickness of misfortunate and exiled people, and the sorrow of all the young girls who are apart from their faithful lovers. The conclusion says that the violet is the companion of sad people; in fact it does not smile at happy people, but rather by its presence stirs up in the mind endearing memories and the joys of the past. The violet reminds people of the brevity of youth, which is short and unfaithful, and does not keep the promises of happiness it seemed to give at first.

BOLOGNA: CITY OF ARCADES

1. *Baedeker's* notes, "The general style of the building is Gothic, but shows many peculiarities." (*Northern Italy*, p. 118)

2. In other words, stained glass windows.

3. Anesaki is describing the Asinelli and Garisenda towers. *Baedeker's* notes that the leaning towers are "the most singular structures in Bologna, though plain square brick buildings. The Torre Asinelli, erected about 1109, by Gherardo degli Asinelli, which looks prodigiously high when seen from the pavement below, is 320 ft. in height and 4 ft. out of the perpendicular. A rough staircase of 447 steps leads to the summit, which commands a fine view. The unfinished Torre Garisenda, begun in 1110 by Filippo and Otoone Garisenda, is 163 ft. high only, but is 10 ft. out of the perpendicular." (*Northern Italy*, p. 372)

4. Although is not certain, it would appear that Anesaki is at the Palazzo del Podesta, on the east side of the Piazza del Netunno.

5. The Romanization "Petronino" is provided in the text, but it seems likely that he is instead referring to San Petronio. Later on, he refers again to this church with yet another variation on the name (this time in *kana*): Petorinino.

6. The building of San Petronio was begun in 1390, but never completed.

7. *Baedeker's* notes, "The Cappella Baciocchi (5th from the altar) contains the monument of Princess Elisa Baciocchi (d. 1820), grand-duchess of Tuscany and sister of Napoleon, and of her husband Felix; opposite to it, that of three of her children, by the two Franzoni. Over the altar a Madonna by Lorenzo Costa (1492), by whom the fine stained-glass windows were also designed. By the pillar to the right of the chapel is the tomb of Bishop Ces. Nacci, by Vinc. Onofri (ca. 1480)." (*Northern Italy*, p. 367)

8. *Baedeker's* notes, "The 8th Chapel, the oldest in the church, consecrated in 1392, contains frescoes of the beginning of the 15th cent.: Paradise and Hell to the left, recalling Dante's poem; altar with sculptures in marble, and stained glass by Jacob of Ulm (?), also worthy of note." (*Northern Italy*, p. 367)

9. Anesaki gives the Romanization "Beviracca," but it seems likely that he is referring to the house of the Duke of Bevilacqua, which gets further mention later on.

10. *Baedeker's* notes, "The early-Gothic church of San Francesco was built by Marco da Brescia (?) in 1246–60. Long used as a military magazine, it was restored to its sacred uses in 1887. The apse has buttresses in the northern style. To the left is a fine brick tower by Ant. Vincenzi (1397–1405). The interior is in the form of a basilica with aisles, and has an ambulatory with nine recently redecorated chapels. It is now being restored by Alf. Rubbiani. The left aisle contains the tomb of Alexander V. (d. 1410), with the recumbent figure of that Pope by Sperandio. The large marble Altar in the Choir, with numerous figures and reliefs, is the earliest known work of the brothers Massegne of Venice (1388)." (*Northern Italy*, p. 371)

11. A *ken* 間 is 1.818 meters (1.99 yards).

12. *Baedeker's* notes, "Dante compares the giant Antæus, who bends towards him, to this tower, 'when a cloud passes over it.'" (*Northern Italy*, p. 372)

13. "Francesco" refers to Francesco Francia (1450–1517). *Baedeker's* notes, "The 6th [chapel] Bentivogio, paved with coloured and glazed tiles, contains a Madonna, with angelic musicians and four saints (1499), the finest work of Fr. Francia." (*Northern Italy*, p. 375)

14. These frescoes had been restored in 1874, but Anesaki thinks that their good condition is due to careful preservation. "Costa" is Lorenzo Costa (1460–1535), a painter from Ferrara. Paintings in the oratory included Francia's *Marriage of St. Cecilia*; Costa's *St. Urbaus converting Valerian*; Tomarocci's *Baptism of Valerian*; Chiodarolo's *Angel crowning Saints Cecilia and Valerian*; Aspertini's *Martyrdom of Sants Valerian and Tiburtius*; Aspertini's *Burial of Saints Valerian and Tiburtius*; Chiodarolo's *Vindication of St. Cecilia*; Tamarocci's *Martyrdom of St. Cecilia in the oil-cask*; Costa's *St. Cecilia bestowing alms* and Francia's *Burial of St. Cecilia*. Long though it is, this list of paintings is useful when Anesaki compares another painting of St. Cecilia the next day to what he saw here.

15. *Baedeker's* notes, "the university [has been] established since 1803 in the old Palazzo Poggi, which was built by Pellegrino Tibaldo and has a court by Bart. Triachni. It possesses five faculties and is attended by about 1500 students." (*Northern Italy*, p. 376). But this location was clearly not the original location or facility of the university. The *Catholic Encyclopedia* provides the following information: "A tradition of the thirteenth century attributed the foundation of this university to Theodosius II (433); but this legend is now generally rejected.

The authentic 'Habita,' issued by Frederick Barbarossa in 1158, was at best only an implicit recognition of the existence of the school at Bologna, and the bull of Clement III (1189), though it speaks of 'masters and scholars,' has no reference to a university organization. The university, in fact, developed out of the 'Schools of the Liberal Arts' which flourished at Bologna early in the eleventh century." (*Catholic Encyclopedia*, "The University of Bologna")

16. *Baedeker's* provides the following description of the same scene: "Chapel of San Domenico (restored 1596–1605), contain[s] the tomb of the saint: a sarcophagus of white marble dating from 1267, with good reliefs from the life of the saint. ... The kneeling Angel to the left, in front, a graceful early-Renaissance work, is by Niccolo dell Arca, who received his surname from this sarcophagus, and who also executed the rich canopy, with its beautiful wreaths of fruit held by putti (1469–73). The angel of the right is an early work of Michael Angelo (1494), who also executed the St. Petronius immediately over the sarcophagus, with the church in his hand." (*Northern Italy*, p. 370)

17. This "Filippo Lippi" is actually Filippino Lippi (ca. 1459–1504), whose painting of the Madonna and saints was done in 1501. Anesaki gives the name of Lippi's father, Fra Filippo Lippi (1406–69), who was also a well-known Italian artist.

18. The Palazzo Bevilacqua, an early Renaissance structure of 1477–84.

19. Also known as the Maruyama-Shijō 円山四条 school of painting. This school, founded by Maruyama Ōkyo 円山応挙 (1733–95), was a prominent movement in Japanese painting in the eighteenth and nineteenth centuries. The school is known for blending both realistic elements (seen as a Western artistic influence) and Japanese techniques and motifs.

20. The main cathedral in Bologna is San Pietro.

21. It is unclear to which painting Anesaki refers here. Masaccio painted such a scene, *Distribution of Alms and the Death of Ananias*, but Lippi apparently did not. It is possible that Anesaki is confusing the two. He views Masaccio's painting in Florence (see entry for April 19, p. 66).

22. Kyōgen 狂言 is the comic theatrical form that functions as a counterpart to Nō drama. It was a popular entertainment in its own right during the Edo 江戸 period (1600–1868).

23. "Petronino" in the text. See Note 5.

24. See Note 25 below.

25. This painting is probably in the Abbondio Chapel. Robert Gibbs (in "Giovanni da Modena") describes the two frescoes there by Giovanni di Modena

as follows: "The frescoes of 1420-1 in the chapel of S. Abbondio in S. Petronio, Bologna, show two mystic crucifixions: one of Christ on a tree between Adam and Eve, prophets, the Virgin and saints, and the other on a cross, the arms of which crown a personification of the Church on one side and stab a personification of the Synagogue on the other (an anti-Semitism aimed at locally established Jewish colonies)." If these are indeed the frescoes that Anesaki saw, then his dates ("sixteenth century") are wrong.

26. Apparently the Pinacoteca Nazionale or Accademia di Belle Arti.

27. Guido Reni (1575–1642), commonly called "Guido," was influenced by Raphael and the Carracci family (see Note 29), and became the leading painter of the Bolognese (or Ecclectic) school after he settled permanently in Bologna in 1622.

28. Reni's pieces on display in this room (Room A) at the time included *Samson, victorious over the Philistines*; *Madonna del Rosario*; *St. Sebastian*; *Madonna della Pietà*; *Sant' Andrea Corsini*; *Crucifixion*; and *Massacre of the Innocents*.

29. The next room, Room B, was dedicated to the art of the Carracci family of Bolognese painters, the brothers Agostino (1557–1602) and Annibale (1560–1609) and their cousin Lodovico (1555–1619).

30. Indeed, it was "the one after that," specifically Room D.

31. "Perugino" is Pietro Perugino (1446–1524), a teacher of Raphael.

32. This painting is also called *Madonna in Glory with the Child and Saints* and shows the Virgin Mary with saints Michael, John, Catharine, and Appollonia. See List of Artworks, #1.

33. See List of Artworks, #2.

34. St. Cecilia is the patron saint of music and musicians in general, not just of this church in particular (as Anesaki implies here).

35. Cimabue, originally named Bencivieni di Pepo (born before 1251, died after 1302) was the last great Italian artist in the Byzantine style. His work influenced Giotto and Duccio.

THE HOME OF FLOWERS; THE CAPITAL OF PAINTINGS

1. This is the beginning of Canto I of the *Paradiso*. Henry Wadsworth Longfellow translated this passage as follows:

> The glory of Him who moveth everything
> Doth penetrate the universe, and shine

In one part more and in another less.
Within that heaven which most his light receives
Was I, and things beheld which to repeat
Nor knows, nor can, who from above descends;
Because in drawing near to its desire
Our intellect ingulphs itself so far,
That after it the memory cannot go.

2. Shūzenji 修善寺 is a hot spring resort located on the Izu 伊豆 Peninsula in Japan.

3. Pracchia is about 600 meters (2,000 feet) above sea level.

4. Giotto di Bondone (1276–1337). Giotto began the construction of the bell tower in 1334–36, and Andrea Pisano and Franc. Talenti completed it in 1387 after Giotto's death.

5. These paintings are referred to as *Scenes from the Life of Saint Francis*: "As in the Peruzzi chapel, three frescoes framed by ornamental bands decorate each wall. But unlike in the former, these are dedicated to just the one saint, St. Francis. The Renunciation of Worldly Goods and the Confirmation of the Rule are situated in the lunettes. In the middle register the Apparition at Arles and the Trial by Fire before the Sultan are depicted. The Death of St. Francis and Inspection of the Stigmata and the Apparition at Aries can be seen at eye level. Above the entrance to the chapel the Stigmatisation is portrayed, as it were, as a summation of the life of the saint. The seraphim from whom Francis receives the stigmata here appears – unlike at Assisi or in the panel in the Musée du Louvre – as the crucified Christ." (*Web Gallery of Art*, "Giotto; Frescoes in the Church of Santa Croce in Florence; Frescoes in the Bardi Chapel; Scenes from the Life of Saint Francis: No. 1–4 [left wall]") See List of Artworks, #3 and #4.

6. "Masaccio" is Tommaso di Ser Giovanni Guidi da Castel San Giovanni (1401–28).

7. The Brancacci Chapel was part of Santa Maria del Carmine. According to *Baedeker's*, it was "embellished after 1423 (?) by Masaccio, probably with the assistance of Masolino, with celebrated frescoes from the traditions regarding the Apostles, especially St. Peter, to which Filippino Lippi added others about 1484." (*Northern Italy*, p. 509)

8. The Church of San Marco is a monastic church first built in 1290 and subsequently rebuilt a number of times, the most recent to Anesaki's visit being in

1780. Anesaki spends most of his time in the Monastery of San Marco, which is adjacent to the church.

9. Saint Antoninus, Archbishop of Florence (1389–1459) and a contemporary of Fra Angelico.

10. Girolamo Savonarola (1452–98) was a Dominican reformer who felt that the Renaissance was too decadent. Anesaki's rejection of worldly Renaissance art the previous day echoes Savonarola's attitude.

11. In 1498 Savonarola was hanged and burned by the church for falsely claiming to have seen visions. Before that he was excommunicated (1497), although he had a large following.

12. Anesaki was likely reading *Life and Times of Girolamo Savonarola* by Pasquale Villari and translated by Linda Villari, which was published in 1888. This very paragraph appears on page 687 of the 12th edition. The rest of the sermon is not included.

13. The description of this monastery in *Baedeker's* fills in the blanks that Anesaki leaves out: "The Monastery of San Marco [was] surpressed in 1867, and now restored and fitted up as the Museo di San Marco. The building was originally occupied by 'Silvestrine' monks, but was transferred under Cosimo the Elder to the Domnicans, who were favoured by the Medici. In 1437–43 it was restored in a handsome style from designs by Michelozzo, and shortly afterwards it was decorated by Fra Giovanni Angelico da Fiesole (1387–1455) with those charming frescos which to this day are unrivalled in their portrayal of profound and devoted piety. The painter Fra Bartolomeo della Porta (1475–1517) was a monk in this monastery from 1500 and the powerful preacher Girolamo Savonarola also once lived here." (*Northern Italy*, p. 491).

14. *Christ on the Cross Adored by St. Dominic* (c.1442) by Fra Angelico, Museo di San Marco. See List of Artworks, #5.

15. This painting, by Fra Angelico, is *Peter Martyr Enjoins Silence* (c.1441), Museo di San Marco. It was located over the doorway to the sacristy. See List of Artworks, #6.

16. St. Thomas Aquinas.

17. *Baedeker's* notes, "The First Cloisters... contain... over the entrance to the 'foresteria', or apartments devoted to hospitality, Christ as a pilgrim welcomed by two Dominican monks ('No scene more true, more noble, or more exquisitely rendered than this, can be imagined' C. & C.)" (*Northern Italy*, p. 491). See List of Artworks, #7.

18. *Resurrection of Christ and Women at the Tomb*. See List of Artworks #8.

19. Anesaki uses the term "meeting room" here.

20. *Baedeker's* notes, "The Chapter house… contains a large crucifixion (Christ between the thieves), surrounded by a group of twenty saints, all lifesize, with busts of Dominicans below, by Fra Angelico. The sympathetic grief of the saints is most poignantly expressed." (*Nothern Italy*, p. 491) See List of Artworks #9.

21. "The giant fresco occupies the entire wall opposite to the entrance of the Chapter Room. The saints depicted are, from the left: Cosmas and Damian, Lawrence, Mark the Evangelist, John the Baptist, the Virgin and the pious women; to the right of the Crucifixion kneeling Dominic, Jerome, Francis, Bernard, John Gualberto and Peter the Martyr, standing Zanobi (or perhaps Ambrose), Augustin, Benedict, Romuald and Thomas of Aquino. Around the fresco, on the border, are the busts of the Prophets and Sybils in ten hexagons; in the centre, above the Crucifixion the pelikan, symbol of the redemption. Below, in the lower frieze there are 17 medallions with portraits of the most illustrious members of the Dominican Order." (*Web Gallery of Art*, "Fra Angelico; Frescoes; Convent of San Marco; Frescoes on the corridors and in the Chapter Room; Crucifixion and Saints") See List of Artworks #10.

22. The figure that Anesaki identifies as St. Albert is otherwise identified (see note above) as Zanobi or Ambrose.

23. Eshin 恵心 is another name for Genshin Shōzu 源信僧都 (942–1017), a major figure in Heian period Pure Land Buddhism.

24. "According to legend, this work was written by Francis of Assisi two years before his death (1226). Written in vulgar Umbrian, 'Cantica' is one of the most ancient landmarks of Italian literature. In rhythmic assonant prose, it praises the Lord through the exaltation of His creations: water, fire, stars, moon, etc., up to Death itself." (http://www.ilnarratore.com/anthology/dassisi/cantico.PDF, Last accessed June 24, 2008)

25. Anesaki is referring to the Senbon 千本寺 temple in Kyoto, where he was born.

26. Anesaki is referring to the fourth painting in the series *Scenes from the Life of St. Francis* by Giotti.

27. It is unclear exactly to what Anesaki is referring. *Baedeker's* notes, "Over the central door [of Santa Croce] is a bas-relief (*Raising of the Cross*), by Giov. Dupré." (*Nothern Italy*, p. 477). It makes no note of what is over the other two doors, and there is clearly a discrepancy between Anesaki's "power" and "raising."

28. It is unclear which sūtra, if any, this paraphrase comes from.

29. These frescoes, by Masaccio, depict the life of St. Peter. Masaccio (1401–1427?) was one of the first significant painters of the Renaissance, but after he fell from favor the paintings were completed by Lippi. There are many scenes, many of which Anesaki conflates as he describes them. The individual scenes depict: *The Temptation* (Masolino); *The Expulsion from the Garden* (Masaccio); *Peter's Calling* (Masaccio); *Tribute Money* (Masaccio); *The Healing of the Cripple and the Raising of Tabitha* (Masolino); *St. Peter Preaching* (Masolino); *Baptism of the Neophytes* (Masaccio); *St. Peter Healing the Sick with his Shadow* (Masaccio); *The Distribution of Alms and the Death of Ananias* (Masaccio); *The Raising of the Son of Theophilus*, and *St. Peter Enthroned* (Masaccio and Filippino Lippi); *St. Paul Visiting St. Peter in Prison* (Filippino Lippi) *Peter Being Freed from Prison* (Filippino Lippi); *Disputation with Simon Magus and Crucifixion of St. Peter* (Filippino Lippi).

30. *The Distribution of Alms and the Death of Ananias*, 1426–27. See List of Artworks #11.

31. Correggio (1490–1534) was an Italian painter, whose pseudonym came from the small town in Emilia where he was born. His real name was Antonio Allegri.

32. "Bernardino di Betto (Benedetto), Italian painter called Il Pinturicchio, was, like Perugino, a native of the district around Perugia and consequently open to the artistic currents common to the Umbrian region. His training and early career are completely unknown; even his date of birth is a matter of speculation. Usually considered to have been born around 1454 on the basis of ambiguous data given by Vasari, he was more likely born a few years later." (*Web Gallery of Art*, "Pinturicchio, Biography")

33. In other words, Masaccio and Lippi. Because Anesaki mentions Lippi only once by name in the earlier paragraphs, it is easy to forget who the second "expert artisan" is.

34. The Palazzo Pitti was begun in 1458. Its function has changed over the centuries from the home of Luca Pitti, a banker (and whose name the Palazzo retains), to the home of the Medici family, to a headquarters of Napoleon, to a royal palace in the late nineteenth century, to its most recent incarnation as an art gallery.

35. Toyotomi Hideyoshi 豊臣秀吉 (1536–1598), the second of the so-called "three unifiers" of Japan – Oda Nobunaga 織田信長 (1534–82), Toyotomi Hideyoshi, and Tokugawa Ieyasu 徳川家康 (1543–1616) – did not succeed in his efforts to politically unify the country. His successor, Tokugawa Ieyasu, did.

Anesaki implies that Ieyasu's aesthetics were inferior to Hideyoshi's, although this is in the eye of the beholder. Ieyasu and his grandson, Iemitsu 家光 (1604–51), are particularly known for their taste for the ornate.

36. The Muromachi 室町 period (1336–1568) and the Momoyama 桃山 period (1568–1600) were both times of internecine war in Japan. The Tokugawa 徳川 period which followed (1600–1868) was a time of peace, albeit under military rule. Anesaki refers here, with his term "vulgarization," to the general trend in the Tokugawa toward brighter, more colorful visual arts. Also perhaps in his mind was a move away from religious focus in painting to more secular pieces. Anesaki developed this observation at length in his 1932 book *Art, Life, and Nature in Japan.*

37. These gardens are extensive, and were the model for many other gardens in Europe, including Versailles. Their construction was begun in the sixteenth century by the Medici. This is the largest park area in Florence, and as Anesaki mentions, affords beautiful views of the surrounding area.

38. This is probably the cypress alley known as the "Viottolone."

39. The Medici family crest, which is usually drawn with six orbs, has varied over the centuries. In the sixteenth century there was a period when the crest had seven orbs, and it is likely that Anesaki is referring to this incarnation.

40. San Domenico di Fiesole, a Dominican monastery founded in 1405.

41. Fiesole Triptych. See List of Artworks #12.

42. This painting, of the Madonna with saints, was in the choir of the church, in the first chapel on the left. It was painted by Fra Angelico in 1424–1430 but then adapted by Lorenzo di Credi in 1501.

43. Probably the Convento di San Francesco, to the northwest of Fiesole. It was later converted to an art museum.

44. The word that Anesaki uses here is 禪定三昧, which comes from the Sanskrit word *samādhi*, which in Mahayana usage means deeper, or trance meditation.

45. The source of this quotation is obscure, although St. Francis admired flowers highly, and saw them as manifestations of the Holy Virgin.

46. *Baedeker's* notes, "In the Cappella Peruzzi Giotto has portrayed the life of the two St. Johns: ...Zacharias at the altar, Nativity of the Baptist (with a very fine figure of Elizabeth), Dancing of the Daughter of Herodias; Vision of the Evangelist in Patmos, from the Apocalypse, Resuscitation of Drusiana, and Ascension of the Evangelist, whose tomb his disciples find empty." (*Northern Italy*, p. 479) See List of Artworks #13.

47. As described in the New Testament, Matthew 14:3–11; Mark 6:17–28; Luke 3:19–20. See List of Artworks #14.

48. The three paintings Anesaki probably saw, although his description here is unclear, depicted scenes from the life of St. John the Evangelist: St. John on Patmos, Raising of Drusiana, and Ascension of the Evangelist. For the last, see List of Artworks #15.

49. The terms that Anesaki uses here for "own power" and "other power" are the Buddhist terms *jiriki* 自力 and *tariki* 他力. The implication is that Christ, like Amida Buddha, provides the "other power" to salvation.

50. Anesaki uses a Buddhist term for "welcoming" here: *raigō* 来迎, which refers to "the coming of Buddhas to meet the dying believer and bid welcome to the Pure Land" (C. Muller, *Digital Dictionary of Buddhism*, http://www.buddhism-dict.net/ddb/)

51. Genshin Shōzu 源信僧都 (942–1017) was a major figure in Heian period Pure Land Buddhism. He is perhaps best known for his famous work, *The Essentials of Salvation* (*Ōjō-yōshū* 往生要集), but he was also a painter who depicted the bliss of the Pure Land in his work.

52. Anesaki is referring to the Accademia di Belle Arti Firenze, founded in 1783. *Baedeker's* comments, "The collection of ancient masters contains few pictures to strike the eye or imagination of the amateur, but it is a most important collection for students of the development of Italian art during the 14th–16th centuries." (*Northern Italy*, p. 492)

53. Bencivieni di Pepo, more commonly called Cimabue (see p. 267, note 35).

54. Each of the pieces in this collection is given a number.

55. John Ruskin (1819–1900), British writer and critic. Ruskin's views on art, architecture, and style in general were widely circulated in his own time, and his influence continued to be felt well into the twentieth century. Ruskin also wrote on the structure and design of books, which probably inspired Anesaki's comment. Anesaki mentions Ruskin one more time, much later, when criticizing Ticiano. See the entry for May 22.

56. See List of Artworks #16

57. Matthew 5:39

58. A paraphrase of Matthew 5:4, "Blessed are the meek, for they shall possess the land."

59. Correggio's painting is titled *Ecce Homo* and is owned by the National Gallery in London (which purchased it in 1834 – it is unclear whether Anesaki misremembers where the painting was, or if he saw a copy of it in Paris). The

painting shows Christ in the center, surrounded by four other figures. It does not seem to matter to Anesaki that the surrounding figures are all partly obscured, and the focus is clearly on Christ.

60. Heinrich Hofmann (1824–1911) was a German painter best known for his depictions of Christ.

61. The Palazzo di Brera, which *Baedeker's* describes as "built for a Jesuit college by Ricchini in 1651 et seq., since 1776 the seat of the Accademia di Belle Arti, and now styled Palazzo di Scienze, Lettere ed Arti." (*Northern Italy*, p. 123). Today it is referred to as the Pinacoteca di Brera. However, Anesaki seems mistaken. Leonardo's *The Last Supper* is located in the Santa Maria delle Grazie church, not the Palazzo di Brera, in Milan.

62. See List of Artworks, #8

63. See List of Artworks, #17

64. Franz Seraph von Lenbach (1836–1904), a portrait artist who, in the course of his career, painted almost one hundred portraits of Bismarck.

65. See List of Artworks, #18

66. *Noli Me Tangere* (1440–1441). See List of Artworks, #19

67. See List of Artworks #20

68. See List of Artworks #21

69. This and the next two poems are written in standard *waka* 和歌 meter.

70. San Domenico di Fiesole, which he had visited earlier.

71. The Convento di San Francesco, which Anesaki also mentions on April 20.

72. The English for *gersomino* is "jasmine" but the English for *fūrosō* 風露草 is "geranium." It is possible that Anesaki mistook *gersomino* for *geranio* which is the Italian for "geranium" which could account for why these flowers looked "nothing like the usual jasmine."

73. In early 1909 the New York Times, quoting the *Journal Officiel*, reported that in France "the [population] figures for the first six months of 1908… show that the births exceed the deaths by 11,000. In the corresponding period of the previous year the deaths exceeded the births by 55,000." (*New York Times*, January 18, 1909). Anesaki appears to be commenting on 1907 figures, which were probably available to him in early 1908.

74. Chūjōhime 中将姫 (Princess Chūjōhime), daughter of Lord Fujiwara Toyonari 藤原豊成 (704?–65), was a devout Buddhist who lived in the eighth century. There are many legends associated with her, most notably those concerning the creation of the Taima *mandala* 當麻曼荼羅.

75. Fusehime is a legendary figure who appears in Takizawa Bakin's 滝沢 馬琴 (1767–1848) neo-Confucian classic *Satomi Hakkenden* 里見八犬伝. What makes her salient here is that she sacrifices herself for her father, and becomes the "wife" of a dog, who impregnates her even though she is a virgin. She also commits suicide to defend her honor as a virgin.

76. Galleria degli Uffizi, the Uffizi Gallery. *Baedeker's* describes it as follows: "The gallery originated with the Medici collections, to which numerous additions have been made down to the most recent times, and it is now one of the greatest in the world, both in extent and value." (*Northern Italy*, p. 457)

ASSISI, BIRTHPLACE OF A SAINT

1. This translation is by Henry Wadsworth Longfellow. In Anesaki's original, he gives Dante's original Italian, and below it a Japanese translation. The passage is from Canto XI.

2. Although "sarcophagus" is an awkward word in the English, "tomb" would be incorrect as Anesaki is specifically referring to the stone coffin, and not the vault or room in which it is placed.

3. "The *Beato*" refers to Fra Angelico.

4. Monte Amiata (elevation 1,738 m) is the highest mountain in the Tuscany region, and the second tallest volcano in Italy. It lies in the southernmost part of Tuscany.

5. Monte Cetona (elevation 1,148 m), formerly known as "Monte Piesi," is located near the city of Ciusi.

6. The city of Perugia was a twenty minute tram ride away from the train station. Although Anesaki is unclear about the details here, he left the train station at Ponte S. Giovanni and went up the hill to Perugia, perhaps by electric tram. In order to return to the station and catch the next train he had to either take another tram or walk; in the interest of time he chose the latter mode of transportation.

7. *Baedeker's Central Italy* describes Perugia as follows: "Perugia... lies on a group of hills about 985 ft. above the valley of the Tiber. The town is built in an antiquated style, partly on the top of the hill, and partly on its slope. Numerous buildings of the 14th–15th cent. (when the town was at its zenith), the paintings of the Umbrian school, and the fine views of the peculiar scenery, make Perugia one of the most interesting places in Italy." (*Central Italy*, p. 60)

8. It is unclear which gate Anesaki sees, as there were many. However, it

seems likely that he saw the Arco d' Augusto, which was relatively well preserved and is thought to be Roman in origin.

9. The Monastery of the Franciscans. It was built on a hill ridge, and was finished in 1228. There are two churches in the compound, one above the other. St. Francis's crypt was built in 1818, when Francis's sarcophagus was re-discovered.

10. "One of the six heavens in the realm of desire 六欲天, it is located at the top of Mt. Sumeru(須彌山. At each of its corners there is a peak, where eight gods dwell, and in the palace lives the Lord of the Heavens (Indra, Śakra)." (Muller, *Digital Dictionary of Buddhism*)

11. Anesaki may be alluding to Francis being a party to the drinking centuries ago, as his biographers all mention the dissipation and wild behavior of his youth before he turned to religion.

12. Kōbō Daishi 弘法大師 (774–835), also known as Kūkai 空海, founded the Shingon 真言 (Tantric) sect of Buddhism in Japan. The seat of this sect is on Mt. Kōya 高野山 in central Japan. An important and well known figure in Japanese history, his name would be immediately recognized by Anesaki's readers.

13. Anesaki mentions Hōnen much earlier (see entry for April 6), but it is not until he reaches Assisi that Hōnen's life and teachings become important. Hōnen 法然 was as famous as Kōbō Daishi (see above); his name would be familiar to any Japanese reader. The Yoshimizu hermitage 吉水の庵 was located north of Kyoto, and was where Hōnen established himself.

14. Dengyō Daishi 伝教大師 (767–822) is credited with establishing Tendai 天台 Buddhism in Japan. Mt. Hiei 比叡山, to the northeast of Kyoto, is home to a vast temple complex and is the seat of Tendai Buddhism in Japan. By using Kōbō Daishi, Hōnen, and Dengyō Daishi as contrast objects, Anesaki is elevating St. Francis to an extremely high level.

15. Paul Sabatier (1858–1928) wrote *The Life of St. Francis of Assisi*. The book was first published in 1894 in French, but was translated soon thereafter into English, Swedish, German, and Italian (the first English translation, published by Charles Scribner and Sons, New York, appeared in 1894). A Japanese translation appeared in 1915 (*Asshishi no sei furanchesuko den* アッシシの聖フランチェスコ伝, Tokyo: Nihon kirisutokyō kōbunkyōkai 日本基督教興文協会), but because Anesaki is writing in 1908, we can assume he was familiar with the original or one of the earlier translations.

16. Although Anesaki uses a Buddhist term here (*hōtō* 法燈), he seems to be applying it to a Christian concept.

17. These levels are commonly referred to as the Upper Basilica (Anesaki's

upper level) the Lower Basilica (Anesaki's central level) and the Tomb of the Saint (Anesaki's lower level).

18. Anesaki refers here to the 48-scroll *Hōnen Shōnin Eden* 法然上人絵伝. As Ive Aaslid describes it, "Commissioned by a retired emperor in 1307, it claims to be the authoritative account of the life and deeds of Hōnen, the early Kamakura period founder of Jōdo Buddhism. Beyond simply recounting the priest's activities, the scroll functions to inspire religious devotion in its viewers. Although the text quotes Hōnen's teachings and writings extensively, the visual narrative provides perhaps the most concrete evidence for the merits of faith in Hōnen's Jōdo doctrine. In an early section of the emaki, Hōnen is visually transformed from a human priest into a deified savior figure. Later sections show people from all walks of life achieving rebirth as a result of Hōnen's teachings." (Ive Aaslid, Abstract of "Memory and Salvation in the 48-scroll Hōnen Shōnin Eden"). For a photograph of the Interior of the Upper Church, see List of Artworks #23

19. See List of Artworks #24

20. See List of Artworks #25

21. This story comes from part 1, chapter 53 of *Fioretti di San Francesco*. In part it reads:

> Then [St. Francis and the peasant] were come to about the midst of the ascent of the mount, because the way was toilsome, and the heat exceeding great, the peasant was overcome with thirst, insomuch that he began to cry after St. Francis saying: "Alas! Alas! I am dying of thirst; unless I have something to drink, I shall presently faint."
>
> Then St. Francis dismounted from the ass, and betook himself to prayer, remaining upon his knees, with hands uplifted up to heaven, until he knew by revelation that his prayer was heard. Then said he to the peasant, "Run quickly to yonder rock, and there thou shalt find a stream of living water, which Jesus Christ of his mercy has caused to flow out from the stone." Then went he to the place which St. Francis had shown to him, and found a beautiful fountain, issuing by virtue of the prayer of St. Francis, from that hard rock; and he drank of it plentifully, and was refreshed. And certain it is that this spring of water flowed forth miraculously at the prayer of St. Francis, for neither before nor after was a spring to be found at that spot, nor any running water save at a great distance therefrom. (*The Little Flowers of St. Francis of Assisi*, trans. Roger Hudleston. Boulder, Colorado: Christian Classics Ethereal Library, 1990)

22. As noted, this is from part 1, chapter 16 of *Fioretti di San Francesco*. The English translation here is from *The Little Flowers of St. Francis of Assisi*, trans. Hudleston. The passage that Anesaki omits makes reference to the story of Noah's Ark, and reads as follows: "Two of all your species he sent into the Ark with Noah that you might not be lost to the world; besides which…" A number of translations of *Fioretti* were published in the late nineteenth and early twentieth centuries, so it is difficult to determine which one Anesaki had read.

23. *Myōga o yorokobu* 冥加を喜ぶ.

24. The Sumiyoshi School 住吉派 was an early Tokugawa school of painting. The Tosa School 土佐派 was a fourteenth and fifteenth century school of painting.

25. Probably the Roman Templo di Minerva (Temple of Minerva).

26. St. Clare (1194–1253) founded the order of Carissines. The church of Santa Chiara was built by de Campello in 1257. Clare is probably one of the most famous disciples of Francis, if not the most famous, for reasons that are fleshed out later by Anesaki.

27. This translation is an approximation at best, as the term that Anesaki uses, *ichinen hokki* 一念發起 refers to one initially having faith in the Buddha, and entering on the Buddhist path. Sabatier writes in his biography of Francis:

Immediately on passing through [*Porta Nuova*] you find yourself in the open country; a fold of the hill hides the city and cuts off every sound that might come from it. Before you lies the winding road to Foligno; at the left the imposing mass of Mount Subasio; at the right the Umbrian plain with its farms its villages, its cloudlike hills, on whose slopes pines, cedars, oaks, the vine, and the olive-tree shed abroad an incomparable brightness and animation. The whole country sparkles with beauty.

Francis had hoped by this sight to recover the delicious sensations of his youth. With the sharpened sensibility of the convalescent he breathed in the odors of the springtime, but springtime did not come to his heart, as he had expected. Nature had for him only a message of sadness. He had believed that the breezes of this beloved countryside would carry away the last shudders of the fever, and instead he felt in his heart a discouragement a thousandfold more painful than any physical illness. The miserable emptiness of his life suddenly appeared before him; he was terrified at his solitude, the solitude of a great soul in which there is no altar.

Memories of the past assailed him with intolerable bitterness. Seized with a disgust of himself, he found that his former ambitions seemed to him ridiculous or despicable. Francis went home overwhelmed with the weight of a new suffering.

In such hours of moral anguish we seek a refuge either in love or in faith. By a holy violence he was to arrive at last at a pure and virile faith, but the road to this point was long and sown thick with obstacles, and at the moment at which we have arrived he had not yet entered upon it; he did not even suspect its existence. All he knew was that pleasure leads to nothingness, to satiety and self-contempt. (Paul Sabatier, *The Road to Assisi: the Essential Biography of St. Francis*, Edited with Intro. and annotations by Jon M. Sweeney, Brewster, Mass.: Paraclete Press, 2003, pp. 9–10.)

28. The reasons for Hōnen's exile to the island of Shikoku are complex, but in sum it was because his interpretation of Buddhism was seen as heretical, and he was considered a harmful influence.

29. The translation of this term, *shimon yūkan* 四問遊觀 is from Muller's *Digital Dictionary of Buddhism*.

30. Kapilavastu was the hometown of the Buddha, and was located in a mountainous region of present-day Nepal.

31. "Arousals of the mind" is *hosshin* 發心.

32. Jichin is another name for Jien 慈円 (1155–1225), a Tendai priest and poet.

33. *The Tale of the Heike* 平家物語 was originally told by blind *biwa* (lute) players known as *biwa hōshi* 琵琶法師.

34. The term Anesaki uses is *daihotsugan* 大發願, which is defined as "To give rise to the intention to save all sentient beings. To arouse the aspiration for enlightenment, or rebirth in the Pure Land." (C. Muller, *Digital Dictionary of Buddhism*). The "hut-like" chapel is the Cappella del Transito, currently located in the right part of the apse of the church of Santa Maria degli Angeli.

35. Anesaki refers here to "Italian Time:" a system of time telling that began in the fourteenth century. In this system, the "first hour" (Anesaki's "one o'clock" here) started at sunset. Hence, seven or eight in the evening according the modern clock would be the first or second hour of the day in Italian Time. *Baedeker's* 1868 edition notes, "The old Italian reckoning from 1 to 24 o'clock is now disused, except by the humbler classes. Ave Maria = 24. The hours are altered every fortnight, being regulated by the sunset. The ordinary reckoning of other nations is termed *ora francese.*" (*Northern Italy, as Far as Leghorn, Florence, and Ancona, and the Island of Corsica*. Leipzig: Karl Baedeker, 1868, p. xxiv.)

36. The term is *hōshōjini* 法性自爾, and this translation is from the *Digital Dictionary of Buddhism*.

37. There are many different versions of this legend. The events took place in 1224, when Francis was in the Verna. Sabatier wrote:

> Francis doubled his fastings and prayers, "quite transformed into Jesus by love and compassion," says one of the legends. He passed the night before the festival alone in prayer, not far from the hermitage. In the morning he had a vision. In the rays of the rising sun, which after the chill of night came to revive his body, he suddenly perceived a strange form. A seraph, with outspread wings, flew toward him from the edge of the horizon and bathed his soul in raptures unutterable. In the center of the vision appeared a cross, and the seraph was nailed upon it.
>
> When the vision disappeared, he felt sharp sufferings mingling with the ecstasy of the first moments. Stirred to the very depths of his being, he was anxiously seeking the meaning of it all when he perceived on his body the stigmata of the Crucified One. (*The Road to Assisi*, p.129–130)

38. Anesaki uses the Buddhist term *honzon* 本尊 (Ch. *benzun*) here. *The Digital Dictionary of Buddhism* elaborates: "A *benzun* is a buddha, bodhisattva, or mandala that is used as an object of worship. A *benzun* that appears externally is referred to as an 'object of veneration with form' 有相本尊, while one that is generated in the mind of the practitioner is called an 'object of veneration without form' 無相本尊. The sutras of Esoteric School 密教 – the Mahāvairocana-sūtra 大日經(and the Yuzhijing 瑜祇經 – mention the *benzun*, but the term has come to be used more generally to describe objects of veneration throughout the various sects of Buddhism. Although the Esoteric school views Mahāvairocana 大日如來(as the original *benzun*, bodhisattvas and other deities have become objects of veneration that manifest one aspect of Mahāvairocana."

39. It is unclear, but the painting that Anesaki seems to be looking at is Giotto's *St. Francis in Glory*, 1316–19.

40. Anna M. Stoddart (1840–1911) published her book *Francis of Assisi* in 1903 (London: Methuen).

41. This event in Francis's life took place some time between 1206 and 1209. Francis had spent days hidden from his father, who was enraged that Francis had taken cloth from his father's stores and sold it to earn money for the chapel San Damiano. Sabatier's account is as follows:

> The seclusion could not last long. Francis perceived this and told himself that for a newly made knight of Christ he was cutting a very pitiful figure. Arming himself, therefore, with courage, he went one day to the city to present himself before his father and make known to him his resolution. It is

easy to imagine the changes wrought in his appearance by these few weeks of seclusion, much of them passed in mental anguish. When he appeared, pale, cadaverous, his clothes in tatters, upon what is now the Piazza Nuova, where hundreds of children play all day long, he was greeted with a great shout, "*Pazzo, Pazzo!*" ("A madman! A madman!") "*Un pazzo ne fa cento*" ("One madman makes a hundred more"), says the proverb, but one must have seen the delirious excitement of the street children of Italy at the sight of a madman to gain an idea how true it is. The moment the magic cry resounds they rush into the street with frightful din, and while their parents look on from the windows, they surround the unhappy sufferer with wild dances mingled with songs, shouts, and savage howls. They throw stones at him, fling mud upon him, blindfold him; if he flies into a rage, they double their insults; if he weeps or begs for pity, they repeat his cries and mimic his sobs and supplications without respite and without mercy. (*The Road to Assisi*, p. 37–38)

42. 雲母坂. This is one of the main routes up Mt. Hiei 比叡山 in Kyoto; particularly in ancient times it was the route that one took to the summit. Hiei is the seat of Tendai Buddhism in Japan, and is home to the vast Buddhist temple complex of Enryakuji 延暦寺.

43. There is a play on words here, which makes the third line of the poem mean both that he is crawling along but also that he may get a glimpse of the saint's footprints.

44. *Baedeker's* comments, "In a ravine of the Monte Subasio, to the east of Assisi, is situated the hermitage *delle carceri* (2300 ft.), to which St. Francis retired for devotional exercises. Near the chapel are a few apartments built in the 14th century, and the rock-bed of the saint. It is reached on foot from the Porta Cappuccini in 1½ [hours], with donkey in 1 hour." (*Central Italy*, p. 75) Anesaki was on foot.

45. Jon Sweeney, in his annotated version of Sabatier's *Lif of St. Francis Assisi*, writes, "Regarding the Carceri, one century-old guide to Assisi writes, 'Even to call such shelters huts is giving them too grand a name, for they were but caverns excavated in the rock, scattered here and there in a deep mountain gorge. They can still be seen, unchanged since the days of St. Francis save for the tresses of ivy growing thick, like a curtain, across the entrance, for now there are none to pass in and out to pray there.'" (*The Road to Assisi*, p. 57)

46. The *yamabushi* 山伏 are followers of *shugendō* 修験道, a religious tradition that advocates an ascetic life in the mountains.

47. *Shōjō no shugyō* 小乗の修行

48. *Shōdō no nangyō* 聖道の難行. The accusation that Hōnen turned to Pure Land because he was unable to follow traditional Buddhist paths to enlightenment was a common view. Here Anesaki refutes that view.

49. *Nembutsu sanmai* 念佛三昧. "The samādhi in which the individual whole-heartedly thinks of the appearance of the Buddha, or of the Dharmakāya, or repeats the Buddha's name. The one who enters into this samādhi, or merely repeats the name of Amitābha, however evil his life may have been, will acquire the merits of Amitābha and be received into Paradise, hence the term." (Soothill's *Dictionary of Chinese Buddhist Terms*).

50. Anesaki uses a neologism here, 念神三昧, which is a variation of the Buddhist term, 念佛三昧. By substituting the character for God 神 for the character for Buddha 佛 in his phrase, he implies that St. Francis's austerities brought him to a state in which he whole-heartedly thought of the appearance of Christ.

51. The term that Anesaki uses for "lion's roar" (siṃhanāda 子吼) is Buddhist, and is defined as "The lion's roar, a term designating authoritative or powerful preaching. As the lion's roar makes all animals tremble, subdues elephants, arrests birds in their flight and fishes in the water, so Buddha's preaching overthrows all other religions, subdues devils, conquers heretics, and arrests the misery of life." (Soothill's *Dictionary of Chinese Buddhist Terms*)

52. In his 1907 travelogue of Italy, J.W. Cruickshank describes the monastery as:

...built on the sides of Monte Subasio. The path leaves Assisi by the gate at the end of the town farthest from S. Francesco, and from this point one or one and a half hours ought to be allowed for the walk.

Originally a little chapel was built here by the Benedictines, and since the time of Francis a network of small chapels, a few sleeping-cells, and a refectory have existed. In the woods round about there are caves associated with the names of the early Franciscans, and to these places they retired for solitary contemplation. Perhaps here more than elsewhere it is possible to realize the daily life of the Franciscans, and nowhere else is the sense of primitive simplicity so complete.

The visitor enters a small courtyard, in the centre of which is a well said to have been built by S. Bernardino of Siena, the spring itself being the result of a miracle worked by St. Francis. From this court we enter the chapel called after S. Bernardino; it is some twenty-one feet long by sixteen feet broad. In it are preserved relics of St. Francis: 1) The tabernacle for the sacrament used in his time, 2) A chalice of the same period, 3) A pillow used by St. Francis, 4) The cord of Brother Egidio, 5) The cross and hair shirt of St. Francis.

At the end of the chapel are five little stalls, the second of which is traditionally assigned to St. Francis.

From this comparatively large chapel we pass into the Cappella Primitiva. This is said to have been the first chapel used by St. Francis; it has no window, and is only about twelve feet long by six feet broad.

To the left, three steps lead up into the choir of S. Bernardino; round it there are twelve stalls, and beside these there is room for nothing but a reading-stand. The sacristy which serves for all these chapels is about six feet by four feet six inches, and it is lighted by a window no larger than a pane of glass. At the entrance to the sacristy there is a trap-door, and passing down about fifteen steps the chamber of St. Francis is reached. Like many other parts of the building, it rests on the live rock. The space occupied by the bed is shown. The room measures about nine feet by six feet. Next to this bed space is an oratory where St. Francis prayed.

The doors by which these chambers are entered are so small that no ordinary person can stand upright, and the width is strictly in proportion. Outside the oratory is an opening leading down into the gorge below it; it was by this passage that the devil escaped when he tempted St. Francis and was beaten off by the saint." (Cruickshank & Cruickshank, *The Umbrian Cities of Italy*, Vol. I. Boston: L. C. Page & Company, 1907, pp. 45–47.)

53. This statue was a bronze copy of Giovanni Dupré's *Statue of St. Francis* in the cathedral, erected in 1882. Anesaki mentions the original later on.

54. A Buddhist concept for which there is no set English translation. Roughly speaking, it means to set aside for the future one's merits earned presently through one's own efforts.

55. This is the Chiesa Nuova. The designation of "new" is relative, in that it was built in the seventeenth century.

56. The "cathedral" is San Rufino, which had been the cathedral of Assisi since the early eleventh century. Anesaki is terse at best in his description. A twenty-first century guidebook describes it as follows: "Note also the façade of the church, this is one of the masterpieces of Romanesque architecture in Umbria and is a riot of exquisitely carved figures mythical and biblical. Around the beautiful rose window are the four animals which represent the evangelists and at the entrance there are two crouching lions, one devouring a man and the other holding a man in his claws, these beasts are meant to put you in a sombre frame of mind before entering the cathedral!" (Judith Dean, *Every Pilgrim's Guide to Assisi*, p. 5)

57. Giovanni Dupré, Italian sculptor, 1817–1882.

58. Probably the Giardino Publicco, now called the Gairdino del Pincio.

59. The term for "silent illumination" (*jakkō* 寂光) is a Buddhist term.

60. Anesaki's interpretation of this famous story is a little odd. In Sabatier's version, we are told that "The poor priest [of San Damiano] was surprised enough when Francis handed over to him the whole product of his sale. He doubtless thought that a passing quarrel had occurred between Bernardone and his son, and for greater prudence refused the gift. But Francis so insisted upon remaining with him that he finally gave him leave to do so. As to the money, now become useless, Francis cast it as a worthless object upon a window-seat in the chapel." (*The Road to Assisi*, p. 37).

61. See entry for April 19, where Anesaki first mentions the *Cantica*.

62. The Portiuncula, or Porziuncula, the chapel that is now located within Santa Maria degli Angeli.

63. In other words, the Blessed Sacrament.

64. Clare died in 1253 and was originally interred in San Damiano. Later her body was moved to the chapel of San Giorgio in the Basilica of Santa Chiara.

65. Sabatier's translation of this passage of the *Cantica del sole* hymn is: "O most high, almighty, good Lord God, to you belong praise, glory, honor, and all blessing! Praised be my Lord God with all Your creatures, and especially our Brother Sun, who brings us the day and who brings us the light. Fair is he and shines with a very great splendor: O Lord, he signifies You to us!" (*The Road to Assisi*, p. 135).

66. Sabatier writes: "[Clare] made him a large cell of reeds in the monastery garden, so that he might be entirely at liberty as to his movements. How could he refuse a hospitality so thoroughly Franciscan? It was indeed, but only too much so: Legions of rats and mice infested this retired spot. At night they ran over Francis's bed with an infernal uproar, such that he could find no rest from his sufferings. But he soon forgot all of that when near his sister-friend. Once again she gave back to him faith and courage. 'A single sunbeam,' he used to say, 'is enough to drive away many shadows.'" (*The Road to Assisi*, pp. 134–135)

67. This poem is in volume 30 of *Chokushūgoden* 勅修御伝.

68. It is hard to imagine this, but Judith Dean's description makes it clearer: "Climb the narrow stairs, noticing about halfway up on your right a small window leading out onto a terrace, grandly called the *giardinetto* (little garden) of St. Clare. By tradition this is the place that St. Francis composed his 'Canticle of the Creatures' while he was spending time at San Damiano recuperating after an

attempted operation to cure his eye problems by cauterization." (*Every Pilgrim's Guide to Assisi and other Franciscan Pilgrim Places*, p.45)

69. Matsuo Bashō 松尾芭蕉 (1644–1694) wrote this poem when he was forty-four years old, while at his retreat in Fukagawa. From there, he heard a temple bell but he could not tell if it was from Tōeisan Kan'ei temple 東叡山寛永寺 in Ueno 上野, or the temple in Asakusa 浅草.

70. This is from Canto XXX of Dante's *Paradiso*, which reads in part:

> There near and far nor add nor take away;
>> For there where God immediately doth govern,
>> The natural law in naught is relevant.
> Into the yellow of the Rose Eternal
>> That spreads, and multiplies, and breathes an odour
>> Of praise unto the ever-vernal Sun, … (trans. Longfellow)

71. Anesaki uses the term *daimyō* 大名 here, which in the Japanese context is usually translated as "provincial lord." The *Catholic Encyclopedia* entry for St. Clare reads, "Cofoundress of the Order of Poor Ladies, or Clares, and first Abbess of San Damiano; born at Assisi, 16 July, 1194; died there 11 August, 1253. She was the eldest daughter of Favorino Scifi, Count of Sasso-Rosso, the wealthy representative of an ancient Roman family, who owned a large palace in Assisi and a castle on the slope of Mount Subasio. Such at least is the traditional account."

72. These frescoes are done in the style of Lorenzetti, but their actual authorship is unclear. Pietro Lorenzetti (c.1280–1348), also called Pietro Laurati, was from Siena.

73. Harold Goad (1878–1956) founded the Laboratorio San Francesco on Via Metastasio for the poor children of Assisi. He later became a published scholar on the Franciscans, and also on the development of the fascist state. When Anesaki met him in Italy, though, he had not yet produced these scholarly works.

74. The Porziuncula Chapel inside the church of Santa Maria degli Angeli.

75. As Sabatier tells it: "One day – it was probably February 24, 1209 – the festival of St. Matthias mass was being celebrated at the Portiuncula. When the priest turned toward him to read the words of Jesus, Francis felt himself overpowered with a profound agitation. He no longer saw the priest; it was Jesus, the Crucified One of San Damiano, who was speaking: 'As you go, proclaim the

good news, the kingdom of heaven has come near. Cure the sick, raise the dead, cleanse the lepers, cast out demons. You received without payment; give without payment. Take no gold, or silver, or copper in your belts, no bag for your journey, or two tunics, or sandals, or a staff; for laborers deserve their food.' These words burst upon him like a revelation, like the answer of Heaven to his sighs and anxieties." (*The Road to Assisi*, pp. 43–44). The Bible passage is from Matthew 10:7–10.

76. Sabatier's version of this passage is: "Be praised, Lord, for our Sister Death of the body, from whom no one may escape. Alas for them who die in a state of mortal sin; happy they are who are found to have conformed to your most holy will, for the second death will do them no harm." (*Road to Assisi*, p. 153).

77. 諸行無常 (*shogyō mujō*)

78. Judith Dean explains, "Throughout Francis' life he was constantly wracked by notions of his own sinfulness and unworthiness and quite understandably he went through periods of doubt and human temptation. This was never more acutely demonstrated than in 1216 after the sudden death of Pope Innocent III whom Francis greatly admired, respected and was very fond of. In a fit of uncertainty and what we might perhaps call depression, Francis' thoughts turned to a life he could have led, warmed by the security and affection of a wife and children. Realizing what he had allowed himself to dwell on he felt enormous remorse and sought to correct himself in the traditional manner through physical penance and he threw himself onto roses that were in the grounds of the Porziuncula. The roses tore at Francis' flesh causing blood to drip onto the plants and tradition has it that from then on the roses grew up thornless and a deep red color." (*Every Pilgrim's Guide to Assisi*, p. 51)

79. The "path of a believing mind through other power" is 他力信心の易行道. These are specifically Buddhist terms.

80. 智慧才覺 (*chiesaikaku*)

81. *Nembutsu*: invoking the name of the Buddha, usually implied to be Amida Buddha. The religious and doctrinal history involved in this passage is complex, but simply put Anesaki is defending Hōnen's support of reciting the *nembutsu* as a means to salvation in lieu of the traditional path of priestly austerities.

82. Paschal Robinson (1870–1948), author of *The Real St. Francis of Assisi* (London: Catholic Truth Society, 1904) *The Writings of Saint Francis of Assisi* (Philadelphia: Dolphin Press, 1906), and *A Short Introduction to Franciscan Literature* (New York: Tennant and Ward, 1907).

83. This poem highlights the salient parts of Clare's life.

From her earliest years Clare seems to have been endowed with the rarest virtues. As a child she was most devoted to prayer and to practices of mortification, and as she passed into girlhood her distaste for the world and her yearning for a more spiritual life increased. She was eighteen years of age when St. Francis came to preach the Lenten course in the church of San Giorgio at Assisi. The inspired words of the Poverello kindled a flame in the heart of Clare; she sought him out secretly and begged him to help her that she too might live "after the manner of the holy Gospel" ...On Palm Sunday Clare, arrayed in all her finery, attended high Mass at the cathedral... That was the last time the world beheld Clare. On the night of the same day she secretly left her father's house, by St. Francis's advice and, accompanied by her aunt Bianca and another companion, proceeded to the humble chapel of the Porziuncula, where St. Francis and his disciples met her with lights in their hands. Clare then laid aside her rich dress, and St. Francis, having cut off her hair, clothed her in a rough tunic and a thick veil, and in this way the young heroine vowed herself to the service of Jesus Christ. This was 20 March, 1212.

Clare was placed by St. Francis provisionally with the Benedictine nuns of San Paolo, near Bastia, but her father, who had expected her to make a splendid marriage, and who was furious at her secret flight, on discovering her retreat, did his utmost to dissuade Clare from her heroic proposals, and even tried to drag her home by force. But Clare held her own with a firmness above her years, and Count Favorino was finally obliged to leave her in peace. (*Catholic Encyclopedia*, "St. Clare of Assisi")

84. These paintings, in the Lower Basilica, are attributed to Giotto. "In the four compartments of the vault the three Franciscan virtues – Poverty, Obedience and Chastity – are pictured and explained by inscriptions on the arches of the wall. Since the work and the writings of St. Bonaventure, Francis has been conceived as the 'angel of the sixth seal.' For this reason these pictures are bound within a framework whose figurative elements allude to the Apocalypse and whose central motif is the apocalyptic Christ on the keystone of the vault." (*Web Gallery of Art*, http://www.wga.hu/frames-e.html?/html/g/giotto/assisi/lower/ crossing/ooallego.html)

85. One of the Franciscan allegories, this is St. Francis in glory. "Worked through with gold, the triumphal procession of St. Francis comes into view. He is enthroned in the centre of the triangular surface and drawn towards heaven by angels. His figure and in particular his face seem to belong to another world.

The golden rays that emanate from him heighten the effect of the gold-embroi-dered dalmatic. The halos and the shimmering hair of the angels sustain this festive vein. The diverse figures of the angels, their music and their dancing – in which they take one another by the hand – lend the representation its liveli-ness." (*Web Gallery of Art,* http://www.wga.hu/frames-e.html?/html/g/giotto/assisi/lower/ceiling/)

  86. This is the allegory of obedience.

    In the chapterhouse of a cloister Obedience rules between two observers, the dual-faced Prudence (Prudentia) and the quiet Humility (Humilitas). Obe-dience commands silence and places the yoke upon the monk who kneels before her. Francis, who stands on the roof of the building like an apparition between two kneeling angels, also bears such a yoke.

    The embodiment of Presumptuousness, the horned centaur, is denied entrance. Two young men, a monk of the order and a layman, will follow in the footsteps of the saint. An angel has already taken one of them by hand. Interestingly, however, it seems to be Prudence who presides over such a decision: with her dual face she sees both past and future. She holds out a mirror, as a symbol of knowledge, towards the kneeling monk, whom the young men are following, and her astrolabe stands for the wider context which she is able to recognize. (*Web Gallery of Art,* http://www.wga.hu/frames-e.html?/html/g/giotto/assisi/lower/ceiling/)

  87. This is the allegory of poverty. "Poverty is a winged gaunt woman dressed only in rags, at whom children throw stones or brandish sticks. Christ himself marries this woman to St. Francis. Numerous angels, as well as the personifica-tions of Hope and Chastity, are present as witnesses. As offerings, two angels carry worldly goods heavenwards. The reactions of the world are depicted at either side: on the left a young man imitates Francis, and on the right the rich express ridicule." (*Web Gallery of Art,* http://www.wga.hu/frames-e.html?/html/g/giotto/assisi/lower/ceiling/)

  88. This is the allegory of chastity. "In a well-fortified castle, Chastity rules: only angels can enter here. In order to reach her, a long path must be followed. The representatives of the three divisions of the Franciscan order (a lay brother, a Franciscan and Clare) have climbed the hill. They too, as the middle scene shows, will be washed and dressed by angels. On the other side the extremely vivid and bizarre figures of demons are being cast into the abyss. They are Unchasteness (Immunditia) with the boar's head, Burning Desire (Ardor) with the flaming head, and Love (Amor) with the clawed feet and the hearts

tied around him. The round is completed by the spider-legged, devilish Death (Mors)." (*Web Gallery of Art*, http://www.wga.hu/frames-e.html?/html/g/giotto/assisi/lower/ceiling/)

89. This is from Canto III of Dante's *Paradiso*.

90. The May Day festival. It has special significance for Anesaki, for it originates in the Roman Floralia festival, when people gathered spring flowers. The flower-gathering theme of the title is thus repeated here.

91. The Chapel of St. Martin is one of the side chapels in the Lower Basilica. "This was built for a powerful Franciscan cardinal at the beginning of the fourteenth century and is particularly noted for the fresco life-cycle of St. Martin by the great Sienese artist, Simone Martini. St. Martin of Tours was often compared with St. Francis because both had started out on their new lives in Christ by giving their possessions away to a poor man...." (*Every Pilgrim's Guide to Assisi*, p. 17)

92. Clare's aunt Bianca took the tonsure with Clare. Clare's mother, Blessed Ortolana, was known for her strict piety.

93. The Société des Bollandistes, a group of hagiographical scholars founded in the seventeenth century.

94. Francesco Petrarch, Italian poet and humanist, born at Arezzo, 20 July, 1304; died at Arquá, 19 July, 1374.

95. The services were held in the Lower Basilica, where Anesaki had viewed the Four Allegories of Francis earlier.

96. Anesaki alludes earlier to Wagner (see entry for April 5), but this is the first explicit mention of his final opera *Parsifal* (premiered in 1882). *Parsifal* involves Wagner's development of the Schopenhauerian concept of compassion, with a plot that combines elements of the Grail legend and various mythological and religious ideas, including references to the life of the Buddha and the life of Christ.

97. Later, while visiting a nunnery in Rome, Anesaki meets a nun who, he says, resembles the Clare in these paintings. See entry for May 11.

98. This sentence is particularly difficult to translate, as Anesaki uses primarily Buddhist terms when speaking of St. Clare. The original reads, "クララが見た聖衆の来迎は光明遍照の天人の群であつたというふが、それを十分に述べ得ない."

99. The word that Anesaki uses for hindrances is traditionally used in Buddhism to refer to the five hindrances to women: inability to become Brahma-kings, Indras, Māra-kings, Caikravarti-kings, or Buddhas.

THE ETERNAL CITY; THE POPE'S THRONE

1. This was apparently a common Japanese expression at the time, but it is no longer in use. Japanese tourists today usually substitute "the food is delicious" or "there are beautiful views" for "there are fields of flowers."

2. *Baedeker's* notes, "The Scala di Spagna, which descends from Santissima Trinità to the Piazza di Spagna by 137 steps, was constructed by Al. Specchi and De Sanctis in 1721–25. Models for artists with their picturesque costumes frequent its vicinity. At the foot of the steps (to the left as we descend) is the house where John Keats died in 1821." (*Central Italy*, p. 160)

3. The measurements of the church were inscribed upon the pavement of the nave.

4. The church of St. Peter's has undergone a number of restorations in its history. *Baedeker's* notes: "In the course of time the edifice had at length become so damaged that Nicholas V. determined on its reconstruction, and in 1452 began the tribune, from the design of the Florentine Bernardo Rossellino... The wall had risen to a height of 4–5 ft. only when the work was interrupted by the death of the Pope (1455). The work was not resumed till 50 years later, when a new impulse was given to the undertaking by the idea of Julius II to erect a tomb for himself during his own lifetime, for which, as there was no sufficient room in the church, it was proposed to add a chapel... The tradition, that Julius II had invited a number of architects, including Giuliano da Sangallo, to submit designs, and that Bramante, who came from Lombardy, was the successful competitor, is probably true. [Bramante's] plan, which had the merit of majestic simplicity, was, it is well known, not adhered to. During the last year of Bramante's (d. 1514) life, Guiliano da Sangallo (d. 1516) was entrusted with the superintendence of the work, and was assisted by Raphael and Fra Giocondo da Verona (d. 1515).... In 1606 the church was completed with the exception of the façade, when Paul V introduced a momentous alteration. Reverting to the idea of a Latin cross, he caused the nave to be lengthened, and the present weak and unsuitable façade to be erected by Carlo Maderna. The effect of the dome, as contemplated by Michael Angelo, is thus entirely lost except from a distance; from the spectator standing in the piazza of St. Peter the drum supporting the dome vanishes behind the façade." (*Central Italy*, pp. 319–320)

5. These are the colonnades around the Piazza di San Pietro, which were erected in 1655–67 by Bernini. There are 162 statues atop these colonnades, all of saints.

6. The Pincio, in northeast Rome, is described by *Baedeker's* as follows: "The Pincio, the *collis hortorum*, or 'hill of gardens', of the ancients, was called *Mons Pincius* from a palace of the Pincii, an influential family of the later period of the empire. Here were once the famous gardens of Lucullus, in which Messalina, the wife of Claudius, afterwards celebrated her orgies. A vineyard belonging to the monastery of Santa Maria del Popolo was converted by Gius. Valadier, the Roman architect, during the Napoleonic regime (1809–14), into the beautiful pleasure-grounds. This is a fashionable resort towards evening, when the Italians pay and receive visits in their carriages. The projecting terrace above the Piazza del Popolo (150 ft.) commands a magnificent view of modern Rome, which however, has been much impaired by the building-over of the Prati di Castello." (*Central Italy*, p. 158)

7. Antonio Fogazarro (1842–1911), Italian novelist and poet. Fogazarro published his novel *Il santo* (The Saint) in 1905, and it was banned shortly thereafter by the Roman Catholic Church. The novel is a political fantasy of sorts, in which the hero, a man who preaches to the common man in Rome, challenges both the Catholic Church and the Italian government, and charges the former with four faults: falsehood, clerical domination, greed, and immobility. As Fogazarro's biographer, Robert A. Hall Jr., notes, "[The hero], as Fogazzaro portrays him, combines the asceticism and self-immolation of a mediaeval mystic with the love of his fellow-men manifested by, say, Saint Francis of Assisi, and the direct outspokenness of a Saint Catherine of Siena or a Savonarola." (*Antonio Fogazzaro*, Boston, p. 81). The connection with St. Francis of Assisi was not lost on Anesaki, it would seem.

8. Bernardino Betti Pinturrichio (1454–1513).

9. The race had taken place on April 11. See Anesaki's entry for that day.

10. Prince Tanehito 栽仁王 (1888–1908), a sub-lieutenant in the navy, died on April 4.

11. *Baedeker's* notes: "The Thermæ of Diocletian, which give name to the piazza, were the most extensive thermæ in Rome, and were completed by Diocletian and his co-regent Maximian in 305–6 A.D. The principal building was enclosed by a peribolos, the outline of the round central portion ('exedra') of which is preserved by the modern houses at the beginning of the Via Nazionale. The corners were occupied by circular domed structures, one of which is now the church of San Bernardo, and another is built into a girls' school on the Via Viminale. The circumference of the baths is said to have been about 2000 yds., or half as much again as that of the Baths of Caracalla, and the number of

daily bathers 3000… Pius IV entrusted Michael Angelo with the task of adapt-
ing part of the Thermæ for a Carthusian Convent. The large vaulted central
hall was accordingly converted into the church of Santa Maria degli Angeli
in 1563–66… The remaining parts of the Thermæ, formerly occupied by the
Carthusians, now accommodate various charitable and educational institutions
and the Museo Nazionale Romano delle Terme Diocleziane." (*Central Italy*, pp.
166–167)

12. The Baths of Diocletian actually covered about eleven to thirteen hect-
ares, which would be about 33,000 to 40,000 *tsubo*.

13. The horse races took place just north of Rome, in Tor di Quinto at the
Ippodromo.

14. Anesaki left Japan in the spring of 1900 (not 1901, as the text implies)
bound for Europe on a trip sponsored by the Japanese Ministry of Education.
"Otowa" is Ōhashi Otowa 大橋乙羽 (1869–1901), an author best known for his
travelogues, who was one of the people that accompanied Anesaki on this earlier journey. Ōhashi died of overwork/exhaustion in early 1901, three months
after returning from the trip to Europe. The play to which Anesaki refers may
have been an on-board production done to celebrate the festival.

15. *Baedeker's* notes that the Basilica of Constantine "was a basilica of three
halls, with vaulting of vast span, which has served as a model to modern architects, as in the case of St. Peter's." (*Central Italy*, p. 264)

16. Anesaki seems slightly mistaken here. *Baedeker's* notes, "After the town
of Romulus had sprung up on the Palatine [where the Colosseum is located], a
second, inhabited by Sabines, was built on the Quirinal, and the two were subsequently united into one community. Whilst each retained its peculiar temples
and sanctuaries, the Forum, situated between them, and commanded by the
castle and the temple of Jupiter on the Capitol, formed the common focus and
place of assembly of the entire state, and the Forum and Capitol maintained this
importance down to the latest period of ancient Rome." (*Central Italy*, p. xxix)

17. Anesaki is correct: in his autobiography, Gibbon wrote, "It was at Rome,
on the 15th of October 1764, as I sat musing amid the ruins of the capitol, while
the bare-footed friars were singing Vespers in the temple of Jupiter [presently
the Church of Santa Maria in Aracœli], that the idea of writing the decline and
fall of the City first started to my mind." (*The Autobiographies of Gibbon*, p. 303)

18. According to *Baedeker*, "The present name ('Church of the Altar of Heav-
en'), dating from the 14th century, is derived from an ancient legend according
to which this is the 'Camera Octaviani'… in which the Sibyl of Tibur appeared

to the emperor, whom the senate proposed to elevate to the rank of a god, and disclosed to him the new Revelation." (*Central Italy*, p. 235)

19. Probably the fresco of the life of San Bernardino of Siena, painted about 1484, located in the first chapel off the right aisle.

20. This is the second chapel of the left aisle, where "a manger (*presepe*) is fitted up at Christmas. This consists of a gorgeous and brilliantly illuminated representation of the Nativity in life-size, with the richly decorated image of *Il Santo Bambino*, or Holy Child. Between Christmas Day and January 6ᵗʰ, from 3 or 4 o'clock daily, children from 5 to 10 years of age here recite little poems, etc., in honour of the Bambino, a carefully studied performance, but usually accomplished with great naturalness of gesture and manner." (*Central Italy*, p. 236)

21. Anesaki makes it sound like the construction was recent, but actually it had started twenty years earlier. "The Franciscan monastery belonging to the church was pulled down in 1888 to make room for the vast Monument of Victor Emmanuel II, designed by Count Gius. Sacconi. The work, which is being erected on the N. end of the Capitol, has already swallowed up about 10½ million francs as the cost of the site, substructures, preliminary operations, etc. The entire cost is estimated at 24½ francs. When finished, it will be over 200 ft. in height, and will include an equestrian statue of the king, rising in the centre of a platform, surrounded by colonnades and approached by massive flights of steps. The colonnades, with columns 50 ft. in height, are being richly decorated with mosaics and paintings, and the apartments in the basement are to be fitted up as a Museo del Risorgimento Italiano." (*Central Italy*, p. 237)

22. Anesaki has already mentioned some of the Seven Hills of Rome, but this is the first time he identifies the category as such. The category includes the Capitoline, Palatine, Aventine, Quirinal, Viminal, Esquiline, and Cælian Hills. Gianicolo Hill, on the western bank of the Tiber, is not included in the group.

23. San Pietro in Montorio was renowned for its panoramic view of Rome and its environs. The 1904 edition of *Baedeker's* contained a pull-out panorama of it more than thirty inches in length.

24. The Regio Palazzo del Quirinale.

25. The "glaring" here is figurative, not literal. Anesaki is referring to the fact that the Italian monarchy chose the Quirinal Palace as the residence of Victor Emmanuel II (1820–1878) when Italy was unified in 1871. The choice of the Quirinal Palace as the royal residence was contentious, as the building had been built by Pope Gregory XIII and was the property of the Pope until the nineteenth century. By the time that Anesaki visited Rome in 1908, the residence

was still in the hands of the monarchy but was used as office space, and not as the king's residence. In any event, it became a symbol of the power and (in some eyes) tyranny of the Italian monarchy vis-à-vis the Pope.

26. The Pincio Hill is actually in the north of Rome. It would have been to Anesaki's left if he was looking out over Rome from the Gianicolo in the direction of the Seven Hills, which may account for his impression that it was in the west.

27. Li Hongzhang 李鴻章 (1823–1901) was a general and political leader during the late Qing Dynasty. He was known for helping China adopt Western industrial technology.

28. The chapel and convent were handed over to the Spanish congregation of the Amadeites, a branch of the Franciscan order, in 1472. With the help of the King Ferdinand and Queen Isabella of Spain, they built a new church there in 1481–1500, designed by Baccio Pontelli and Meo del Caprina. (Chris Nyborg, "Pietro montorio" of "Churches of Rome")

29. Giuseppe Garibaldi (1807–1882), prominent military leader and popular hero of the age of Italian unification known as the *Risorgimento*. Garibaldi was anti-clerical, and openly stated venomous opinions of the church. That said, most of what Garibaldi said was aimed at the organizational side of religion, not the spiritual side of it. Although he is writing over twenty years after Garibaldi's death, given Anesaki's apparent hostility to the institutions created by the *Risorgimento*, it seems odd that he does not state an opinion on its leading figure.

30. The observatory on Monte Mario is north of the Vatican.

31. If Anesaki means to say that this was where Petrarch died, then he is mistaken here. Petrarch died near Padua. It is possible that Anesaki is confusing Petrarch with Torquato Tasso (1544–1595), an Italian poet who is often compared to Petrarch, and who did die in Sant' Onofrio on April 25, 1595.

32. Shinmura Izuru 新村出 (1876–1967), a linguist and the editor of one of the major Japanese dictionaries, the *Kōjien* 広辞苑.

33. The building was erected in 1508–1511 by Bald. Peruzzi, for the papal banker Agostino Chigi. Later the villa changed hands and was owned by Cardinal A. Farnese and his family until 1731. The King of Naples owned it until 1861, when it was let by Francis II for 99 years to the Duke of Ripalda.

34. There had been alterations made to the course of the Tiber River.

35. *Baedeker's* describes the painting: "The ceiling, with its pendentives and spandrels, was decorated from the designs of Raphael (1516–18) by Giulio Romano, Francesco Penni, and Giovanni da Udine (who executed the enclosing garlands), with twelve illustrations of the myth of Psyche, which are among the

most charming creations of the master." (*Central Italy*, p. 369) Anesaki's reference to "Amore" is to "Amor," the Latin translation of the Greek "Eros," or Cupid, who is the other central figure in the myth alongside Psyche.

36. See also the entry for April 19, in which Anesaki makes a similar argument.

37. Arnold Böcklin (1827–1901), a Swiss Symbolist painter. "Böcklin... was an energetic figure devoid of the languid melancholy of 'decadence'. Italy's light and aura of antiquity were decisive in his early development; his paintings quickly came to be populated with mythological figures, with centaurs and naiads. Not until his fiftieth year did he begin to paint the powerfully atmospheric works associated with his name today." (Michael Gibson, *Symbolism*, p. 125)

38. *Baedeker's* notes that the "colossal head in grisaille" described here is incorrectly attributed to Michelangelo (*Central Italy*, p. 370). The piece has more recently been attributed to Sebastiano Luciani, also known as Sebastiano del Piombo (1485–1547) or Baldassare Peruzzi (1481–1536).

39. This is the basilica of San Giovanni in Laterano. It "was the principal church of Rome after the time of Constantine the Great. The emperor presented Pope Sylvester I with a large palace, which had hitherto belonged to the wealthy family of the Laternai, and fitted up a church within it. It was called the Basilica Constantiniana after its founder, and sometimes Basilica Sancti Salvatoris, or Aula Dei, as being a second Zion, and gradually became privileged to grant the most ample indulgences." (*Central Italy*, p. 303)

40. Born 2 March, 1810, at Carpineto; elected Pope 20 February, 1878; died 20 July, 1903, at Rome.

41. These cloisters were constructed in the thirteenth century. The columns had numerous small spiral and inlaid columns.

42. Anesaki refers here to the Lateran Councils, "a series of five important councils held at Rome from the twelfth to the sixteen century. From the reign of Constantine the Great until the removal of the papal Court to Avignon, the Lateran palace and basilica served the bishops of Rome as residence and cathedral. During this long period the popes had occasion to convoke a number of general councils, and for this purpose they made choice of cities so situated as to reduce as much as possible the inconveniences which the bishops called to such assemblies must necessarily experience by reason of long and costly absence from their sees. Five of these councils were held in the Lateran palace, and are known as the First (1123), Second (1139), Third (1179), Fourth (1215), and Fifth Lateran Councils." (*Catholic Encyclopedia*, "Lateran Councils.")

43. According to legend, Dominic and Francis met in Rome during the Fourth Lateran Council in 1215. Other sources indicate that the two met in 1218.

44. The Alban hills lie to the southeast of Rome.

45. This is the Lateran Baptistery. The octagonal building dates to the fourth century; it has porphyry columns and is about twenty meters in diameter. See Amanda Claridge, *Rome: An Oxford Archaeological Guide*, pp. 347–349. *Baedeker's* 1890 edition describes is as follows: "From the piazza we at once enter the precincts of the BAPTISTERY itself. It is divided into a central space and surrounding passage by eight large columns of porphyry with an antique architrave in marble, which are said to have been presented by Constantine. In the centre is the font in green basalt. The frescoes are by A. Saccchi, Maratta, and others. — Adjacent, to the right, is the oratory of JOHN THE BAPTIST, containing a statue of the saint in bronze by L. Valadier, executed in 1772 (after Donatello), and placed between two columns of serpentine. The bronze doors, presented by Hilarius, are said to have been brought from the Thermæ of Caracalla." (*Central Italy (1890)*, p. 265).

46. Marcus Aurelius Antoninus (188–217), known as Caracalla, was Roman emperor from 198–217. The Baths of Caracalla were begun by his father, the emperor Septimius Severus (emperor from 193–211) in 206 and completed in 216.

47. *Baedeker's* was less than enthusiastic about the artistic quality of these statues: "At the foot of the steps are two insipid marble groups by Jacometti, Christ and Judas, and Christ before Pontius Pilate; also a kneeling statue of Pius IX" (*Central Italy*, p. 311)

48. *Baedeker's* notes: "Opposite the N.E. corner of the Lateran is the edifice containing the Scala Santa. The Two-storied portico was erected by Sixtus V. The Scala Santa is a flight of twenty-eight marble steps from the palace of Pilate at Jerusalem, which our Saviour is said to have once ascended. They were brought to Rome in the period of the crusades, and may be ascended only on the knees. They are now protected with wood. The four adjoining flights are for the descent." (*Central Italy*, p. 311)

49. Luigi Luzzatti (1841–1927) was an Italian political leader and economist. In his career he held the posts of Minister of Finance and Prime Minister (1910–11).

50. What Anesaki does not say – but which is salient here – is that Luzzatti was Jewish. Luzzatti's book *God in Freedom: Studies in the Relations Between Church and State* (English translation by Alfonso Arbib-Costa; New York: Mac-

millan, 1930) considered to be a landmark work in the advocacy of religious toleration. Luzzatti held that liberty of faith was of utmost importance. John T. McNeill, in his review of Luzzatti's book, wrote that Luzzatti "sympathetically examined all the higher religions, and his work exhibits a special admiration for Christianity, not in its institutional but in its spiritual manifestations. This is nowhere more evident than in the summary of his debate with Professor Formichi on the topic 'Buddha vs. Christ' in which Luzzatti, who is always a great admirer of Buddhist religious toleration, nevertheless affirms vigorously the superiority of the Christian way." ("Freedom as Religious Principle" in *The Journal of Religion*, Vol. 11, No. 2 (April 1931), pp. 296-7)

51. Alessandro Costa (1857–1953) was not only a musician but also a scholar of Buddhism. He published *Il Buddha e la sua doctrina* in 1903 (Torino: Fran-telli Bocca) and *Una curiosa polemica: Brevi cenni sul presente stato della critica e dell' arte musicale in Italia* in 1881 (Rome: Tip. di Roma). He also published an article on Schopenhauer in Bignami's magazine *Cœnobium* ("La Religiosita nella Filosofia di Arturo Schopenhauer" in vol. 1, no. 5), which later became a book-length study published as *Il pensiero religioso di Arturo Schopenhauer (esposizione critica)* (Rome: Formiggini, 1935).

52. Anesaki uses a string of Buddhist terms here: 中世の様な観念三昧、信心帰敬の祈念三昧を欠く.

53. Rafael Cardinal Merry del Val y Zulueta (October 10, 1865 – February 26, 1930) was a Roman Catholic Cardinal (Cardinal Priest of Basilica di Santa Prassede) from 1903 until his death.

54. William Henry O'Connell (1859–1944). O'Connell did not have much support in Boston, but depended on the Vatican to gain his office in 1907. He also had a connection with Japan. He was named special papal envoy to the emperor of Japan in August of 1905 and was given the Grand Cordon of the Sacred Treasure by the Meiji Emperor in December of the same year. (*Who's Who in New England*, p. 799). Anesaki knew O'Connell, and received letters of introduction from him on his first trip to Europe (See *Teiunshū*, p. 189)

55. Cardinal Merry del Val was born in London to Spanish diplomatic parents and lived in the United Kingdom until 1878, so it is no surprise that his English was fluent.

56. See notes to May 4 entry.

57. This is Yokoi Tokio 横井時雄 (1857–1928), an educator and politician who traveled twice (1889–1890 and 1894–1896) to Yale University in the United States to study religion.

58. This large statue, the *Statua di Goethe*, is located at the Porta Pinciana entrance to Villa Borghese. A gift from Kaiser Wilhelm II of Germany in 1904 to the city of Rome, it was meant to represent friendship between Germany and Rome. Johann Wolfgang von Goethe (1749–1832) was relatively well-known in Japan, particularly for his *The Sorrows of Young Werther* (1774). He visited Rome twice, once from November 1786 to February 1787 and once from June 1787 to April 1788.

59. This church was consecrated in 324 and underwent multiple re-buildings and restorations over the centuries. When Anesaki saw it there were still rebuilding projects underway.

60. The openwork screen above the sliding partitions between two rooms in traditional Japanese architecture.

61. This is the Pyramid of Caius Cestius (in Italian, Piramide di Caio Cestio or Piramide Cestia). Architecturally unusual in Rome, this funerary monument, dedicated to Caius Cestius, was built in about 18–12 B.C. Its design was modeled on Egyptian pyramids. See Amanda Claridge, *Rome: An Oxford Archaeological Guide*, pp. 364–366.

62. John Keats (1795–1821); Percy Bysshe Shelley (1792–1822); Joseph Severn (1793–1879).

63. Shelley's epitaph is taken from Shakespeare's *The Tempest*, I.ii.402–404.

64. In 1899, a writer identified by the initials C.M.R. wrote the following in an article for the New York Times:

> Perhaps there is something about the surroundings, something about the influence of Rome – the Eternal City – which makes its little Protestant cemetery, where the graves of Keats and Shelley are, so peculiarly impressive... When a girl swings open the great iron gate one of the prettiest views, I think, in Italy is disclosed. It is that of a little garden, sown in heartache, but planted in love, that it may seem nearer home, and watered, you know, by tears. The ground rises steadily from the entrance in the further wall, so that it is all laid before you at once, but the distant city wall is so ivy-covered and tree-hidden that you hardly know the garden stops there. From your feet straight up to the wall leads the broad central path of the garden, with cypress trees on either side throwing it into shadow. A southern sun gleams on white stones and flowers that are beyond the trees, and the May morning I was there the azaleas were veritable shrubs and bushes of blossoms, and the air, already sweet with box, was sweeter still with roses.
>
> Shelley's grave lies at the further side of the cemetery. One goes up the

central path, and at the end turns to the left for a few yards. A well-defined path leads to it and the inscription on the stone is clear... The grave of Keats is not near Shelley's, and it is with quite a pang of disappointment that one learns that it is outside the garden.... Steps must be retraced and the entrance passed again. Then it is a walk along the dusty road beyond the wall. At the right of the little cemetery one enters a field, where the grass has grown high and which the wild flowers deck in nature's free-hand gardening. The only path is that which has been worn by the seekers of the unnamed grave; but it goes direct and sure, and far in the distant corner, "close to the city wall," it stops before the stone with that inscription of which one phrase is to often quoted. The words complete are:

This grave contains all that was mortal of a young English poet, who on his deathbed, in the bitterness of his heart at the malicious power of his enemies, desired these words to be engraven on his tombstone: 'Here lies one whose name was writ in water.' Feb. 24, 1821. (C.M.R. "Three Graves in Italy" *New York Times*, May 27, 1899, Saturday Review of Books and Art, Page BR344.)

65. Anesaki is mistaken: the shards are from olive oil jugs, not wine jugs. But *Baedeker's* indicates that at the time of Anesaki's travels, "the hill [was] honeycombed with cellars, in some of which wine is sold" which may explain Anesaki's impression about the shards. "Recent excavations confirm that the Testaccio was a dump used exclusively to gather the shards of olive oil amphorae. The olive oil was brought to the city under the control of the *annona* to be distributed at regulated prices to the urban plebs. The earliest amphorae were brought probably in the late 70s BC, to bring olive oil from the Brindisi hinterland. The Testaccio dump was in use for hundreds of years, always growing under the control of the authorities, as the excavations reveal how the hill was built with shards in a planned way." (Pedro Paulo A Funari, "Review of *El Monte Testaccio y la llanura subaventina. Topografía extra portam Trigeminam. Rome, Consejo Superior de Investigaciones Científicas*")

66. The House of Crescentius, "commonly called Casa di Rienzi, or di Pilato, [was] constructed of brick with a singular admixture of antique fragments. On the east side, Via del Ricovero, a long metrical Latin inscription records that 'this lofty house was erected by Nicholas, son of Crescens, foremost and descended from the foremost, not from motives of ambition, but to revive the ancient glory of Rome.' The Crescentii were the most powerful noble family in Rome at the close of the 10th century, but no scion of the name of Nicholas can be traced, and the house, the oldest existing specimen of mediæval domestic architecture in

Rome, perhaps not earlier than the 11th or 12th century. The building was originally much larger, and was intended to command the bridge over the Tiber. It
has nothing to do with Cola di Rienzo, 'the last of the tribunes,' who was born in
the Rione Regola." (*Central Italy*, pp. 285–286)

67. Anesaki puts these *haiku* in quotation marks, implying that they are not
his, but it would seem that he was the composer, given the content.

68. This was Bagni, "the station for the sulphur-baths of Acque Albule, the
Roman Acquae Albulae, which were much frequented in ancient times, and
were again fitted up for the reception of patients in 1879.... The water, the
unpleasant smell of which is due to its strong impregnation with sulphuretted
hydrogen, rises from the tufa rock and is probably the outlet of a subterranean
source from the Apennines." (*Central Italy*, p. 418)

69. Taira no Kiyomori 平清盛 (1118–1181), the leader of the Taira clan at the
end of the Heian period. He was largely known for his ruthlessness and over-
bearing pride, so Anesaki's choice of him here indicates that Hadrian, too, was
in someway a flawed and/or fated leader. (Kiyomori's clan lost the Gempei war
of 1180–1185, throwing Japan into its medieval, feudal era.)

70. *Baedeker's* notes: "The now neglected Villa d'Este, to the west of the
town, one of the finest of the Renaissance period, was laid out by Pirro Ligorio
in 1549 for Cardinal Ippolito d'Este, and belongs now to archduke Francis Ferdinand of Austria-Este. The entrance is in the Piazza San Francesco. In the casino
are frescoes by Fed. Zuccaro and Muziano (damaged). The garden contains ter-
races, grottoes with cascades, densely-shaded avenues, magnificent groups of
cypresses, and charming points of view." (*Central Italy*, p. 424)

71. This is the garden surrounding the Villa Gregoriana, built in the early
nineteenth century for Pope Gregory XVI.

72. It seems what Anesaki means is that some of the rock formation comes
from lime in the mountain streams.

73. It is difficult to reconcile Anesaki's account perfectly with the description
in *Baedeker's*, but it helps shed some light on his description: "On week-days
the only entrance to the Waterfalls is by the iron gate on the other (east) side
betweent the Porta Sant'Angelo and the Ponte Gregoriano. The path directly
opposite the entrance leads to the upper end of the Traforo Gregoriano, which
consists of two shafts, 290 and 330 yards long respectively, driven through the
rock of Monte Catillo in 1826–35 by the engineer Folchi, to protect the town
from inundations by providing a sufficient outlet for the Anio even in time of
flood. Near it is an arch of an ancient bridge in 'opus reticulatum'. As however,

the cutting can only be entered from the lower end, visitor [*sic.*] entering the grounds usually turn at once to the left, pass (to the left again) through an archway below the road, and follow the margin of the valley, enjoying a view of the two temples on the left. We then reach a Terrace planted with young stone-pines, whence we obtain a charming view of the temple of the Sibyl, above us, and below of the New Waterfall (354 ft. high), by which the Anio emerges from the Traforo Gregoriano. Passing through a door, which a custodian opens, we may proceed to the fall and the entrance of the tunnel (372 paces long; the walk by the roaring stream is far from pleasant). From the terrace we retrace our steps for a short distance, and then bearing constantly to the right, follow the footpath (not the stone steps) descending to the valley; to the left are some Roman sub-structures; halfway down, near some cypresses, a path descends to the right to a platform of masonry, immediately above the new fall. We now return to the cypresses and then descend the path, at first in zigzags and afterwards in steps. We descend to the lowest point to which it leads, finally by a flight of stone steps, wet with spray, to the fantastically-shaped Sirens' Grotto. From the grotto we return to the point where the paths cross, and ascend the path on the other side of the valley to a gallery hewn in the rock, the apertures of which we observe some time before reaching it. At the end of the gallery the path again divides; the branch to the left leads across an iron bridge to the Grotto of Neptune, formerly the channel of the main branch of the Anio. The new works drew off the greater part of the water from this channel, but the fall is still very fine." (*Central Italy*, pp. 423–424)

74. This church was the largest of the eighty churches in Rome dedicated to the Holy Virgin.

75. *Baedeker's* notes, "The Basilica Liberiana [said to have been built in the 4th century] was re-erected by Sixtus III (432–40), who named the church Sancta Maria Mater Dei, shortly after the Council of Ephesus had sanctioned this appellation of the Virgin (431). Of this edifice the nave with its ancient marble columns and mosaics is still preserved. In the 12th century the church was farther altered in the medieval style. Eugene III added a new porch, Nicholas IV a new tribune adorned with mosaics, and Gregory XI gave the campanile its present form and its pointed roof. About the end of the 15th century began a new period in the history of the church, when the irregularities of the medieval additions were removed, and symmetrical straight lines were formed by the erection of accessory buildings and masking walls. The two large side-chapels, covered with domes, were added by Sixtus V in 1586 and Paul V in 1611. The exterior of

the tribune was remodeled to its present form by Clement X, and the final restoration was entrusted by Benedict XIV to Fuga." (*Central Italy*, p. 180–1)

76. *Baedeker's* notes, "According to a legend which cannot be traced farther back than the 13th century, the Virgin appeared simultaneously in 352 A.D. to the devout Roman patrician Johannes and to Pope Liberius in their dreams, commanding them to erect a church to her on the spot where they should find snow on the following morning (5th August)." (*Central Italy*, p. 180)

77. This is either the basin of porphyry said to be the tomb of the Patrician Johannes, or the Confessione di San Matteo.

78. Anesaki praises the chapels with this terse sentence, but what he saw was much more complex. *Baedeker's* notes:

RIGHT AISLE: First chapel: Baptistery with fine ancient font of porphyry. Adjacent, to the right, is the Sacristy, with an altar of the school of Andrea Bregno and further portions of the ciborium by Mino da Fiesole. A pillar in the open space to the left of the baptistery commemorates the conversion to Roman Catholicism of Henri IV of France. Farther on is the Cappella del Crocifisso with 10 columns of porphyry. In the right transept is the sumptuous Sixtine Chapel, constructed by Dom Fontana under Sixtus V, and gorgeously restored; in the niche on the left, an altar-piece (St. Jerome) by Ribera; on the right, occupying the whole wall, the monument of Sixtus V, with a statue of the pope by Valsoldo; on the left, monument of Pius V by Leonardo da Sarzana. Over the altar, a canopy in gilded bronze represents angels bearing the chape; in the 'Confessio' under the staircase a statue of San Gaetano, by Bernini, and by the altar a group of the Holy Family, by Cecchino da Pietrasanta (1480). At the end of the right aisle, the Gothic monument of Card. Consavi (Gunsalvus, d. 1299), by Johannes Cosmas.

LEFT AISLE: Tomb of De Levis, composed of two monuments, by a pupil of Andrea Bregno. 1st Chapel (of the Cesi): Martyrdom of St. Catharine, altar-piece by Girol. Da Sermoneta; on the right and left two recumbent bronze statues to the memory of cardinals of the family. 2nd Chapel (of the Pallavicini-Sforza), said to have been designed by Michelangelo: Assumption of Mary, altar-piece by Sermoneta. In the Left Transept, opposite the Sixtine Chapel, is the Borghese Chapel, constructed by Flaminio Ponzio in 1611, and also covered with a dome. Over the altar, which is gorgeously decorated with lapis lazuli and agate, is an ancient and miraculous picture of the Virgin (almost black), painted according to tradition by St. Luke, which was carried by Gregory I as early as 590 in solemn procession through the city. The frescoes in the large arches are by Guido Reni, Lanfranco, Cigoli, etc. The monuments of the Popes Paul V. (Camillo Borghese, d. 1621) and Clement VIII (Aldobrandini, d. 1605) are by pupils of Bernini. (*Central Italy*, p. 182)

79. Unidentified church. There are three churches dedicated to St. Charles in Rome: San Carlo ai Catinari, San Carlo al Corso, and San Carlo alle Quattro Fontane, but none of them seems to match Anesaki's description. However, San Carlo al Corso is the closest to Anesaki's next destination, Augustus's mausoleum.

80. The mausoleum of Augustus was used in the nineteenth and early twentieth century as a concert hall.

81. Program music is "music that, most often explicitly, attempts to express or depict one or more nonmusical ideas, images, or events." (*The Harvard Dictionary of Music*, "Program Music"). The term "program music" was introduced by Franz Liszt (1811–1886) to refer to the passages of explanatory text he appended to his own symphonies. Although the concept of expressing literary ideas or images in music is much older than the nineteenth century, the concept of program music was often taken up by composers associated with the Romantic movement. The *Symphonie Fantastique* (Fantastic Symphony) of Hector Berlioz (1803–1869) was premiered in 1830, and is a representative work of French Romanticism. Its various sections (such as the "March to the Scaffold" and "Witches' Sabbath") are meant to depict fantastical and dream-like images in the music.

82. These are orchestral passages from Wagner's opera *Tristan und Isolde* (1865).

83. This piece, also by Wagner, was first performed in 1845.

84. It was founded in 1622 by Pope Gregory XV.

85. *Baedeker's* notes, "The printing office (Tipografía Poliglotta) of the college was formerly celebrated as the richest in type for foreign languages." (*Central Italy*, p. 160)

86. Anesaki does not give more information, but perhaps he is referring here to the case of Edward McGlynn (1837–1900) who was excommunicated from the Church for his political activities, most notably his support of a tax system that he felt would help his impoverished parishioners in the United States.

87. The Gyōsei School 曉星学校 is a private Christian School in Tokyo, founded in 1881.

88. The Franciscan Missionaries of Mary was founded by Blessed Mary of the

Passion, born Hélène Marie Philippine de Chappotin de Neuville (1839–1904), a French woman. Mary established her group of missionaries in the mid-1880s, and sent nuns worldwide as part of the mission. It is still extant and active today. Later, Anesaki provides more information about the order.

89. Simone Martini (1283–1344). The painting referred to here is probably *St. Clare and St. Elizabeth of Hungary* (1317) in Cappella di San Martino, Lower Church, San Francesco, Assisi.

90. Anesaki implies that such method of production in which individuals specialize in a certain area was a modern development. However, he need not have looked further than his own history to find a contradiction to this idea: the wood-block print artists of the Tokugawa period (1600–1868) likewise divided up the process from drawing to final production.

91. *Lohengrin* (first produced in 1850) is an opera by Richard Wagner. The character whom Anesaki calls "Eliza" is actually Elsa, who is devout and who appeals to God to prove her innocence when she is falsely accused of murder.

92. This is a branch of the "Sister of the Assumption." It is "a congregation of French nuns devoted to the teaching of young girls. It was founded in 1839 by Eugénie Milleret de Bron, in religion Mère Marie-Eugénie de Jesus (1817–1898), under the direction of the Abbé Combalot, a well-known orator of the time, who had been inspired to establish the institute during a pilgrimage to the shrine of Sainte-Anne d'Auray in 1825... The motto of the congregation is 'Thy Kingdom Come', and the aim to combine with a thorough secular education a moral and religious training which will bear fruit in generations to come." (*Catholic Encyclopedia*, "Sister of the Assumption")

93. This event actually happened in 1870, not 1871.

94. The order of the Ursulines was founded by St. Angela de Merici (1474–1540) for the purpose of educating young girls. It was initially popular in Germany, France and Italy, but later spread around the world.

95. John Duns Scotus, "Surnamed Doctor Subtilis, died 8 November, 1308; he was the founder and leader of the famous Scotist School, which had its chief representatives among the Franciscans." (*Catholic Encyclopedia*, "Blessed John Duns Scotus")

96. "Michael Wadding, mystical theologian, born at Waterford, Ireland, in 1591; died in Mexico, Dec. 1644... Michael Wadding was distinguished by his profound knowledge of the supernatural states and by rare prudence in the direction of souls." (*Catholic Encyclopedia*, "Michael Wadding").

97. Presumably the painting depicted events of the late sixteenth and early

seventeenth centuries, when Franciscans and Jesuits were persecuted in Japan under the shoguns Toyotomi Hideyoshi and later Tokugawa Ieyasu.

98. The church of Santa Maria della Vittoria.

99. *Baedeker's* notes, "In the left transept is the notorious group of St. Theresa by Bernini, the execution of which is masterly, whatever may be thought of the spirit" (*Central Italy*, p. 165). A more objective description of the sculpture is provided by the online guide to churches of Rome: "The most famous work of art in the church can be seen in it: Bernini's *Ecstasy of St. Teresa of Avila*, also from 1646. It is considered one of the best Baroque sculptures in Rome, and is one of Bernini's best and most well-known works. An angel is about to pierce St. Teresa's heart with a dart of divine love, a scene described in her mystical writings. The persons witnessing her ecstasy are the donor Cardinal Francesco Cornaro and his family." (Chris Nyborg, "Maria Vittoria" of "Churches of Rome")

100. See entry for May 4, when Anesaki first visited Pincio Park.

101. Hibiya 日比谷 is a neighborhood in Tokyo. Anesaki mentions it here because of an incident three years earlier, on September 5, 1905, in which riots, originating in Hibiya, spread across the city. The protestors were against the Treaty of Portsmouth, which ended the Russo-Japanese war. On September 6 the government declared martial law, and the rioting ceased the following day.

102. Presumably this is the Quirinal, but Anesaki is not specific.

103. *Baedeker's* notes, "The Cappella di Niccolò V. [is] decorated by Fra Angelico da Fiesole with frescoes from the lives of SS. Lawrence and Stephen. They are the last and maturest works of that master, executed about 1450–55, restored under Gregory XIII and Pius VII." (*Central Italy*, p. 342) Today art historians believe that Angelico had many assistants while working on these frescoes, and attribute some of the work to them, specifically Benozzo Gozzoli. The frescoes of Lawrence and Stephen's lives cover the north, east, and west walls. The paintings on the south wall are no longer extant, but it is thought that they portrayed the entombment of Christ. Anesaki's description here becomes confusing because he neglects to indicate which paintings he is referring to from sentence to sentence, thus I have added more parenthetical information than usual.

104. In order, from the west wall, across the north wall, and finishing with the east wall: *St. Peter Consecrates Stephen as Deacon, St. Stephen Distributing Alms, St. Peter Consecrates St. Lawrence as Deacon, The Sermon of St. Stephen, Dispute before Sanhedrin, St. Sixtus Entrusts the Church Treasures to Lawrence, St. Lawrence Distributing Alms, St. Stephen Being Led to his Martyrdom, The*

Stoning of St. Stephen, Condemnation of St. Lawrence by the Emperor Valerian, Martyrdom of St. Lawrence.

105. In the Santa Maria del Carmine church in Florence. See Anesaki's entry for April 19, when he visited the chapel.

106. *Baedeker's* notes, "Also on the wall below [St. Stephen and St. Lawrence]: L. St. Bonaventura, R. St. John Chrysostom. In the vaulting: L. St. Augustine, R. St. Gregory. On the lower part of the right wall: L. St. Athanasius, R. St. Thomas Aquinas. On the vaulting: L. St. Leo, R. St. Ambrose. On the ceiling the Four Evangelists. Though thus in immediate proximity to the boundless energy of Michael Angelo and the lovely forms of Raphael, the frescoes of Fra Angelico yet hold their ground in virtue of their air of perfect devotion and calm contemplative worship." (*Central Italy*, p. 342)

107. The Temple of Jupiter Victor, not the Temple of Jupiter Capitolinus. Not much remained of it when Anesaki saw it. *Baedeker's* comments: "To the west of the imperial palace, between the Nymphaeum and the House of Livia, lies a ruined temple, of which only the sub-structures remain. This is apparently the Temple of Jupiter Victor, erected in consequence of a vow made by Favius Maximus at the Battle of Sentium, B.C. 295. The nearly square podium is approached by 26 steps in five flights. A round pedestal with an inscription, on the fourth landing, was the lower part of a votive offering of Domitius Calvinus, who triumphed over Sapin in B.C. 36." (*Central Italy*, p. 280)

108. Also known as the Domus Augustana.

109. This building is the Great Synagogue of Rome (Tempio Maggiore di Roma). Anesaki seems disappointed that it obstructs his view of St. Peter's dome, but what he does not tell us is that the building, erected between 1901 and 1904, was an architectural masterpiece built on the former premises of the Jewish ghetto. It was designed by Vincenzo Costa and Osvaldo Armanni, and it combined Roman, Greek, Assyro-Babylonian, and Egyptian architectural elements. L. Scott Lerner writes, "A square-shouldered structure crowned by a brilliant aluminum cupola, the building communicates stability, permanence, and strength. With a lateral facade facing the river and the principal facade rising above a small square, it cuts the figure of a modern fortress and its fiefdom. Along with the Synagogue of Florence (1882), the principal reference for the Roman project was the main synagogue of Paris on the rue de la Victoire (1874). The latter in many respects is more impressive than the Great Synagogue of Rome, yet to an onlooker moving about either capital the Parisian synagogue, whose 90-foot-high facade is largely obscured on a narrow street, hardly makes

a greater statement about the new and equal space of the modern Jew than its very visible 150-foot counterpart on the Tiber." (L. Scott Lerner, "Narrating Over the Ghetto of Rome" *Jewish Social Studies* Volume 8, Numbers 2 & 3)

110. This is the Villa Mills, actually part of the Domus Augustana. To clarify Anesaki's chronology: the building was first part of Domus Augustana, *then* was bought by Charles Andrew Mills (1760–1846) in 1820, *then* was converted into the Convent of the Order of the Visitation in 1856, *then* was taken over by the Italian government in the early twentieth century. (See H.B. Morton, *A Traveller in Rome*. Rome: De Capo Press, 2002, pp. 417–420 and Thomas Ashby, "Recent Excavations in Rome" in *The Classical Quarterly*, Vol. 2 No. 2 (1908), p. 147)

111. The Domus Tiberiana is actually on the other (western) side of the Domus Augustana.

112. The Terme di Antonino Caracalla. *Baedeker's* describes its opulence: "These baths were begun in A.D. 212 by Caracalla, extended by Heliogabalus, and completed by Alexander Severus. They contained 1600 marble baths, but could accommodate a much larger number of bathers at once. Their magnificence was unparalleled. Numerous statues, including the Farnese Bull, Hercules, and Flora at Naples, mosaics, etc., have been found here, while the massive walls, notwithstanding the destruction of the roof, still bear testimony to the technical perfection of the structure. The bathing establishment proper, surrounded by a wall with porticoes, a race-course, etc., forming a square, was 240 yards in length and 124 yards in breadth, while the entire enclosure was 360 yards long and as many broad." (*Central Italy*, pp. 291–2)

113. One of the tombs to which Anesaki refers was probably the Tomb of the Scipios (Sepolcro dei Scipioni), located beyond Caracalla's bath on the Via Appia. In addition to this, there were many other tombs along the Via Appia, largely occupied by patrician Roman families. Some, although not many, were preserved and/or restored in Anesaki's time.

114. The so-called "Wall of Romulus," a small fragment of an ancient stone wall. Its origins are unclear, but it is thought to be part of a wall enclosing the ancient city. It remains a major tourist attraction in Rome today.

115. This passage is unclear, but it would seem that Anesaki is commenting on what he can see *from* the dome of St. Peter's, i.e., the residences of the Swiss Guard and other citizens of the Vatican. The reference to houses built upon houses, or houses built upon roofs, is probably meant to be a comment on multi-storied buildings, something that did not appear in traditional Japanese architecture.

116. *Baedeker's* notes, "For the Ascent of the Dome... visitors knock at the door in the left aisle. An easy spiral inclined plane ascends to the roof. The walls bear memorial-tablets of royal personages who have made the ascent. On the roof a number of domes and other small structures are seen, some of which serve as dwellings for the workmen and custodians. The view from the roof ranges over the entire city and the Campagna from the Apennines to the sea. ...The Dome rises 308 ft. above the roof, and is 630 ft. in circumference. The visitor will observe the huge hoops of iron by which the dome was strengthened in the 18th century, when threatening fissures had begun to appear. The gallery within the drum affords a striking view of the interior. An easy staircase ascends between the outer and inner domes to the Lantern, which commands a view of the whole church and its environs. A perpendicular iron ladder ascends to the copper ball on the summit, which can contain 16 persons, but affords no view; the ascent is not worth the trouble, and is quite unsuitable for ladies." (*Central Italy*, p. 328)

117. The "salvation" here (Anesaki uses the Buddhist term *tokudō* 得道) refers to Pius X's ordination, and the commemoration here is the jubilee celebration of that ordination.

118. Here Anesaki obliquely sums up the previous four decades and Italian unity: when Italy was united under Victor Emmanuel II the Papal States were eliminated, leaving the Pope with Vatican City. The French government had initially supported the Pope, but in the end withdrew that support and left the pontiff to fend for himself.

119. *The Creation* (1798) is one of many oratorios composed by Franz Josef Haydn (1732–1809).

120. A reference to the last scene of *Götterdämmerung* (*Twilight of the Gods*), the final opera in Richard Wagner's cycle of four dramas *Der Ring des Nibelungen* (*The Ring of the Nibelung*, first performed in its entirety at the first Beyreuth Festival in 1876). Contrary to Anesaki's summary of the plot, it is actually Valhalla, the hall of the gods, that is destroyed at the end of the opera, not the human world as well.

121. Pietro Perugino (1446–1524), teacher of Raphael, and Alessandro Botticelli, (1446–1510).

122. There are many paintings in the series: "Left: 1. (by the altar) Perugino and Pinturicchio, Moses, with his wife Zipporah journeying to Egypt, Zipporah circumcises her son; 2. Sandro Botticelli, Moses kills the Egyptian, drives the shepherds from the well, kneels before the burning bush; 3. Piero di Cosimo and

pupils of Cosimo Rosselli, Pharaoh's destruction in the Red Sea; 4. C. Rosselli, Moses receives the Law on Mt. Sinai, Worship of the golden calf; 5. S. Botticelli, Destruction of the company of Korah and of Dathan and Abiram (perhaps a reference to the schism of the Archbishop of Carniola); in the background is the Arch of Constantine. 6. Luca Signorelli and Bart. Della Gatta, Moses as a law-giver (the nude youth in the centre personifies the tribe of Levi), Investiture of Joshua, Mourning over the body of Moses. Right: 1. Perugino and Pinturic-chio, Baptism of Christ; 2. S. Botticelli, Sacrifices in cleansing a leper (Levit. xiv. 2–7) and Christ's Temptation; in the background is the then recently com-pleted Ospedale di Santo Spirito; 3. Dom. Ghirlandajo, Vocation of Peter and Andrew, in a dignified and severe monumental style; 4. C. Rosselli, Sermon on the Mount, Cure of the leper; 5. Perugino, Christ giving the keys to Peter, one of the master's finest monumental works in spite of defects in the composition (the figure with the T square on the right is that of the architect Giov. De Dolci); 6. C. Rosselli, Last Supper." (*Central Italy*, p. 331)

123. The Gesù, built by Vignola (Giacomo Barozzi, 1507–73) and Giacomo Della Porta (1541–1604) in 1568–75. By all accounts this church was visually spectacular, but Anesaki does not mention the art work at all, presumably because it post-dated Angelico and Giotto, and thus was beneath his notice.

124. The Museo Nazionale Romano delle Terme Diocleziane. The museum is built on part of what was the Baths (Thermæ) of Diocletian. Later, under Pius IV, parts of the baths were converted into a convent for the Carthusians. Eventu-ally, part of the convent was made into a national museum that houses works discovered on public property within the city limits.

125. Madeleine-Sophie Barat (1779–1865), the Foundress of the Society of the Sacred Heart, was later canonized in 1925. She is sometimes also known as Mary Magdalen, which perhaps explains why Anesaki refers to her as "Marie" rather than the conventional "Mother Barat."

126. This is the first specific mention of the Swiss Guards at the Vatican. The Swiss Guards have policed the Vatican since the fifteenth century. The corps was formalized in 1505 by Julius II. Their uniforms, in red, yellow, and black, have remained the same since the sixteenth century.

127. The word that Anesaki uses for "vessel" is *gan* 龕 which refers to a niche or an alcove for a Buddhist image.

128. Émile Zola (1840–1902), the French naturalist writer, had many views similar to Anesaki's on the Catholic Church. Although the specific reference here is unclear, one finds, for example, Anesaki's description of visiting St.

Peter's Basilica remarkably similar to Zola's depiction of (the fictional) Abbé Pierre Froment's visit to the same place in his novel *Rome*. Furthermore, Zola had a strong influence on Japanese intellectuals and artists of the late nineteenth and early twentieth centuries. It is likely that Anesaki had read many of Zola's works.

129. It appears that Anesaki is contrasting the deep faith of the Shinshū believers in Kaga who "took refuge" in the leader of their religion (just like Catholics took refuge in and expressed adoration for the Pope), with the way that scholars view such things as a rather embarrassing aspect of religion. My thanks to Mark Blum, for the background information on this passage.

130. The Yasukuni Shrine in Tokyo is dedicated to the spirits and memory of Japan's post-1868 war dead. The analogy that Anesaki makes here indicates that Imperial recognition of the war dead in Japan raises their status in the same way that Papal recognition of a nun does at the Vatican. This is perhaps more salient a point today than it was in Anesaki's time; some recent Japanese Prime Ministers have visited Yasukuni Shrine on August 15, the anniversary of Japan's surrender at the end of World War II, but have received great international criticism for doing so because it is seen as condoning Japan's actions during the war years.

131. This play is likely *The Blind Prophet: A Dramatic Poem* which Goad published in 1903 with Rivingtons in London.

FROM ROME TO VENICE

1. Japan was victorious in the Russo-Japanese war of 1904–5.

2. Japan was also victorious in the Sino-Japanese war of 1894–5. Anesaki did not fight in either the Russo-Japanese war or the Sino-Japanese war.

3. *Inferno*, Canto V.

4. This is the only hotel that Anesaki mentions by name. It was centrally located in the city, and was the first hotel listed in the 1904 *Baedeker's* guide to northern Italy.

5. The Cathedral of Sant' Orso, or Basilica Ursiana.

6. The *anatra* bird is a wild duck or goose (J. *kamo* 鴨). The question mark in parentheses is Anesaki's, who apparently was not sure what sort of bird it was in the piece.

7. The Baptistery of the Orthodox, or San Giovanni in Fonte.

8. More specifically, *Baedeker's* notes, "The cupola is decorated with mosa-

ics of the 5th century (partly restored), the best and most ancient at Ravenna, respresenting the Baptism of Christ (with a beard) and with the river-god of Jordan on a gold ground and the twelve Apostles on a blue ground. Under these runs a broad frieze, on which, between the groups of light columns, are represented four altars with the open books of the gospels, and thrones with crosses. The upper arcades of the wall are adorned with sixteen figures of prophets (?), and architectonic enrichments in stucco. On the lower section of the wall are admirable mosaics of gold festoons on a blue ground with statues of prophets (?) at the corners." (*Northern Italy*, pp. 388–9)

9. Anesaki is mistaken. It is not "the emperor Maximilian" but rather St. Maximian, who consecrated the church in 547. The paintings depict Archbishop Maximian.

10. Anesaki's interpretation differs from *Baedeker's*: "The interior... is adorned with beautiful mosaics of the 5th century on a dark blue ground: in the dome, a Latin cross between the symbols of the four Evangelists; in the four arches eight apostles, between whom are doves drinking out of a vase; under the vaulting of the right and left transept are the other four apostles in gilded mosaic; beside them are stags at a spring. Over the door is Christ as a young shepherd, with long hair; opposite is the triumph of Christian faith, in which Christ (?) is committing to the flames an open book, probably heretical; the adjacent cabinet contains the gospels." (*Northern Italy*, p. 391)

11. San Giovanni Evangelista. It was "erected in 424 by the Empress Galla Placida in consequence of a vow made during a voyage from Constantinople, but almost wholly rebuilt in 1747, except the tower. The court in front has retained the form of the ancient atrium. Above the beautiful portal of the latter (1316) are reliefs in allusion in the foundation of the church." (*Northern Italy*, p. 392)

12. *Baedeker's* notes, "The vaulting of the 4th chapel on the left is adorned with frescoes of the four Evangelists, with their symbols above them, and the four fathers of the church, saints Gregory, Ambrose, Augustine, and Jerome, by Giotto (who had come to Ravenna between 1317 and 1320 on a visit to his friend Dante)." (*Northern Italy*, p. 392)

13. The Ospedale civile di Ravenna. Although it is unclear, the reference to a monastery may refer to the Convento delle Monache del Corpus Domini, which existed on the square until 1812.

14. The Piazza Anita Garibaldi, which has a monument by Cesare Zocchi (1851–1922) dedicated in 1888 to all Italian war dead.

15. *Baedeker's* notes:

At the corner of the Via Alberoni, a few paces to the south of S. Apollinare Nuovo, some remains of the Palace of Theodoric are still extant, unless indeed, as is possible, these date from an addition erected in the time of the exarchs.

The remains include a narrow façade with round-arched blind arcades and with a central niche (exedra) in the upper story (disengaged in 1898 and at the same time freely restored) a colonnade in two stories, the bases of two round towers, etc. The palace was plundered by Belisarius in 539, and in 784 its treasures of art and most of its columns were removed to Aix-la-Chappelle by Charlemagne. The palace and its gardens extended east to the Viale Pallavicino, and down to 1098 the sea adjoined it at the back. The massive principal tower was standing until 1295. (*Northern Italy*, p. 393)

16. Anesaki omits or abbreviates much of what he saw. *Baedeker's* notes, "The interior of [San' Apollinare Nuovo] contains twenty-four marble columns brought from Constantinople. On the right is an ancient ambo. The walls of the nave are adorned with interesting mosaics of the 6th century, partly of the Arian, and partly of the Roman Catholic period, afterwards frequently restored (most recently in 1898–99): on the left the town of Classis with its Roman buildings, the sea and ships, twenty-two virgins with the Magi (the east half badly restored); on the right is the city of Ravenna with its churches and the palace of Theodoric, and twenty-six saints with wreaths approaching Christ enthroned between angels (a group which has also been freely restored). These last mosaics betray a tendency to the showy style of the later period, but the 16 single figures of the teachers of the church above them, between the windows, are executed in a more independent and pleasant manner. Above the windows, on the upper part of the wall, on each side, are thirteen interesting compositions from the New Testament. On the left, the sayings and miracles of Christ (without a beard); on the right, the history of the Passion from the Last Supper to the Resurrection (Christ with a beard)." (*Northern Italy*, pp. 392–3)

17. The castle was "an ancient and picturesque edifice with four towers, surrounded by a moat. It was built after 1385 by Bartolino da Novara for Niccolò II, and partly restored after a fire in 1554, and [was then] occupied by the prefect and other local authorities." (*Baedeker's*, p. 356) The House of Este is famous in Italy and beyond for its role in the development of art and science.

18. *Baedeker's* notes, "The Sala del Consiglio and the adjacent Sala di Napoli, in the apartments of the prefecture, contain frescoes of the school of Dosso

Dossi, representing wrestling-matches of the ancient palæastra. The Sala dell' Aurora contains a fine frieze with children. Adjacent is a cabinet with three Bacchanalia by followers of Garófalo." (*Northern Italy*, p. 356)

19. *Baedeker's* also notes that one could tour the dungeon of the palace "at the base of the 'lion tower', where the Margrave Nicholas III confined his faithless wife Parisina Malatesta and his natural son Hugo, her paramour, before beheading them on May 21st, 1425…. Visitors also see the prison in which Alphonso I confined for life his brother Julius and the Prince Ferrante d'Este after their conspiracy in 1506." (*Northern Italy*, p. 356)

20. San Giorgio.

21. *Baedeker's* notes, "The cathedral has an imposing façade with three series of round arches, one above the other, an admirable example of the Lombard style. The lower part of the front and the lateral façades date from 1135; the upper part is of the 13th century, the sculptures mainly of the 13th and 14th. The projecting portal, embellished with two lions, was added at a later period; the reliefs are of an earlier date, some of them being probably by Nicolaus." (*Northern Italy*, p. 357)

22. "The fine interior, with its aisles and double transept, does not correspond with the façade, as it was modernized in the baroque style by Mazzarelli in 1712. In the 2nd transept on the right: Martyrdom of St. Lawrence by Guercino; on the altar at the back, Crucifix, with the Virgin, St. John, St. George, and St. Maurelius, five figures in bronze, by Niccolò Baroncelli and Dom. Di Paris (1453–66); terracotta figures of Christ and the Apostles in both transepts by Alfonso Lombardi. In the choir, to the right, Annunciation; to the left, St. George, by Cosimo Tura. 6th altar to the left, Coronation of the Virgin, saints below, by Fr. Francia. 3rd altar on the left, Madonna enthroned with saints, by Garofalo (1524). On the right and left of the principal door, saints Peter and Paul, in fresco, by the same master. In the rooms adjoining the sacristy, Garofalo, Annunciation; Dom. Panetti, Madonna, with two donors; Giacomo da Siena, Statue of the Madonna (1408)" (*Northern Italy*, p. 357)

23. What Anesaki really says is that he "ate some *udon*," a thick Japanese wheat pasta usually served in a broth. One imagines that his Italian *udon* was a bit different. Much earlier on the trip he mentions eating "Italian *udon*" also. Apparently the term *pasta* had not entered the Japanese lexicon yet.

24. The Piazza Vittorio Emanuele Secondo, formerly the Prato della Valle.

25. These statues were done in 1865 by by the Swiss sculptor Vincenzo Vela (1820–1891).

26. The church was "begun by Girol. Da Brescia in 1501, continued by Al. Leopardi in 1521–22, and completed in 1532 by Morone of Bergamo." (*Northern Italy*, p. 254)

27. "The sepulchral church of St. Anthony of Padua (b. at Lisbon, d. 1231; an associate of St. Francis of Assisi) commonly called 'Il Santo', was begun in 1232; the nave was completed in 1307, and the remainder in 1424. The church was restored in 1749 after a fire and whitewashed in the interior." (*Northern Italy*, p. 251)

28. The building measures 115 by 55 meters (126 by 60 yards).

29. Anthony is buried beneath the altar in the left transept.

30. Altichiero (c.1330–c.1390) was born in Zevio, near Verona, and is considered to be the founder of the Veronese school of early Renaissance art.

31. Donato di Niccolò di Betto Bardi, 1386–1466. Anesaki's description is slightly confusing: the sculpture depicts Christ on the Cross, and beneath him stands the Virgin Mary. On either side of Mary stand St. Francis and St. Anthony. Next to Francis and Anthony stand two more saints each, St. Daniel, St. Justina, St. Louis, and St. Prosdocimo.

32. The depiction of Antonio's life is a compilation of many artists' work: "Ordination of St. Anthony, by Antonio Minello (1512); 2. Murder of a woman, afterwards resuscitated by the saint, by Giovanni Dentone; 3. Resuscitation of a youth, by Girolamo Campagna; 4. Resuscitation of a suicide surrounded by women, by Jac. Sansovino; 5. Resuscitation of a child, by Minello and Sansovino (1528); 6, 7. Tullio Lombardo (1525), Discovery of a stone in the corpse of a miser instead of a heart, and Cure of a broken leg; 8. Miracle with a glass, by Gian Maria da Padova and Paolo Stella (1529); 9. St. Anthony causes a child to bear witness in favour of its mother, by Antonio Lombardo (1505)." (*Northern Italy*, p. 251)

33. This statue, by Donatello, is the equestrian Statue of Gattamelāta (Erasmo da Narni; d. 1443), general of the army of the Republic of Venice in 1438–41. *Baedeker's* notes that it was "the first great equestrian monument cast in bronze in Italy since antiquity, completed in 1453." (*Northern Italy*, p. 252)

34. The statue on the Capitoline Hill was of Marcus Aurelius. The bronze original was erected in the second century. It was moved to the Capitoline museum in 1981 for restoration and preservation and replaced by a copy in the square. The statue is a rare example of early Roman bronze sculpture; most early statues were later melted for their bronze, but this particular one was preserved because the mounted figure was mistaken for Constantine and thus preserved for its supposed Christian connection.

35. The bronze statue of Kusunoki Masashige (1294–1336) is located outside of the Imperial Palace in Tokyo. Kusunoki was a *samurai* who became legendary in the Meiji Period. He was symbolic of loyalty to one's master. Anesaki finds the statue distasteful for artistic reasons, but would have found it even more so had he been able to predict the future: in the years leading up to World War II, the government made full use of the example of Kusunoki because he exemplified the virtues of undying loyalty to the emperor that they expected from their soldiers. The statue was installed on the Imperial Palace Grounds in 1900.

36. The Museo Civico, "rebuilt in 1881 by Boito, with a fine façade and staircase, containing the civic library, archives, and collections of antiquities and paintings." (*Northern Italy*, p. 253)

37. More specifically, "in the cloisters are columns, friezes, and other remains of a Roman temple, excavated near the Caffe Pedrocchi; also numerous Roman tombstones, the Monument of the Volumnii (discovered at Monselice in 1879), medieval coats-of-arms, memorial stones, etc." The upper floors contain paintings, tapestries, and coins and medals. (*Northern Italy*, p. 253)

38. Although Anesaki refers to it as "one work," it really comprises a number of panels with twenty-three separate scenes from the life of Christ.

39. *Baedeker's* notes, "The Eremitani, an old Augustine church of the middle of the 13th century, restored in 1880, is a long building with painted vaulting of wood, containing frescoes by Andrea Mantegna and his contemporaries of the school Squarcione, which are among the most important examples of Northern Italian art." (*Northern Italy*, p. 255). Clearly Anesaki did not share this view of the importance of Mantegna's work. Much of the Eremitani, including Mantegna's frescoes, was destroyed in the Second World War. Only fragments of the frescoes survive.

FAREWELL TO ITALY; TWO DAYS IN VENICE

1. "Dragon Palaces," also known as "Sea God's Palaces" are mythical places from the Chinese tradition. In Chinese mythology, there are four Dragon Kings who rule the seas. They live in crystal palaces, the opulence of which is often described in traditional literature. Anesaki mentions the Dragon Kings and their palaces here not only because of their mythical nature, but also because they are so closely associated with water, as is Venice, and because they are associated with decadence.

2. Joseph Mallord William Turner (1775–1851) was a well-known British

landscape artist who visited Venice multiple times and produced a number of paintings of it.

3. *Baedeker's* notes, "The Ponte di Rialto, built in 1588–92 by Giovanni da Ponte on the site of an earlier wooden bridge, is 158 ft. long and 90 ft. wide, and consists of a single marble arch of 74 ft. span and 32 ft. in height, resting on 12,000 piles. It is situated midway between the Dogana di Mare and the railway-station, and down to 1854 was the sole connecting link between the east and west quarters of Venice." (*Northern Italy,* p. 294)

4. Anesaki uses the word "soprano" here, but he is probably referring to male vocal harmony (involving, for example, tenor and bass voices) rather than male and female (as the word "soprano" implies).

5. *Baedeker's* notes, "The foundation of the Eastern supremacy of Venice was laid by Doge Enrico Dandolo (1192–1205), who conquered Constantinople in 1204. In consequence of this Venice gained possession of numerous places on the coasts of the Adriatic and the Levant, from Durazzo to Trebisond, and of most of the Greek islands, including Candia, which was administered on the model of the mother-city. During the conquest and administration of these new territories there arose a class of nobles, who declared themselves hereditary in 1297 and excluded the rest of the people from all share in the government." (*Northern Italy,* p. 266). Anesaki's criticism here is not unlike his criticism of Pius X; he dislikes elitism of any kind. Also, although he does not mention it explicitly, it would not have been lost on Anesaki that the rise of elitism in Venice happened during the lifetime of St. Francis of Assisi.

6. According to *Baedeker's,* the gondolas were painted black in conformity with a law passed in the fifteenth century (*Northern Italy,* p. 261).

7. Taira no Kiyomori, the leader of the Taira clan, dedicated the main building of the Itsukushima Shrine on Miyashima Island in 1168. The shrine sits on pillars that are sunk into the water, effectively making it a building on the sea.

8. The Accademia di Belle Arti.

9. Ticiano or Tiziano Vecelli da Cadore, is also known by his Latinized name, Titian. He lived c.1477–1576, and, as Anesaki notes, is widely considered the most famous painter in the Venetian School.

10. Bartolomé Esteban Murillo (b. 1617, Sevilla, d. 1682, Sevilla). Murillo painted more than one painting of the Immaculate Conception, and it is unclear here whether Anesaki is referring to one specific version or of Murillo's depiction of the event as a whole. Anesaki may also be criticizing, albeit indirectly, a doctrinal issue: "The theme of the Virgin of the Immaculate Conception was of

unsurpassed importance to the faithful of Seville in the seventeenth century. The dispute over the immaculacy of the Virgin Mary was one of the most divisive in the history of the Renaissance church. There were two parties to the debate: the immaculist, lead by the Franciscan order, who believed that the Virgin had been miraculously conceived without original sin, and the sanctification party, lead by the Dominicans, who held that Mary had been conceived in sin and subsequently sanctified, or purified, in the womb of her mother. From the late Middle Ages the church of Castile had been an ardent proponent of the immaculist doctrine and repeatedly attempted to persuade the popes to elevate it to the status of a dogma. Finally in 1661 Pope Alexander VII issued a constitution declaring the immunity of Mary from original sin and forbidding further discussions of the issue. News of the papal ruling intensified in Seville the demand for images of the Virgin Immaculate. Murillo's rendition, executed for the Escorial, is faithful to the spirit of the times: the youthful Mary is a lovely creation, her physical beauty a sufficient expression of her purity; only a few putti are needed as supporting players. Murillo's appealing vision of the Immaculate Conception became canonical." (*Web Gallery of Art,* "Immaculate Conception (1665–70)" under "Murillo, Bartolomé Esteban")

11. Paolo Caliari Veronese (b. 1528, Verona, d. 1588, Venezia).

12. The painting was *originally* called *The Last Supper* but was later renamed *Supper in the house of Levi.* Nonetheless, Anesaki calls it *The Last Supper* here, apparently viewing the content and not any placard associated with the painting.

13. That is, the sixteenth century. Venice reached it peak before this, and in the course of the sixteenth century lost control of various territories, including Nauplia, the islands of Chios, Paros, and Cyprus.

14. The history of this painting is worth noting. "This work, painted for the Dominican order of SS. Giovanni e Paolo to replace an earlier work by Titian destroyed in the fire of 1571, is the last of the grandiose 'suppers' painted by Veronese for the refectories of Venetian monasteries. ...The expressive hedonism so alien to the religious context – the subject in fact appears to be a purely pagan one in exaltation of love of life in 16th century Venice – aroused the suspicions of the Inquisition. On July 18th 1573 Veronese was summoned by the Holy Office to appear before the Inquisition accused of heresy. If the questions of the inquisitors show the first signs of the rigors of the Counter-reformation, Veronese's answers show clearly his unfailing faith in the creative imagination and artistic freedom. Not wishing to yield to the injunction of the Inquisition

to eliminate the details which offended the religious theme of the Last Supper, he changed the title to 'Feast in the House of Levi,' a subject which tolerated the presence of fools and armed men dressed up 'alla tedesca.'" (*Web Gallery of Art*, "Feast in the House of Levi" under "Veronese, Paolo")

15. John Ruskin (1819–1900), British writer and critic. See also entry for April 21. In his multi-volume work *Modern Painters*, Ruskin makes such comments as "the massy leaves of the Titian forest are among the most sublime of the conceivable forms of material things" (p. 78) and "For three hundred years back, trees have been drawn with affection by all the civilized nations of Europe, and yet I repeat boldly, what I before asserted, that no men but Titian and Turner ever drew the stem of a tree." (p. 387)

16. Probably Ticiano's *Pietà* (1576). This painting was originally meant to decorate Ticiano's grave, but he died before it was finished. It was completed by Palma il Giovane. Anesaki was thus correct that the painting was among his last.

17. Anesaki's impressions were not unique. *Baedeker's* quotes Ruskin: "Mr. Ruskin, in the 'Stones of Venice,' lays great stress upon the colouring of St. Mark's, reminding the reader 'that the school of incrusted architecture is the only one in which perfect and perment chromatic decoration is possible.' And again: – 'the effects of St. Mark's depend not only upon the most delicate sculpture in every part, but, as we have just stated, eminently on its colour also, and that the most subtle, variable, inexpressible colour in the world, – the colour of glass, of transparent alabaster, of polished marble, and lustrous gold.'" (*Northern Italy*, p. 272)

18. Anesaki actually wrote "Rido" in both *katakana* and Romanization. It should be, of course, "Lido."

19. The Campanile di San Marco, a clock tower, collapsed on July 14, 1902. It was erected again, and completed on April 25, 1912. The cause of the collapse was simple structural deterioration, not a surprise given that the tower had first been constructed almost a thousand years earlier.

20. Richard Wagner wrote in his autobiography, *My Life*, "It was very difficult for Ritter to induce me to interrupt my daily arrangements even to visit a gallery or a church, though, whenever we had to pass through the town, the exceedingly varied architectonic peculiarities and beauties always delighted me afresh. But the frequent gondola trips towards the Lido constituted my chief enjoyment during practically the whole of my stay in Venice. It was more especially on our homeward journeys at sunset that I was always over-powered by unique impressions." (Richard Wagner, *My Life*, vol. II)

21. The Madonna dell' Orto, also called San Cristoforo Martire.

22. Tintoretto was also known as Jacobo Robusti (1518–1594). It is unclear why Anesaki says he had seen enough of such paintings, as this is the first mention he makes in the travelogue of Tintoretto. Other painters whose works were in this church at that time included Cima da Conegliano, Daniel van Dyck, Palma Vecchio, Girolamo da Santa Croce, Palma Giovane, Alessandro Vittoria, Lor. Lotto, and Giov. Bellini.

23. This is the second mention that Anesaki makes of Böcklin (the first was when he was in Rome, on May 6). The painting in question here, *The Isle of the Dead* (*Die Toteninsel*) was painted in 1883. Michael Gibson describes it as follows: "Among the most famous [of his paintings] is the painting known as *The Isle of the Dead* (1880), which Böcklin himself entitled 'A tranquil place'. It was clearly important to him; he made five different versions of the composition. The new title was suggested by the white-draped coffin on the boat, the funerary presence of the cypresses, and the overwhelming impression of immobility and silence. The white figure vividly lit by a setting sun in contrasted with the dark, vertical forms of the trees, impervious to the slanting rays of the sun. Like a dream, the painting condenses a number of contradictory sensations and emotions." (*Symbolism*, p. 125) See List of Artworks #25

24. This is the second mention that Anesaki makes of laundry hanging from windows of what used to be elegant architecture. Similarly, earlier he notes that the mansions of the rich and powerful have become factories. One interpretation of this is that he is using poverty and decay as symbols of impermanence and the inevitable decline of wealth and power.

25. Giuseppe Revere was born in Trieste (Northern Italy) in 1812. He died in Rome in 1889. He was an Italian writer and active patriot, and was very close to the great patriot and political thinker Giuseppe Mazzini, with whom he fought for the unification of Italy against the Austrians. His poetry is filled with religious and philosophical symbols, combined with descriptions of landscapes.

Venice

Venice was the breath of the sea
Never had the world ever seen a more beautiful thing;
and when Italy was weeping as a servant
Venice was free and was spreading her joyful anthem.

Venice had her mystical wedding with the sea,

the deep waves embraced her as the maid chosen by Fate,
In the middle of the raging storm
victory opened her fertile bosom.
But now the sea denies Venice its stormy embraces
And since its love for her is broken,
the sea gives now its unfaithful embrace to other lands.
Venice, with her scattered hair covered with seaweed,
and her shining eyes steadily focused on her vanished fleet,
is stretching her arms and is joining herself to the Shore.

HOW CHRISTIANITY APPEALS TO A JAPANESE BUDDHIST

[The notes to this section are by Masaharu Anesaki. –Ed.]

1. This means leaving the world at death and returning again, out of compassion, in order to teach and save his fellow-beings.

2. A system of Buddhist philosophy founded upon the idea of the identity of Buddha and the Dharma has been developed in Japan into an enthusiastic faith in the incarnate Dharma. Another later development of Buddhism into a belief in one personal redeemer, Amita Buddha, in whose representative acts and through whose grace men are to be saved, has struck a firm root in our country. These two forms of Buddha's religion, the former called the *Hokke* (Saddharma-puṇḍarīka) and the latter the *Jōdo* (Sukhāvatī) Buddhism, are no accidental modifications of it, but the developments of its religious essence. Japan, where these forms of Buddhism are most influential, is furnishing a good soil for the acceptance of Christianity. It is no exaggeration to say that Christianity was prepared for in Japan before the introduction of the Cross. On the other hand, no Buddhist will remain unastonished on noticing the very Buddhistic expression of Christianity, as shown in Thomas à Kempis's *Imitation* or in St. Francis's religion of humility and meekness.

3. This school of painting flourished from the eleventh century to the fourteenth, just coinciding with the rise of the two forms of Buddhism alluded to in the previous note. For the facsimilies of the paintings belonging to this school, see *Selected Relic of Japanese Art* (Kyoto, 1900–1905), Part iv. Plate 17, Part vi. Plate 13; and *The Kokka* (Tokyo, 1889–1905), Nos. 3, 25, 61, etc.

4. Nāgārjuna, in his Prajñā-paramita-çāstra.

Bibliography

Aaslid, Ive. Abstract of "Visual Memory and Salvation in the 48-scroll Hōnen Shōnin Eden" presented for the Asian Studies Conference Japan, 2000. Last accessed June 13, 2006. http://www.meijigakuin.ac.jp/~ascj/2000/200007.htm

A Funari, Pedro Paulo, Review of *El Monte Testaccio y la llanura subaventina. Topografía extra portam Trigeminam. Rome, Consejo Superior de Investigaciones Científicas* by Antonio Aguilera. in *Mirabilia: Revista Eletrōnica de História Antiga e Medieval (Journal of Ancient and Medieval History)*, No. 3 (December 2003). Available online at http://www.revistamirabilia.com/ Numeros/Num3/resenhas/res1.htm Last accessed May 8, 2008.

Anesaki Masaharu 姉崎正治. *Hanatsumi Nikki* 花つみ日記. Tokyo: Hakubunkan 博文館, 1909.

———. *History of Japanese Religion, with Special Reference to the Social and Moral Life of the Nation.* London: Kegan Paul International, 1930.

———. "How Christianity Appeals to a Japanese Buddhist." *The Hibbert Journal,* Vol. IV (1905-6), pp. 1–18.

———. "Takayama Chogyū ni kotōru no sho," 高山樗牛に答ふるの書 reprinted in *Takayama Chogyū, Saitō Nonohito, Anesaki Chōfū, Tobari Chikufū shū* 高山樗牛・斉藤野の人・姉崎嘲風・登張竹風集 in *Meiji Bungaku Zenshū* 明治文学全集, vol. 40. Tokyo: Chikuma Shobō 筑摩書房, 1970, pp. 210–220.

———. *Teiunshū* 停雲集. Tokyo: Hakubunkan 博文館, 1911.

———. *Waga shōgai: Anesaki Masaharu sensei no gyōseki* わが生涯・姉崎正治先生の業績. Tokyo: Ōzorasha 大空社, 1993.

Arrivabene, Charles. *I Poeti Italiani: Selections from the Italian Poets: Forming an Historical View of the Development of Italian poetry from the earliest times to the present ; with biographical notices.* London: P. Roalndi, 1855.

Ashby, Thomas. "Recent Excavations in Rome." *The Classical Quarterly,* Vol. 2 No. 2 (1908), pp. 142–150.

Baedeker, Karl. *Northern Italy, as Far as Leghorn, Florence, and Ancona, and the Island of Corsica.* Leipzig: Karl Baedeker, 1868.

———. *Italy Handbook for Travellers: Central Italy and Rome.* Tenth Edition. Leipzig: Karl Baedeker, 1890.

————. *Italy Handbook for Travellers: Central Italy and Rome.* Fourteenth Edition. Leipzig: Karl Baedeker, 1904.

————. *Italy Handbook for Travellers: Northern Italy.* Twelfth Remodeled Edition. Leipzig: Karl Baedeker, 1903.

————. *Italy Handbook for Travellers: Southern Italy and Sicily with Excursions to the Lipari Islands, Malta, Sardinia, Tunis, and Corfu.* Fourteenth Edition. Leipzig: Karl Baedeker, 1903.

Baumann, Martin. "Buddhism in Switzerland." *Journal of Global Buddhism*, 1 (2000), pp. 154–5.

Blashfield, Edwin H. and Evangeline W. *Italian Cities*, vol. II. New York: Charles Scribner's Sons, 1908.

The Catholic Encyclopedia, online version. Last accessed April 25, 2008. http://www.newadvent.org/cathen/

Claridge, Amanda et al. *Rome: An Oxford Archaeological Guide.* Oxford: Oxford University Press, 1998.

Coffin, David R. *The Villa D'Este at Tivoli.* Princeton: Princeton University Press, 1960.

Coggiatti, Stelvio. "An Introduction to Camellias in Italy." *International Camellia Journal*, Vol. 1 (1973), pp. 68–70.

————. "Camellias in Rome a Century Ago." *International Camellia Journal*, Vol. 1 (1973), pp. 11–14.

Cruickshank, J.W. & A.M. Cruickshank. *The Umbrian Cities of Italy*, Vol. I. Boston: L. C. Page & Company, 1907.

Dante Alighieri, *The Divine Comedy*, trans. Henry Wadsworth Longfellow. Project Gutenburg, Ebook #1004, Release date 1997-08-01. Last accessed June 12, 2006. http://www.gutenberg.org/dirs/etext97/0ddc110.txt

Dean, Judith. *Every Pilgrim's Guide to Assisi and other Franciscan Pilgrim Places.* Norwich: Canterbury Press, 2002.

Emiliani-Guidici, Paolo. *Florilegio dei Lirici Più Insigni d'Italia: Preceduto da un Discorso*, vol. 1. Florence: Poligrafia Italiana, 1846.

Gibbon, Edward. *The Autobiographies of Edward Gibbon.* London: John Murray, 1897.

Gibbs, Robert. "Giovanni da Modena [Giovanni di Pietro Falloppi]," in *The Dictionary of Art*, vol. 12, pp. 703–704. Jane Turner, editor. New York: MacMillian/Grove, 1996.

Gibson, Michael. *Symbolism.* Köln & London: Taschen, 1995.

Hall, Robert A. *Antonio Fogazzaro.* Boston: Twayne Publishers, 1978.

Hudleston, Roger. *The Little Flowers of St. Francis of Assisi: In the First English Translation*. Grand Rapids, Mich.: Christian Classics Ethereal Library; Boulder: NetLibrary, [1990?].

Ishibashi Tomonobu and H. Kishimoto. "Principal Works by Masaharu Anesaki," in *Monumenta Nipponica*, Vol. 6, No. 1/2. (1943), pp. vi–x.

Isomae Jun'ichi 磯前順一 and Hidetaka Fukasawa 英隆深澤. *Kindai Nihon ni okeru chishikijin to shūkyō: Anesaki Masaharu no kiseki* 日本における知識人と宗教・姉崎正治の軌跡. Tokyo: Tōkyōdō shuppan, 2002.

Kertzer, David I. *Prisoner of the Vatican: the Popes' Secret Plot to Capture Rome from the New Italian State*. Boston: Houghton Mifflin, 2004.

Korom, Frank J. "A Review of *Deutsche Buddhisten: Geschichte und Gemeinschaften*." *Journal of Buddhist Ethics*, Vol. 5 (1998), pp. 433–435.

Lerner, L. Scott. "Narrating Over the Ghetto of Rome." *Jewish Social Studies* Volume 8, Numbers 2 & 3), pp. 1–38.

Marquis, Albert Nelson, ed. *Who's Who in New England*, Second Edition. Chicago: A. N. Marquis and Company, 1916.

Matsuo Bashō 松尾芭蕉. *Bashō bunshū* 芭蕉文集. Tokyo: Iwanami Shoten, 1959.

McCullough, Helen *Kokin Wakashū: the First Imperial Anthology of Japanese Poetry, with Tosa Nikki and Shinsen Waka*. Stanford: Stanford University Press, 1985.

McDonald, William L. and John A. Pinto. *Hadrian's Villa and Its Legacy*. New Haven: Yale University Press, 1995.

Morton, H. B. *A Traveller in Rome*. Cambridge, Mass.: Da Capo Press, 2002.

Muller, Charles. *Digital Dictionary of Buddhism*. Last accessed April 25, 2008. http://www.buddhism-dict.net/ddb/

Nyborg, Chris. *Churches of Rome*. Last accessed April 24, 2008. http://romanchurches.wikia.com/wiki/Main_Page

Olga's Gallery, Olga Mataev, editor. Last accessed October 15, 2008. http://www.abcgallery.com

Randel, Don Michael, ed. *The Harvard Dictionary of Music*, Fourth Edition. Cambridge: Belknap Press of Harvard University Press, 2003.

Ruskin, John. *Modern Painters*, vol. I. New York: John Wiley & Son, 1872.

———. *Modern Painters*, vol. IV. London: Smith, Elder & Co., 1873.

Sabatier, Paul. *Life of St. Francis of Assisi*. New York: Charles Scribner's Sons, 1917.

Sabatier, Paul. *The Road to Assisi: The Essential Biography of St. Francis*, edited with introduction and annotations by Jon M. Sweeney. Brewster, Mass.: Paraclete Press, 2003.

Sato, Hiroaki. "Record of an Autumn Wind: The Travel Diary of Arii Shokyū," *Monumenta Nipponica* 55:1, pp. 1–43.

Soothill, William E. and Lewis Hodous. *A Dictionary of Chinese Buddhist Terms.* London: K. Paul, Trench, Trubner & Co., 1937.

"Three Graves in Italy" (byline C.M.R.). *New York Times* 27 May 1899, "Saturday Review of Books and Art" section, page BR344.

Villari, Pasquale. *Life and Times of Girolamo Savonarola*, trans. Linda Villari. New York: Scribner's, 1898.

Wagner, Richard. *My Life*. Project Gutenburg, Ebook #5144, Release date February 2004. Last accessed June 9, 2006. http://www.gutenberg.org/dirs/etexto4/wglf210.txt

Web Gallery of Art, Emil Krén, editor. Last accessed April 25, 2008. http://www.wga.hu/index1.html

Zola, Émile. *Rome*, trans. Ernest Alfred Vizetelly. Project Gutenburg, Ebook #8726, Release date August 2005. Last accessed June 9, 2006. http://www.gutenberg.org/dirs/etexto5/rome610.txt

List of Artworks

NOTE: Last accessed 4 November 2008.

1. *Madonna in Glory with the Child and Saints* (PERUGINO, Pietro)
   http://www.wga.hu/html/p/perugino/madonna/m_glory.html
2. *St. Cecilia* by RAFFAELLO Sanzio (Raphael)
   http://www.wga.hu/html/r/raphael/5roma/2/06cecil.html
3. *Scenes from the Life of Saint Francis*: No. 1–4 (left wall) by Giotto
   http://www.wga.hu/html/g/giotto/s_croce/2bardi/scenes_1/index.html
4. *Scenes from the Life of Saint Francis*: No. 1–4 (right wall) by Giotto
   http://www.wga.hu/html/g/giotto/s_croce/2bardi/scenes_2/index.html
5. *Saint Dominic Adoring the Crucifixion* by Fra Angelico
   http://www.wga.hu/html/a/angelico/09/corridor/dominic.html
6. *Peter Martyr Enjoins Silence* by Fra Angelico
   http://www.abcgallery.com/A/angelico/angelico43.html
7. *Christ as Pilgrim Received by Two Dominicans* by Fra Angelico
   http://www.abcgallery.com/A/angelico/angelico45.html
8. *Resurrection of Christ and Women at the Tomb* by Fra Angelico
   http://www.wga.hu/cgi-bin/highlight.cgi?file=html/a/angelico/09/cells/08_women.html
   &find=resurrection
9. *Crucifixion and Saints* by Fra Angelico
   http://www.wga.hu/html/a/angelico/09/corridor/crucifi.html
10. *The Annunciation* by Fra Angelico
    http://www.wga.hu/html/a/angelico/09/corridor/annunci.html
11. *The Distribution of Alms and the Death of Ananias*, 1426–27 by Masaccio
    http://www.wga.hu/tours/brancacc/distrib.html
12. *Fiesole Triptych* by Fra Angelico
    http://www.abcgallery.com/A/angelico/angelico4.html
13. *Scenes from the Life of St John the Baptist: 2. Birth and Naming of the Baptist*
    by Giotto   http://www.wga.hu/html/g/giotto/s_croce/1peruzzi/baptis2.html
14. *Scenes from the Life of St John the Baptist: 3. Feast of Herod* by Giotto
    http://www.wga.hu/html/g/giotto/s_croce/1peruzzi/baptis3.html

15. *Scenes from the Life of St John the Evangelist: 3. Ascension of the Evangelist*
by Giotto   http://www.wga.hu/html/g/giotto/s_croce/1peruzzi/evang3.html
16. *The Mocking of Christ* by Fra Angelico
http://www.wga.hu/html/a/angelico/09/cells/07_chris.html
17. *Transfiguration* by Fra Angelico
http://www.wga.hu/html/a/angelico/09/cells/06_trans.html
18. *Coronation of the Virgin* by Fra Angelico
http://www.wga.hu/html/a/angelico/09/cells/09_coron.html
19. *Noli Me Tangere* by Fra Angelico
http://www.wga.hu/html/a/angelico/09/cells/01_nolim.html
20. *Entombment* by Fra Angelico
http://www.abcgallery.com/A/angelico/angelico53.html
21. *Annunciation* by Fra Angelico
http://www.wga.hu/html/a/angelico/09/cells/03_annun.html
22. *Interior of Upper Church in Assisi*
http://www.wga.hu/html/g/giotto/assisi/upper/00view.html
23. *Legend of St Francis: 15. Sermon to the Birds*
http://www.wga.hu/html/g/giotto/assisi/upper/legend/scenes_2/franc15.html
24. *Legend of St Francis: 14. Miracle of the Spring*
http://www.wga.hu/html/g/giotto/assisi/upper/legend/scenes_2/franc14.html
25. *Isle of the Dead* by Arnold Böcklin
http://www.arnoldbocklin.com/ab_isleofthedead.htm

Index

Printed in the United States
138824LV00001B/186/P